BATMAN KNIGHT AND SQUIRE

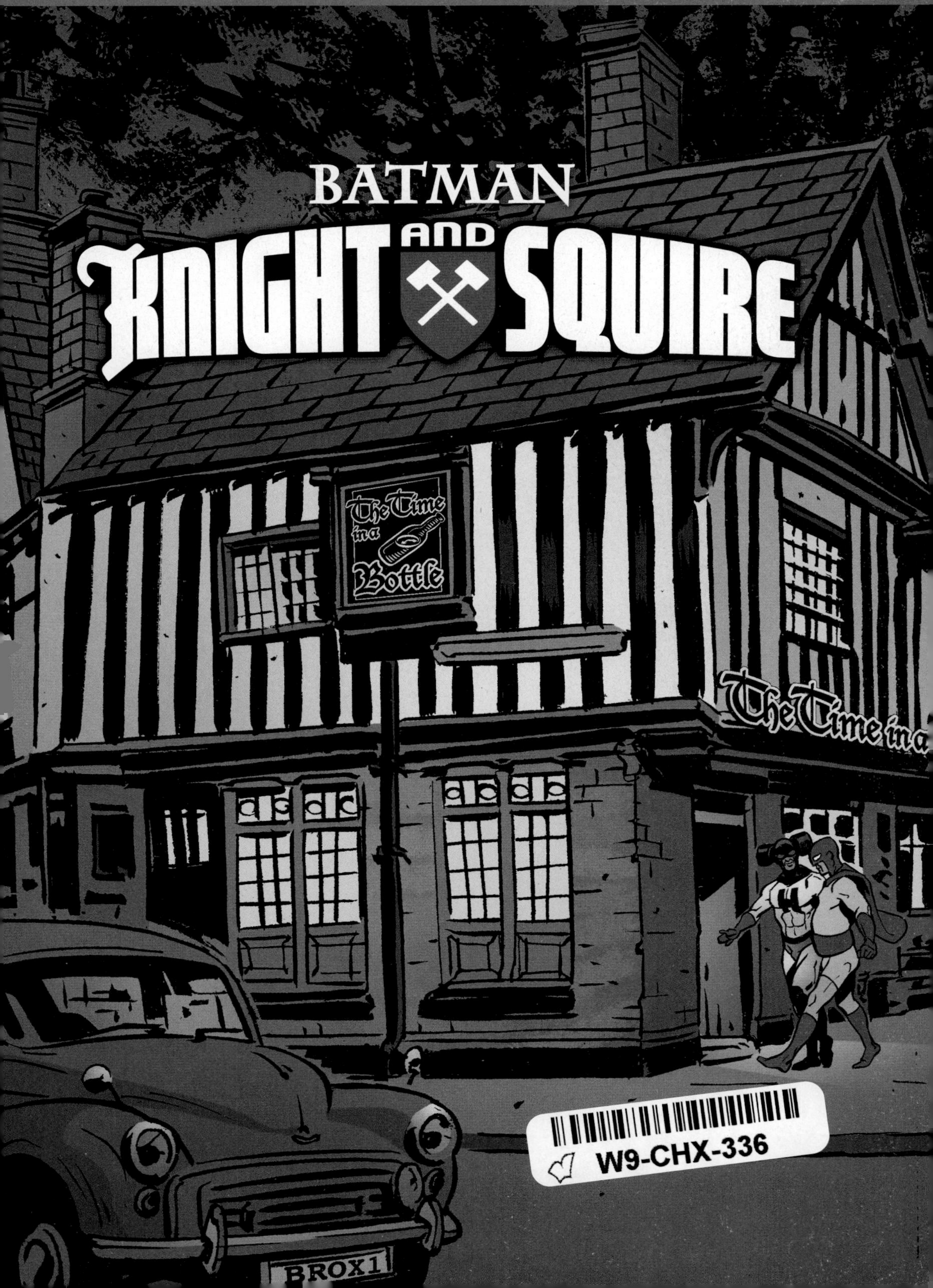
The Time in a Bottle
The Time in a
BROX1

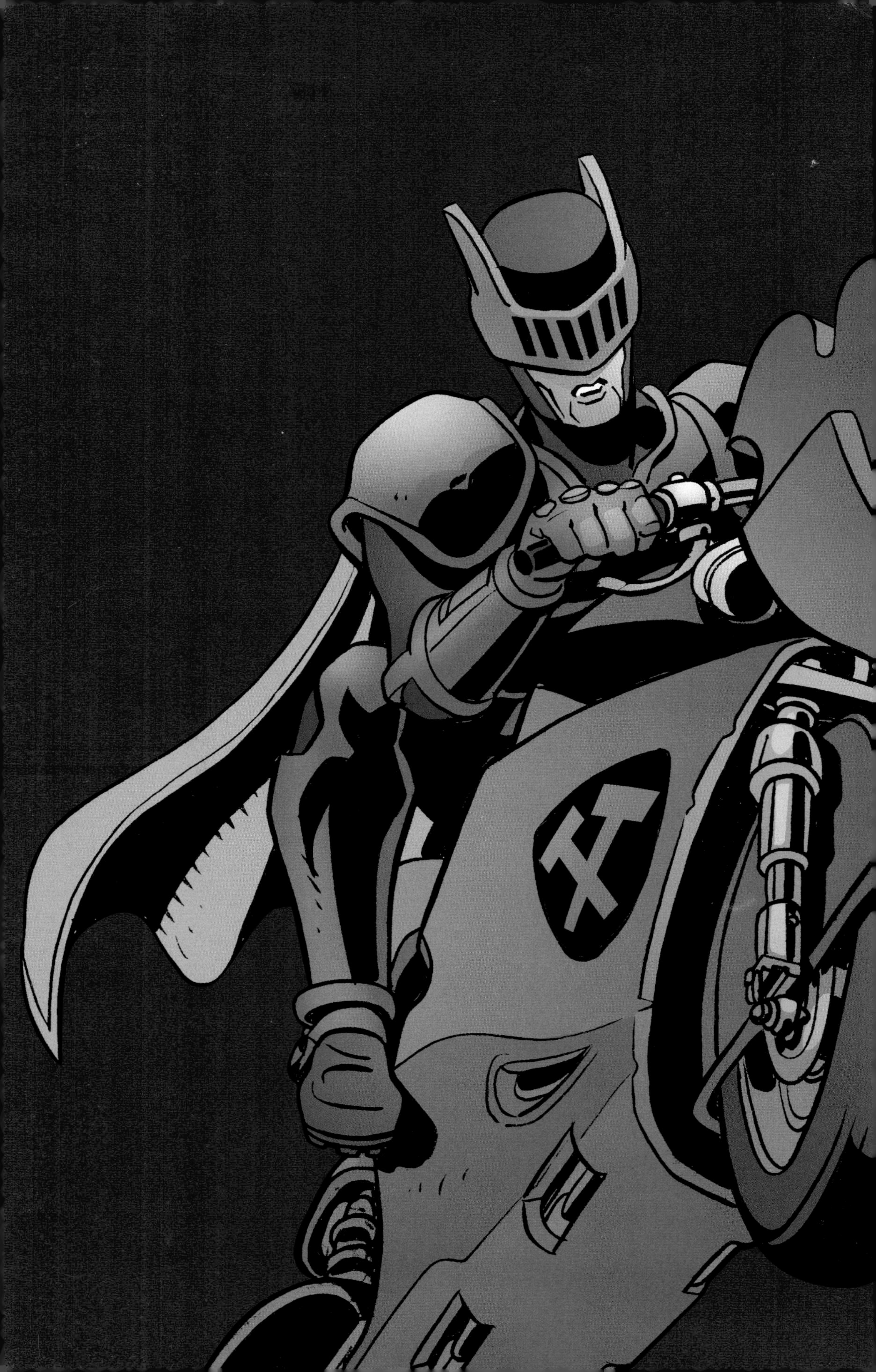

Paul Cornell
Writer

Jimmy Broxton
Artist

Staz Johnson
Issue #4 Layouts

Guy Major
Colorist

Steve Wands
Letterer

Yanick Paquette and **Michel Lacombe**
Cover Artists

Nathan Fairbairn
Cover Colorist

Billy Tucci
Issue #1 Variant Cover Artist

Hi-Fi
Issue #1 Variant Cover Colorist

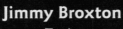
BATMAN

KNIGHT AND SQUIRE

Batman *created by* **Bob Kane**

Janelle Siegel
Editor – Original Series

Katie Kubert
Assistant Editor – Original Series

Ian Sattler
Director Editorial, Special Projects and Archival Editions

Scott Nybakken
Editor

Robbin Brosterman
Design Director – Books

Eddie Berganza
Executive Editor

Bob Harras
VP – Editor in Chief

Diane Nelson
President

Dan DiDio and **Jim Lee**
Co-Publishers

Geoff Johns
Chief Creative Officer

John Rood
Executive VP – Sales, Marketing and Business Development

Amy Genkins
Senior VP – Business and Legal Affairs

Nairi Gardiner
Senior VP – Finance

Jeff Boison
VP – Publishing Operations

Mark Chiarello
VP – Art Direction and Design

John Cunningham
VP – Marketing

Terri Cunningham
VP – Talent Relations and Services

Alison Gill
Senior VP – Manufacturing and Operations

David Hyde
VP – Publicity

Hank Kanalz
Senior VP – Digital

Jay Kogan
VP – Business and Legal Affairs, Publishing

Jack Mahan
VP – Business Affairs, Talent

Nick Napolitano
VP – Manufacturing Administration

Ron Perazza
VP – Online

Sue Pohja
VP – Book Sales

Courtney Simmons
Senior VP – Publicity

Bob Wayne
Senior VP – Sales

BATMAN: KNIGHT AND SQUIRE

Published by DC Comics. Cover and compilation Copyright © 2011 DC Comics. All Rights Reserved.

Originally published in single magazine form in KNIGHT AND SQUIRE 1-6. Copyright © 2010, 2011 DC Comics.
All Rights Reserved. All characters featured in this issue, the distinctive likenesses thereof and related elements are trademarks of DC Comics.
The stories, characters and incidents mentioned in this magazine are entirely fictional.
DC Comics does not read or accept unsolicited submissions of ideas, stories or artwork.

DC Comics, 1700 Broadway, New York, NY 10019
A Warner Bros. Entertainment Company
Printed by Quad/Graphics, Dubuque, IA, USA. 5/27/11. First Printing.
ISBN: 978-1-4012-3071-5

SUSTAINABLE
FORESTRY
INITIATIVE
Certified Chain of Custody
Promoting Sustainable
Forest Management

Fiber used in this product line meets the
sourcing requirements of the SFI program.
www.sfiprogram.org SGS-SFICOC-0130

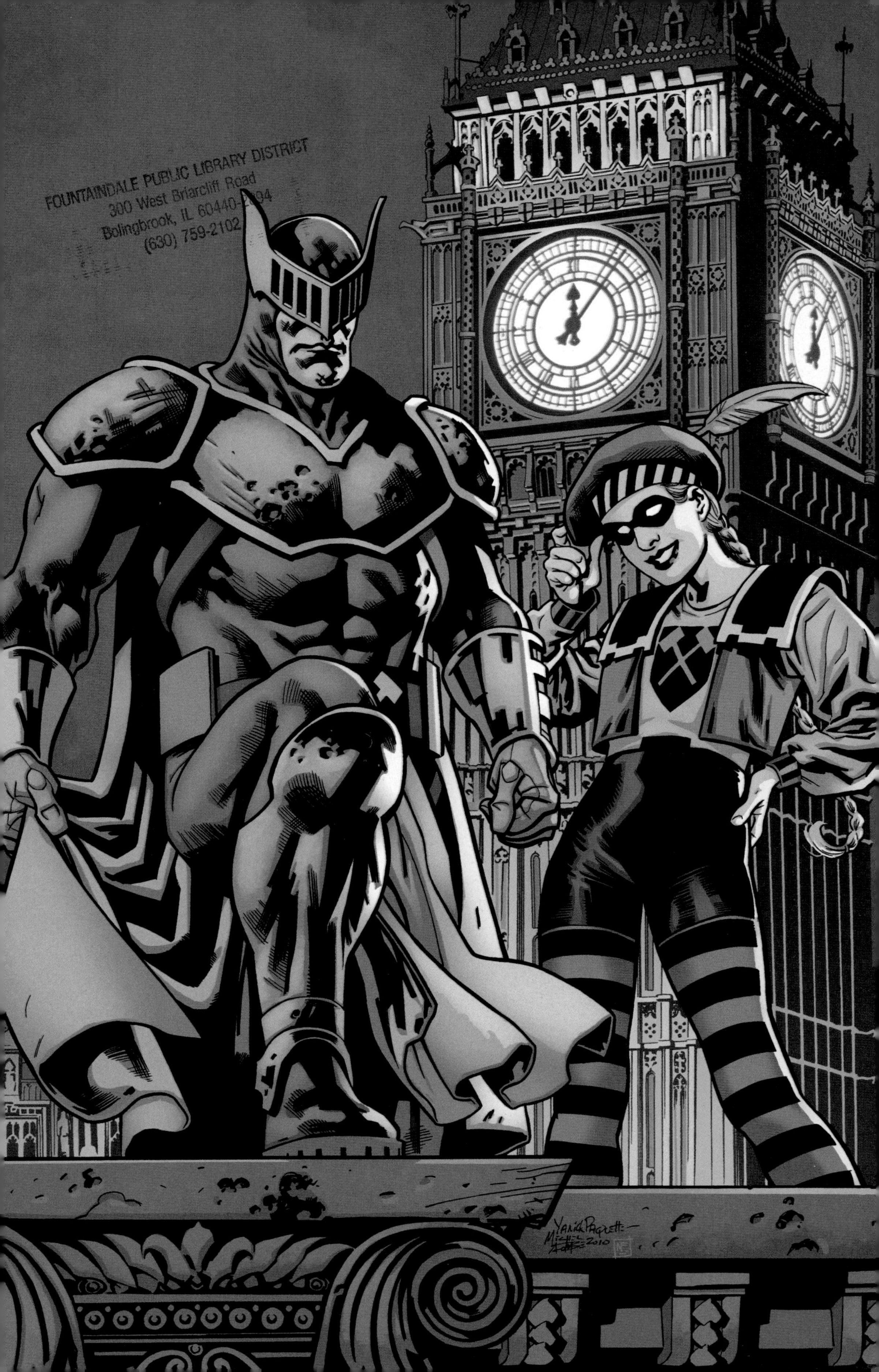

YANICK PAQUETTE
MICHEL LACOMBE 2010

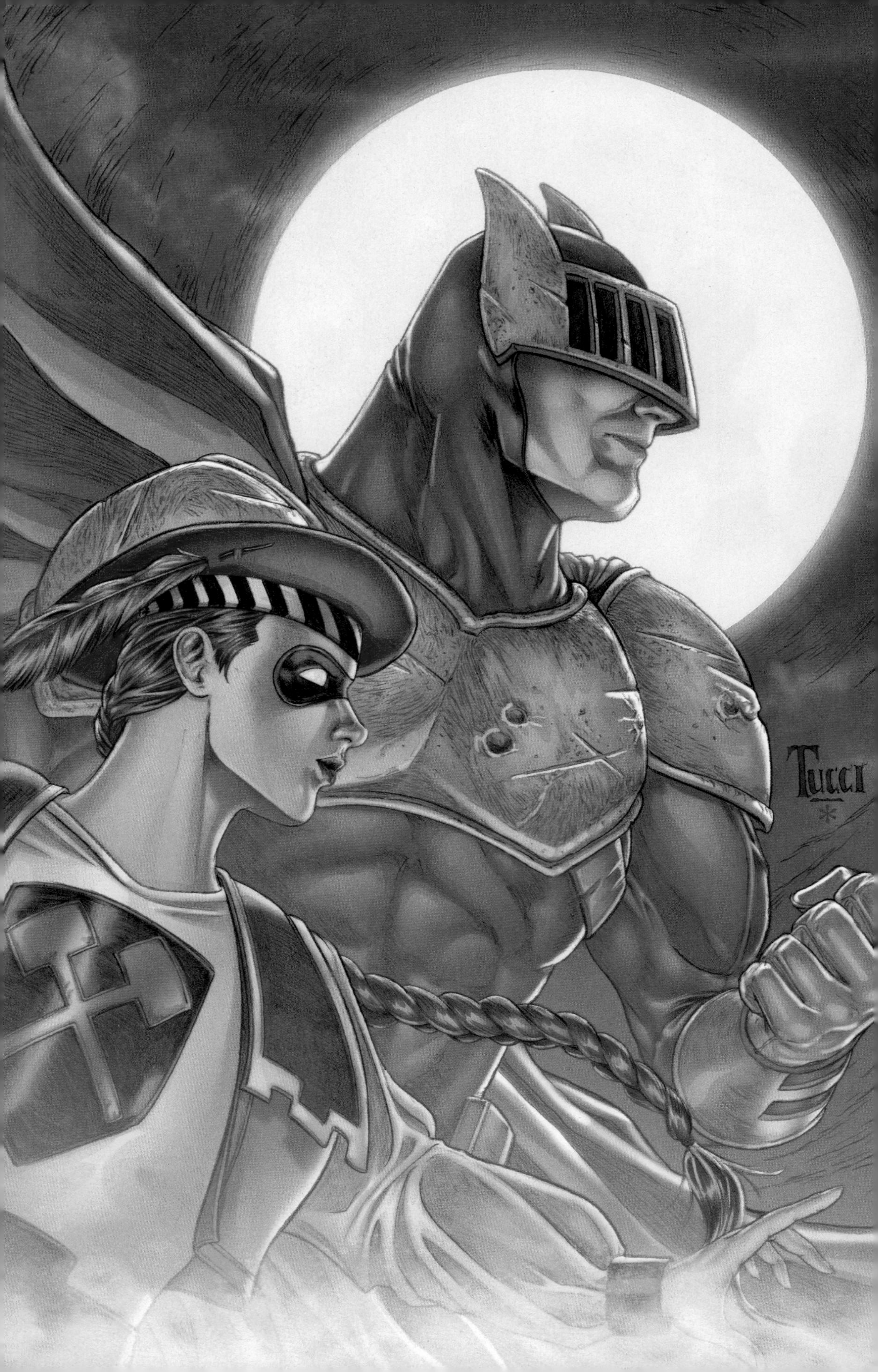
TUCCI

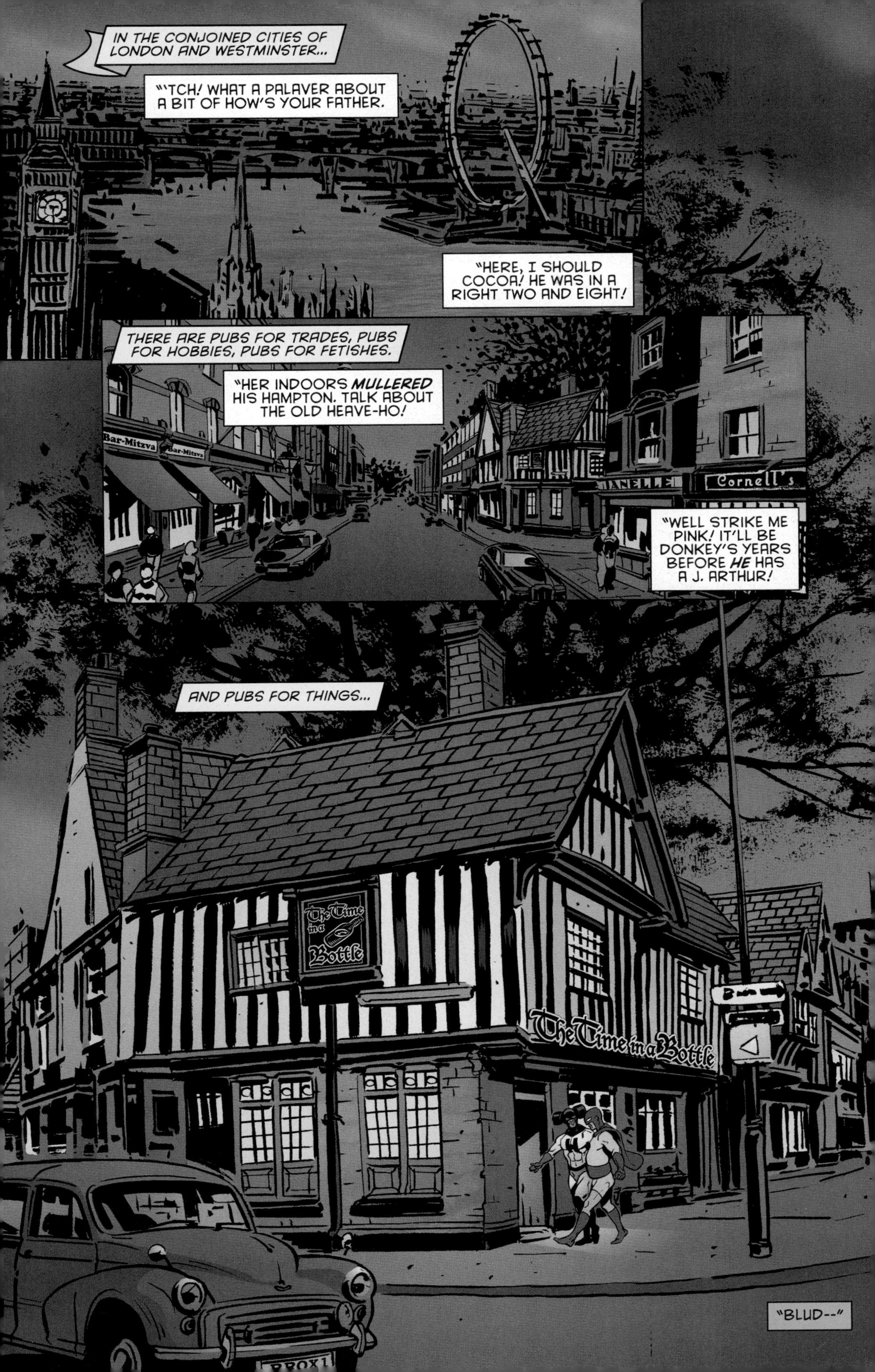
IN THE CONJOINED CITIES OF LONDON AND WESTMINSTER...
"'TCH! WHAT A PALAVER ABOUT A BIT OF HOW'S YOUR FATHER.
"HERE, I SHOULD COCOA! HE WAS IN A RIGHT TWO AND EIGHT!
THERE ARE PUBS FOR TRADES, PUBS FOR HOBBIES, PUBS FOR FETISHES.
"HER INDOORS MULLERED HIS HAMPTON. TALK ABOUT THE OLD HEAVE-HO!
Bar-Mitzva
Bar-Mitzva
Cornell's
"WELL STRIKE ME PINK! IT'LL BE DONKEY'S YEARS BEFORE HE HAS A J. ARTHUR!
AND PUBS FOR THINGS...
The Time in a Bottle
The Time in a Bottle
"BLUD--"

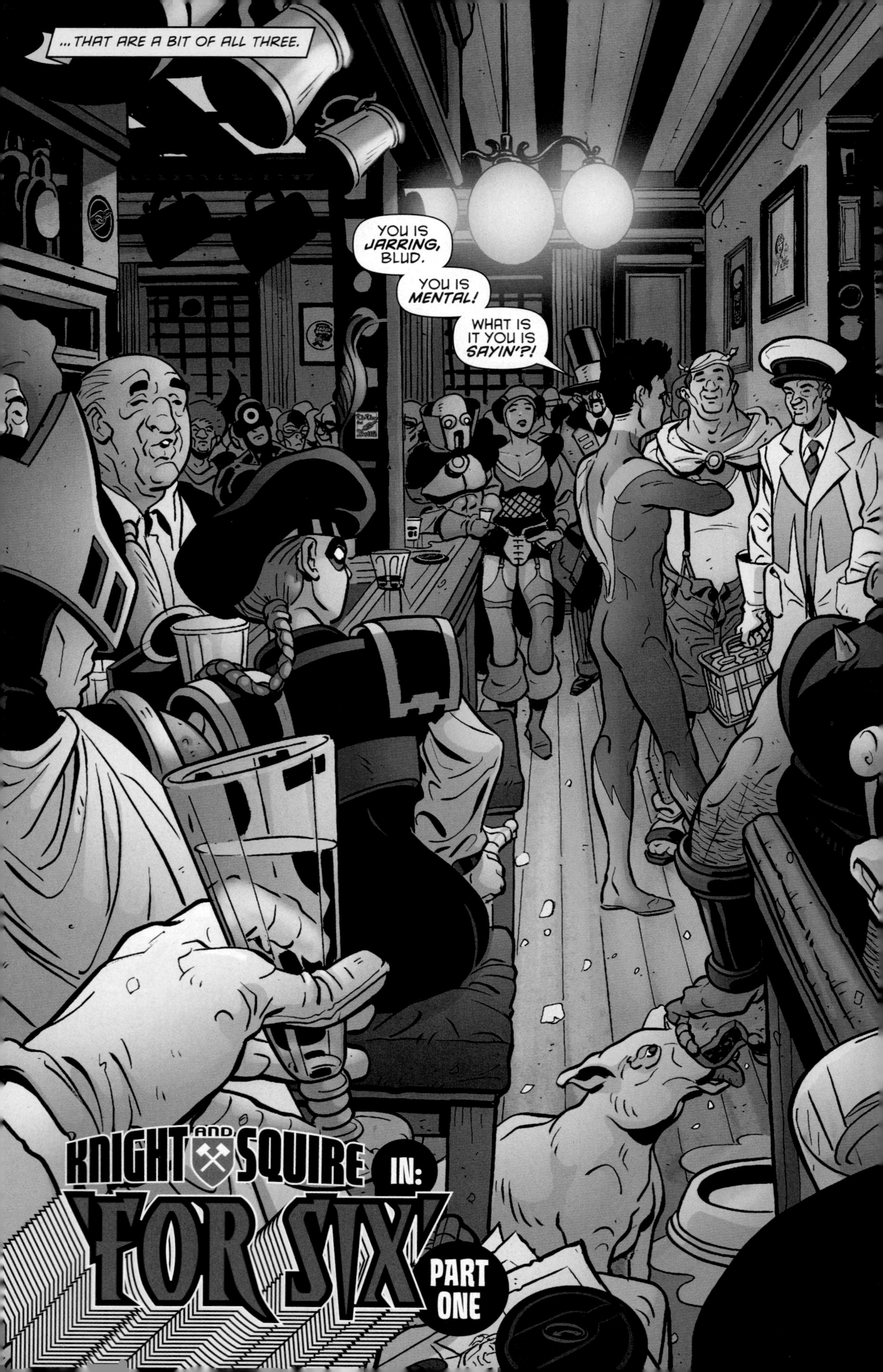
...THAT ARE A BIT OF ALL THREE.
YOU IS JARRING, BLUD.
YOU IS MENTAL!
WHAT IS IT YOU IS SAYIN'?!
KNIGHT AND SQUIRE IN:
'FOR SIX'
PART ONE

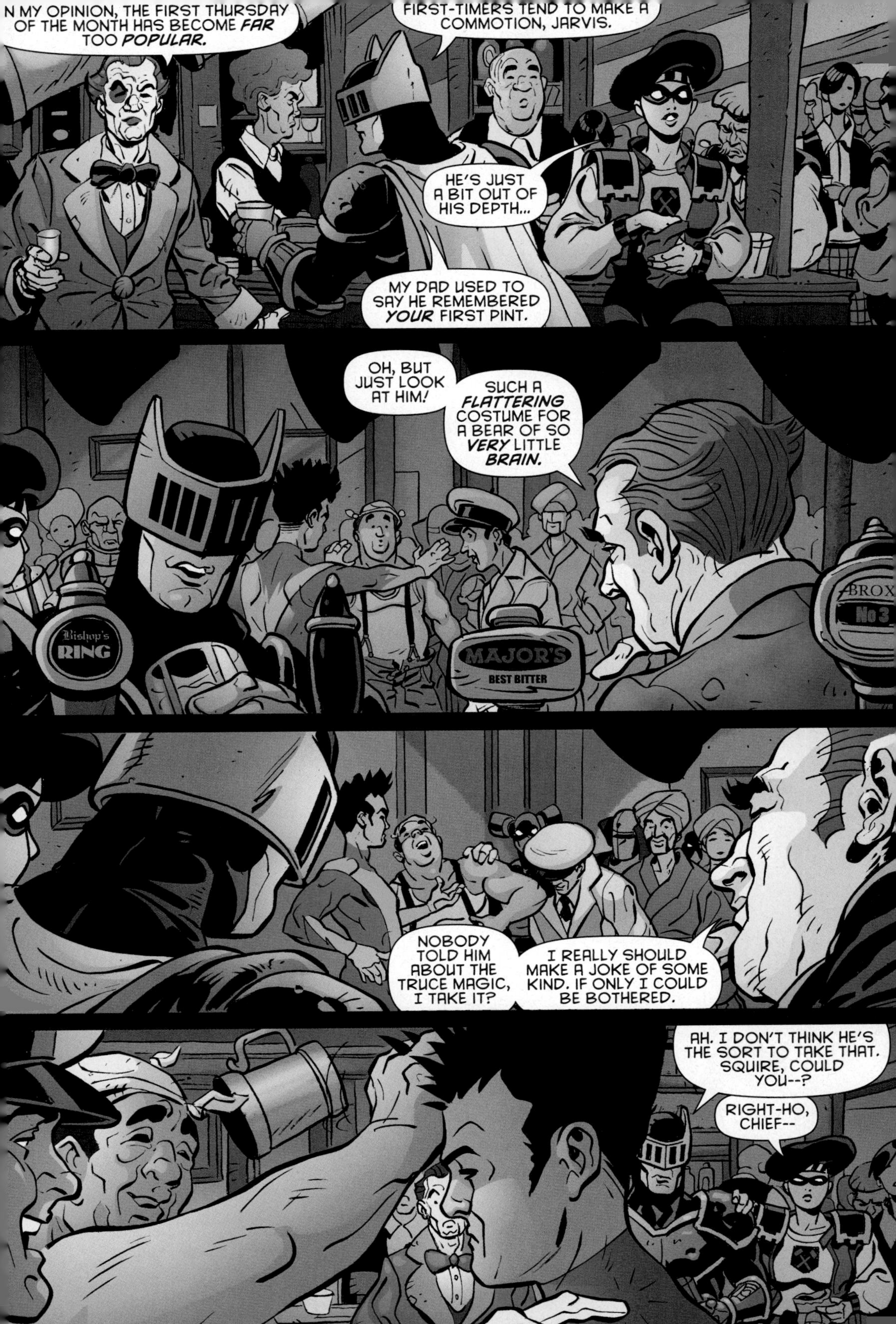
N MY OPINION, THE FIRST THURSDAY OF THE MONTH HAS BECOME FAR TOO POPULAR.
FIRST-TIMERS TEND TO MAKE A COMMOTION, JARVIS.
HE'S JUST A BIT OUT OF HIS DEPTH...
MY DAD USED TO SAY HE REMEMBERED YOUR FIRST PINT.
OH, BUT JUST LOOK AT HIM!
SUCH A FLATTERING COSTUME FOR A BEAR OF SO VERY LITTLE BRAIN.
Bishop's RING
MAJOR'S BEST BITTER
BROX No 3
NOBODY TOLD HIM ABOUT THE TRUCE MAGIC, I TAKE IT?
I REALLY SHOULD MAKE A JOKE OF SOME KIND. IF ONLY I COULD BE BOTHERED.
AH. I DON'T THINK HE'S THE SORT TO TAKE THAT. SQUIRE, COULD YOU--?
RIGHT-HO, CHIEF--

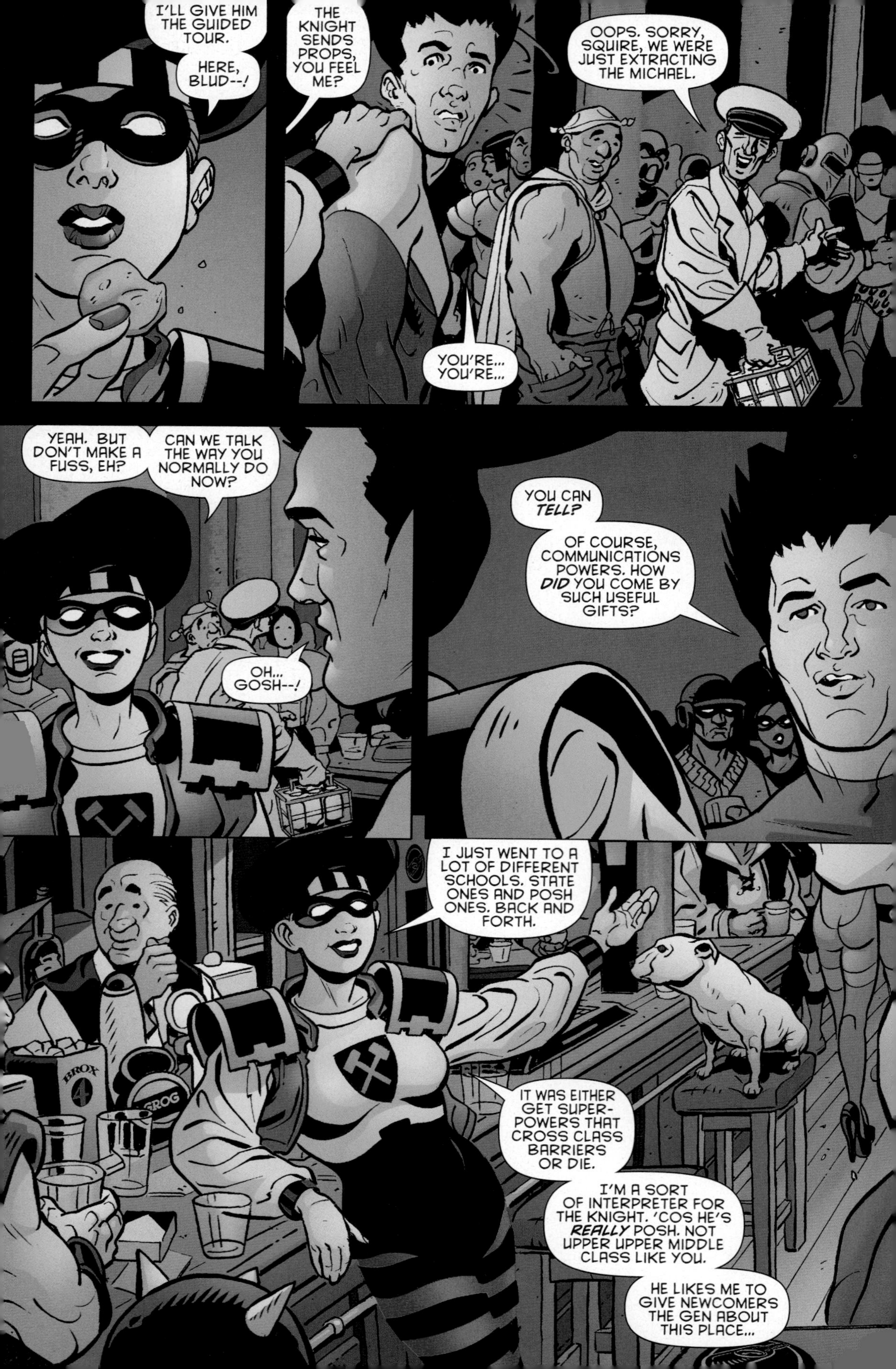

I'LL GIVE HIM THE GUIDED TOUR.
HERE, BLUD--!
THE KNIGHT SENDS PROPS, YOU FEEL ME?
OOPS. SORRY, SQUIRE, WE WERE JUST EXTRACTING THE MICHAEL.
YOU'RE... YOU'RE...
YEAH. BUT DON'T MAKE A FUSS, EH?
CAN WE TALK THE WAY YOU NORMALLY DO NOW?
OH... GOSH--!
YOU CAN *TELL?*
OF COURSE, COMMUNICATIONS POWERS. HOW *DID* YOU COME BY SUCH USEFUL GIFTS?
I JUST WENT TO A LOT OF DIFFERENT SCHOOLS. STATE ONES AND POSH ONES. BACK AND FORTH.
IT WAS EITHER GET SUPER-POWERS THAT CROSS CLASS BARRIERS OR DIE.
I'M A SORT OF INTERPRETER FOR THE KNIGHT. 'COS HE'S *REALLY* POSH. NOT UPPER UPPER MIDDLE CLASS LIKE YOU.
HE LIKES ME TO GIVE NEWCOMERS THE GEN ABOUT THIS PLACE...
BROX 4
GROG

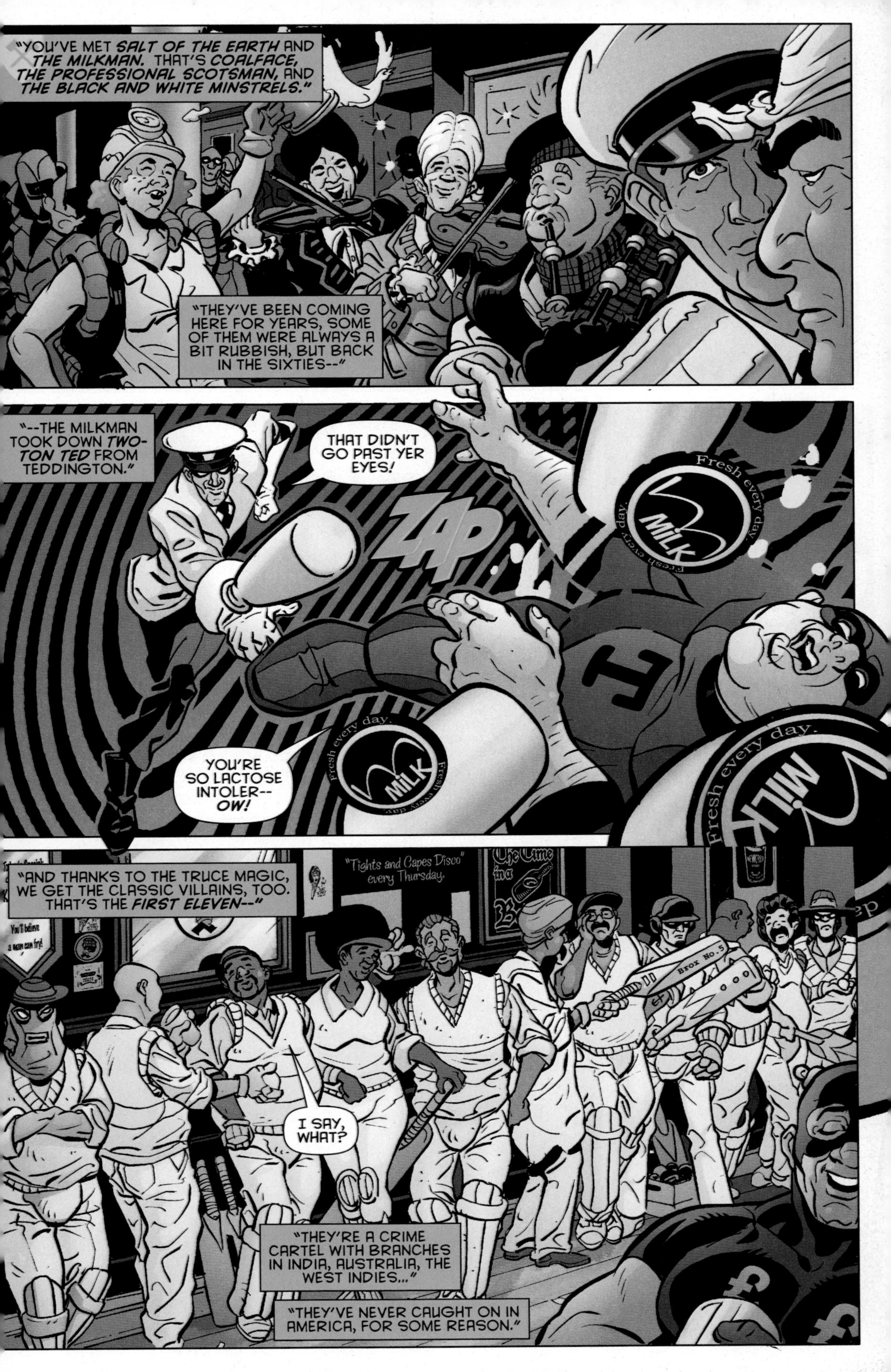
"YOU'VE MET SALT OF THE EARTH AND THE MILKMAN. THAT'S COALFACE, THE PROFESSIONAL SCOTSMAN, AND THE BLACK AND WHITE MINSTRELS."
"THEY'VE BEEN COMING HERE FOR YEARS, SOME OF THEM WERE ALWAYS A BIT RUBBISH, BUT BACK IN THE SIXTIES--"
"--THE MILKMAN TOOK DOWN TWO-TON TED FROM TEDDINGTON."
THAT DIDN'T GO PAST YER EYES!
ZAP
Fresh every day.
MILK
YOU'RE SO LACTOSE INTOLER-- OW!
"AND THANKS TO THE TRUCE MAGIC, WE GET THE CLASSIC VILLAINS, TOO. THAT'S THE FIRST ELEVEN--"
"Tights and Capes Disco" every Thursday.
You'll believe a man can fry!
Brox No. 5
I SAY, WHAT?
"THEY'RE A CRIME CARTEL WITH BRANCHES IN INDIA, AUSTRALIA, THE WEST INDIES..."
"THEY'VE NEVER CAUGHT ON IN AMERICA, FOR SOME REASON."

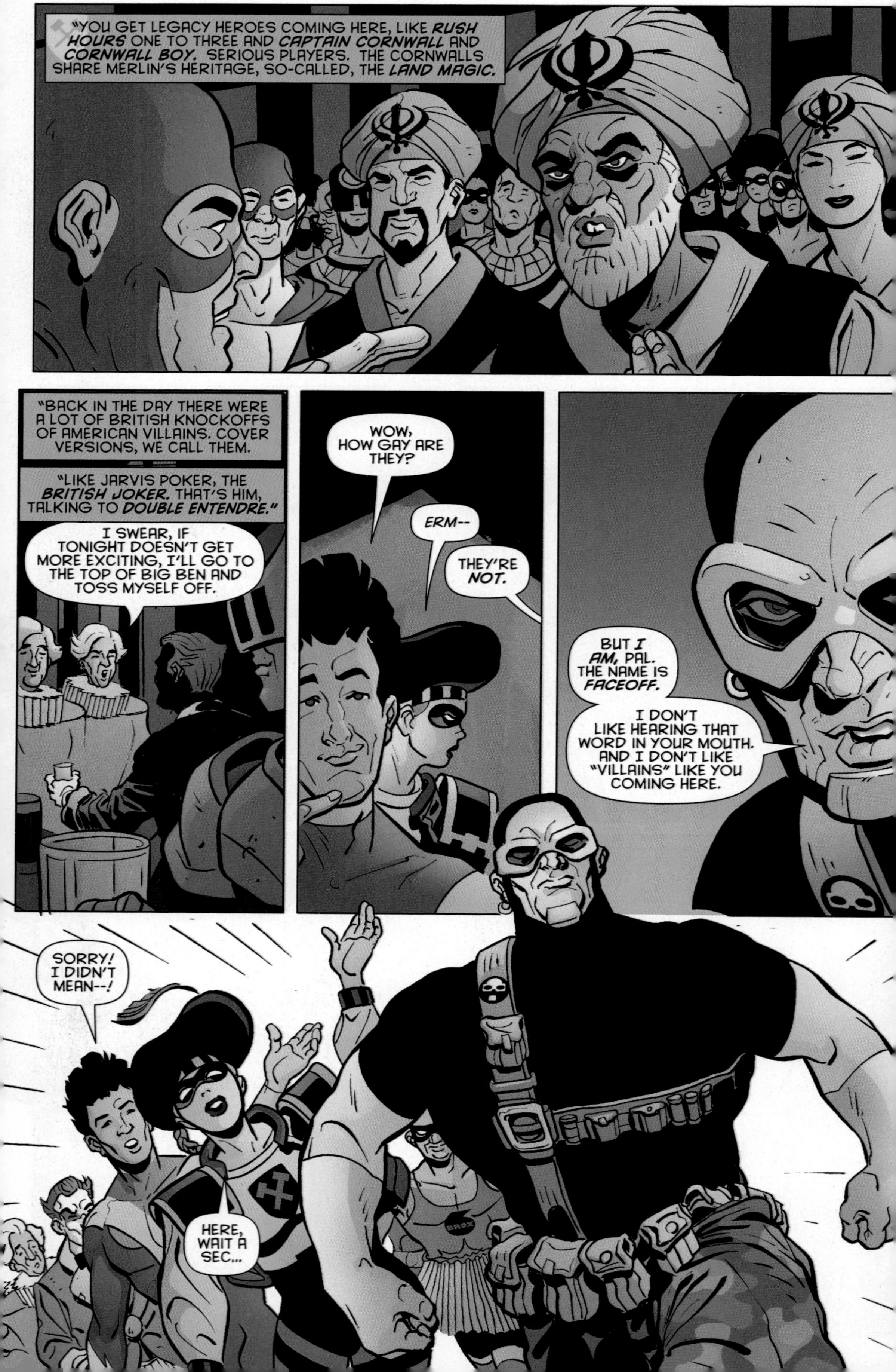
"YOU GET LEGACY HEROES COMING HERE, LIKE RUSH HOURS ONE TO THREE AND CAPTAIN CORNWALL AND CORNWALL BOY. SERIOUS PLAYERS. THE CORNWALLS SHARE MERLIN'S HERITAGE, SO-CALLED, THE LAND MAGIC.
"BACK IN THE DAY THERE WERE A LOT OF BRITISH KNOCKOFFS OF AMERICAN VILLAINS. COVER VERSIONS, WE CALL THEM.
"LIKE JARVIS POKER, THE BRITISH JOKER. THAT'S HIM, TALKING TO DOUBLE ENTENDRE."
I SWEAR, IF TONIGHT DOESN'T GET MORE EXCITING, I'LL GO TO THE TOP OF BIG BEN AND TOSS MYSELF OFF.
WOW, HOW GAY ARE THEY?
ERM--
THEY'RE NOT.
BUT I AM, PAL. THE NAME IS FACEOFF.
I DON'T LIKE HEARING THAT WORD IN YOUR MOUTH. AND I DON'T LIKE "VILLAINS" LIKE YOU COMING HERE.
SORRY! I DIDN'T MEAN--!
HERE, WAIT A SEC...

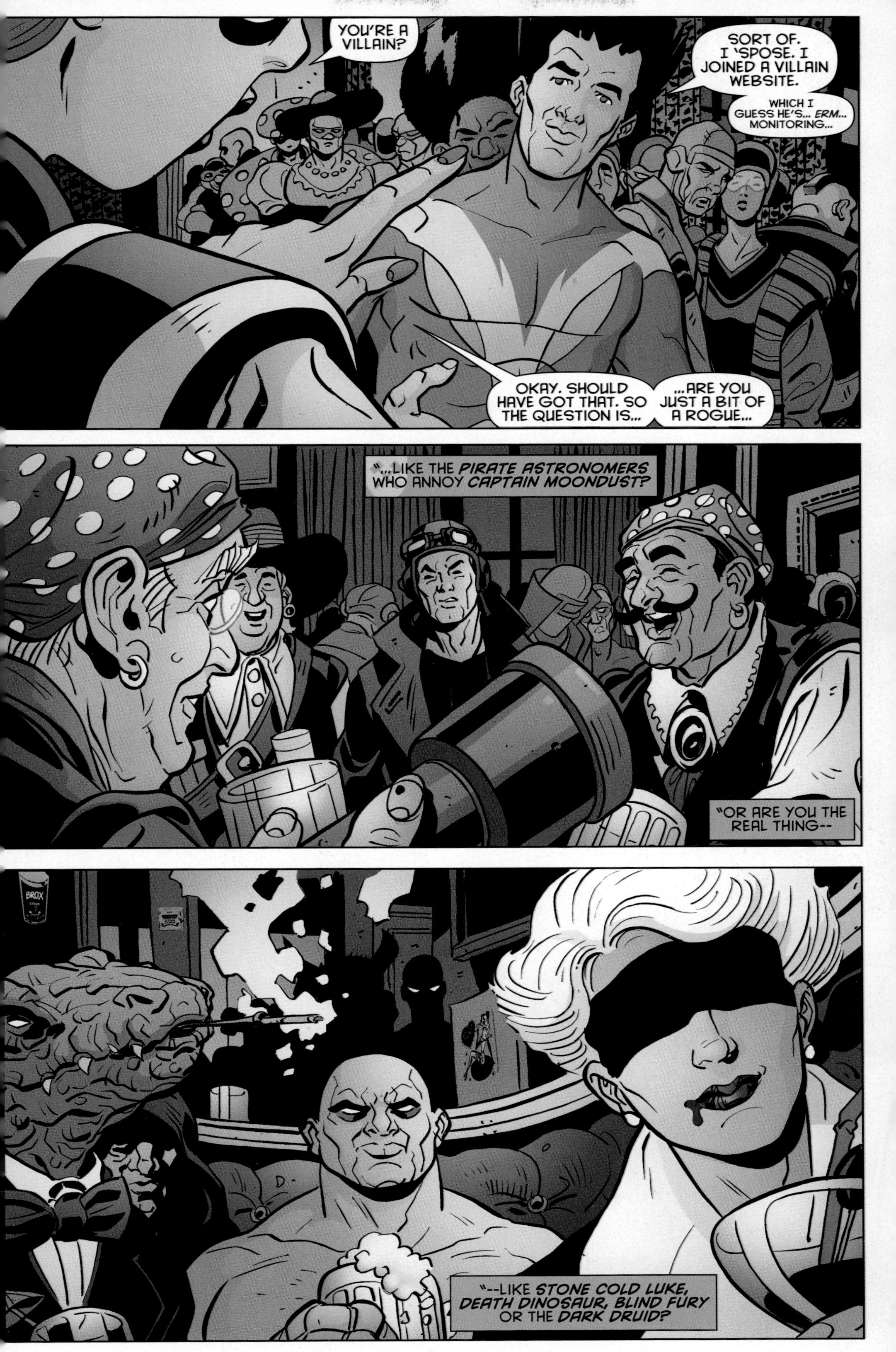
YOU'RE A VILLAIN?
SORT OF. I 'SPOSE. I JOINED A VILLAIN WEBSITE.
WHICH I GUESS HE'S... *ERM*... MONITORING...
OKAY. SHOULD HAVE GOT THAT. SO THE QUESTION IS...
...ARE YOU JUST A BIT OF A ROGUE...
"...LIKE THE *PIRATE ASTRONOMERS* WHO ANNOY *CAPTAIN MOONDUST*?
"OR ARE YOU THE REAL THING--
BROX
"--LIKE *STONE COLD LUKE, DEATH DINOSAUR, BLIND FURY* OR THE *DARK DRUID*?

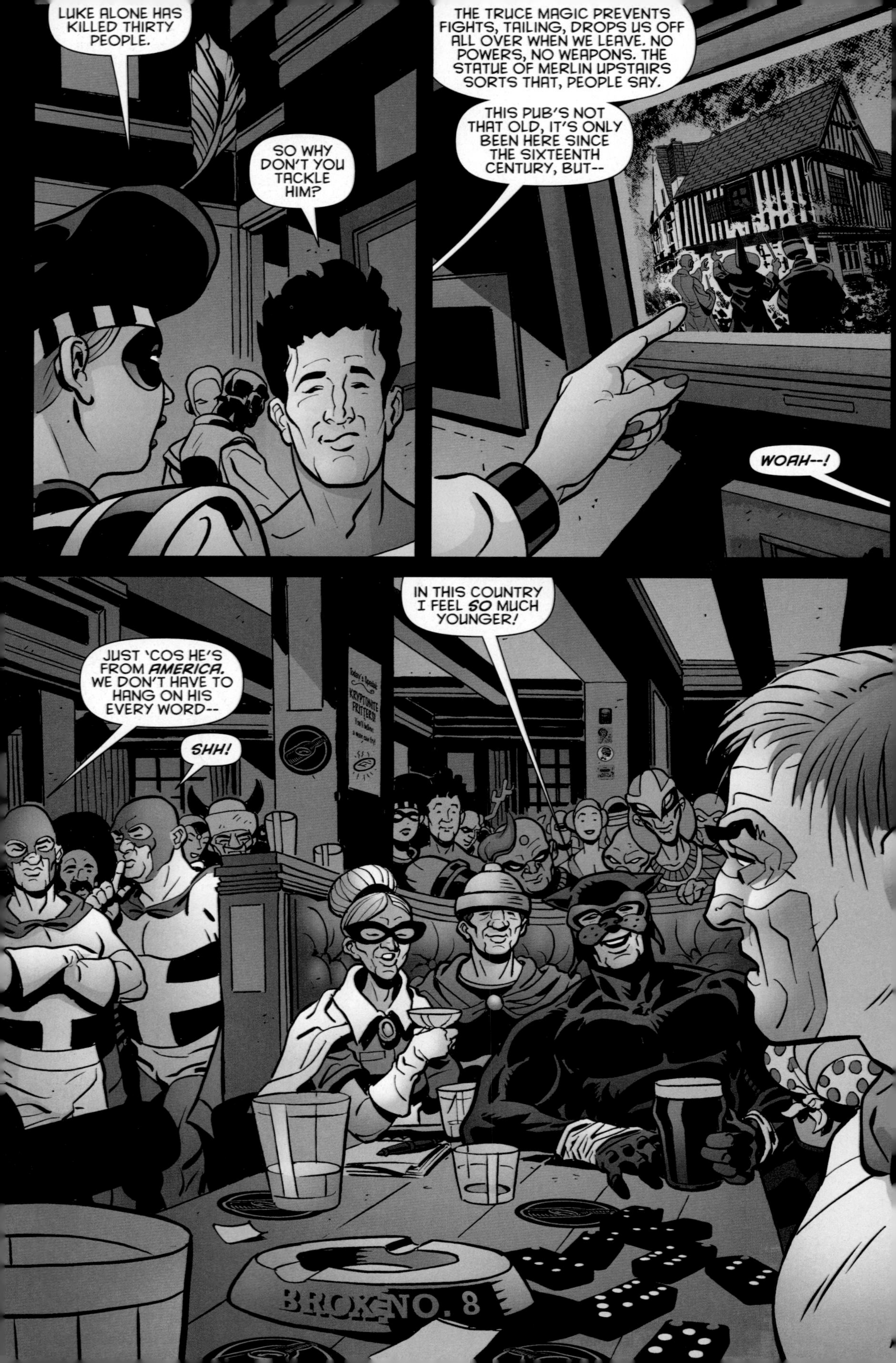
LUKE ALONE HAS KILLED THIRTY PEOPLE.
SO WHY DON'T YOU TACKLE HIM?
THE TRUCE MAGIC PREVENTS FIGHTS, TAILING, DROPS US OFF ALL OVER WHEN WE LEAVE. NO POWERS, NO WEAPONS. THE STATUE OF MERLIN UPSTAIRS SORTS THAT, PEOPLE SAY.
THIS PUB'S NOT THAT OLD, IT'S ONLY BEEN HERE SINCE THE SIXTEENTH CENTURY, BUT--
WOAH--!
JUST 'COS HE'S FROM *AMERICA.* WE DON'T HAVE TO HANG ON HIS EVERY WORD--
SHH!
IN THIS COUNTRY I FEEL *SO* MUCH YOUNGER!
KRYPTONITE FRITTERS
BROK-NO. 8

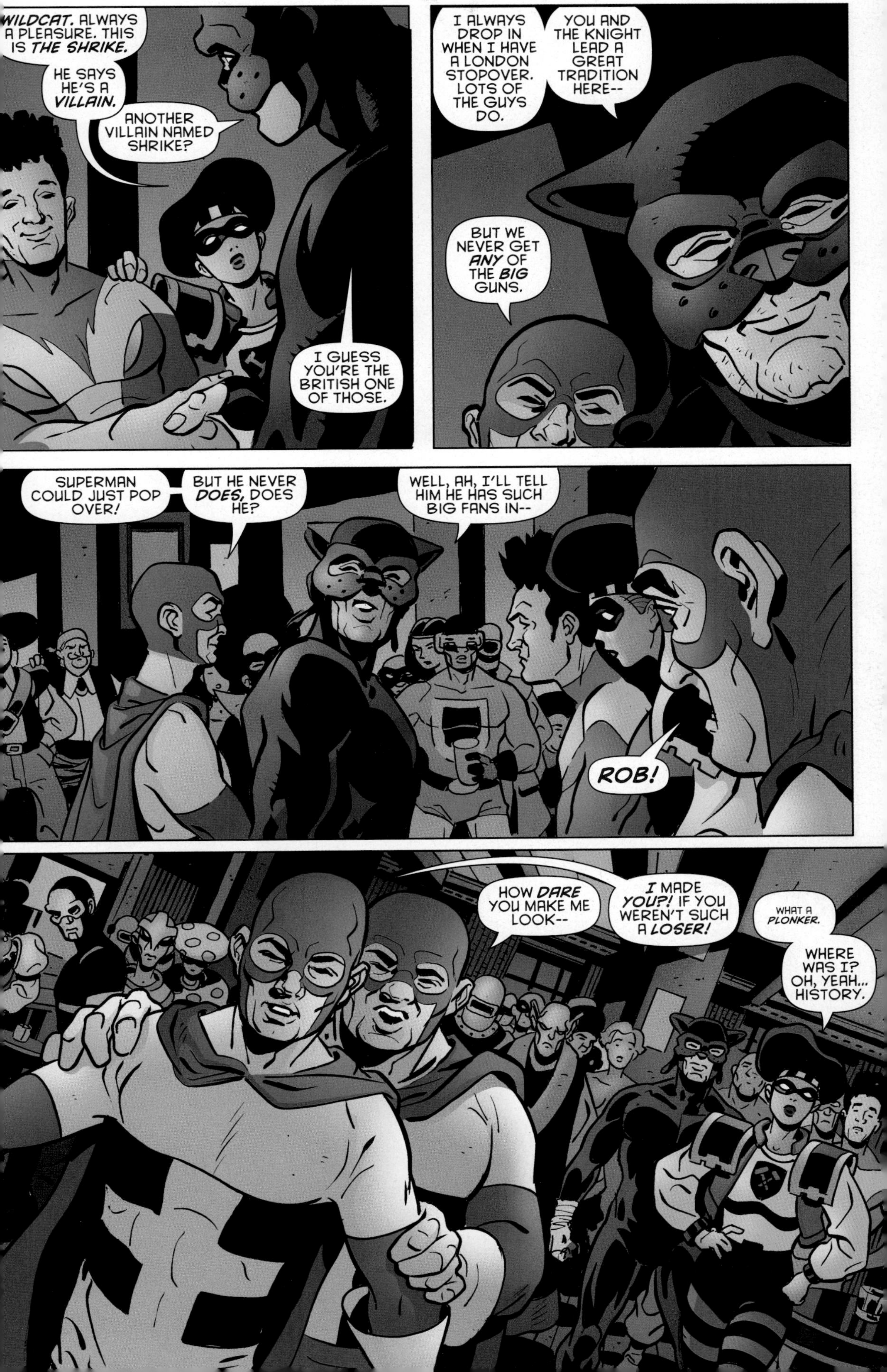
WILDCAT. ALWAYS A PLEASURE. THIS IS THE SHRIKE.
HE SAYS HE'S A VILLAIN.
ANOTHER VILLAIN NAMED SHRIKE?
I GUESS YOU'RE THE BRITISH ONE OF THOSE.
I ALWAYS DROP IN WHEN I HAVE A LONDON STOPOVER. LOTS OF THE GUYS DO.
YOU AND THE KNIGHT LEAD A GREAT TRADITION HERE--
BUT WE NEVER GET ANY OF THE BIG GUNS.
SUPERMAN COULD JUST POP OVER!
BUT HE NEVER DOES, DOES HE?
WELL, AH, I'LL TELL HIM HE HAS SUCH BIG FANS IN--
ROB!
HOW DARE YOU MAKE ME LOOK--
I MADE YOU?! IF YOU WEREN'T SUCH A LOSER!
WHAT A PLONKER.
WHERE WAS I? OH, YEAH... HISTORY.

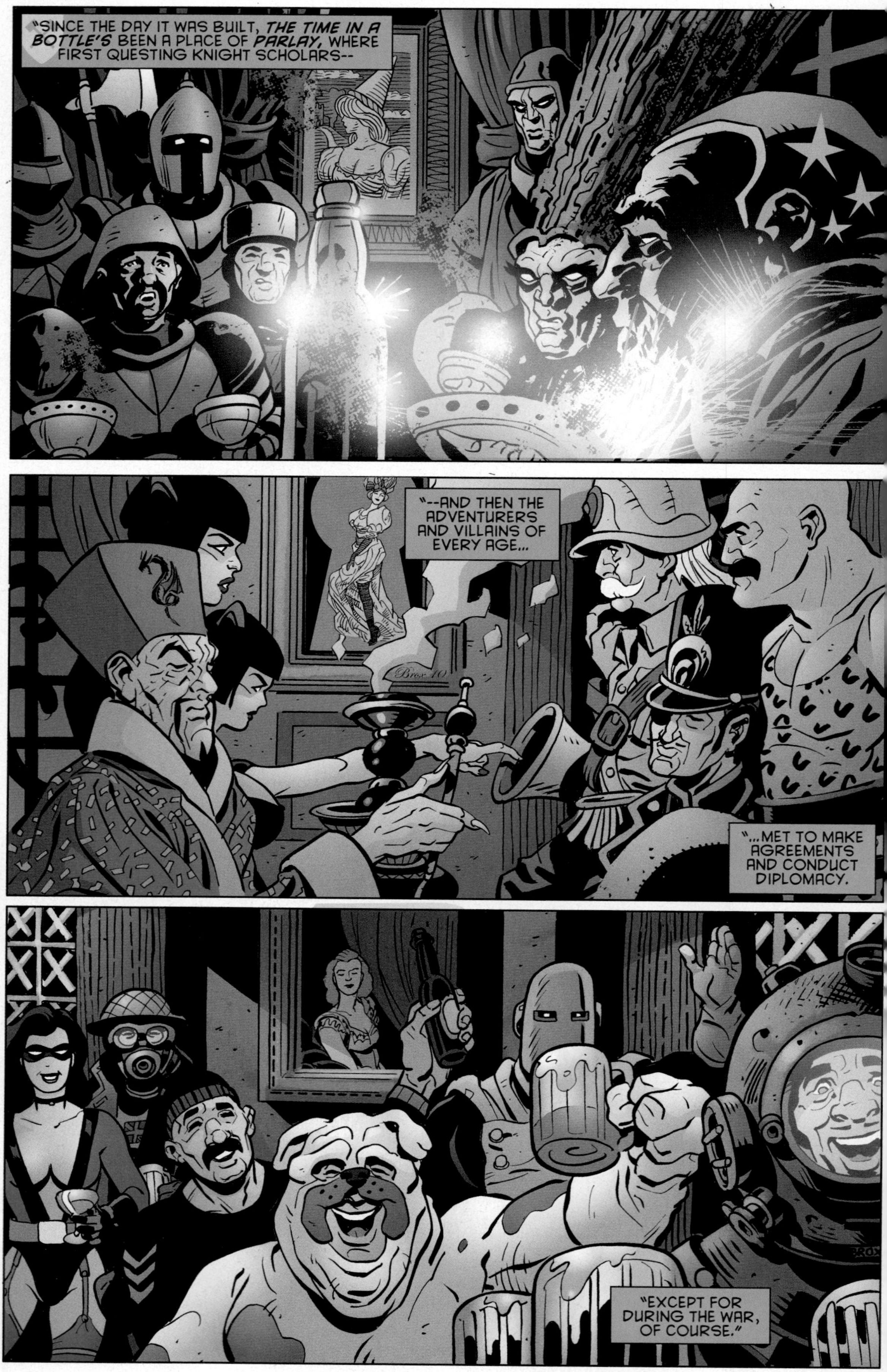
"SINCE THE DAY IT WAS BUILT, *THE TIME IN A BOTTLE'S* BEEN A PLACE OF *PARLAY,* WHERE FIRST QUESTING KNIGHT SCHOLARS--
"--AND THEN THE ADVENTURERS AND VILLAINS OF EVERY AGE...
"...MET TO MAKE AGREEMENTS AND CONDUCT DIPLOMACY.
"EXCEPT FOR DURING THE WAR, OF COURSE."

"THIS IS WHERE THE SO-CALLED MARTIANS CAME TO SIGN THE TREATY TO STOP INVADING BRITAIN AND TRY OTHER PLACES, TOO.

"WHERE THE CHURCH OF BLOOD OF ENGLAND CAME TO ANNOUNCE THEY WERE NOW ONLY SACRIFICING VIRGINS *METAPHORICALLY.*

The Church of Blood

The Church of Blood of England...
the business with the virgins, an...

"WHERE THE *RATTLES* SPLIT INTO THEIR GOOD AND EVIL FACTIONS. SO THIS IS WHERE *DARK WINGS* STARTED!

"AND LOOK..."

...*THAT* IS WHERE ALEISTER CROWLEY BUMPED HIS BONCE.

I SUPPOSE HE'LL FIT IN SOMEWHERE. AMONG THE FUNNY AND THE SERIOUS, THE HORRIFIC AND WHIMSICAL, ALL PUSHED TOGETHER...

ARE YOU TALKING ABOUT THE PUB OR BRITAIN?

BOTH. BUT I *WORRY*...

...IF WE GET A FEW MORE LIKE THAT LAD "FACE-OFF"--

--ONE DAY HE'LL *HAVE* SOMEONE'S FACE OFF. LORD, THAT'S NOT EVEN FUNNY.

BUT, THIS *BEING* BRITAIN, THERE'S A SENSE OF *MODERATION* HERE. *YOU* COULD HAVE BEEN MORE LIKE THE *ORIGINAL* JOKER--

OH, I SUPPOSE. I DO RATHER WORSHIP HIS STYLE--

I JUST CAN'T BRING MYSELF TO COMMIT *CRIMES*.

TOO DREARY FOR ME. TOO INFRA DIG. *TASTE* HAS ALWAYS BEEN MY *CURSE*.

OH DEAR. KNIGHT, MY DEAR OLD MUCKER, I'VE BEEN COMING HERE FIFTY YEARS--

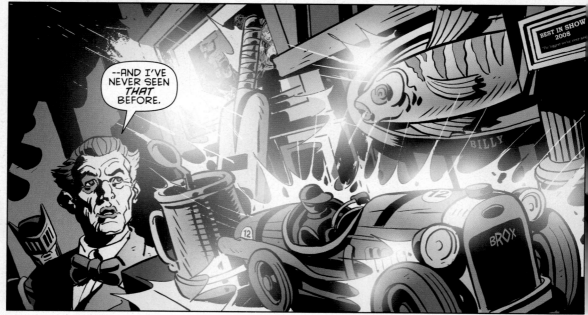

--AND I'VE NEVER SEEN *THAT* BEFORE.

BEST IN SHOW 2008

BILLY

BROX

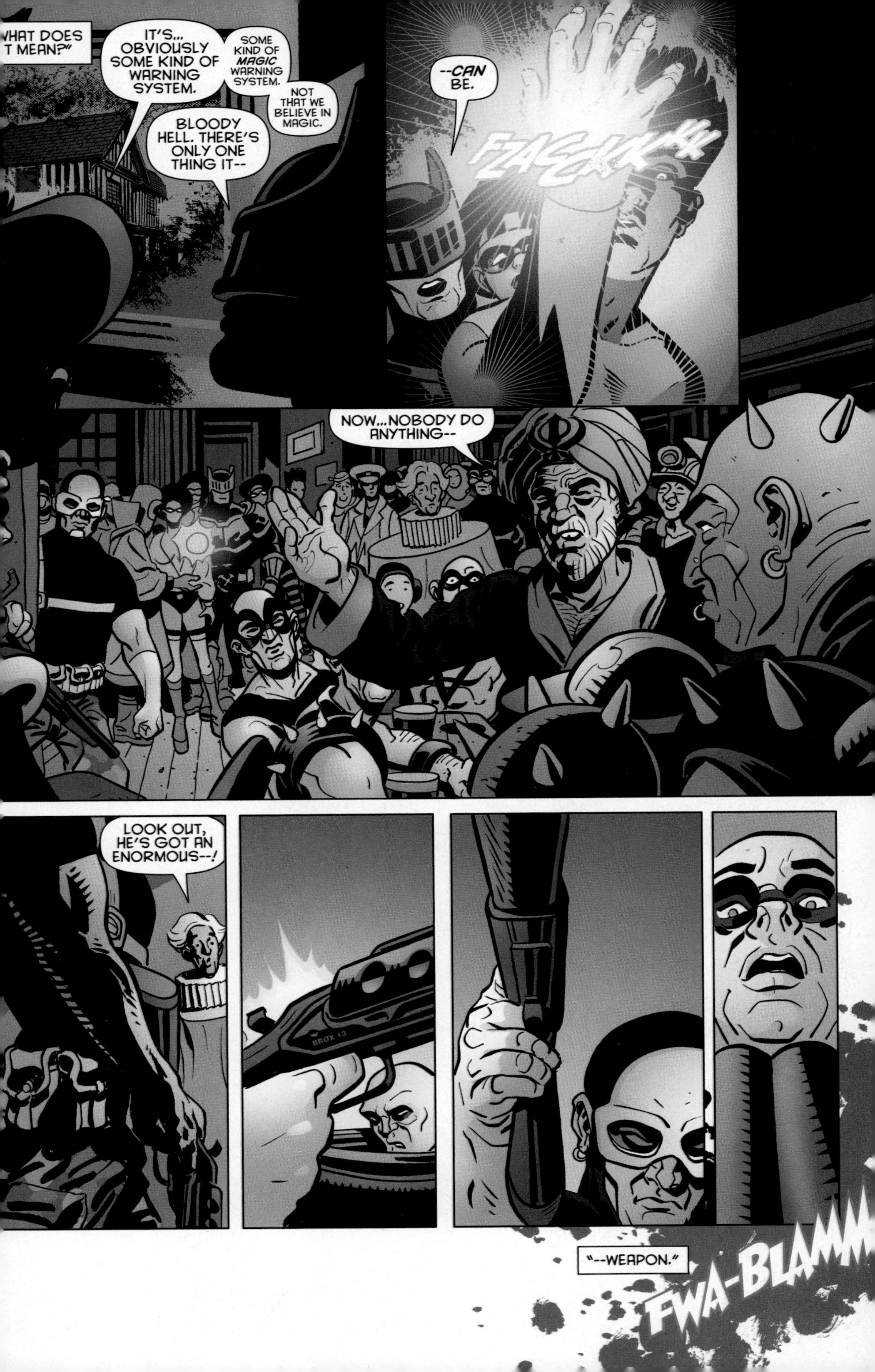

WHAT DOES T MEAN?"
IT'S... OBVIOUSLY SOME KIND OF WARNING SYSTEM.
SOME KIND OF MAGIC WARNING SYSTEM.
NOT THAT WE BELIEVE IN MAGIC.
BLOODY HELL. THERE'S ONLY ONE THING IT--
--CAN BE.
FZAAAK
NOW...NOBODY DO ANYTHING--
LOOK OUT, HE'S GOT AN ENORMOUS--!
BROX 13
"--WEAPON."
FWA-BLAMM

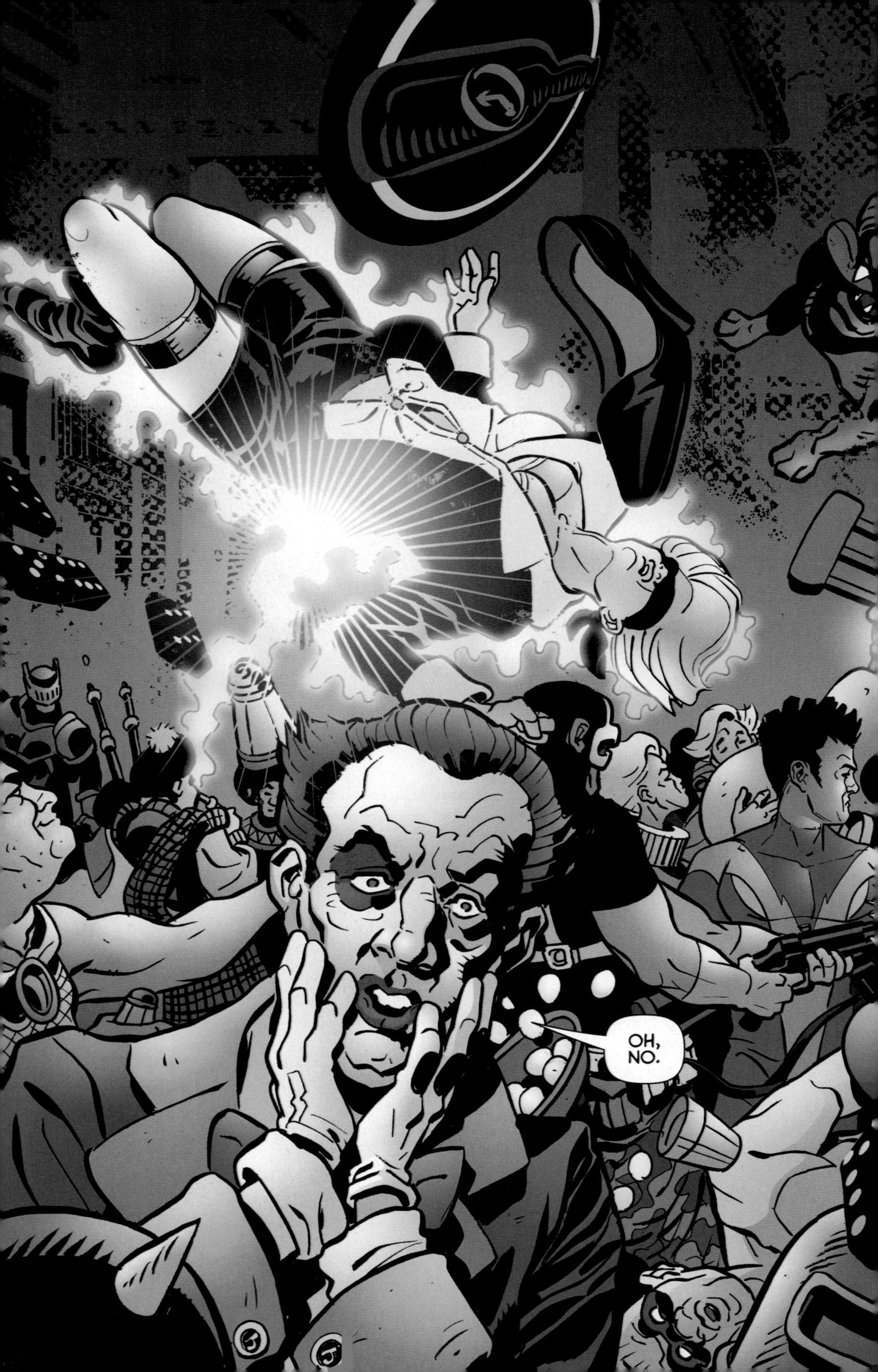
OH, NO.

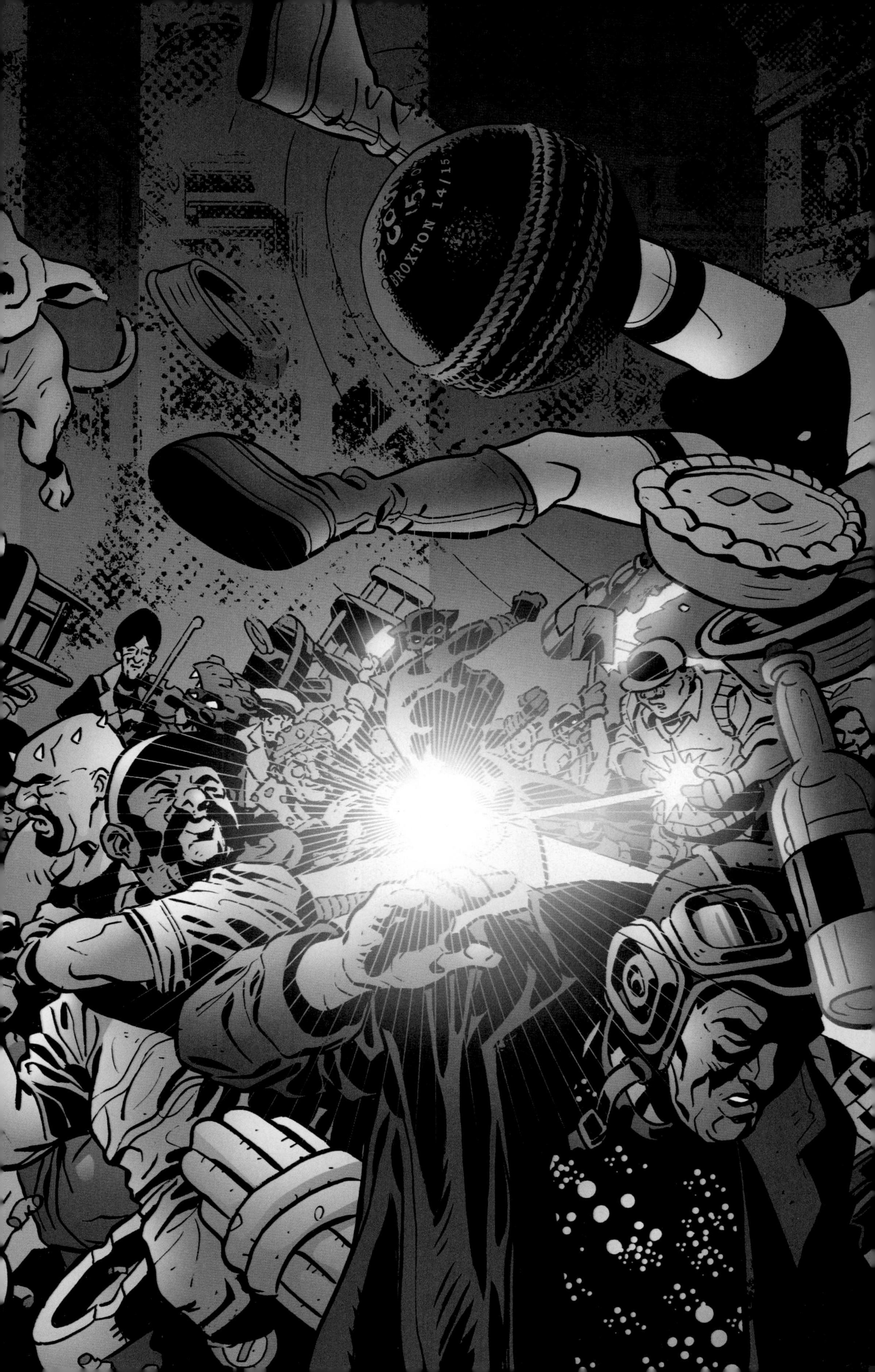
BROXTON 14/15

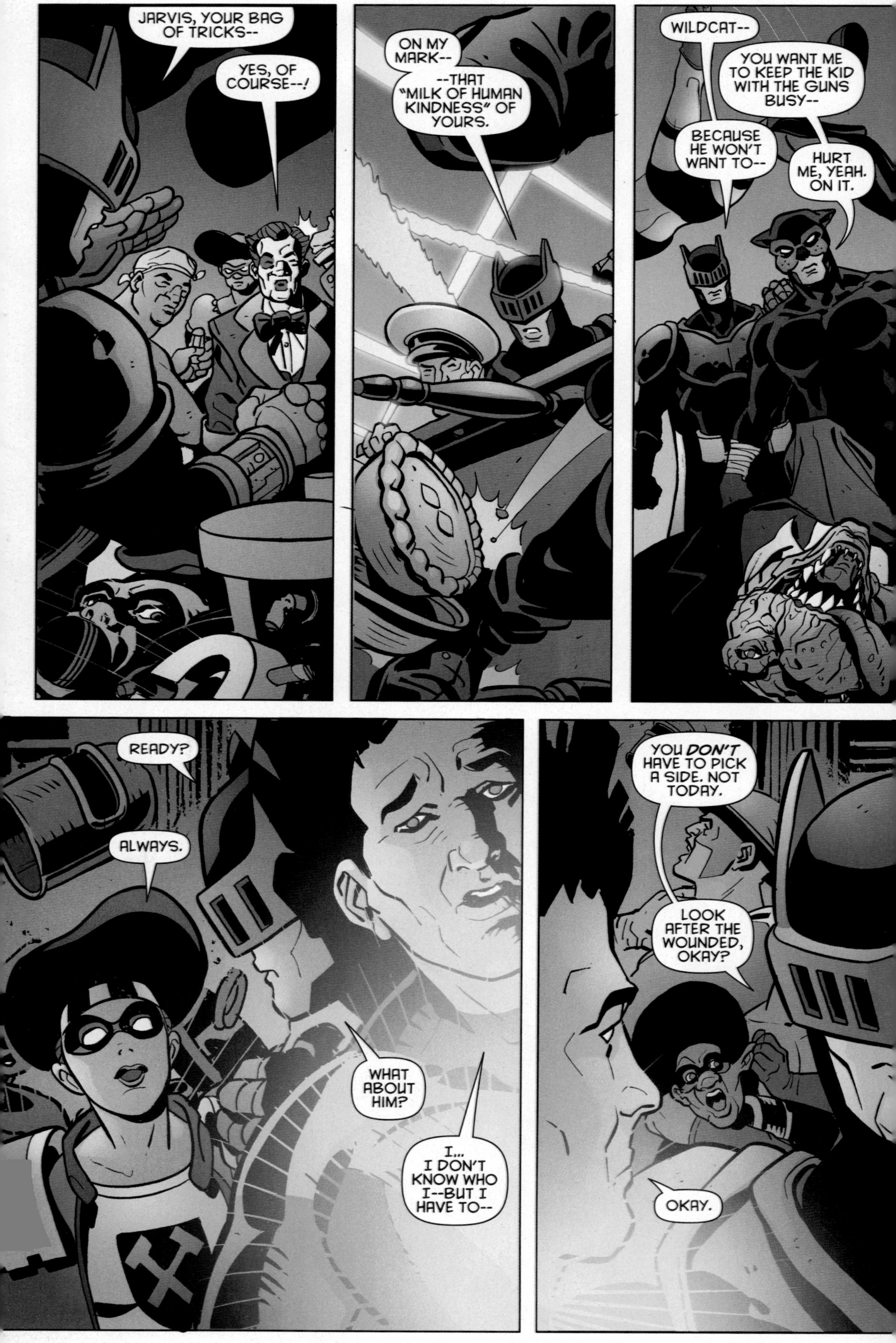

JARVIS, YOUR BAG OF TRICKS--
YES, OF COURSE--!
ON MY MARK--
--THAT "MILK OF HUMAN KINDNESS" OF YOURS.
WILDCAT--
YOU WANT ME TO KEEP THE KID WITH THE GUNS BUSY--
BECAUSE HE WON'T WANT TO--
HURT ME, YEAH. ON IT.
READY?
ALWAYS.
WHAT ABOUT HIM?
I... I DON'T KNOW WHO I--BUT I HAVE TO--
YOU DON'T HAVE TO PICK A SIDE. NOT TODAY.
LOOK AFTER THE WOUNDED, OKAY?
OKAY.

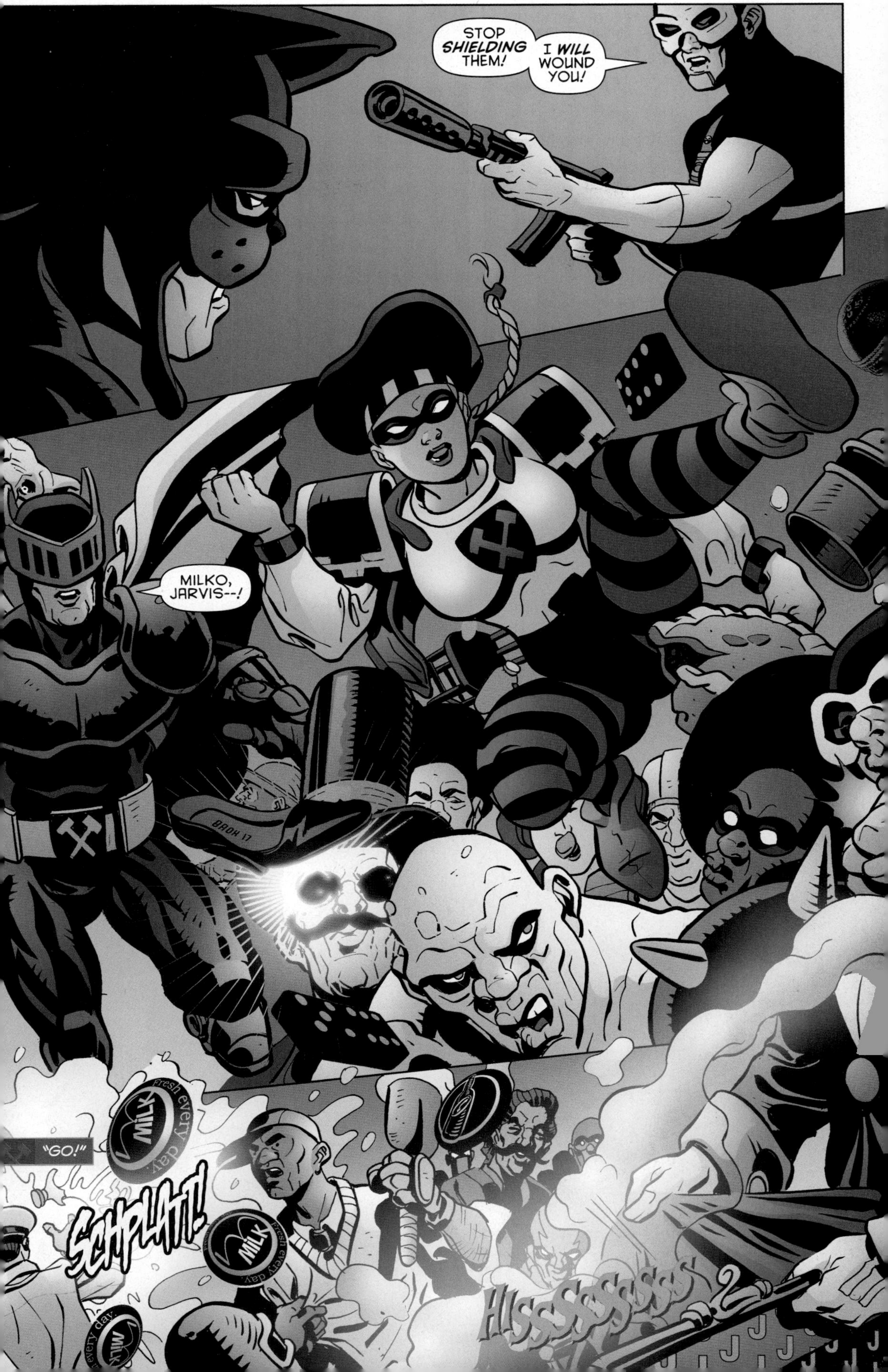
STOP SHIELDING THEM!
I WILL WOUND YOU!
MILKO, JARVIS--!
"GO!"
SCHPLATT!
HISSSSSSSSS
MILK Fresh every day.

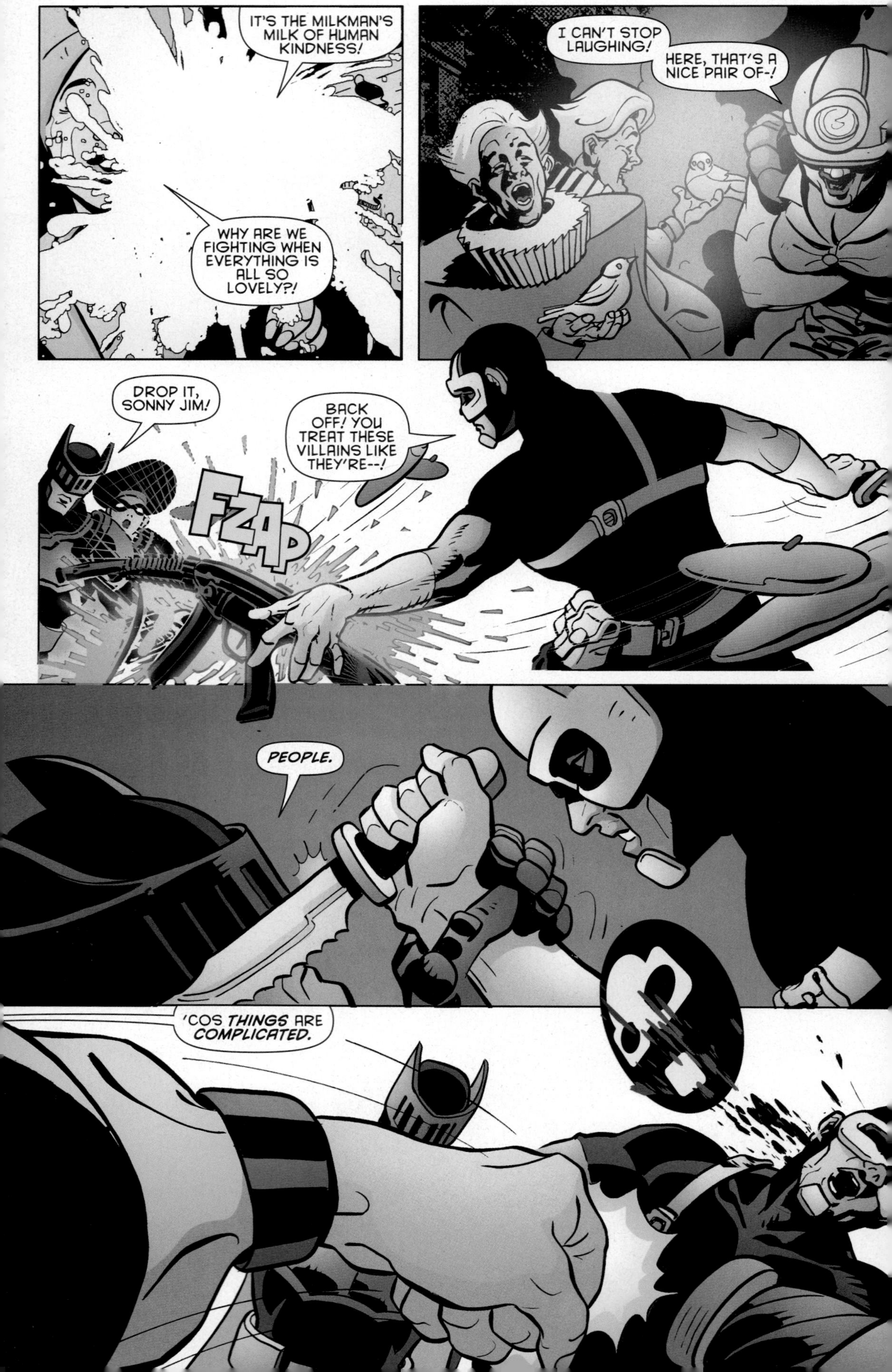
IT'S THE MILKMAN'S MILK OF HUMAN KINDNESS!
WHY ARE WE FIGHTING WHEN EVERYTHING IS ALL SO LOVELY?!
I CAN'T STOP LAUGHING!
HERE, THAT'S A NICE PAIR OF-!
DROP IT, SONNY JIM!
BACK OFF! YOU TREAT THESE VILLAINS LIKE THEY'RE--!
FZAP
PEOPLE.
'COS THINGS ARE COMPLICATED.

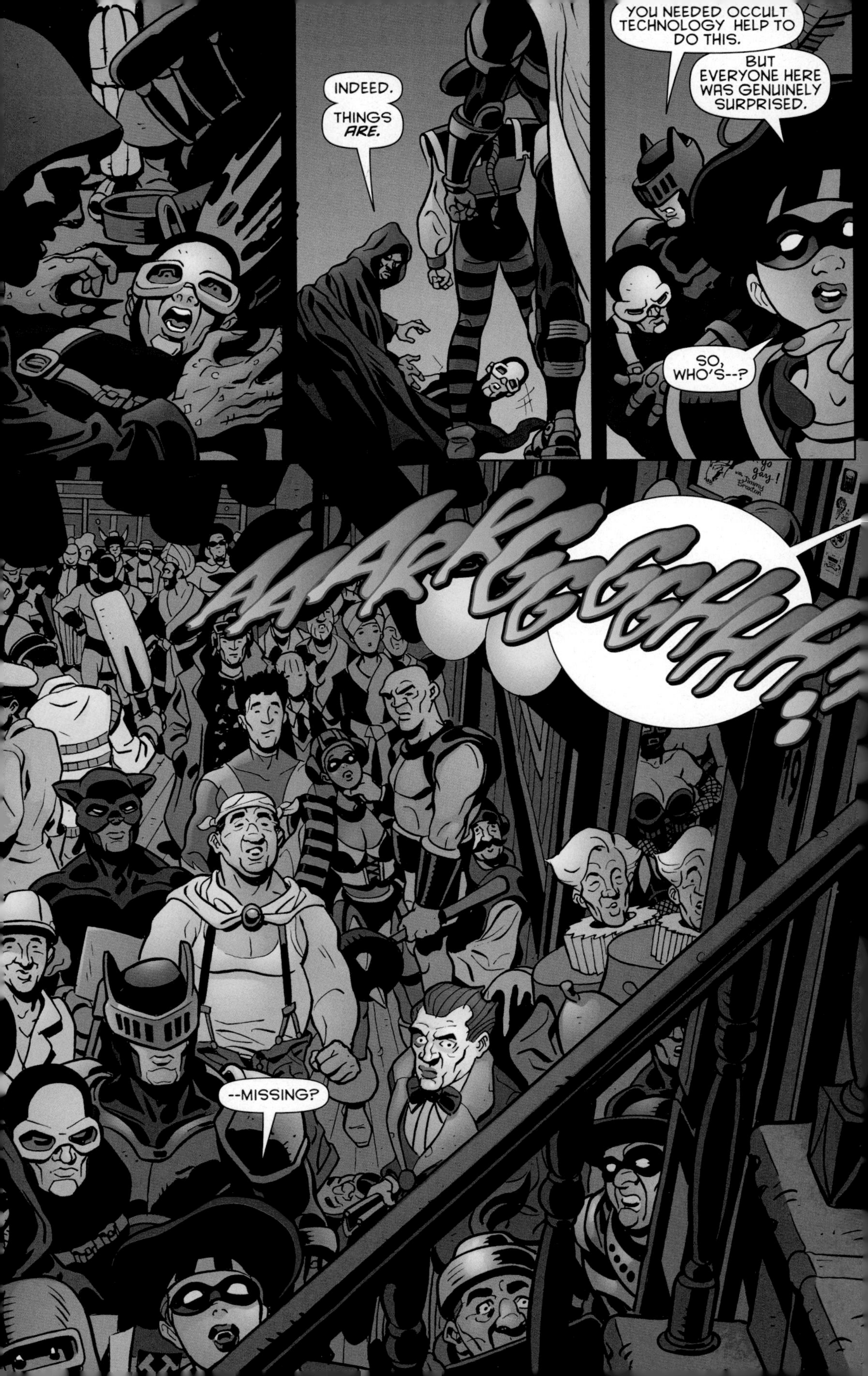

INDEED.
THINGS *ARE.*
YOU NEEDED OCCULT TECHNOLOGY HELP TO DO THIS.
BUT EVERYONE HERE WAS GENUINELY SURPRISED.
SO, WHO'S--?
AAARRGGGHH!!
--MISSING?

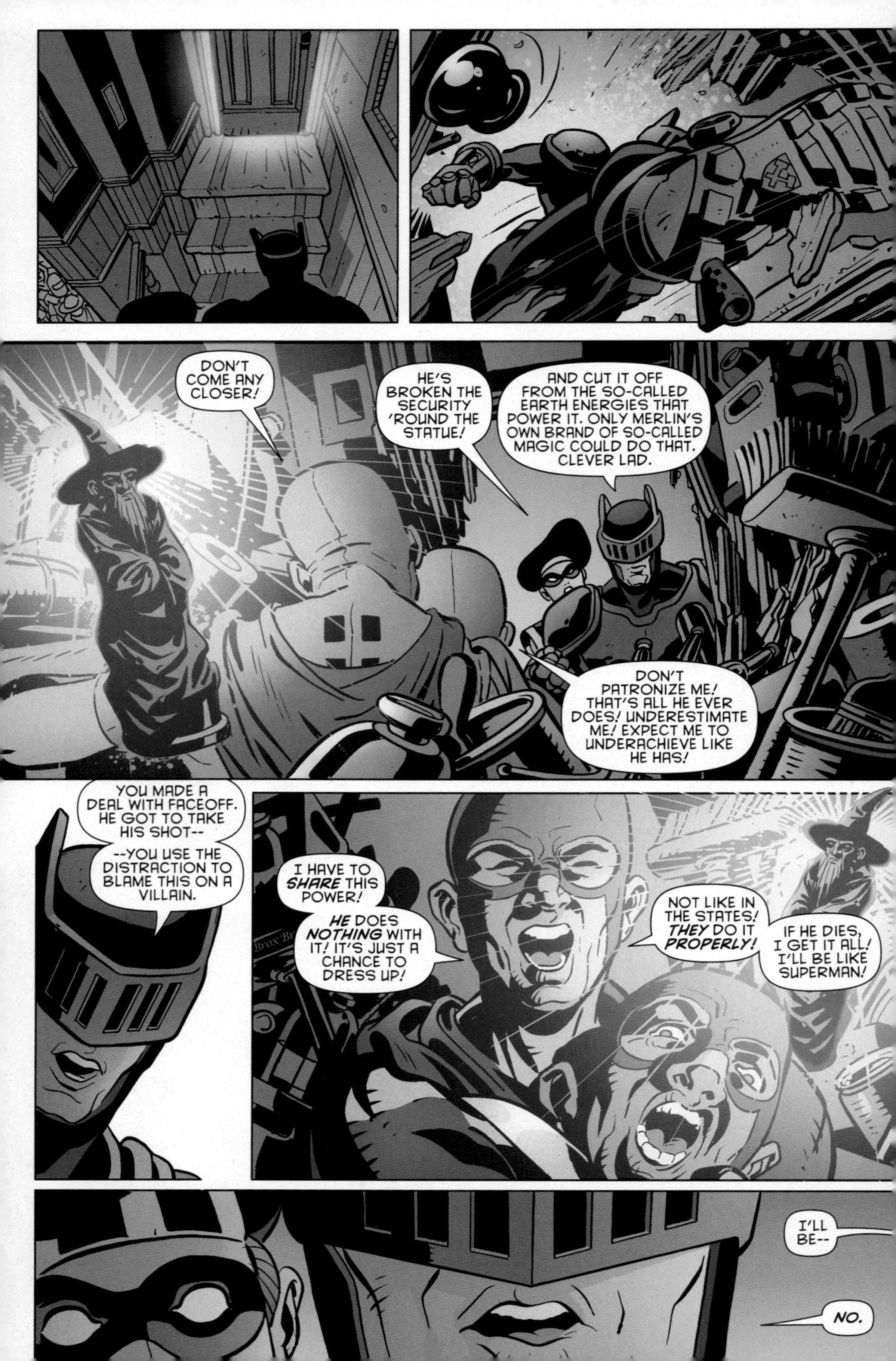

DON'T COME ANY CLOSER!
HE'S BROKEN THE SECURITY 'ROUND THE STATUE!
AND CUT IT OFF FROM THE SO-CALLED EARTH ENERGIES THAT POWER IT. ONLY MERLIN'S OWN BRAND OF SO-CALLED MAGIC COULD DO THAT. CLEVER LAD.
DON'T PATRONIZE ME! THAT'S ALL HE EVER DOES! UNDERESTIMATE ME! EXPECT ME TO UNDERACHIEVE LIKE HE HAS!
YOU MADE A DEAL WITH FACEOFF. HE GOT TO TAKE HIS SHOT--
--YOU USE THE DISTRACTION TO BLAME THIS ON A VILLAIN.
I HAVE TO SHARE THIS POWER!
HE DOES NOTHING WITH IT! IT'S JUST A CHANCE TO DRESS UP!
NOT LIKE IN THE STATES! THEY DO IT PROPERLY!
IF HE DIES, I GET IT ALL! I'LL BE LIKE SUPERMAN!
I'LL BE--
NO.

THE ONLY THING THAT STOPS US BEING *ANYTHING* IS *US.*

WE SAY THAT'S AN AMERICAN THING SO WE DON'T HAVE TO TRY.

IF YOU WERE GOING TO KILL HIM, YOU'D HAVE DONE IT TEN MINUTES AGO.

YOU DON'T NEED *POWER.*

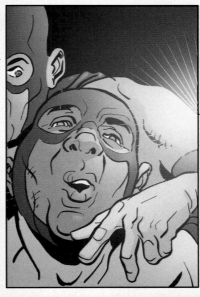

YOU NEED *MODERATION.*

WHICH WE'LL PROVIDE COURTESY OF JAIL TIME--

IF WE RUN INTO YOU WHEN IT'S NOT A PUB NIGHT.

IN THE MEANTIME, I THINK YOU TWO NEED TO SORT A FEW THINGS OUT.

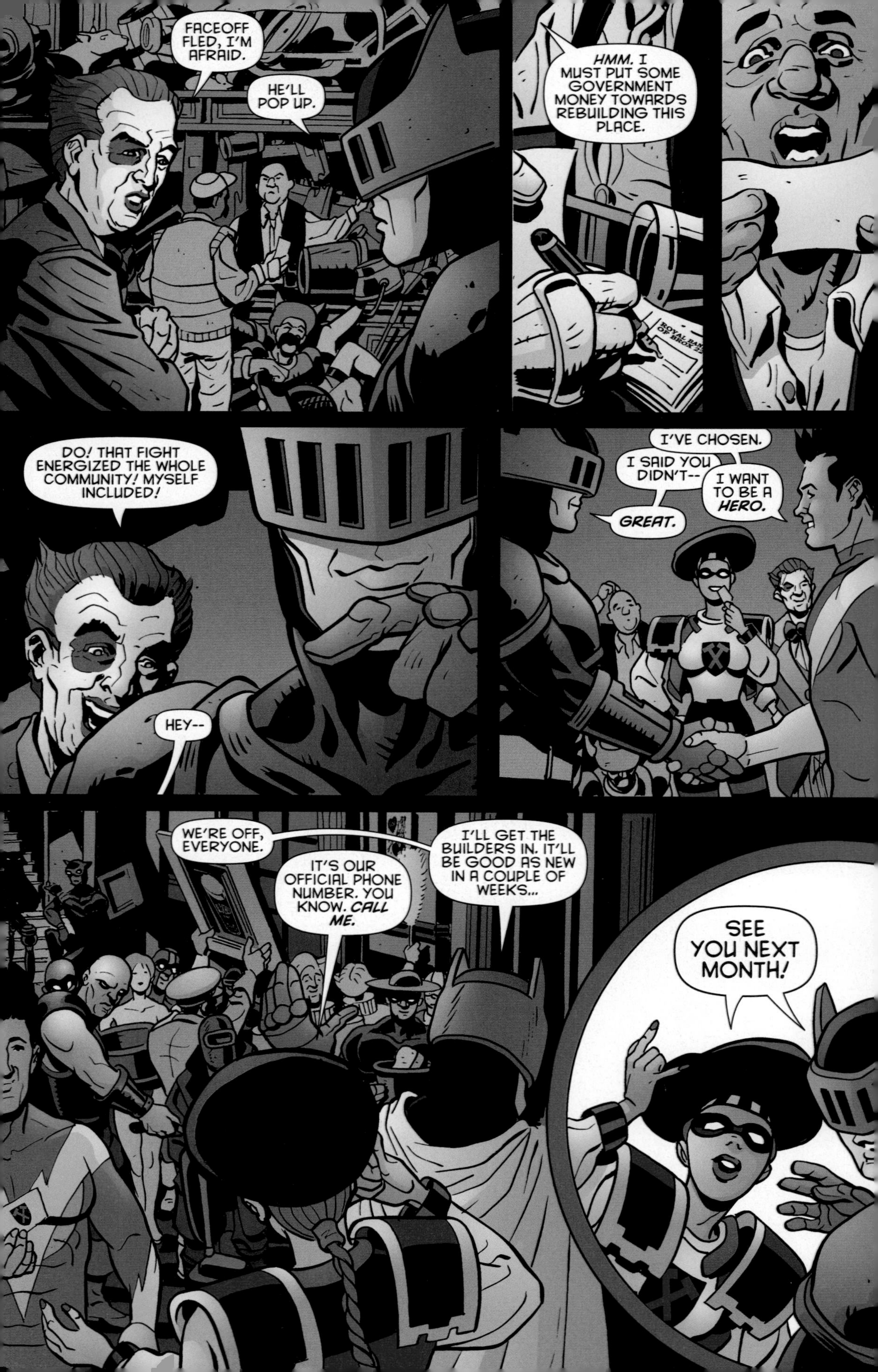
FACEOFF FLED, I'M AFRAID.
HE'LL POP UP.
HMM. I MUST PUT SOME GOVERNMENT MONEY TOWARDS REBUILDING THIS PLACE.
ROYAL BANK OF BROX
DO! THAT FIGHT ENERGIZED THE WHOLE COMMUNITY! MYSELF INCLUDED!
HEY--
I'VE CHOSEN.
I SAID YOU DIDN'T--
I WANT TO BE A HERO.
GREAT.
WE'RE OFF, EVERYONE.
IT'S OUR OFFICIAL PHONE NUMBER. YOU KNOW. CALL ME.
I'LL GET THE BUILDERS IN. IT'LL BE GOOD AS NEW IN A COUPLE OF WEEKS...
SEE YOU NEXT MONTH!

What You Missed If You're A Non-Brit
(not that there's anything wrong with that).

WE'RE AWARE THAT, THROUGH NO FAULT OF THEIR OWN, MANY (MOST EVEN, IF WE'RE LUCKY) OF OUR READERS ARE FROM THE COLONIES. SO WE THOUGHT THAT A QUICK GUIDE TO SOME OF THE CULTURAL REFERENCES MIGHT GIVE YOU A BETTER APPRECIATION OF THIS ISSUE'S CONTENTS.

- "A BEAR OF VERY LITTLE BRAIN" IS HOW WINNIE-THE-POOH THOUGHT OF HIMSELF.

- JARVIS POKER FOLLOWS THE BRITISH COMIC TRADITION OF HAVING ONE'S JOB DESCRIPTION RHYME WITH ONE'S NAME, REVIVED MORE RECENTLY BY VIZ.

- SALT OF THE EARTH IS A SEASIDE POSTCARD IMAGE OF THE BRITISH WORKING MAN ON HOLIDAY, LATER TAKEN UP BY MONTY PYTHON AND THE SEX PISTOLS.

- THE BLACK AND WHITE MINSTRELS: NAMED AFTER AN UNFORTUNATE BRITISH TV BLACKED-UP "MINSTREL SHOW" WHICH RAN UNTIL 1978 (!)

- TWO TON TED FROM TEDDINGTON: FAMILIAR TO THOSE WHO SENT BENNY HILL'S 'ERNIE: THE FASTEST MILKMAN IN THE WEST' SINGLE TO NUMBER ONE IN 1971.

- THE LEADER OF THE PIRATE ASTRONOMERS, WITH HIS MONOCLE, LOOKS A BIT LIKE BRITISH TV ASTRONOMY LEGEND PATRICK MOORE.

- DEATH DINOSAUR IS REMINISCENT OF A STRANGELY WELL-DRESSED MONSTER FROM A 1970s TOP TRUMPS "HORROR" CARD GAME PACK.

WE TRUST THE REFERENCES TO MERLIN (WHO'S IN HERE SOMEWHERE, IN A FAMILIAR GUISE), ALEISTER CROWLEY, PAUL McCARTNEY AND THE CHURCH OF ENGLAND WON'T PASS BY THOSE OF EVEN SLIGHTLY ANGLOPHILE BENT. MUCH OF THE SLANG REMAINS UNTRANSLATED TO SPARE YOUR BLUSHES (AND THOSE OF OUR LADY EDITOR).

UNTIL NEXT ISSUE, CHEERIO!
- PAUL CORNELL

rought to you by

KNIGHT AND SQUIRE

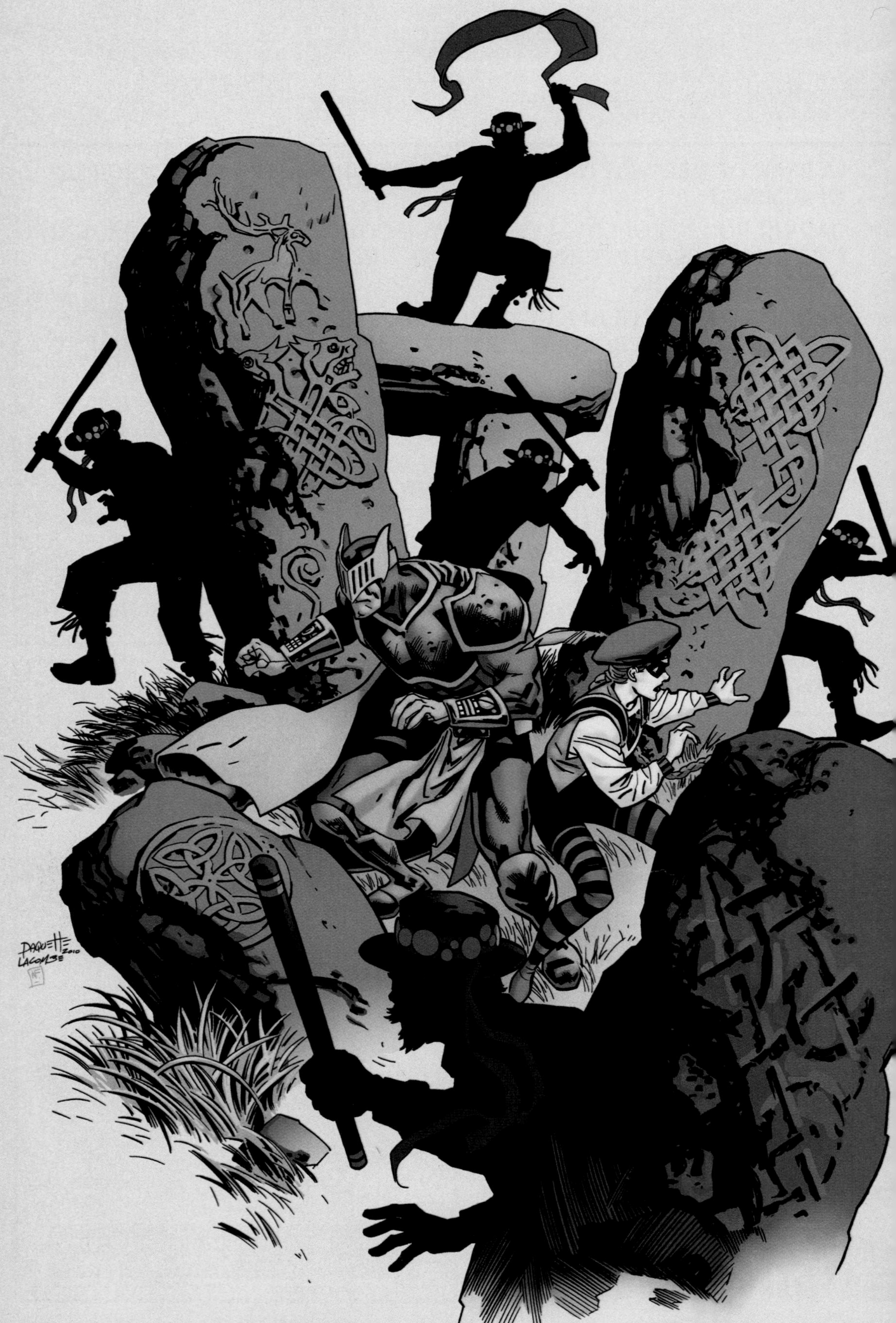
PAQUETTE 2010
LACOMBE

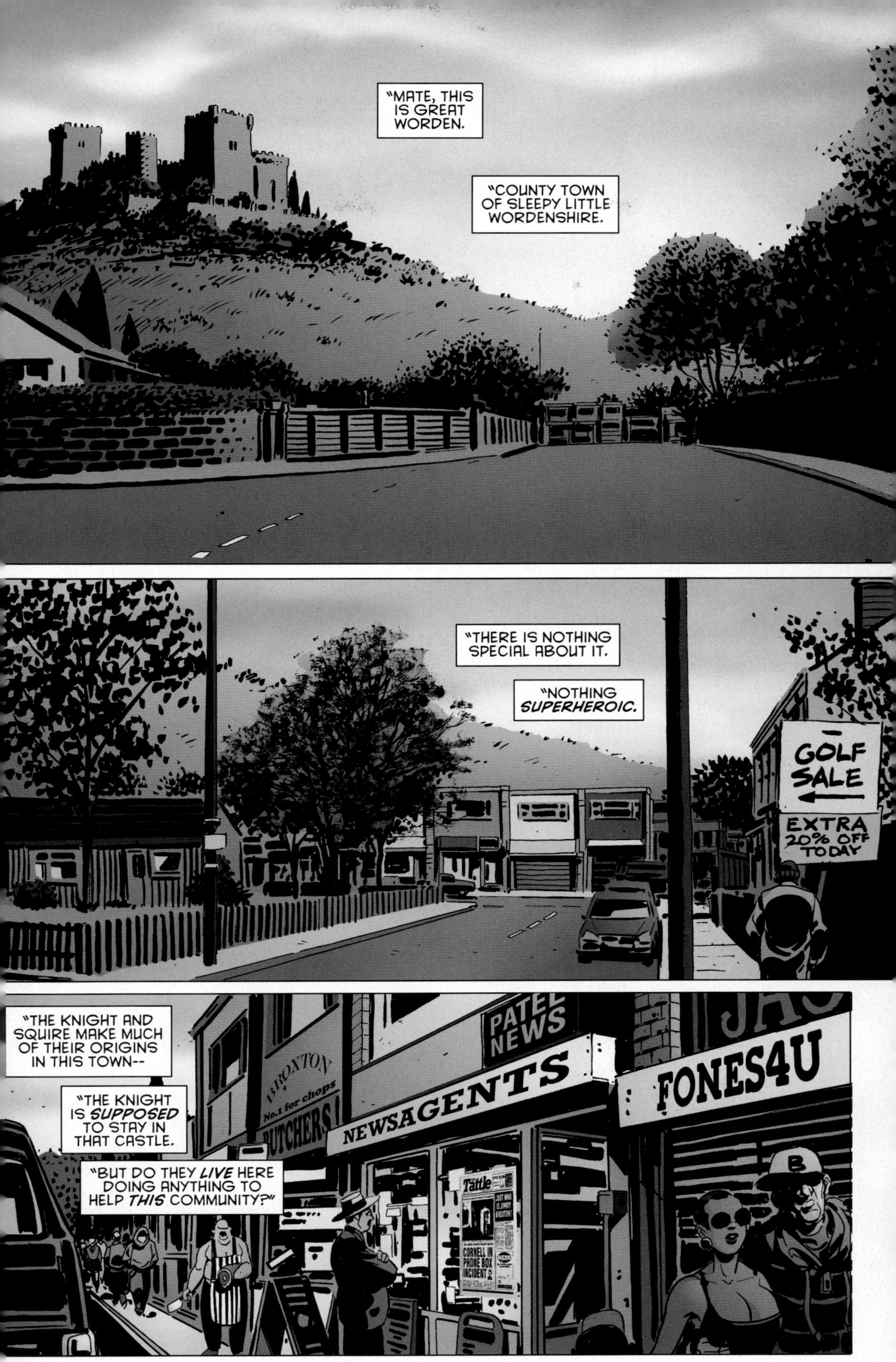
"MATE, THIS IS GREAT WORDEN.
"COUNTY TOWN OF SLEEPY LITTLE WORDENSHIRE.
"THERE IS NOTHING SPECIAL ABOUT IT.
"NOTHING *SUPERHEROIC.*
GOLF SALE
EXTRA 20% OFF TODAY
"THE KNIGHT AND SQUIRE MAKE MUCH OF THEIR ORIGINS IN THIS TOWN--
"THE KNIGHT IS *SUPPOSED* TO STAY IN THAT CASTLE.
"BUT DO THEY *LIVE* HERE DOING ANYTHING TO HELP *THIS* COMMUNITY?"
BROXTON No.1 for chops BUTCHERS
PATEL NEWS
NEWSAGENTS
FONES4U
Tattle
JUST WHO IS JIMMY BROXTON?
CORNELL IN PHONE BOX INCIDENT

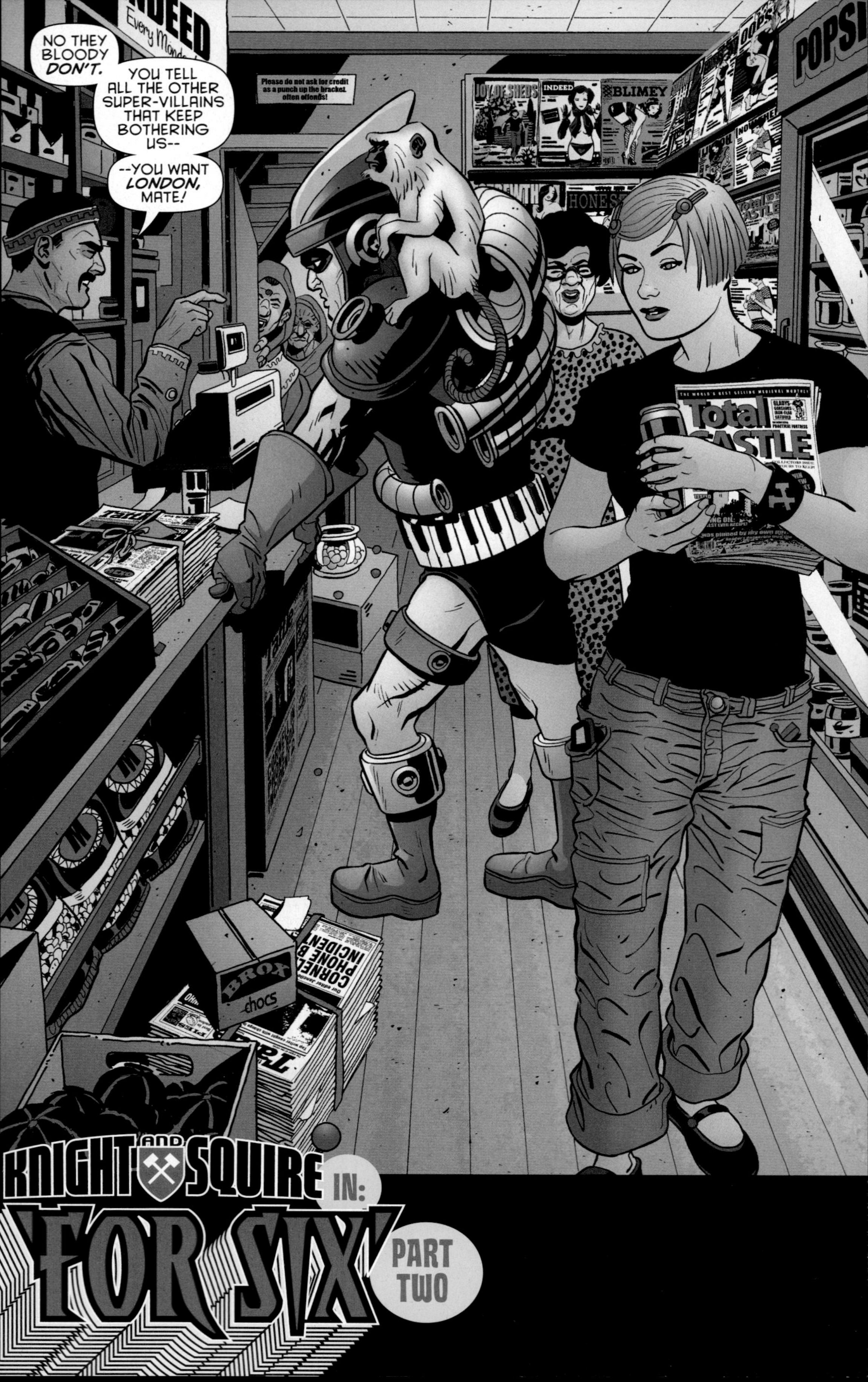

NO THEY BLOODY DON'T.
YOU TELL ALL THE OTHER SUPER-VILLAINS THAT KEEP BOTHERING US--
--YOU WANT LONDON, MATE!
INDEED Every Monday
Please do not ask for credit as a punch up the bracket often offends!
JOY OF SHEDS
INDEED
BLIMEY
POPS
Total CASTLE
BROX chocs
KNIGHT AND SQUIRE IN:
'FOR SIX' PART TWO

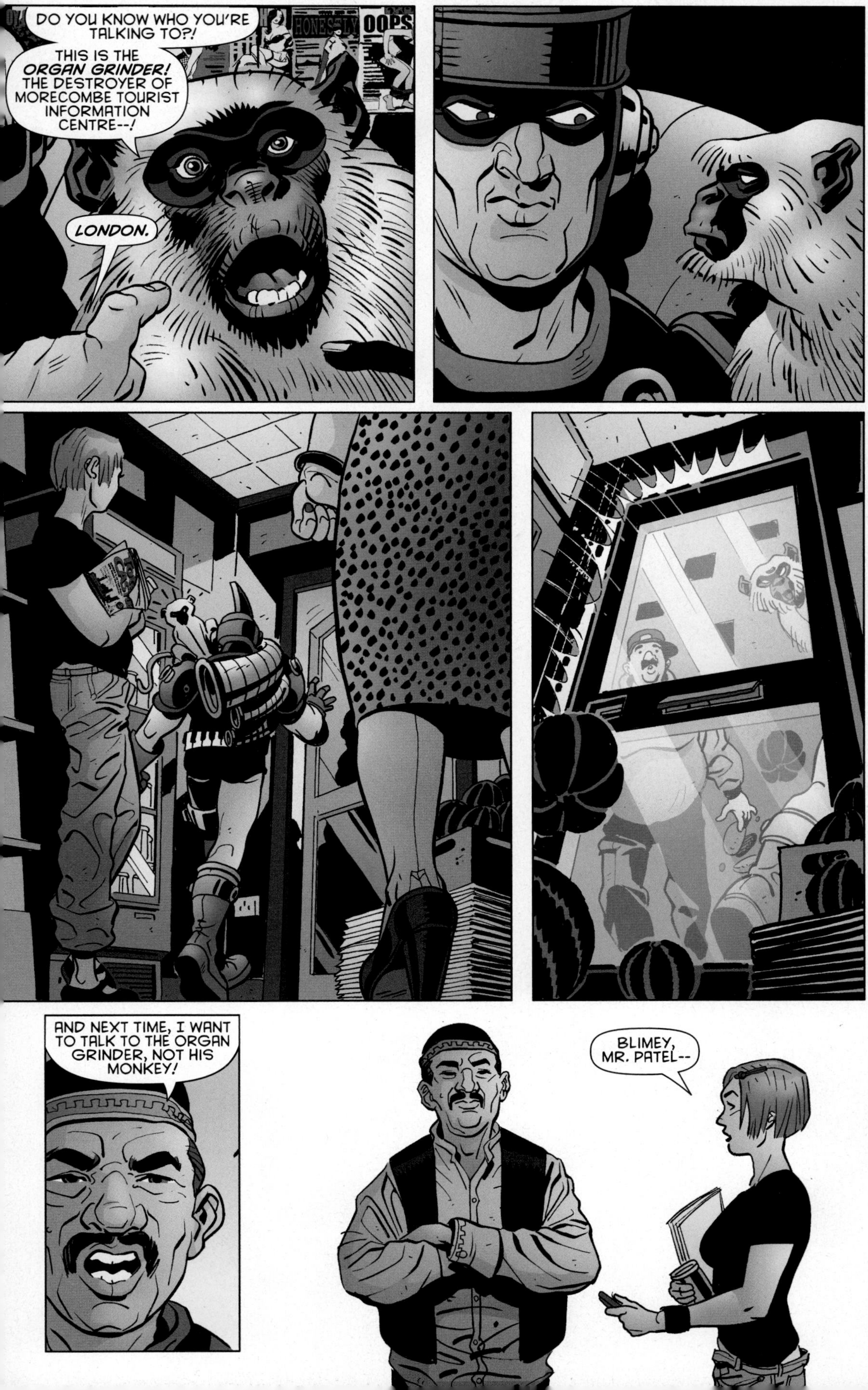
DO YOU KNOW WHO YOU'RE TALKING TO?!
THIS IS THE *ORGAN GRINDER!* THE DESTROYER OF MORECOMBE TOURIST INFORMATION CENTRE--!
LONDON.
HONESTLY
OOPS
AND NEXT TIME, I WANT TO TALK TO THE ORGAN GRINDER, NOT HIS MONKEY!
BLIMEY, MR. PATEL--

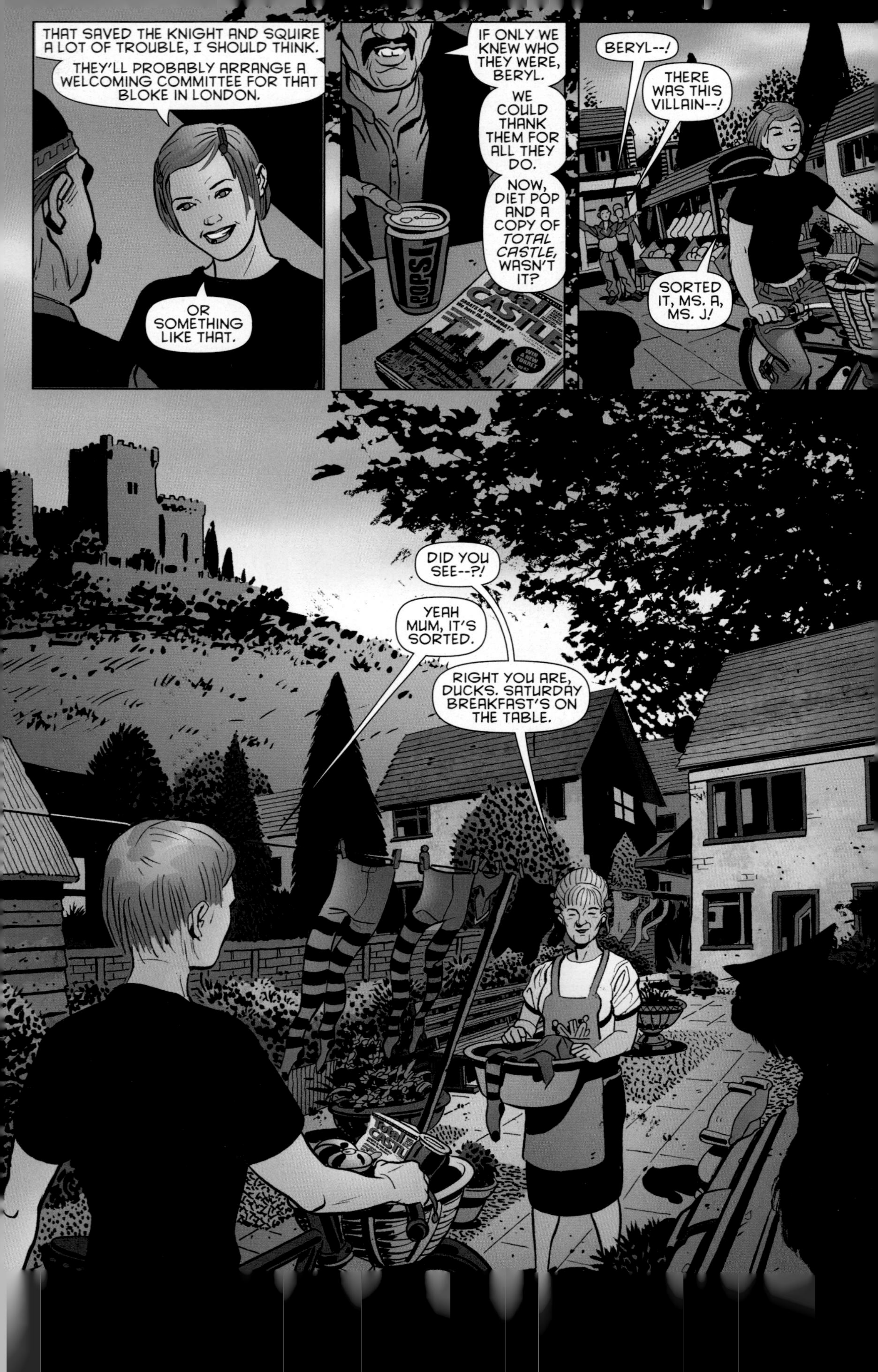
THAT SAVED THE KNIGHT AND SQUIRE A LOT OF TROUBLE, I SHOULD THINK.
THEY'LL PROBABLY ARRANGE A WELCOMING COMMITTEE FOR THAT BLOKE IN LONDON.
OR SOMETHING LIKE THAT.
IF ONLY WE KNEW WHO THEY WERE, BERYL.
WE COULD THANK THEM FOR ALL THEY DO.
NOW, DIET POP AND A COPY OF *TOTAL CASTLE*, WASN'T IT?
POPSI
TOTAL CASTLE
BERYL--!
THERE WAS THIS VILLAIN--!
SORTED IT, MS. A, MS. J!
DID YOU SEE--?!
YEAH MUM, IT'S SORTED.
RIGHT YOU ARE, DUCKS. SATURDAY BREAKFAST'S ON THE TABLE.

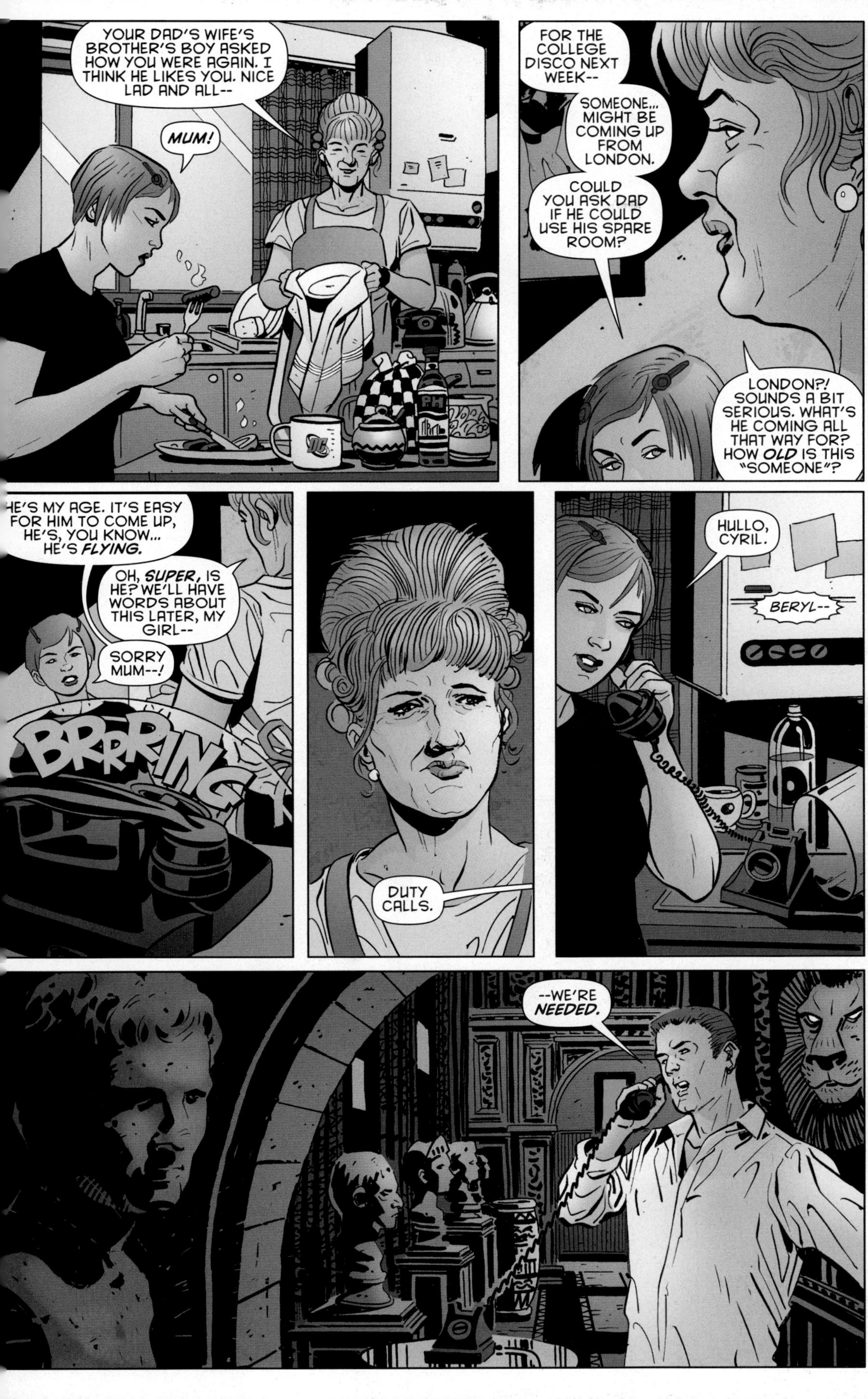
YOUR DAD'S WIFE'S BROTHER'S BOY ASKED HOW YOU WERE AGAIN. I THINK HE LIKES YOU. NICE LAD AND ALL--
MUM!
FOR THE COLLEGE DISCO NEXT WEEK--
SOMEONE... MIGHT BE COMING UP FROM LONDON.
COULD YOU ASK DAD IF HE COULD USE HIS SPARE ROOM?
LONDON?! SOUNDS A BIT SERIOUS. WHAT'S HE COMING ALL THAT WAY FOR? HOW OLD IS THIS "SOMEONE"?
HE'S MY AGE. IT'S EASY FOR HIM TO COME UP, HE'S, YOU KNOW... HE'S FLYING.
OH, SUPER, IS HE? WE'LL HAVE WORDS ABOUT THIS LATER, MY GIRL--
SORRY MUM--!
BRRRING
DUTY CALLS.
HULLO, CYRIL.
BERYL--
--WE'RE NEEDED.

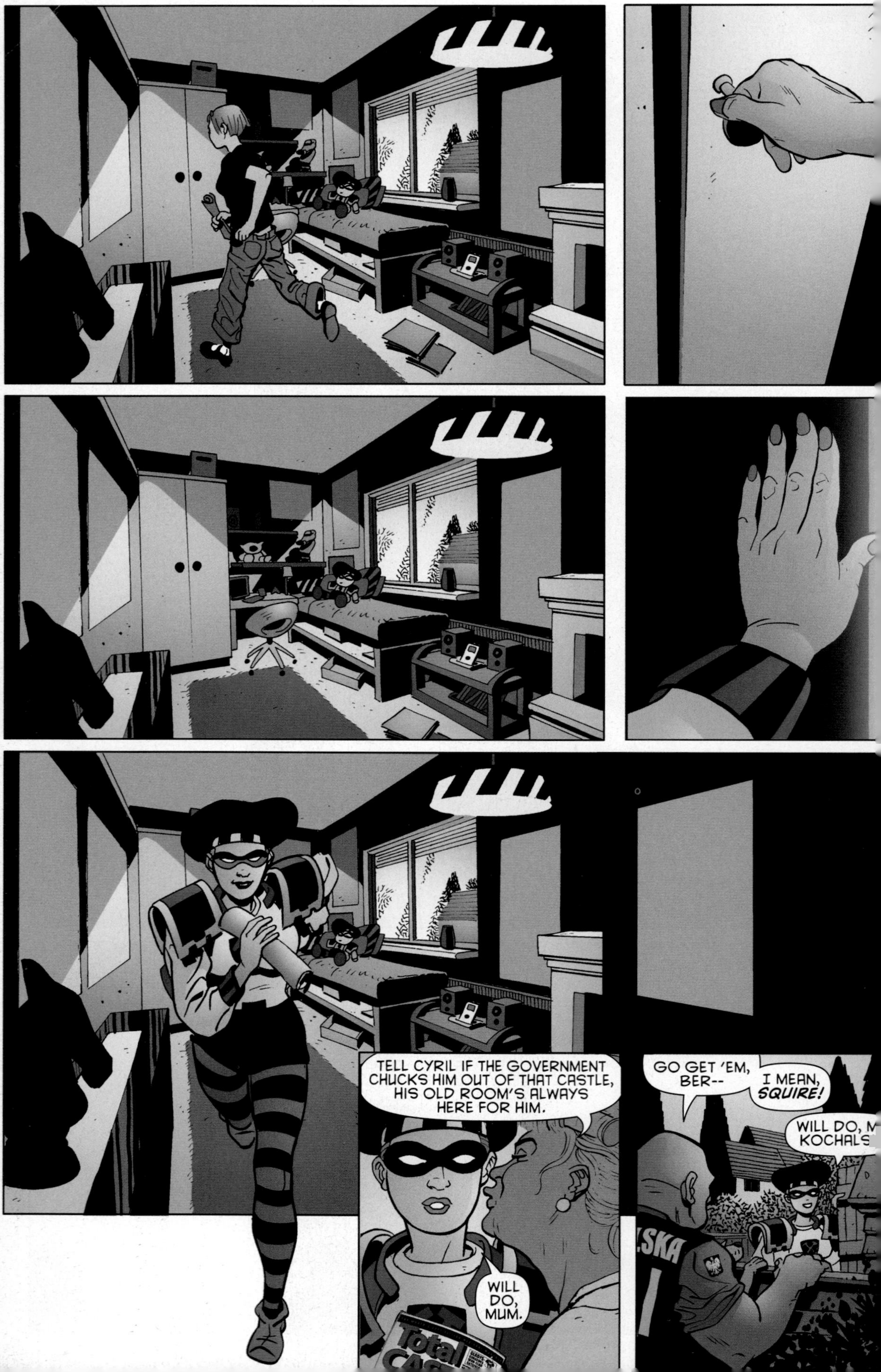
TELL CYRIL IF THE GOVERNMENT CHUCKS HIM OUT OF THAT CASTLE, HIS OLD ROOM'S ALWAYS HERE FOR HIM.
WILL DO, MUM.
GO GET 'EM, BER--
I MEAN, SQUIRE!
WILL DO, M
KOCHALS

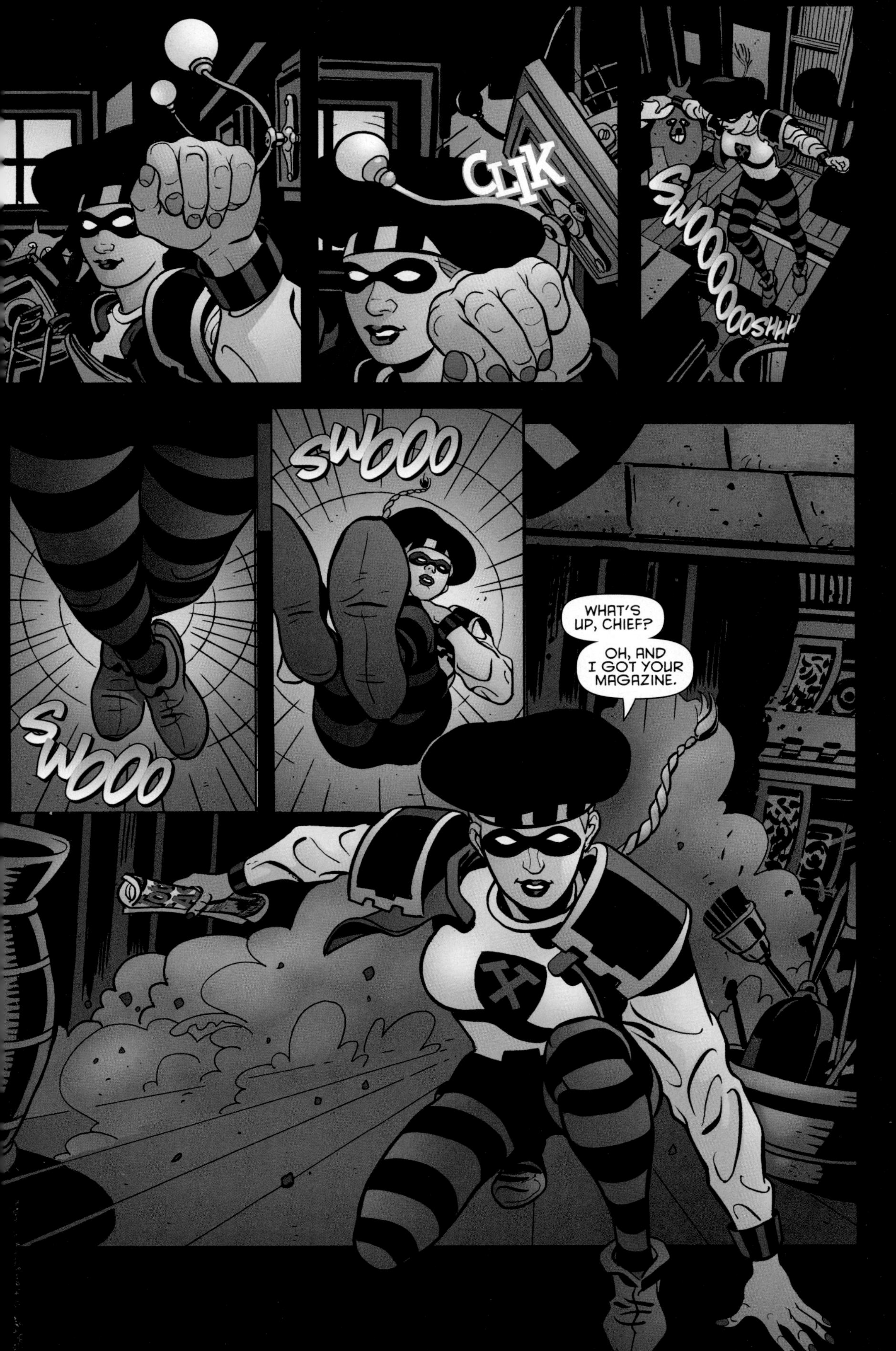
CLIK
SWOOOOOOOSHHH
SWOOO
SWOOO
WHAT'S UP, CHIEF?
OH, AND I GOT YOUR MAGAZINE.

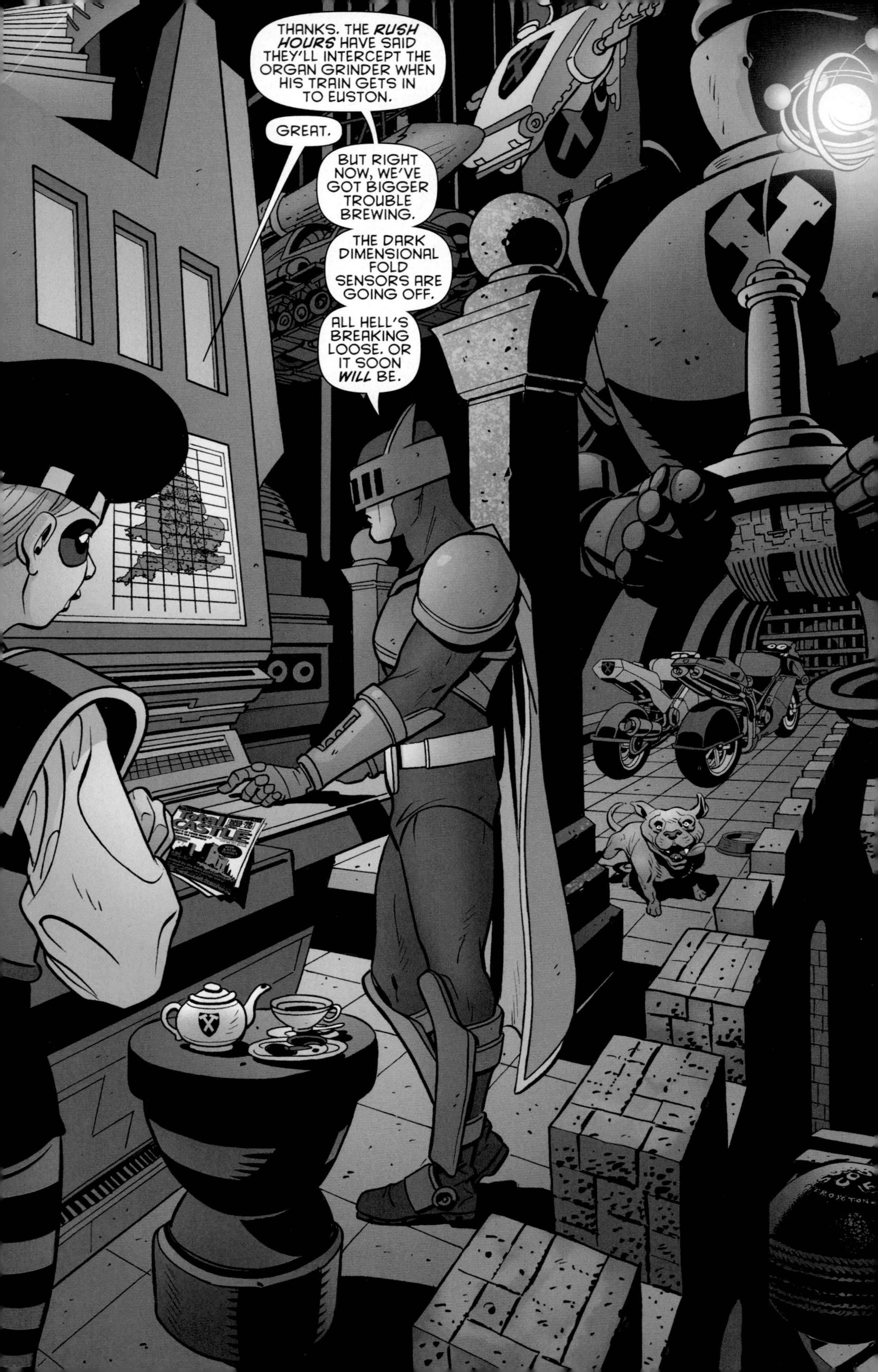
THANKS. THE RUSH HOURS HAVE SAID THEY'LL INTERCEPT THE ORGAN GRINDER WHEN HIS TRAIN GETS IN TO EUSTON.
GREAT.
BUT RIGHT NOW, WE'VE GOT BIGGER TROUBLE BREWING.
THE DARK DIMENSIONAL FOLD SENSORS ARE GOING OFF.
ALL HELL'S BREAKING LOOSE. OR IT SOON WILL BE.

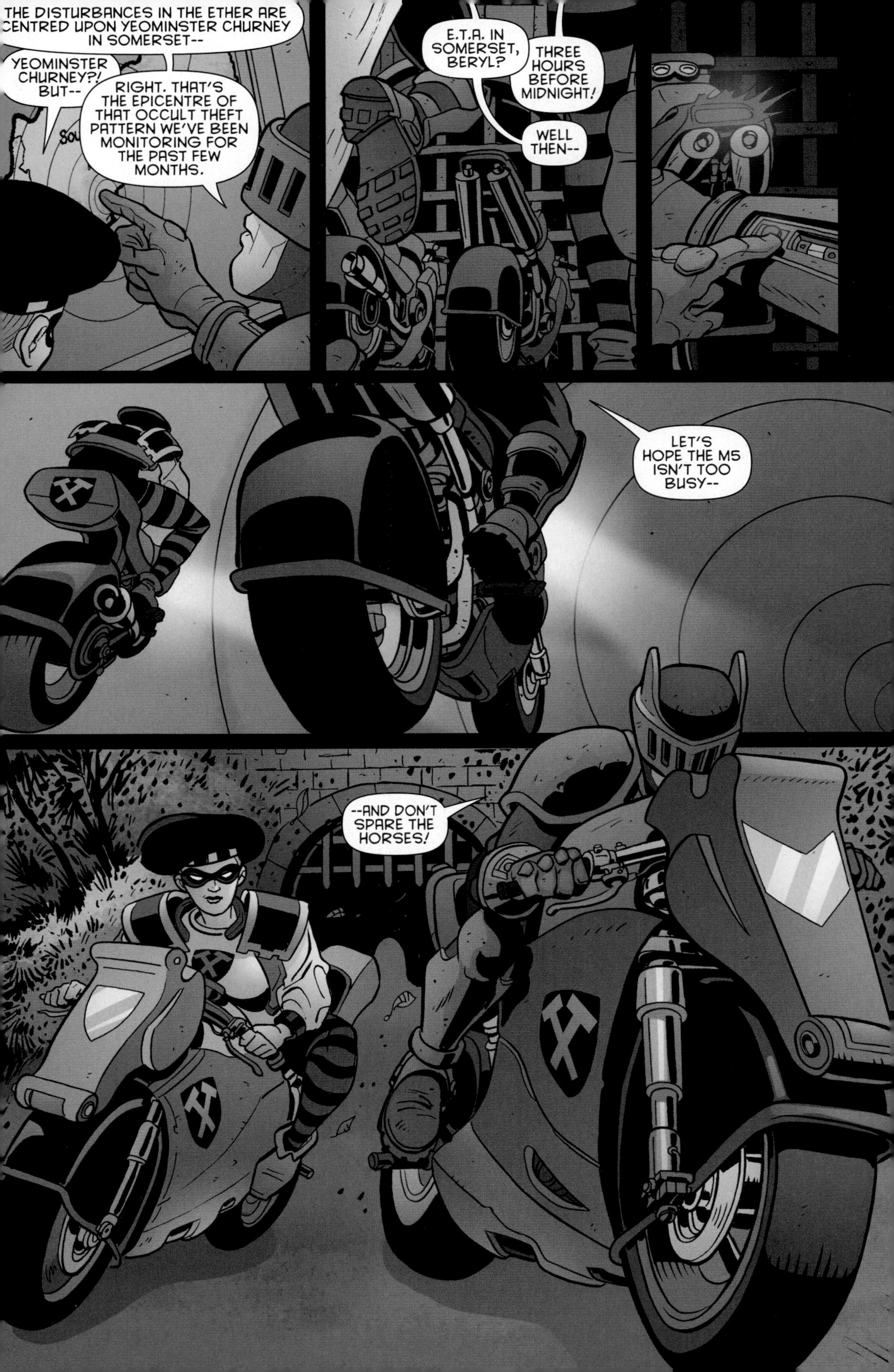
THE DISTURBANCES IN THE ETHER ARE CENTRED UPON YEOMINSTER CHURNEY IN SOMERSET--
YEOMINSTER CHURNEY?! BUT--
RIGHT. THAT'S THE EPICENTRE OF THAT OCCULT THEFT PATTERN WE'VE BEEN MONITORING FOR THE PAST FEW MONTHS.
E.T.A. IN SOMERSET, BERYL?
THREE HOURS BEFORE MIDNIGHT!
WELL THEN--
LET'S HOPE THE M5 ISN'T TOO BUSY--
--AND DON'T SPARE THE HORSES!

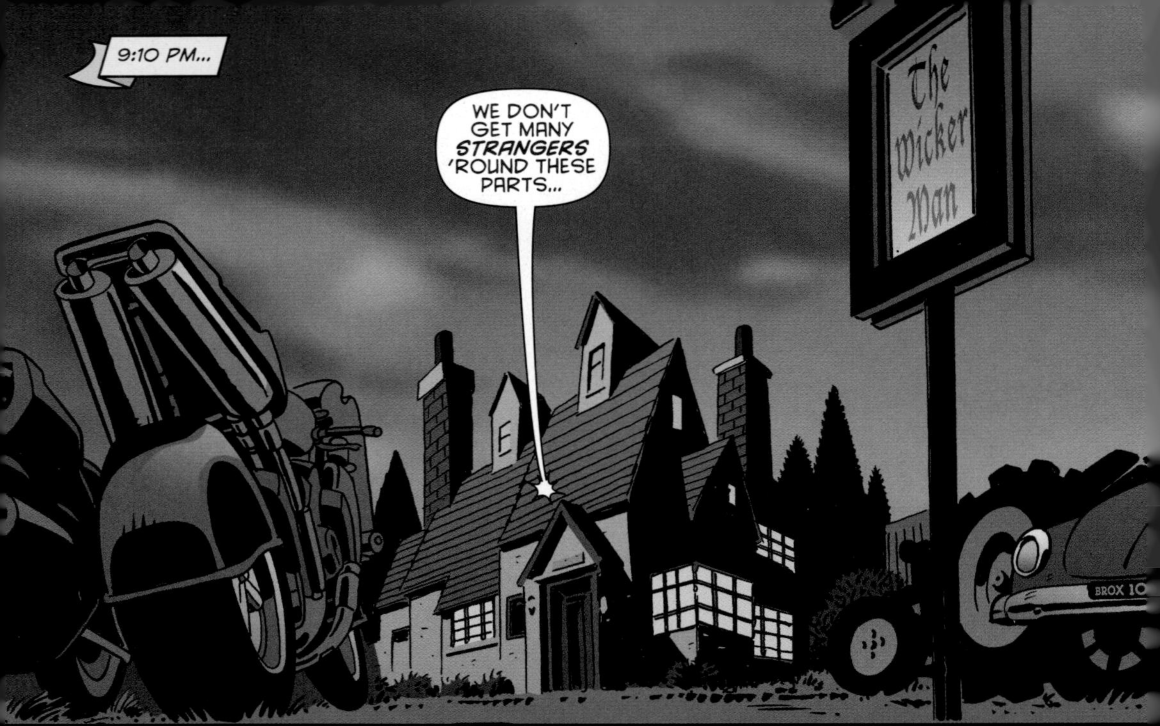
9:10 PM...
WE DON'T GET MANY STRANGERS 'ROUND THESE PARTS...
The Wicker Man
BROX 10

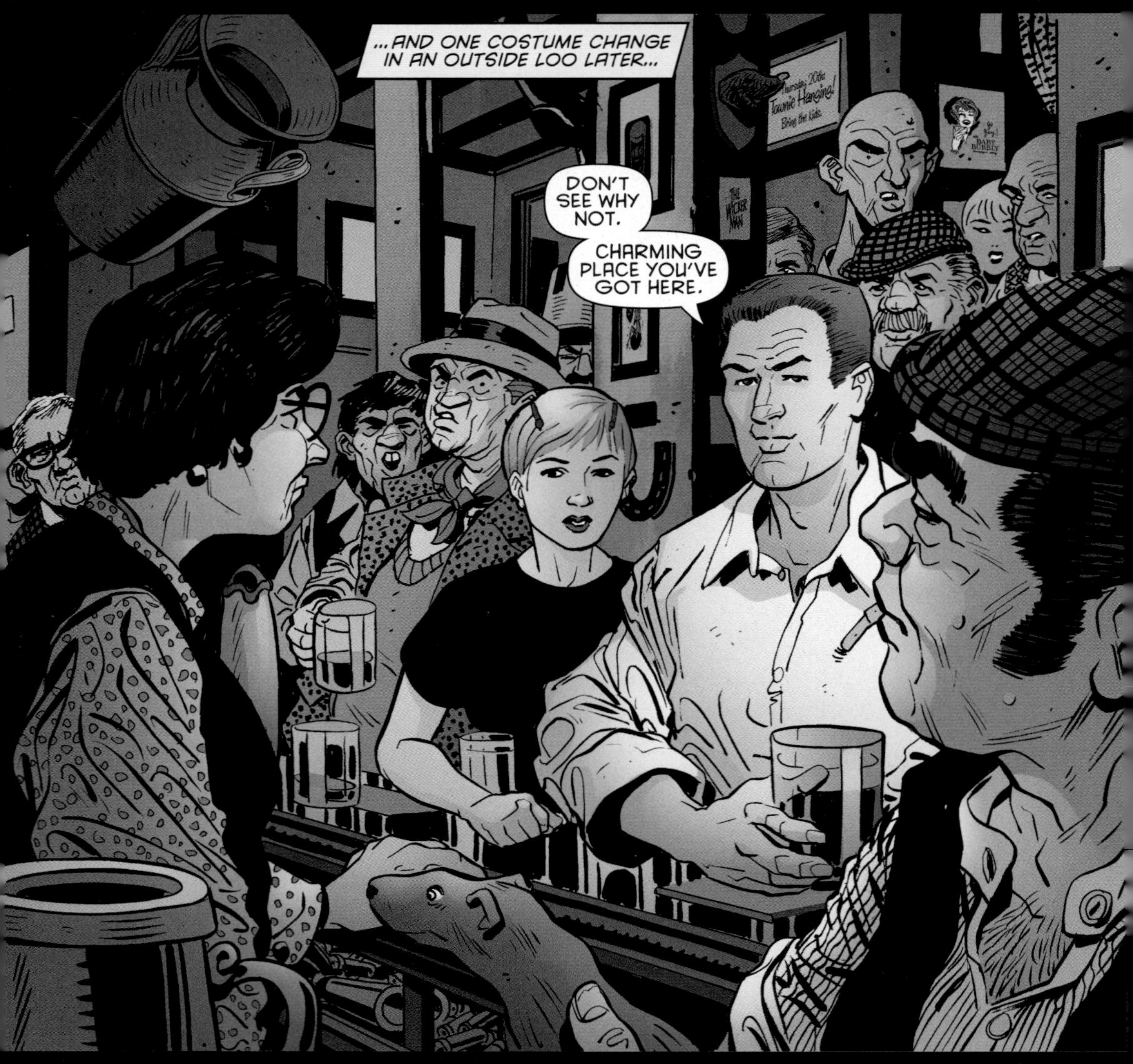
...AND ONE COSTUME CHANGE IN AN OUTSIDE LOO LATER...
Thursday 20th Townie Hanging! Bring the kids.
BABY BUBBLY
THE WICKER MAN
DON'T SEE WHY NOT.
CHARMING PLACE YOU'VE GOT HERE.

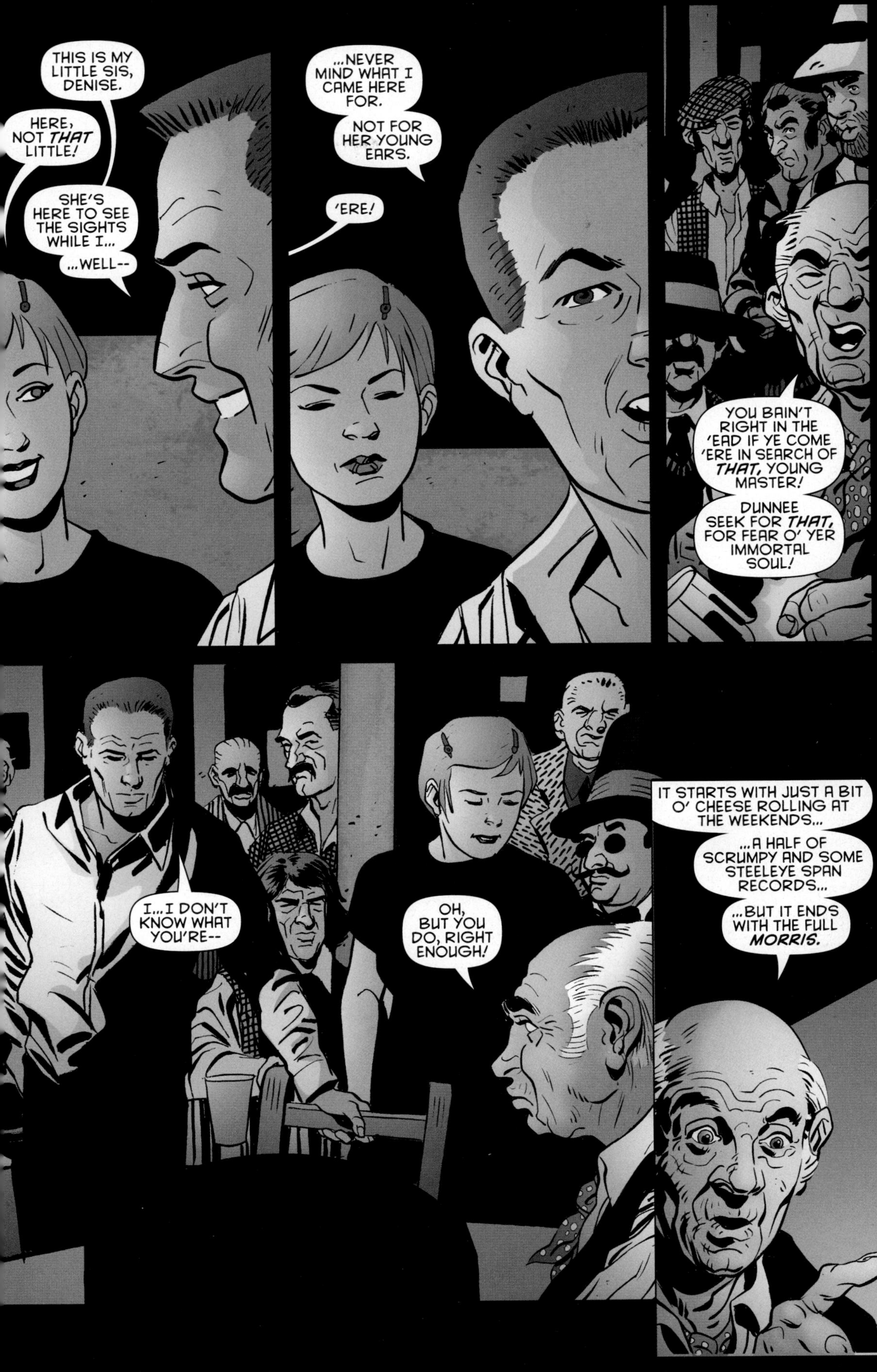
THIS IS MY LITTLE SIS, DENISE.
HERE, NOT *THAT* LITTLE!
SHE'S HERE TO SEE THE SIGHTS WHILE I...
...WELL--
...NEVER MIND WHAT I CAME HERE FOR.
NOT FOR HER YOUNG EARS.
'ERE!
YOU BAIN'T RIGHT IN THE 'EAD IF YE COME 'ERE IN SEARCH OF *THAT,* YOUNG MASTER!
DUNNEE SEEK FOR *THAT,* FOR FEAR O' YER IMMORTAL SOUL!
I...I DON'T KNOW WHAT YOU'RE--
OH, BUT YOU DO, RIGHT ENOUGH!
IT STARTS WITH JUST A BIT O' CHEESE ROLLING AT THE WEEKENDS...
...A HALF OF SCRUMPY AND SOME STEELEYE SPAN RECORDS...
...BUT IT ENDS WITH THE FULL ***MORRIS.***

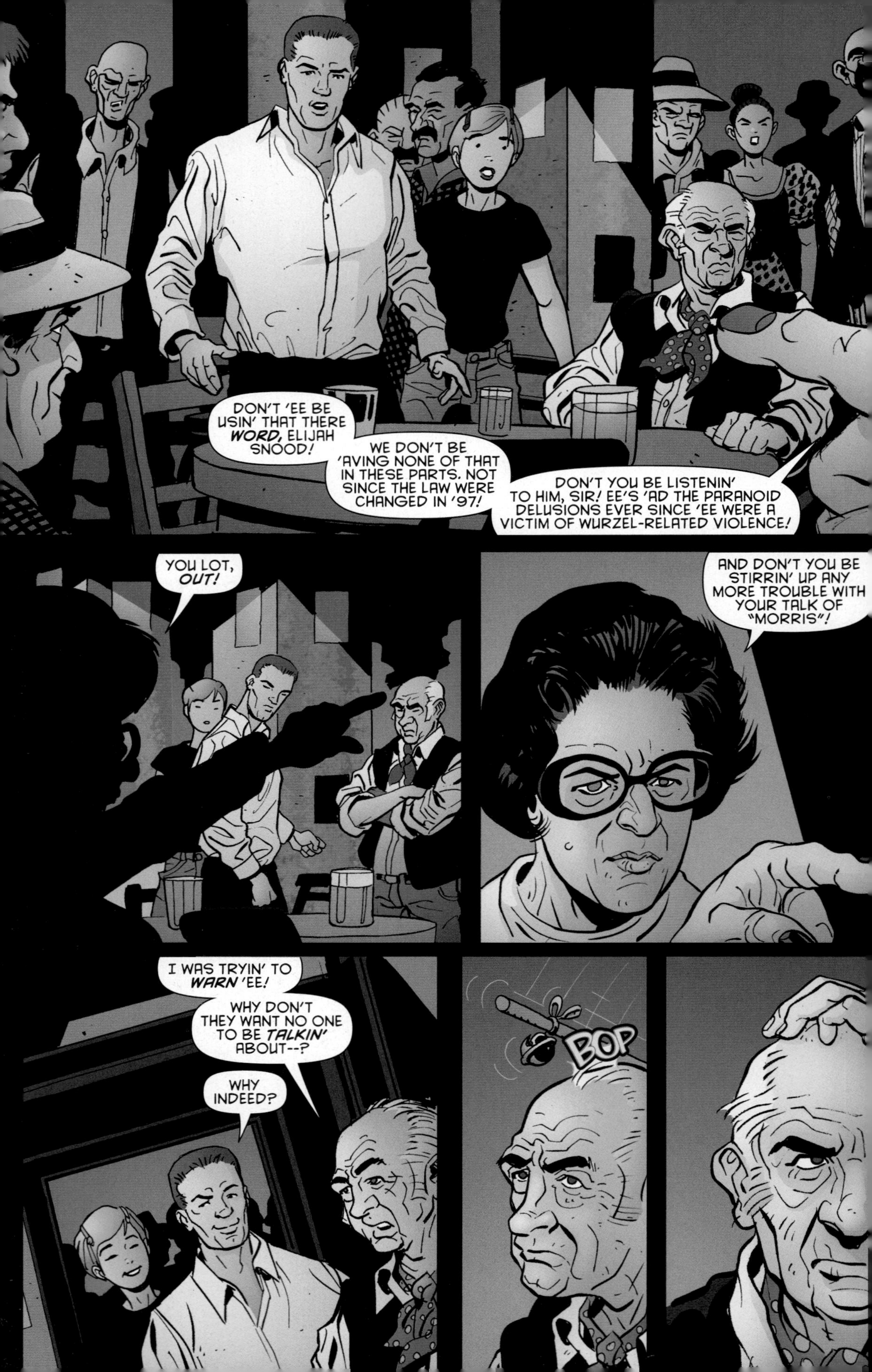
DON'T 'EE BE USIN' THAT THERE WORD, ELIJAH SNOOD!
WE DON'T BE 'AVING NONE OF THAT IN THESE PARTS. NOT SINCE THE LAW WERE CHANGED IN '97!
DON'T YOU BE LISTENIN' TO HIM, SIR! EE'S 'AD THE PARANOID DELUSIONS EVER SINCE 'EE WERE A VICTIM OF WURZEL-RELATED VIOLENCE!
YOU LOT, OUT!
AND DON'T YOU BE STIRRIN' UP ANY MORE TROUBLE WITH YOUR TALK OF "MORRIS"!
I WAS TRYIN' TO WARN 'EE!
WHY DON'T THEY WANT NO ONE TO BE TALKIN' ABOUT--?
WHY INDEED?
BOP

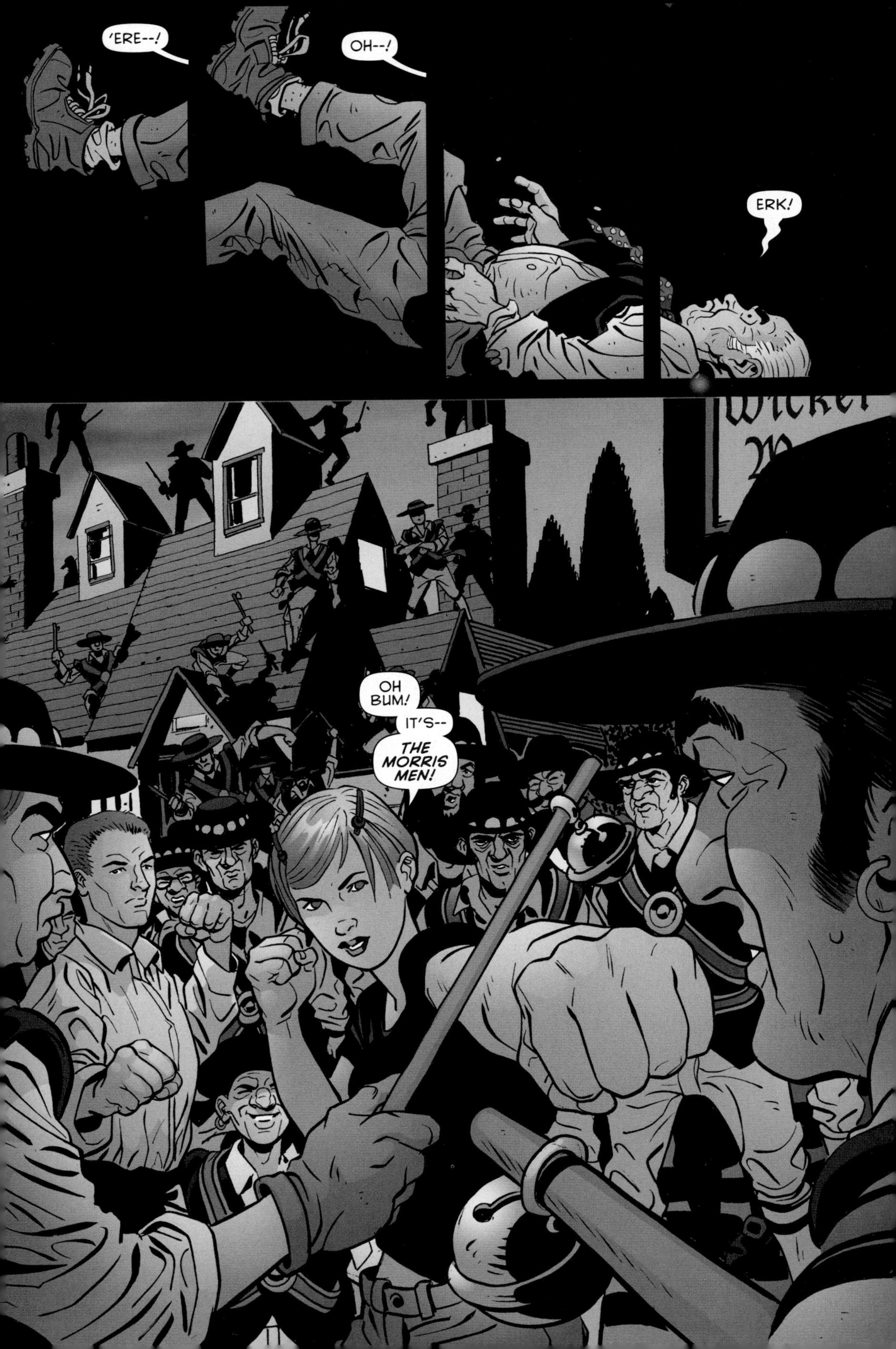
'ERE--!
OH--!
ERK!
Wicker
OH BUM!
IT'S--
THE MORRIS MEN!

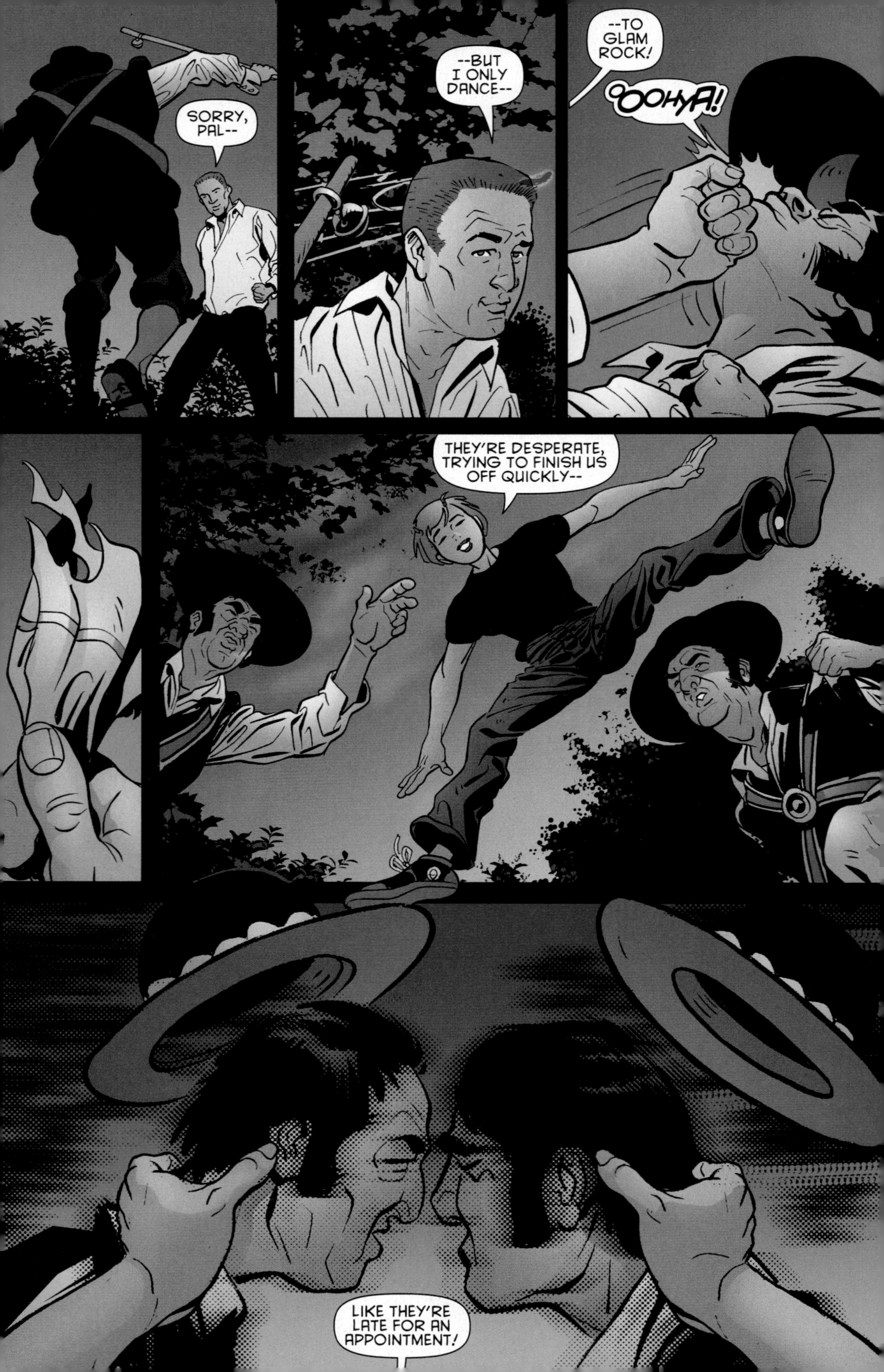
SORRY, PAL--
--BUT I ONLY DANCE--
--TO GLAM ROCK!
OOHYA!
THEY'RE DESPERATE, TRYING TO FINISH US OFF QUICKLY--
LIKE THEY'RE LATE FOR AN APPOINTMENT!

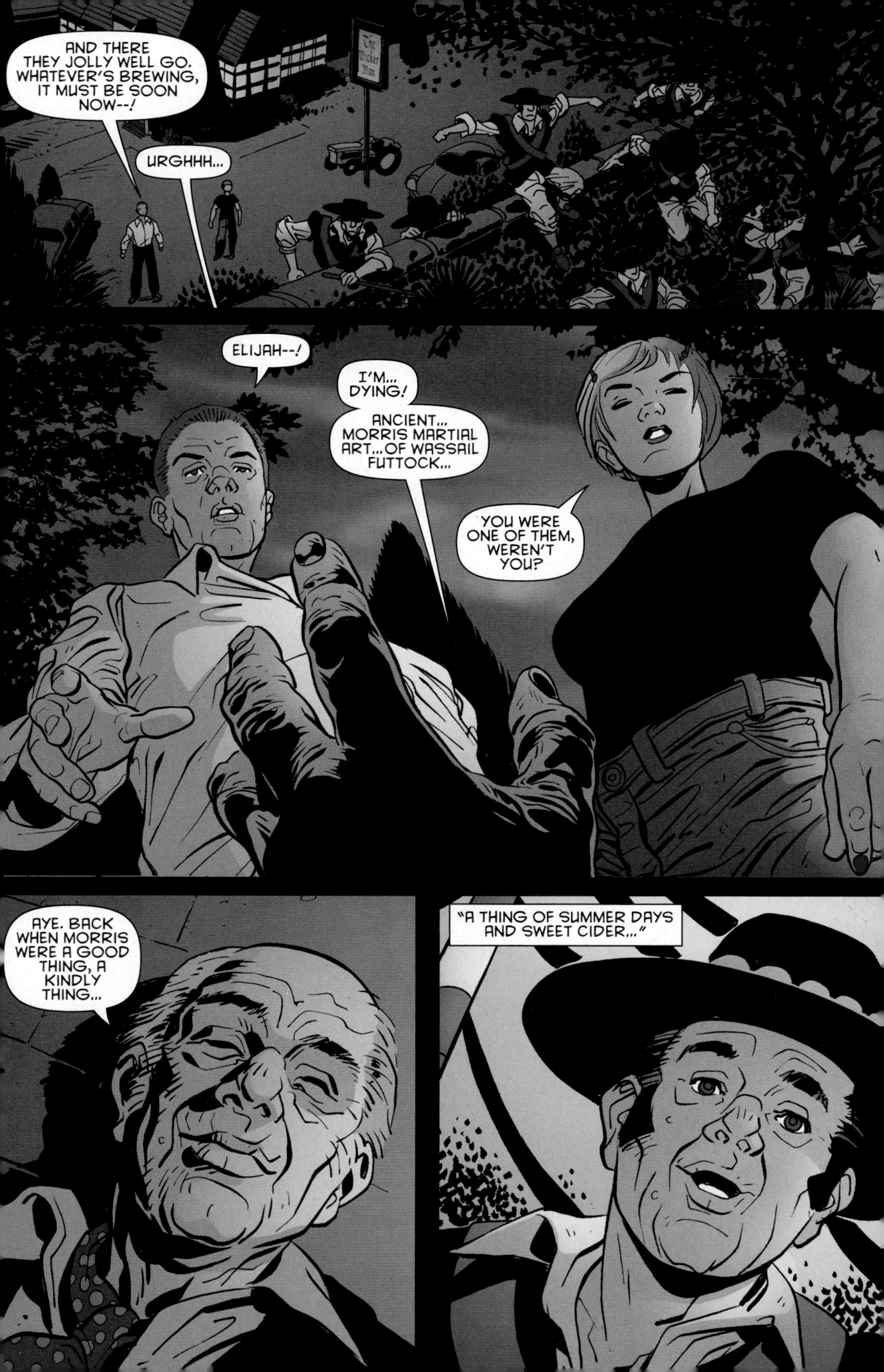
AND THERE THEY JOLLY WELL GO. WHATEVER'S BREWING, IT MUST BE SOON NOW--!
URGHHH...
ELIJAH--!
I'M... DYING!
ANCIENT... MORRIS MARTIAL ART... OF WASSAIL FUTTOCK...
YOU WERE ONE OF THEM, WEREN'T YOU?
AYE. BACK WHEN MORRIS WERE A GOOD THING, A KINDLY THING...
"A THING OF SUMMER DAYS AND SWEET CIDER..."

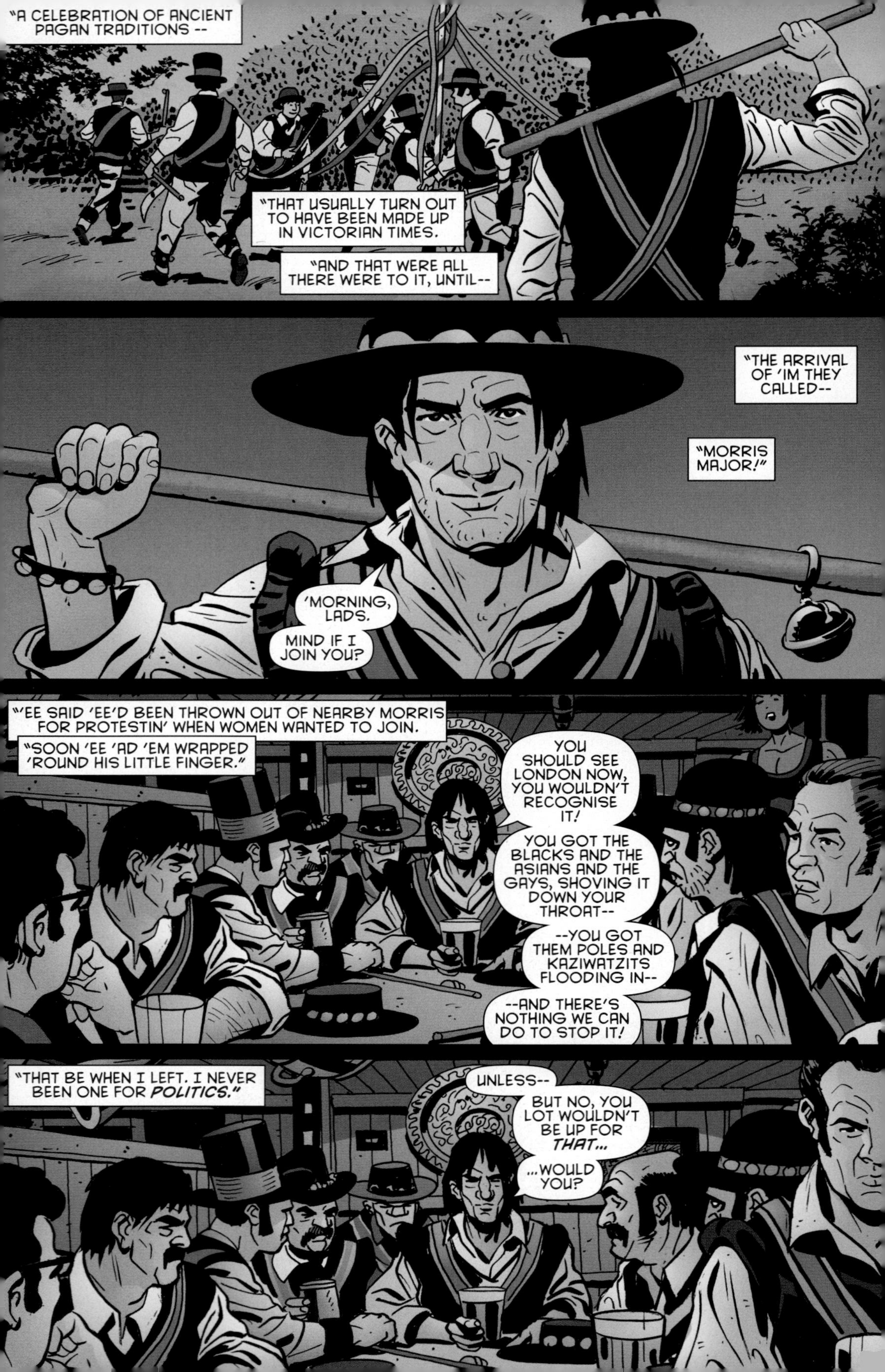
"A CELEBRATION OF ANCIENT PAGAN TRADITIONS --
"THAT USUALLY TURN OUT TO HAVE BEEN MADE UP IN VICTORIAN TIMES.
"AND THAT WERE ALL THERE WERE TO IT, UNTIL--
"THE ARRIVAL OF 'IM THEY CALLED--
"MORRIS MAJOR!"
'MORNING, LADS.
MIND IF I JOIN YOU?
"'EE SAID 'EE'D BEEN THROWN OUT OF NEARBY MORRIS FOR PROTESTIN' WHEN WOMEN WANTED TO JOIN.
"SOON 'EE 'AD 'EM WRAPPED 'ROUND HIS LITTLE FINGER."
YOU SHOULD SEE LONDON NOW, YOU WOULDN'T RECOGNISE IT!
YOU GOT THE BLACKS AND THE ASIANS AND THE GAYS, SHOVING IT DOWN YOUR THROAT--
--YOU GOT THEM POLES AND KAZIWATZITS FLOODING IN--
--AND THERE'S NOTHING WE CAN DO TO STOP IT!
"THAT BE WHEN I LEFT. I NEVER BEEN ONE FOR POLITICS."
UNLESS--
BUT NO, YOU LOT WOULDN'T BE UP FOR THAT...
...WOULD YOU?

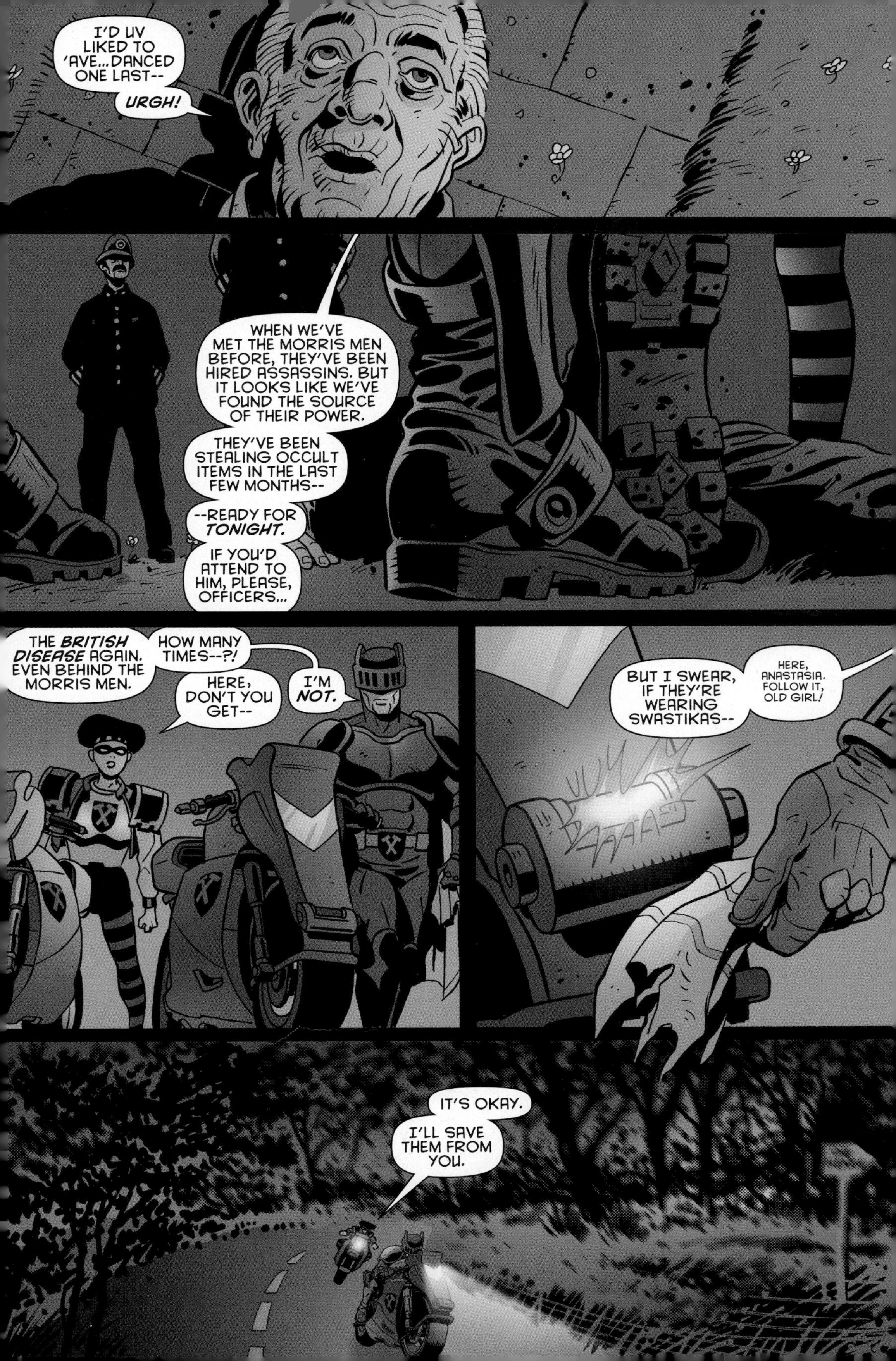

I'D UV LIKED TO 'AVE...DANCED ONE LAST--
URGH!
WHEN WE'VE MET THE MORRIS MEN BEFORE, THEY'VE BEEN HIRED ASSASSINS. BUT IT LOOKS LIKE WE'VE FOUND THE SOURCE OF THEIR POWER.
THEY'VE BEEN STEALING OCCULT ITEMS IN THE LAST FEW MONTHS--
--READY FOR TONIGHT.
IF YOU'D ATTEND TO HIM, PLEASE, OFFICERS...
THE BRITISH DISEASE AGAIN. EVEN BEHIND THE MORRIS MEN.
HOW MANY TIMES--?!
HERE, DON'T YOU GET--
I'M NOT.
BUT I SWEAR, IF THEY'RE WEARING SWASTIKAS--
HERE, ANASTASIA. FOLLOW IT, OLD GIRL!
IT'S OKAY.
I'LL SAVE THEM FROM YOU.

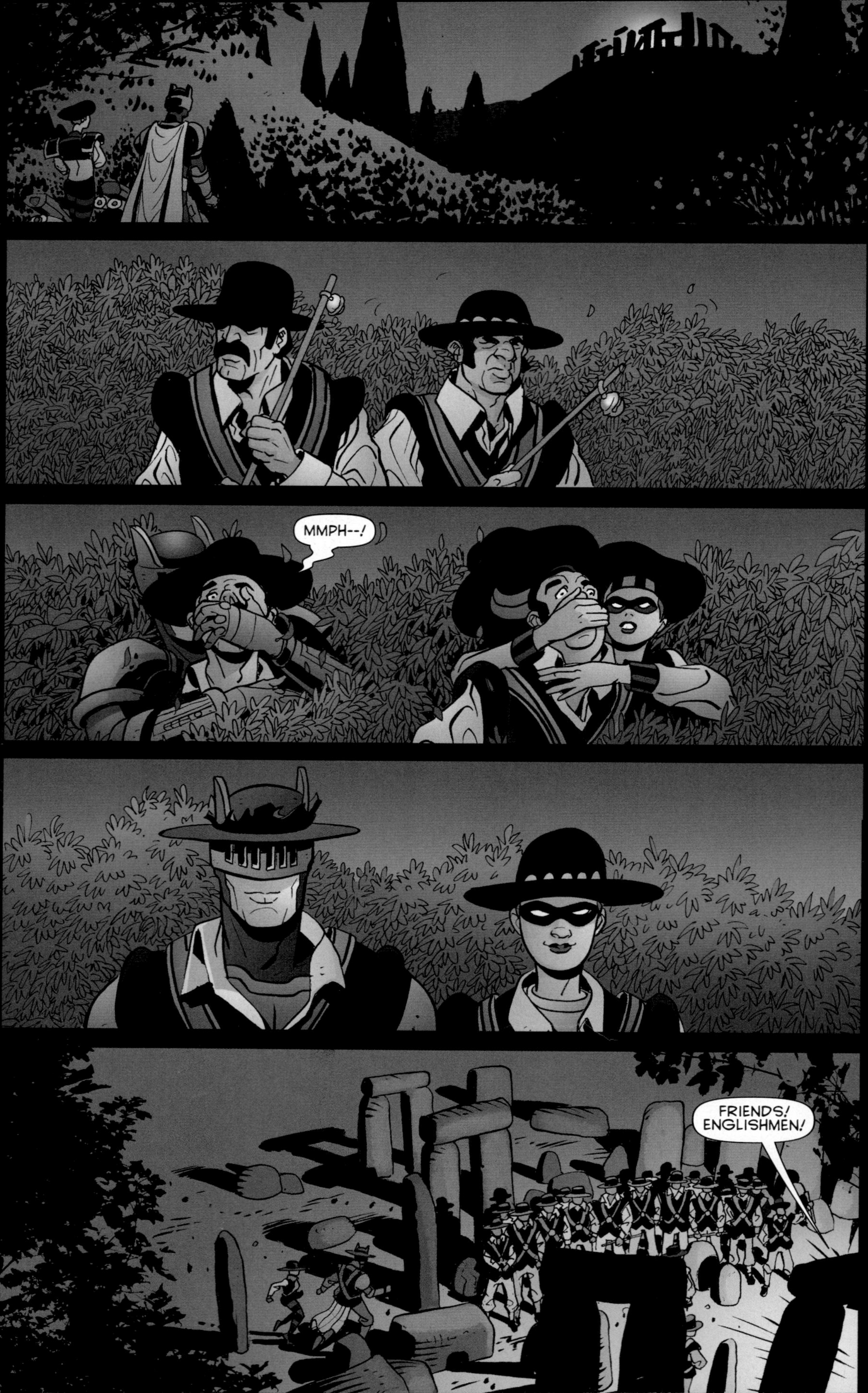
MMPH--!
FRIENDS! ENGLISHMEN!

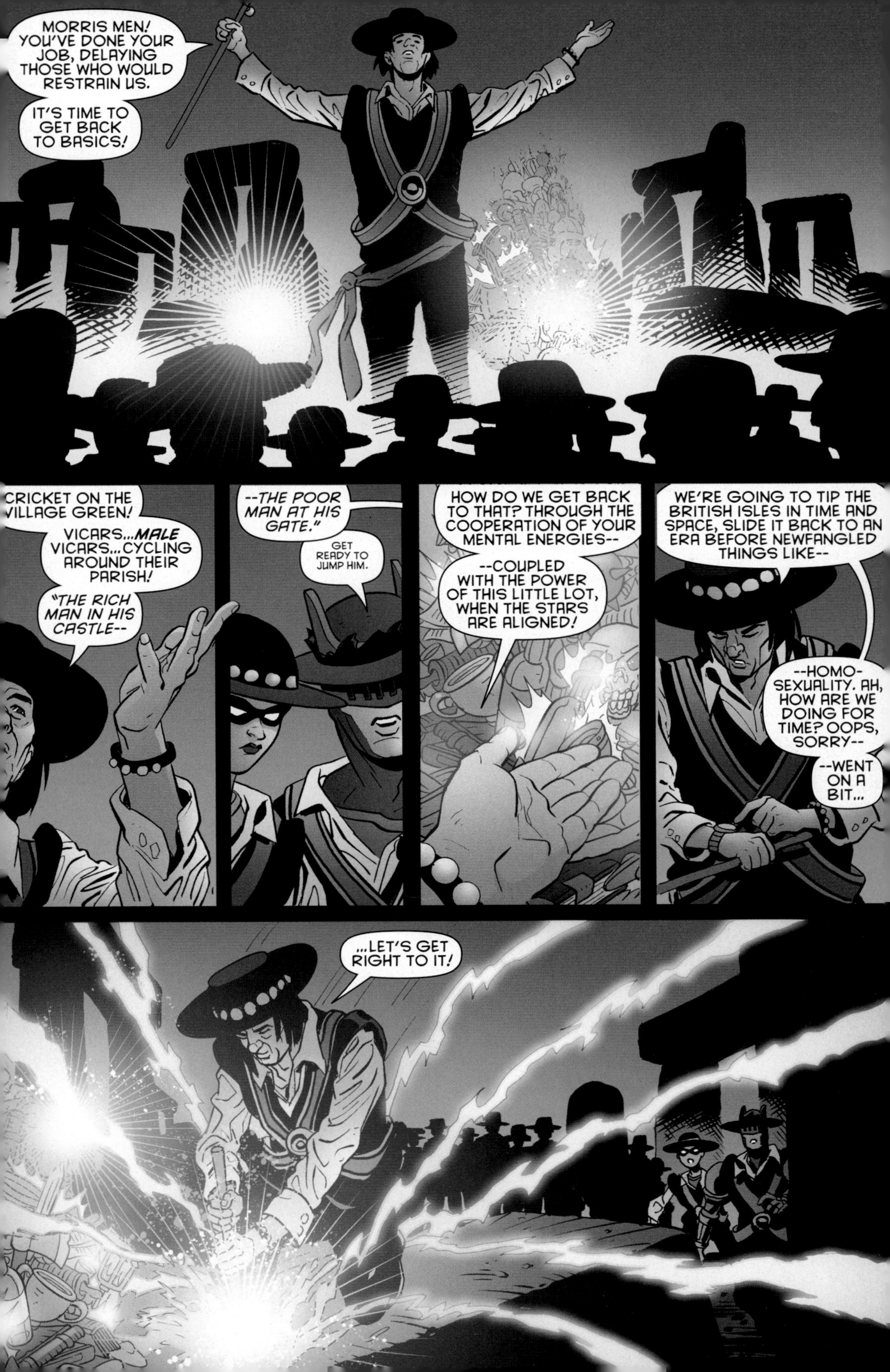
MORRIS MEN! YOU'VE DONE YOUR JOB, DELAYING THOSE WHO WOULD RESTRAIN US.
IT'S TIME TO GET BACK TO BASICS!
CRICKET ON THE VILLAGE GREEN!
VICARS...*MALE* VICARS...CYCLING AROUND THEIR PARISH!
"THE RICH MAN IN HIS CASTLE--
--THE POOR MAN AT HIS GATE."
GET READY TO JUMP HIM.
HOW DO WE GET BACK TO THAT? THROUGH THE COOPERATION OF YOUR MENTAL ENERGIES--
--COUPLED WITH THE POWER OF THIS LITTLE LOT, WHEN THE STARS ARE ALIGNED!
WE'RE GOING TO TIP THE BRITISH ISLES IN TIME AND SPACE, SLIDE IT BACK TO AN ERA BEFORE NEWFANGLED THINGS LIKE--
--HOMO-SEXUALITY. AH, HOW ARE WE DOING FOR TIME? OOPS, SORRY--
--WENT ON A BIT...
...LET'S GET RIGHT TO IT!

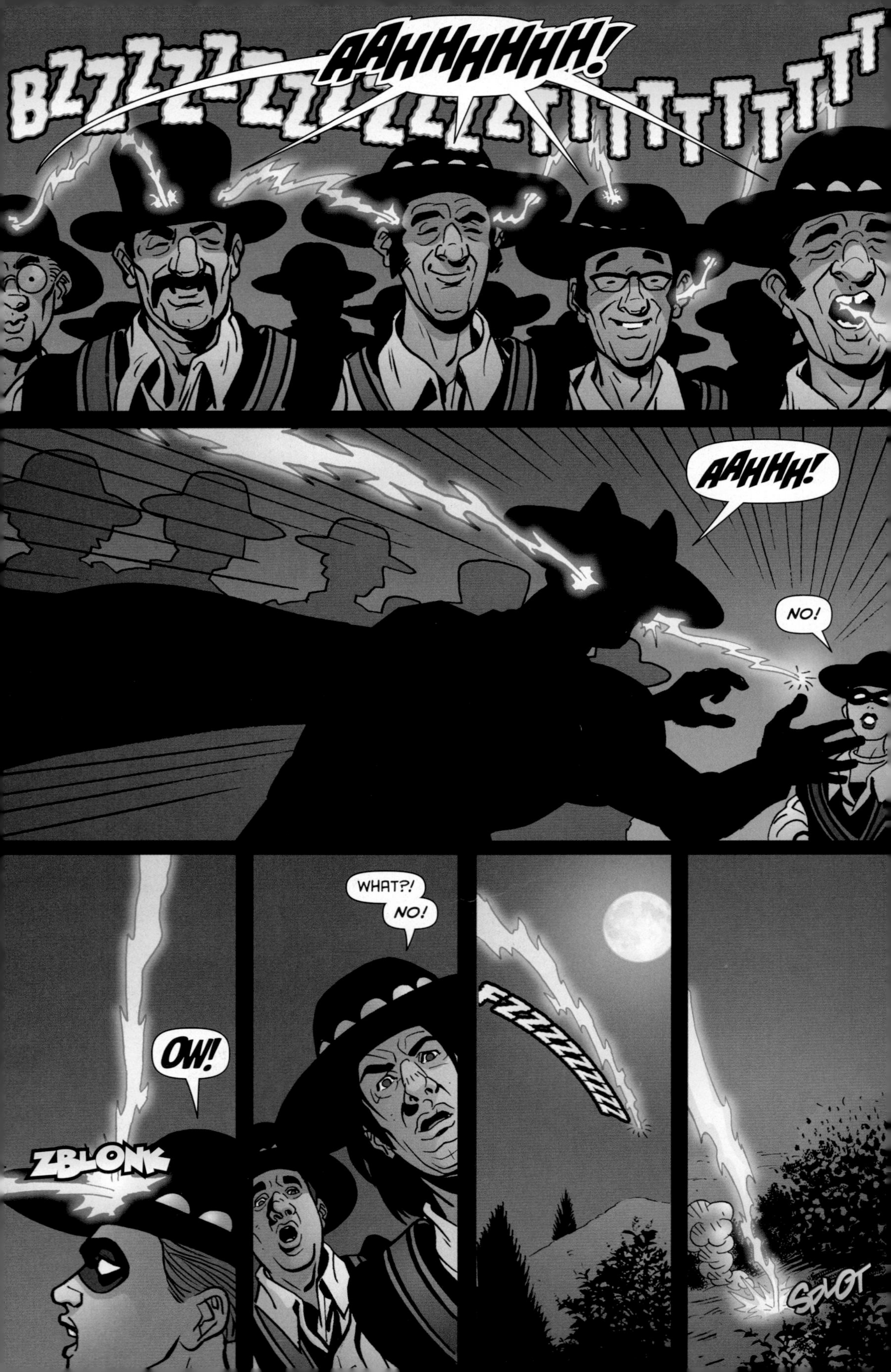
BZZZZZ-ZZZZZZZTTTTTTTTTT
AAHHHHHH!
AAHHH!
NO!
ZBLONK
OW!
WHAT?!
NO!
FZZZZZZZZ
SPLOT

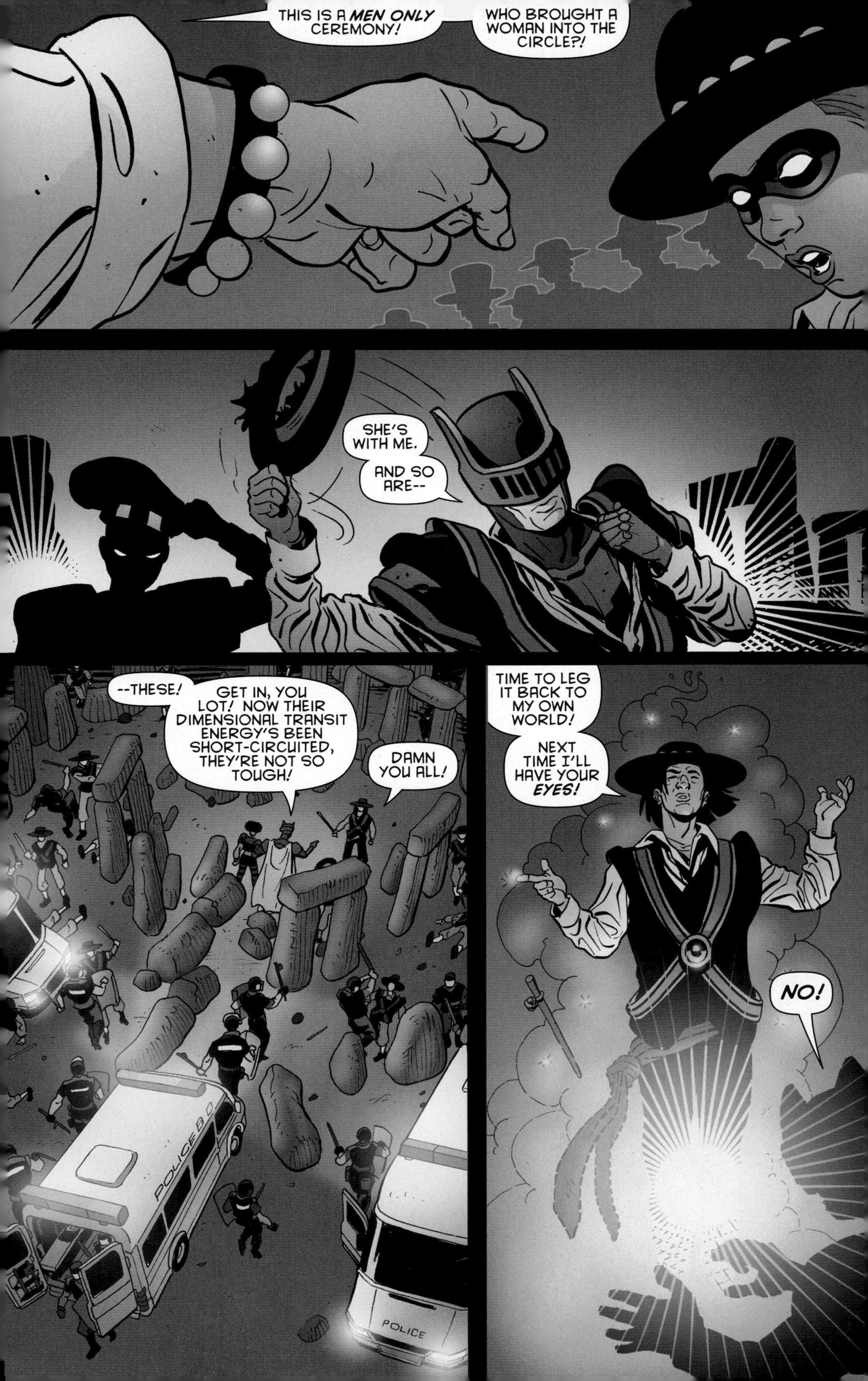
THIS IS A MEN ONLY CEREMONY!
WHO BROUGHT A WOMAN INTO THE CIRCLE?!
SHE'S WITH ME.
AND SO ARE--
--THESE!
GET IN, YOU LOT! NOW THEIR DIMENSIONAL TRANSIT ENERGY'S BEEN SHORT-CIRCUITED, THEY'RE NOT SO TOUGH!
DAMN YOU ALL!
POLICE
POLICE
TIME TO LEG IT BACK TO MY OWN WORLD!
NEXT TIME I'LL HAVE YOUR EYES!
NO!

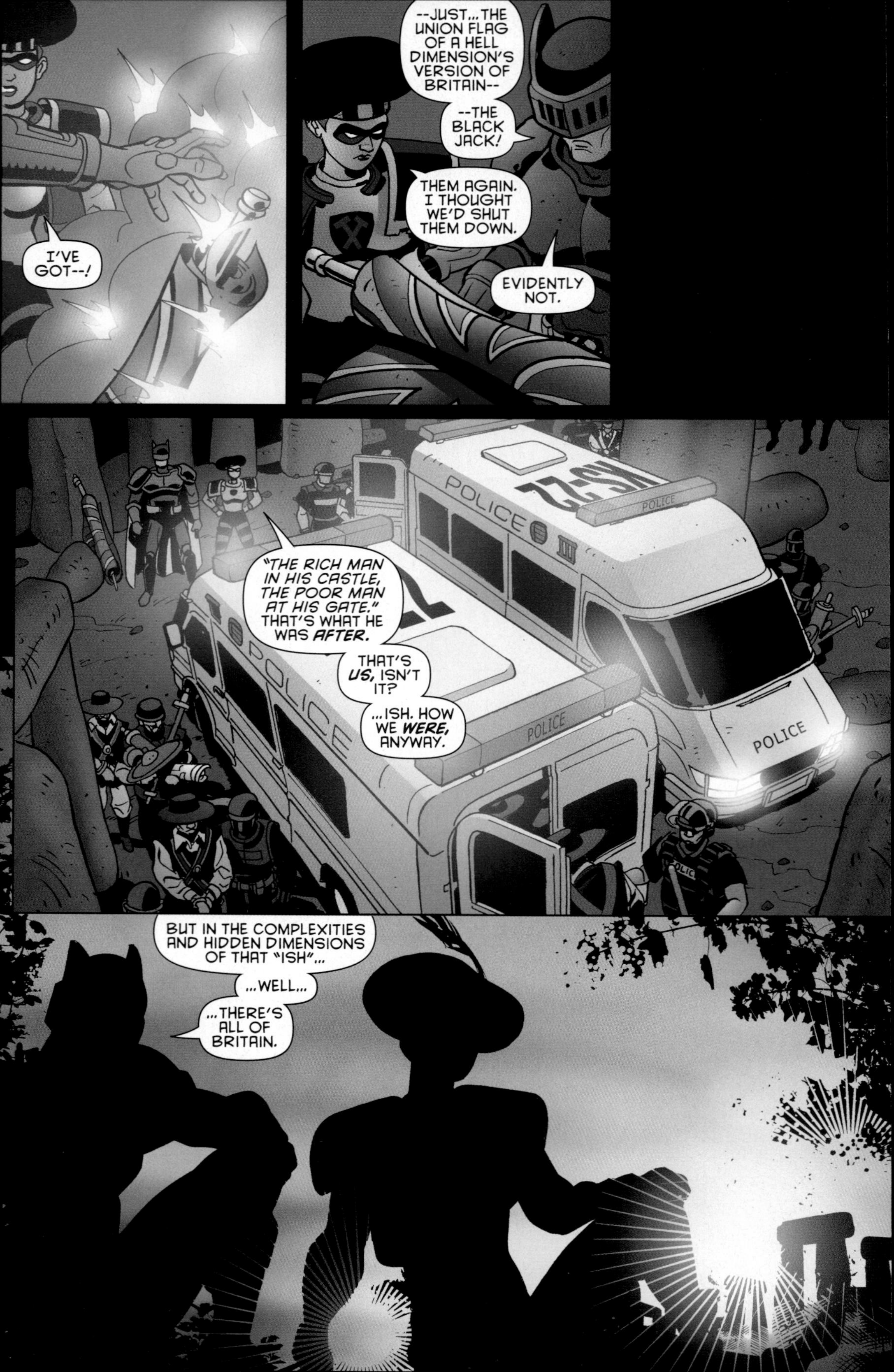
I'VE GOT--!
--JUST... THE UNION FLAG OF A HELL DIMENSION'S VERSION OF BRITAIN--
--THE BLACK JACK!
THEM AGAIN. I THOUGHT WE'D SHUT THEM DOWN.
EVIDENTLY NOT.
POLICE
"THE RICH MAN IN HIS CASTLE, THE POOR MAN AT HIS GATE." THAT'S WHAT HE WAS AFTER.
THAT'S US, ISN'T IT?
...ISH. HOW WE WERE, ANYWAY.
BUT IN THE COMPLEXITIES AND HIDDEN DIMENSIONS OF THAT "ISH"...
...WELL...
...THERE'S ALL OF BRITAIN.

What Morris Men are Like

WELL, LOVELY, GENERALLY. AND NOT AT ALL FASCISTIC. MORRIS DANCING IS FOLK TRADITION INVOLVING DANCERS DRESSED IN RIBBONS AND BELLS ~ENTLY HITTING EACH OTHER WITH SMALL STICKS. IT HAPPENS IN MARKET QUARES AND ON VILLAGE GREENS ON FESTIVAL DAYS. GENUINELY ANCIENT ~RIGINS ARE CLAIMED, BUT IT CERTAINLY DATES BACK TO BEFORE THE ENGLISH IVIL WAR. IT'S THOUGHT IT WAS ORIGINALLY A SWORD DANCE, CREATED IN SPAIN ~ THE VICTORY CELEBRATIONS WHEN THE MOORS WERE DRIVEN OUT. HENCE, ~MOORISH DANCE." IN RECENT YEARS THERE HAVE BEEN RUCTIONS IN THE ~RADITIONALLY ALL-MALE MORRIS COMMUNITY ABOUT LETTING WOMEN DANCE.

THE INITIAL THOUGHT BEHIND THIS STORY WAS READING NEWS REPORTS ~BOUT FOLK AGAINST FASCISM, A MOVEMENT IN BRITISH FOLK MUSIC THAT ~GHTS FAR RIGHT ORGANISATIONS CO-OPTING (OFTEN STRIDENTLY LEFT WING) ~OLK GROUPS AND PERFORMANCES. I BECAME VERY WORRIED, BEFORE THE LAST ~ENERAL ELECTION, THAT THE EXTREMISTS MIGHT CONTROL A LONDON COUNCIL, ~R EVEN GET AN MP. TO MY IMMENSE RELIEF, ELECTORAL TURNOUT WAS ~NORMOUS AND THEY WERE ALL KICKED OUT.

MORRIS MAJOR'S "CRICKET ON THE VILLAGE GREEN" SPEECH MAY REMIND ~RITISH READERS OF FORMER TORY PRIME MINISTER JOHN MAJOR'S NOSTALGIC ~EARNINGS. MAJOR WAS A MODERATE, BUT THE SPEECH WOULD DOUBTLESS ~ESONATE WITH PEOPLE LIKE MORRIS, WHOSE NAME ALSO INVOKES A BRITISH CAR.

"WE'RE NEEDED" WILL BE FAMILIAR TO FANS OF THE AVENGERS. STEELEYE ~PAN ARE A BRITISH FOLK BAND OF THE 1960s, CHEESE-ROLLING IS A FOLK ~PORT WHERE ROUND CHEESES ARE CHASED DOWNHILL (NO, REALLY), SCRUMPY IS ~NOTHER NAME FOR ALCOHOLIC CIDER (OF COURSE, ALL BRITISH CIDER IS ~LCOHOLIC), "WURZEL" IS ANOTHER NAME FOR A TURNIP, A DEROGATORY TERM ~OR COUNTRY FOLK AND THE NAME ~F A COMEDY FOLK BAND. "WASSAIL ~UTTOCK" SOUNDS A BIT LIKE ~VASSAILING, THAT IS, A FOLK ~RADITION INVOLVING APPLES, AND ~HE SORT OF THING YOU MIGHT HEAR ~N RADIO COMEDY "ROUND THE ~ORNE." ANASTASIA WAS THE NAME ~F DAN DARE'S SPACESHIP. "THE ~ICH MAN AT HIS CASTLE, THE POOR ~AN AT HIS GATE" IS FROM THE HYMN ~LL THINGS BRIGHT AND BEAUTIFUL ~VHICH MAKES THE EXTRAORDINARY ~LAIM THAT SOCIAL INEQUALITY IS ~OW GOD LIKES IT.

I'M FROM WURZEL COUNTRY ~MYSELF, SO I'M ALLOWED TO TAKE ~HE MICKEY.

UNTIL NEXT ISSUE, CHEERIO!
- PAUL CORNELL

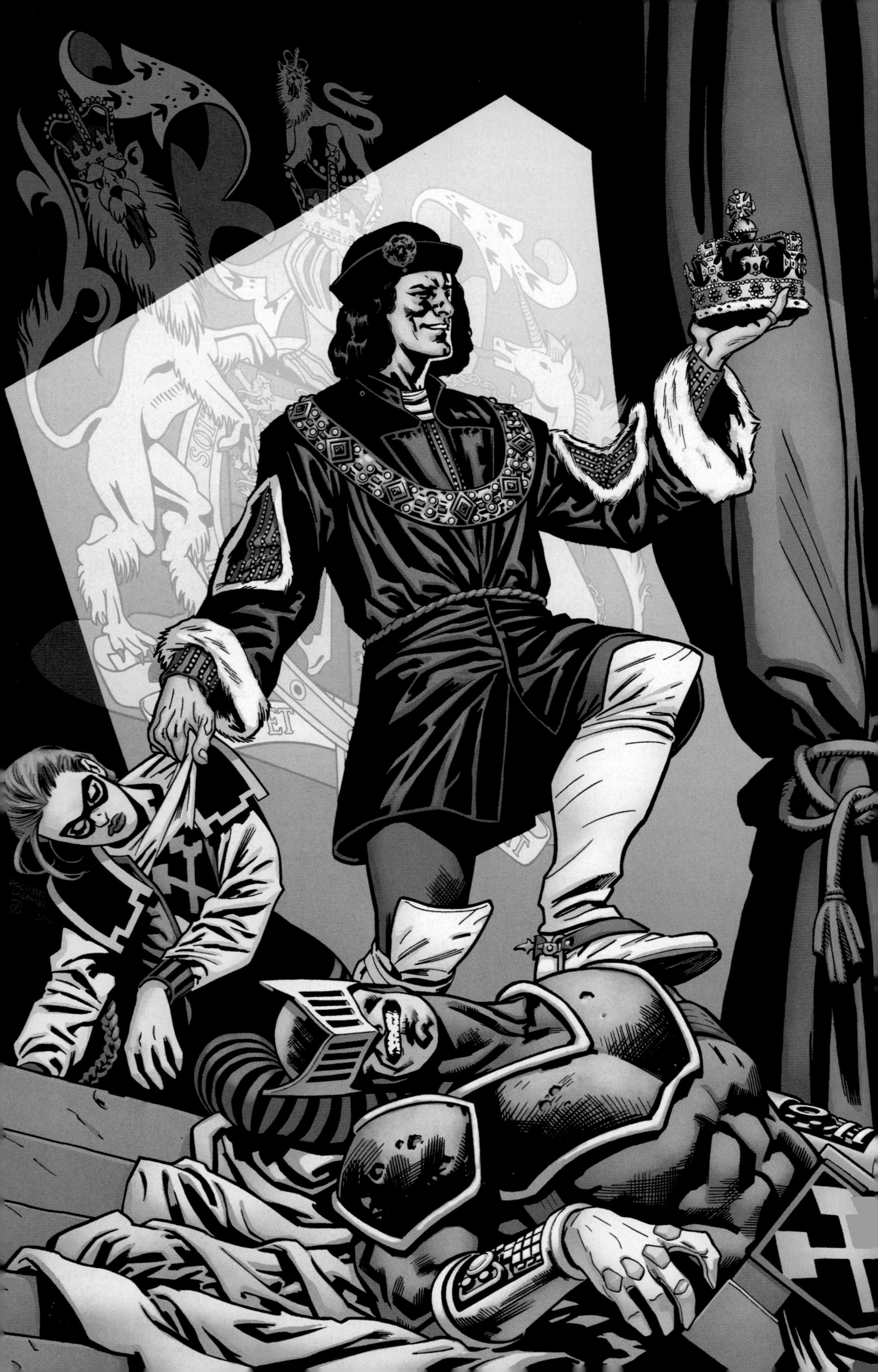

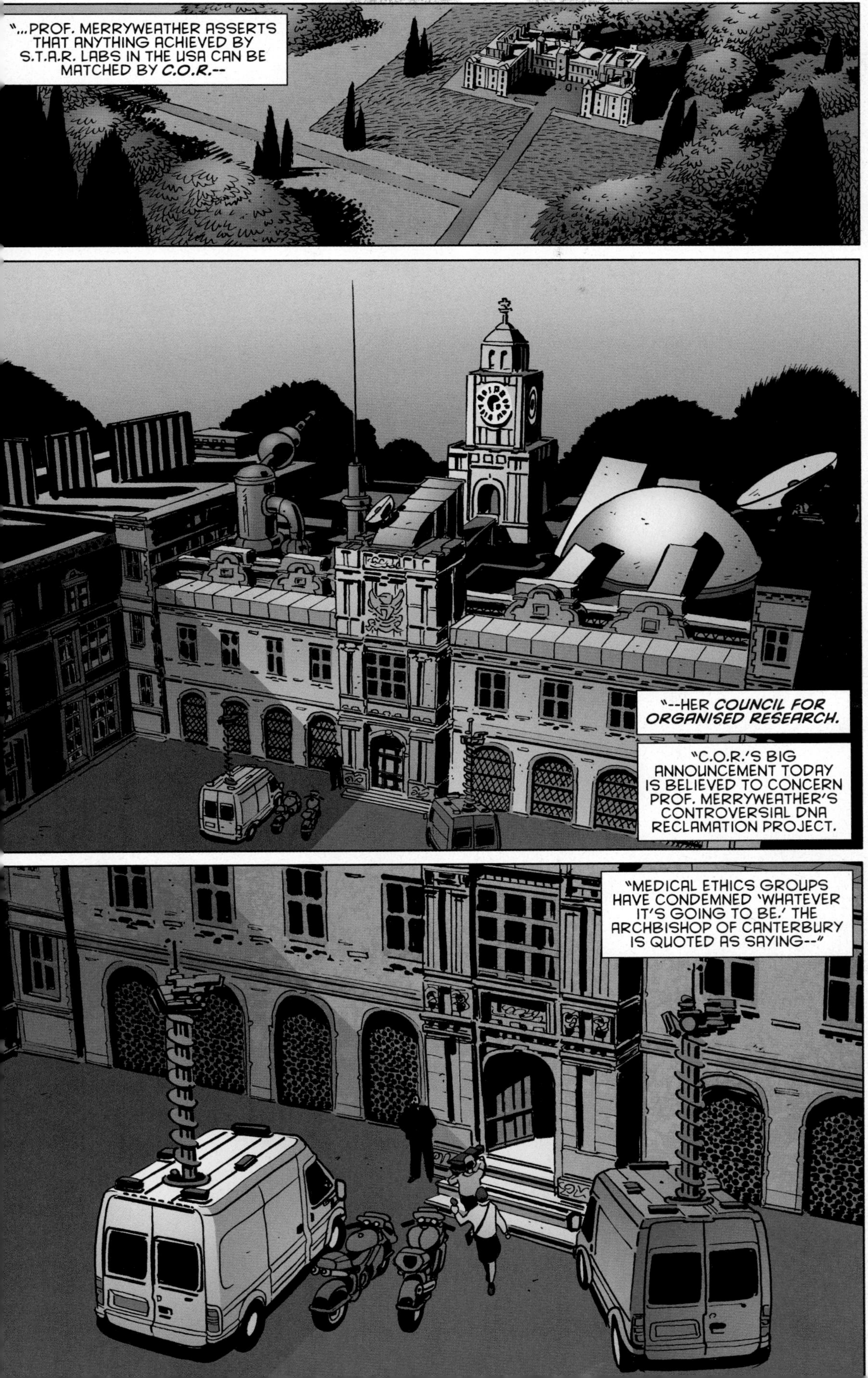
"...PROF. MERRYWEATHER ASSERTS THAT ANYTHING ACHIEVED BY S.T.A.R. LABS IN THE USA CAN BE MATCHED BY C.O.R.--
"--HER COUNCIL FOR ORGANISED RESEARCH.
"C.O.R.'S BIG ANNOUNCEMENT TODAY IS BELIEVED TO CONCERN PROF. MERRYWEATHER'S CONTROVERSIAL DNA RECLAMATION PROJECT.
"MEDICAL ETHICS GROUPS HAVE CONDEMNED 'WHATEVER IT'S GOING TO BE.' THE ARCHBISHOP OF CANTERBURY IS QUOTED AS SAYING--"

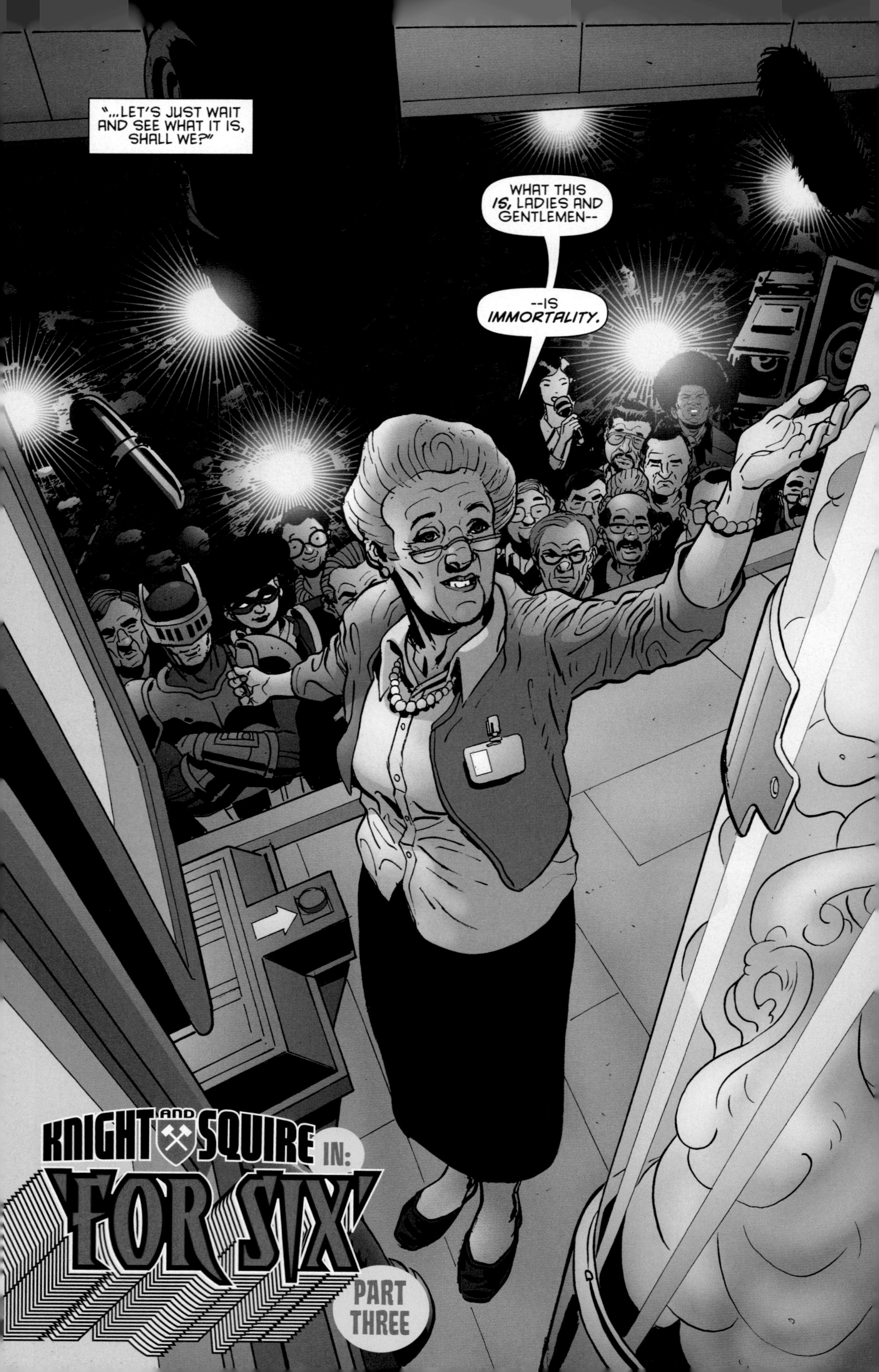
"...LET'S JUST WAIT AND SEE WHAT IT IS, SHALL WE?"
WHAT THIS *IS*, LADIES AND GENTLEMEN--
--IS *IMMORTALITY.*
KNIGHT AND SQUIRE IN:
'FOR SIX'
PART THREE

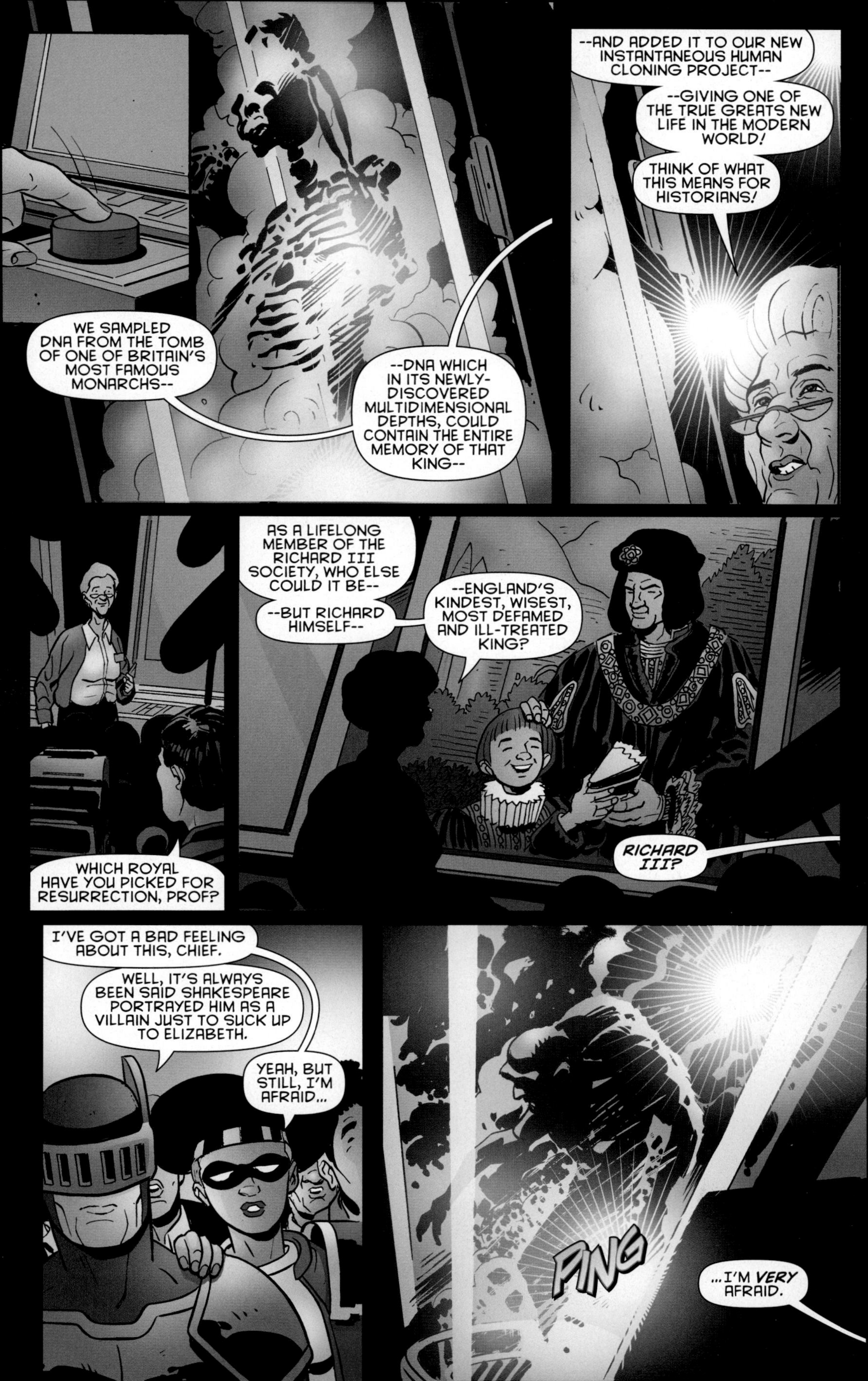
WE SAMPLED DNA FROM THE TOMB OF ONE OF BRITAIN'S MOST FAMOUS MONARCHS--
--DNA WHICH IN ITS NEWLY-DISCOVERED MULTIDIMENSIONAL DEPTHS, COULD CONTAIN THE ENTIRE MEMORY OF THAT KING--
--AND ADDED IT TO OUR NEW INSTANTANEOUS HUMAN CLONING PROJECT--
--GIVING ONE OF THE TRUE GREATS NEW LIFE IN THE MODERN WORLD!
THINK OF WHAT THIS MEANS FOR HISTORIANS!
WHICH ROYAL HAVE YOU PICKED FOR RESURRECTION, PROF?
AS A LIFELONG MEMBER OF THE RICHARD III SOCIETY, WHO ELSE COULD IT BE--
--BUT RICHARD HIMSELF--
--ENGLAND'S KINDEST, WISEST, MOST DEFAMED AND ILL-TREATED KING?
RICHARD III?
I'VE GOT A BAD FEELING ABOUT THIS, CHIEF.
WELL, IT'S ALWAYS BEEN SAID SHAKESPEARE PORTRAYED HIM AS A VILLAIN JUST TO SUCK UP TO ELIZABETH.
YEAH, BUT STILL, I'M AFRAID...
FING
...I'M VERY AFRAID.

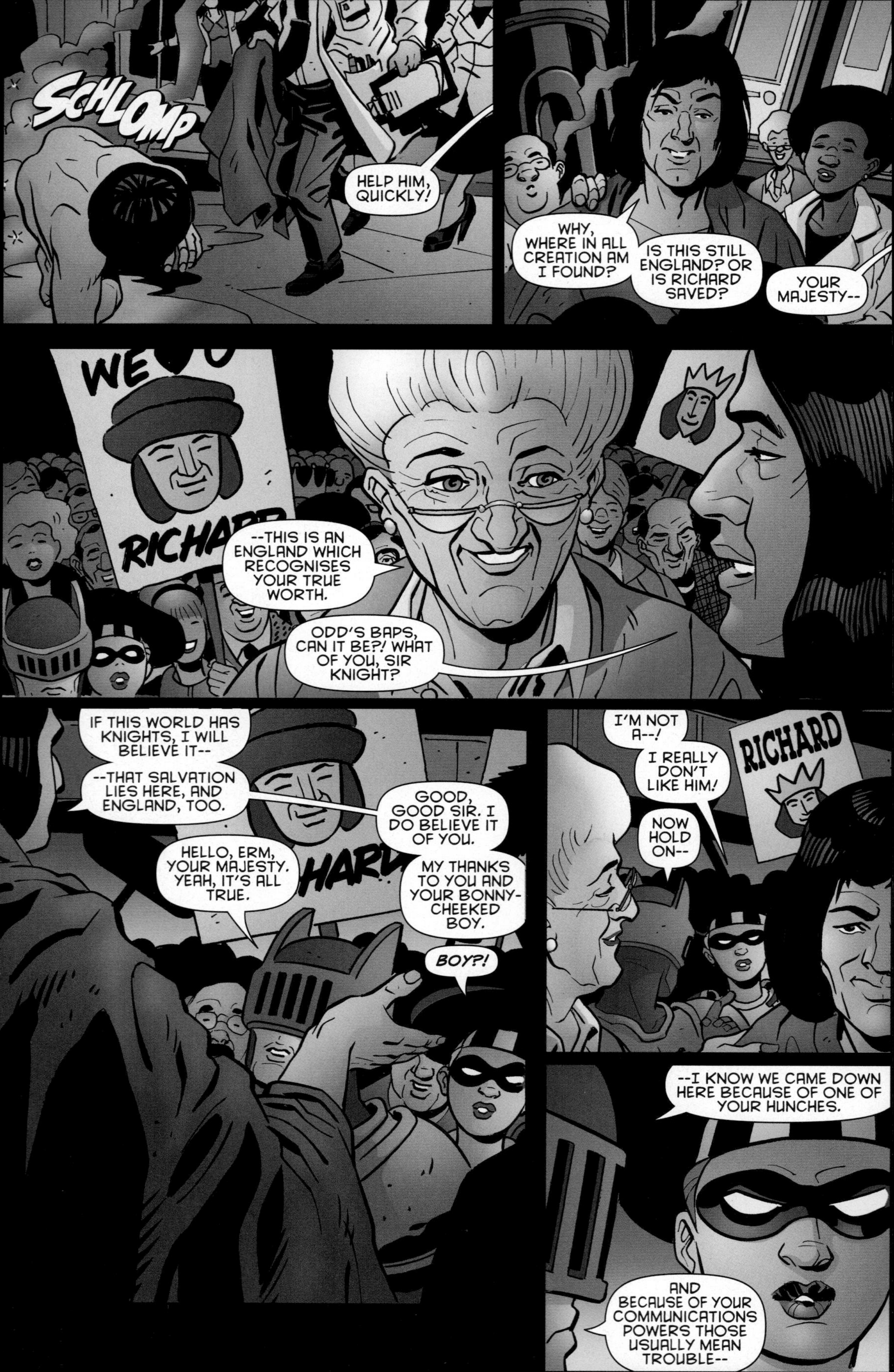
SCHLOMP
HELP HIM, QUICKLY!
WHY, WHERE IN ALL CREATION AM I FOUND?
IS THIS STILL ENGLAND? OR IS RICHARD SAVED?
YOUR MAJESTY--
WE
RICHARD
--THIS IS AN ENGLAND WHICH RECOGNISES YOUR TRUE WORTH.
ODD'S BAPS, CAN IT BE?! WHAT OF YOU, SIR KNIGHT?
IF THIS WORLD HAS KNIGHTS, I WILL BELIEVE IT--
--THAT SALVATION LIES HERE, AND ENGLAND, TOO.
GOOD, GOOD SIR. I DO BELIEVE IT OF YOU.
HELLO, ERM, YOUR MAJESTY. YEAH, IT'S ALL TRUE.
HARD
MY THANKS TO YOU AND YOUR BONNY-CHEEKED BOY.
BOY?!
I'M NOT A--!
I REALLY DON'T LIKE HIM!
RICHARD
NOW HOLD ON--
--I KNOW WE CAME DOWN HERE BECAUSE OF ONE OF YOUR HUNCHES.
AND BECAUSE OF YOUR COMMUNICATIONS POWERS THOSE USUALLY MEAN TROUBLE--

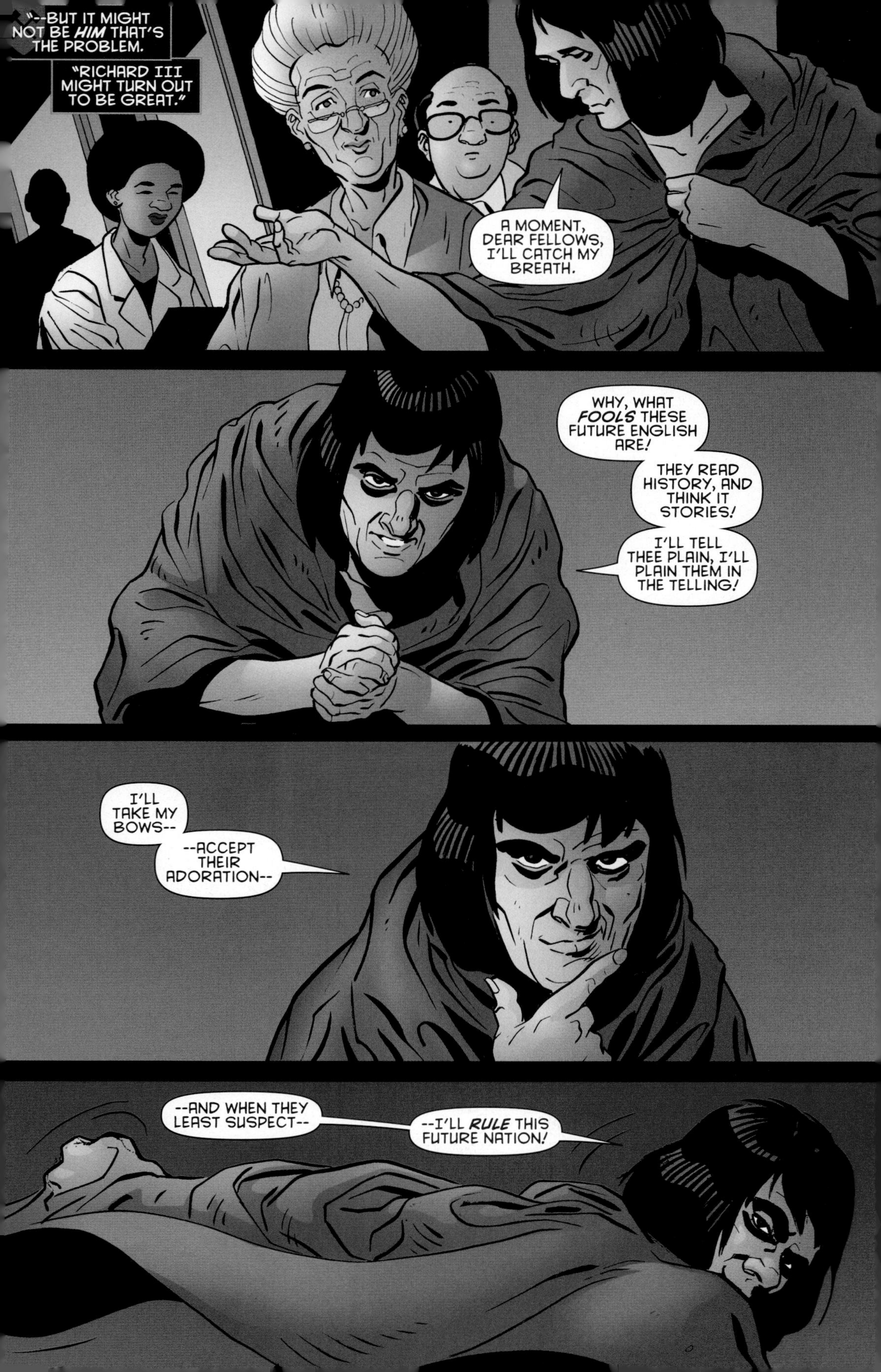

"--BUT IT MIGHT NOT BE *HIM* THAT'S THE PROBLEM.
"RICHARD III MIGHT TURN OUT TO BE GREAT."
A MOMENT, DEAR FELLOWS, I'LL CATCH MY BREATH.
WHY, WHAT *FOOLS* THESE FUTURE ENGLISH ARE!
THEY READ HISTORY, AND THINK IT STORIES!
I'LL TELL THEE PLAIN, I'LL PLAIN THEM IN THE TELLING!
I'LL TAKE MY BOWS--
--ACCEPT THEIR ADORATION--
--AND WHEN THEY LEAST SUSPECT--
--I'LL *RULE* THIS FUTURE NATION!

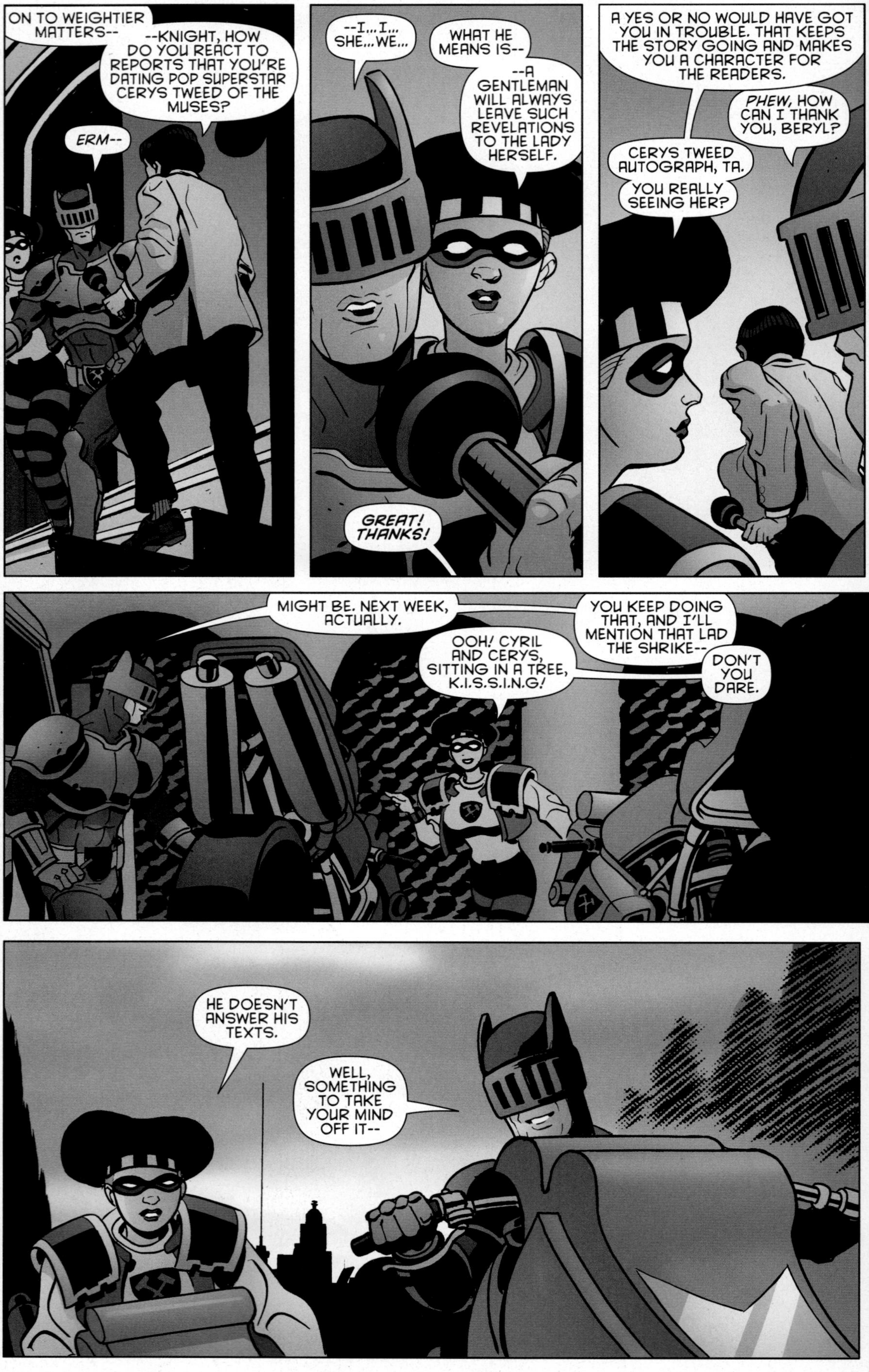
ON TO WEIGHTIER MATTERS--
--KNIGHT, HOW DO YOU REACT TO REPORTS THAT YOU'RE DATING POP SUPERSTAR CERYS TWEED OF THE MUSES?
ERM--
--I... I... SHE...WE...
WHAT HE MEANS IS--
--A GENTLEMAN WILL ALWAYS LEAVE SUCH REVELATIONS TO THE LADY HERSELF.
GREAT! THANKS!
A YES OR NO WOULD HAVE GOT YOU IN TROUBLE. THAT KEEPS THE STORY GOING AND MAKES YOU A CHARACTER FOR THE READERS.
PHEW, HOW CAN I THANK YOU, BERYL?
CERYS TWEED AUTOGRAPH, TA.
YOU REALLY SEEING HER?
MIGHT BE. NEXT WEEK, ACTUALLY.
OOH! CYRIL AND CERYS, SITTING IN A TREE, K.I.S.S.I.N.G!
YOU KEEP DOING THAT, AND I'LL MENTION THAT LAD THE SHRIKE--
DON'T YOU DARE.
HE DOESN'T ANSWER HIS TEXTS.
WELL, SOMETHING TO TAKE YOUR MIND OFF IT--

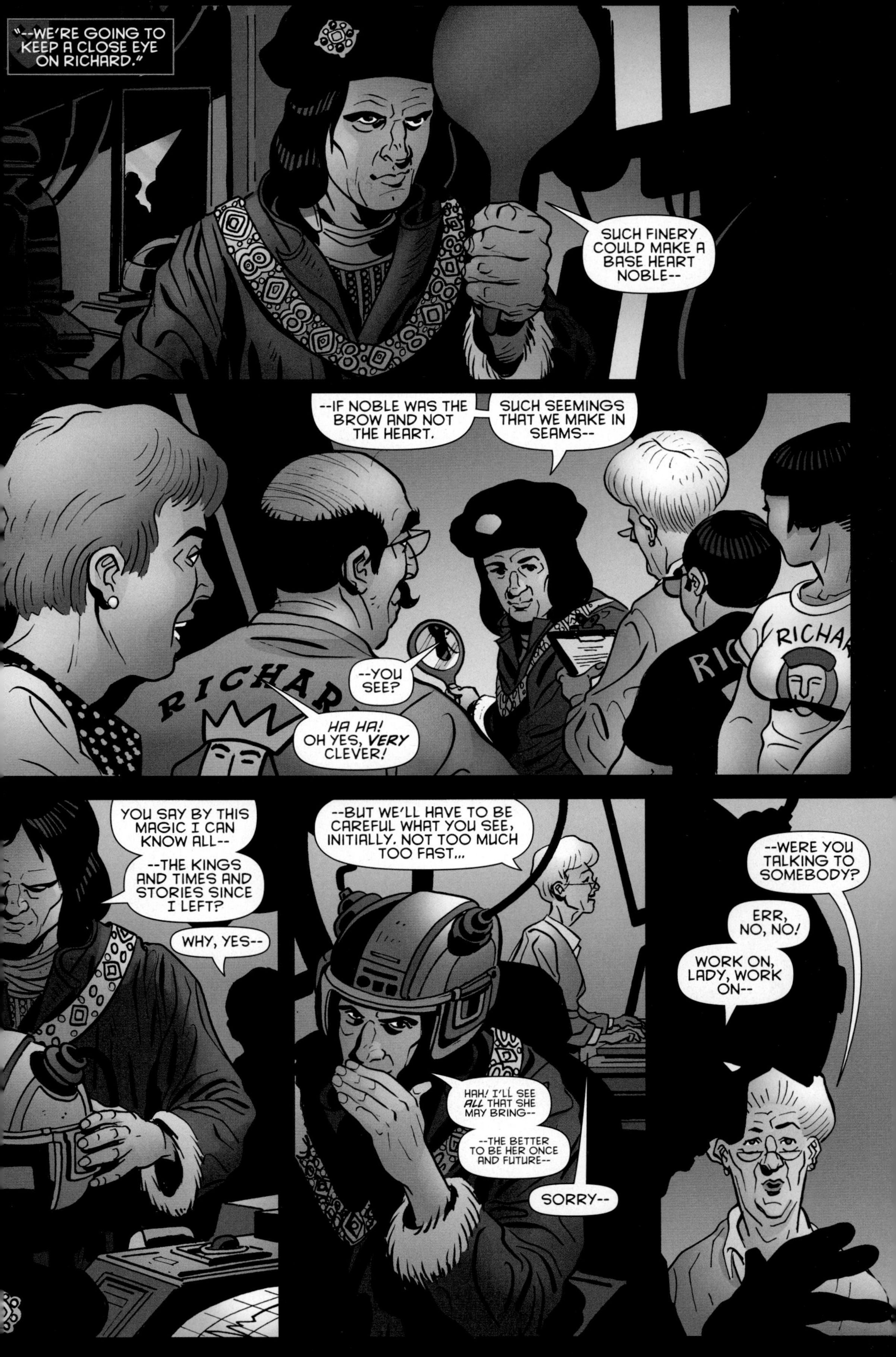
"--WE'RE GOING TO KEEP A CLOSE EYE ON RICHARD."
SUCH FINERY COULD MAKE A BASE HEART NOBLE--
SUCH SEEMINGS THAT WE MAKE IN SEAMS--
--IF NOBLE WAS THE BROW AND NOT THE HEART.
--YOU SEE?
HA HA! OH YES, *VERY* CLEVER!
RICHAR
RIC
RICHAR
YOU SAY BY THIS MAGIC I CAN KNOW ALL--
--THE KINGS AND TIMES AND STORIES SINCE I LEFT?
WHY, YES--
--BUT WE'LL HAVE TO BE CAREFUL WHAT YOU SEE, INITIALLY. NOT TOO MUCH TOO FAST...
HAH! I'LL SEE *ALL* THAT SHE MAY BRING--
--THE BETTER TO BE HER ONCE AND FUTURE--
SORRY--
--WERE YOU TALKING TO SOMEBODY?
ERR, NO, NO!
WORK ON, LADY, WORK ON--

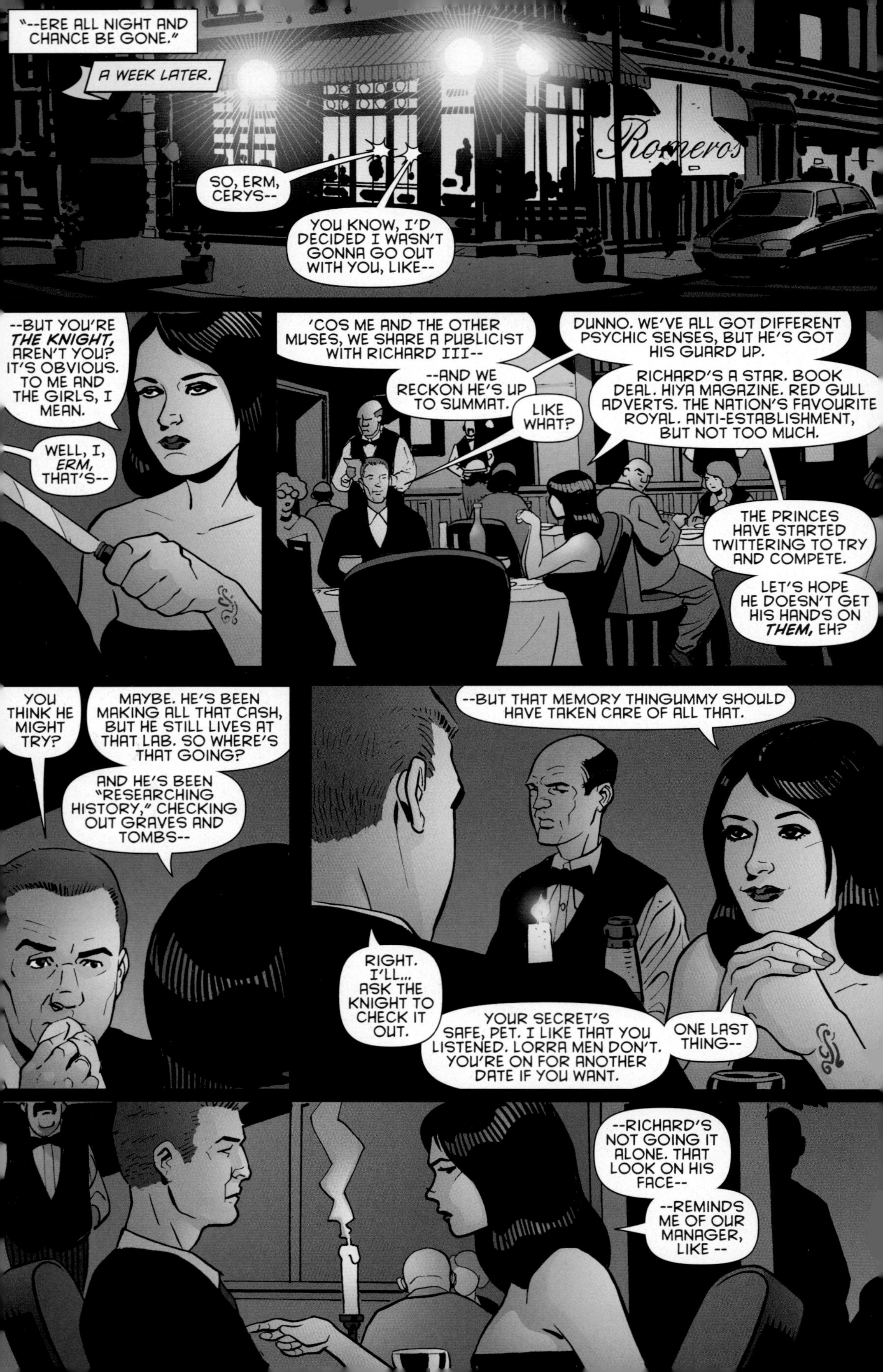
"--ERE ALL NIGHT AND CHANCE BE GONE."
A WEEK LATER.
Romeros
SO, ERM, CERYS--
YOU KNOW, I'D DECIDED I WASN'T GONNA GO OUT WITH YOU, LIKE--
--BUT YOU'RE *THE KNIGHT,* AREN'T YOU? IT'S OBVIOUS. TO ME AND THE GIRLS, I MEAN.
WELL, I, *ERM,* THAT'S--
'COS ME AND THE OTHER MUSES, WE SHARE A PUBLICIST WITH RICHARD III--
--AND WE RECKON HE'S UP TO SUMMAT.
LIKE WHAT?
DUNNO. WE'VE ALL GOT DIFFERENT PSYCHIC SENSES, BUT HE'S GOT HIS GUARD UP.
RICHARD'S A STAR. BOOK DEAL. HIYA MAGAZINE. RED GULL ADVERTS. THE NATION'S FAVOURITE ROYAL. ANTI-ESTABLISHMENT, BUT NOT TOO MUCH.
THE PRINCES HAVE STARTED TWITTERING TO TRY AND COMPETE.
LET'S HOPE HE DOESN'T GET HIS HANDS ON *THEM,* EH?
YOU THINK HE MIGHT TRY?
MAYBE. HE'S BEEN MAKING ALL THAT CASH, BUT HE STILL LIVES AT THAT LAB. SO WHERE'S THAT GOING?
AND HE'S BEEN "RESEARCHING HISTORY," CHECKING OUT GRAVES AND TOMBS--
--BUT THAT MEMORY THINGUMMY SHOULD HAVE TAKEN CARE OF ALL THAT.
RIGHT. I'LL... ASK THE KNIGHT TO CHECK IT OUT.
YOUR SECRET'S SAFE, PET. I LIKE THAT YOU LISTENED. LORRA MEN DON'T. YOU'RE ON FOR ANOTHER DATE IF YOU WANT.
ONE LAST THING--
--RICHARD'S NOT GOING IT ALONE. THAT LOOK ON HIS FACE--
--REMINDS ME OF OUR MANAGER, LIKE --

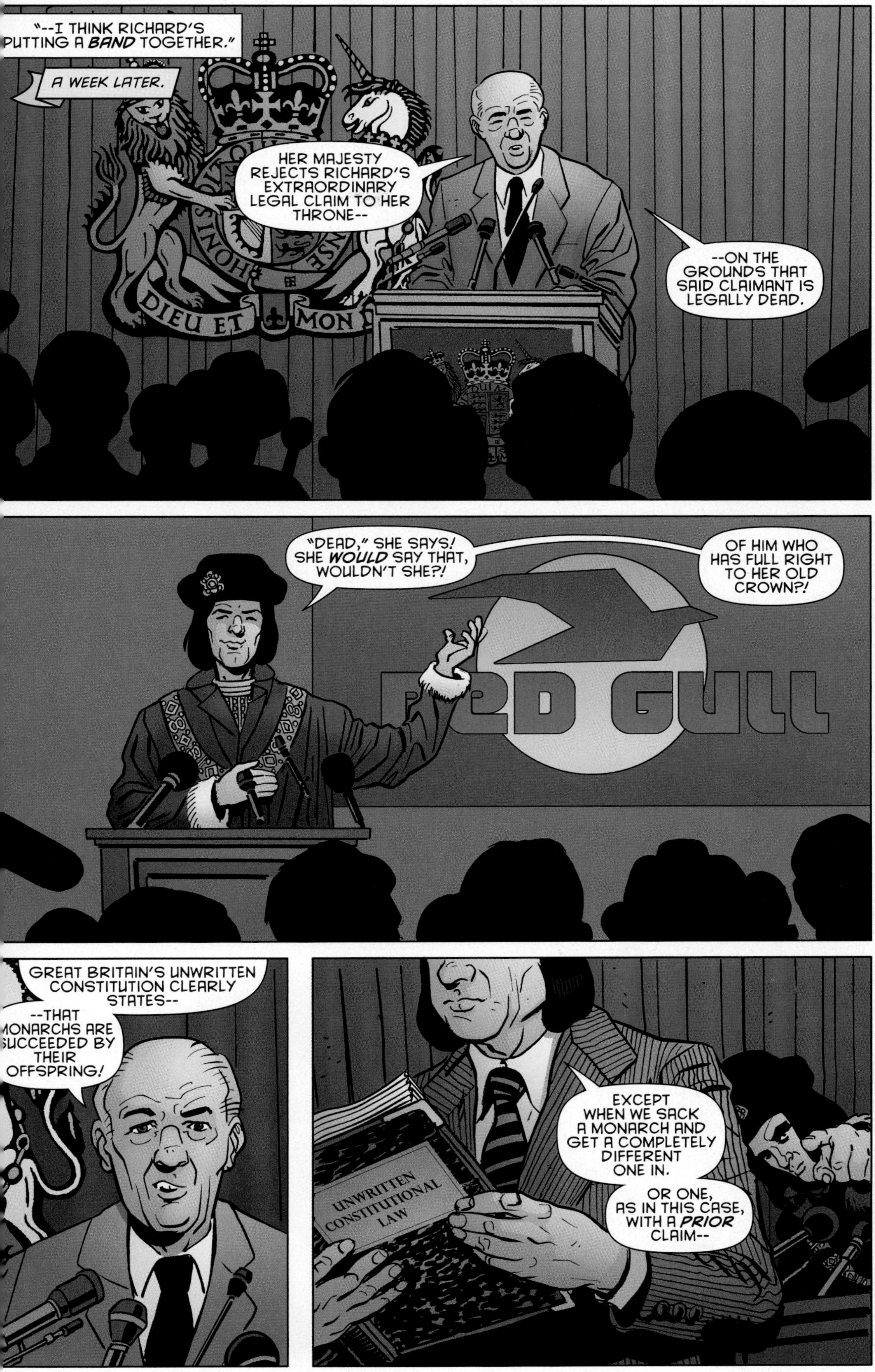
"--I THINK RICHARD'S PUTTING A *BAND* TOGETHER."
A WEEK LATER.
HER MAJESTY REJECTS RICHARD'S EXTRAORDINARY LEGAL CLAIM TO HER THRONE--
--ON THE GROUNDS THAT SAID CLAIMANT IS LEGALLY DEAD.
DIEU ET MON D
"DEAD," SHE SAYS! SHE *WOULD* SAY THAT, WOULDN'T SHE?!
OF HIM WHO HAS FULL RIGHT TO HER OLD CROWN?!
GREAT BRITAIN'S UNWRITTEN CONSTITUTION CLEARLY STATES--
--THAT MONARCHS ARE SUCCEEDED BY THEIR OFFSPRING!
UNWRITTEN CONSTITUTIONAL LAW
EXCEPT WHEN WE SACK A MONARCH AND GET A COMPLETELY DIFFERENT ONE IN.
OR ONE, AS IN THIS CASE, WITH A *PRIOR* CLAIM--

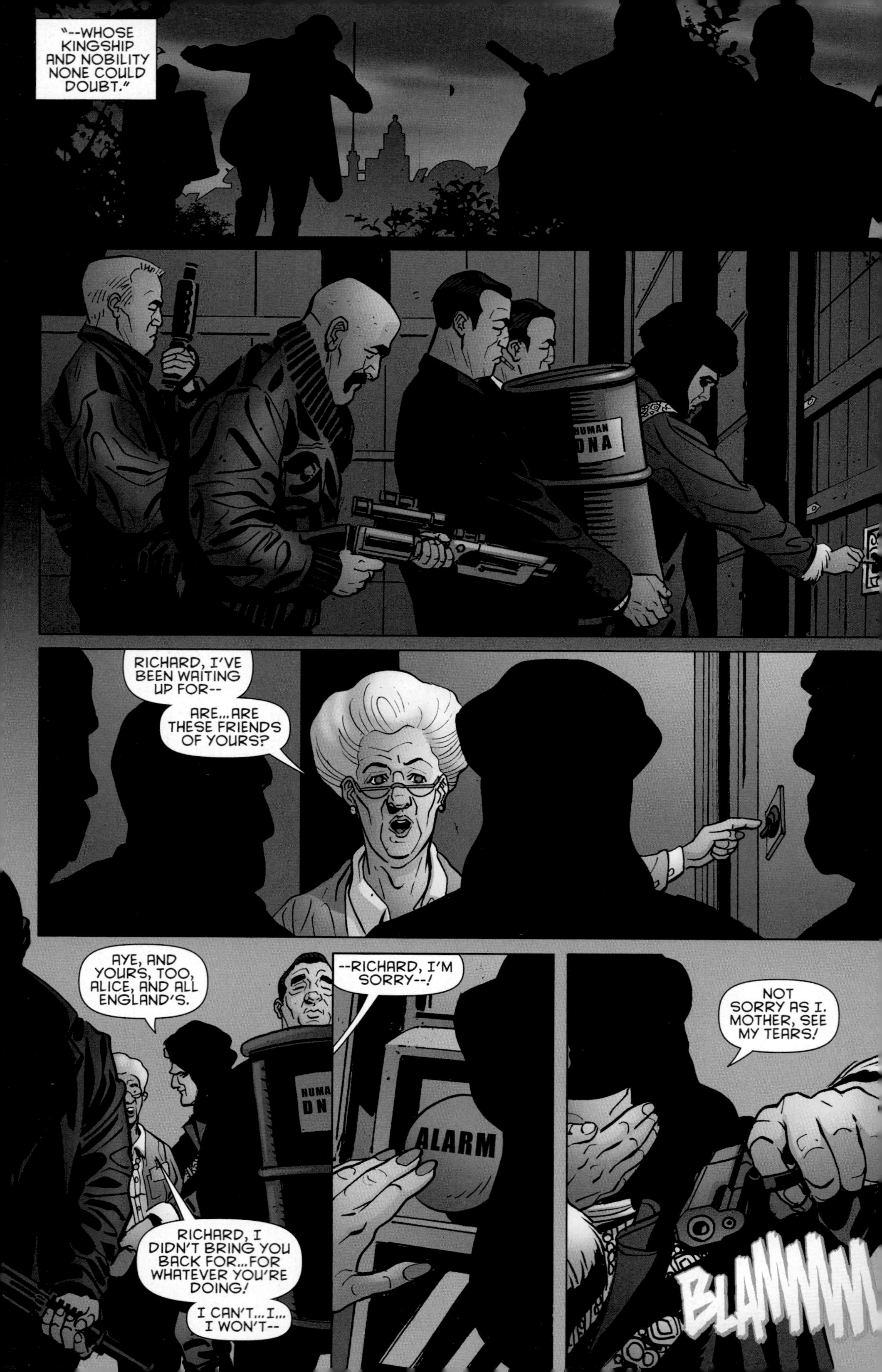
"--WHOSE KINGSHIP AND NOBILITY NONE COULD DOUBT."
HUMAN DNA
RICHARD, I'VE BEEN WAITING UP FOR--
ARE... ARE THESE FRIENDS OF YOURS?
AYE, AND YOURS, TOO, ALICE, AND ALL ENGLAND'S.
RICHARD, I DIDN'T BRING YOU BACK FOR... FOR WHATEVER YOU'RE DOING!
I CAN'T... I... I WON'T--
--RICHARD, I'M SORRY--!
ALARM
NOT SORRY AS I. MOTHER, SEE MY TEARS!
BLAMMM

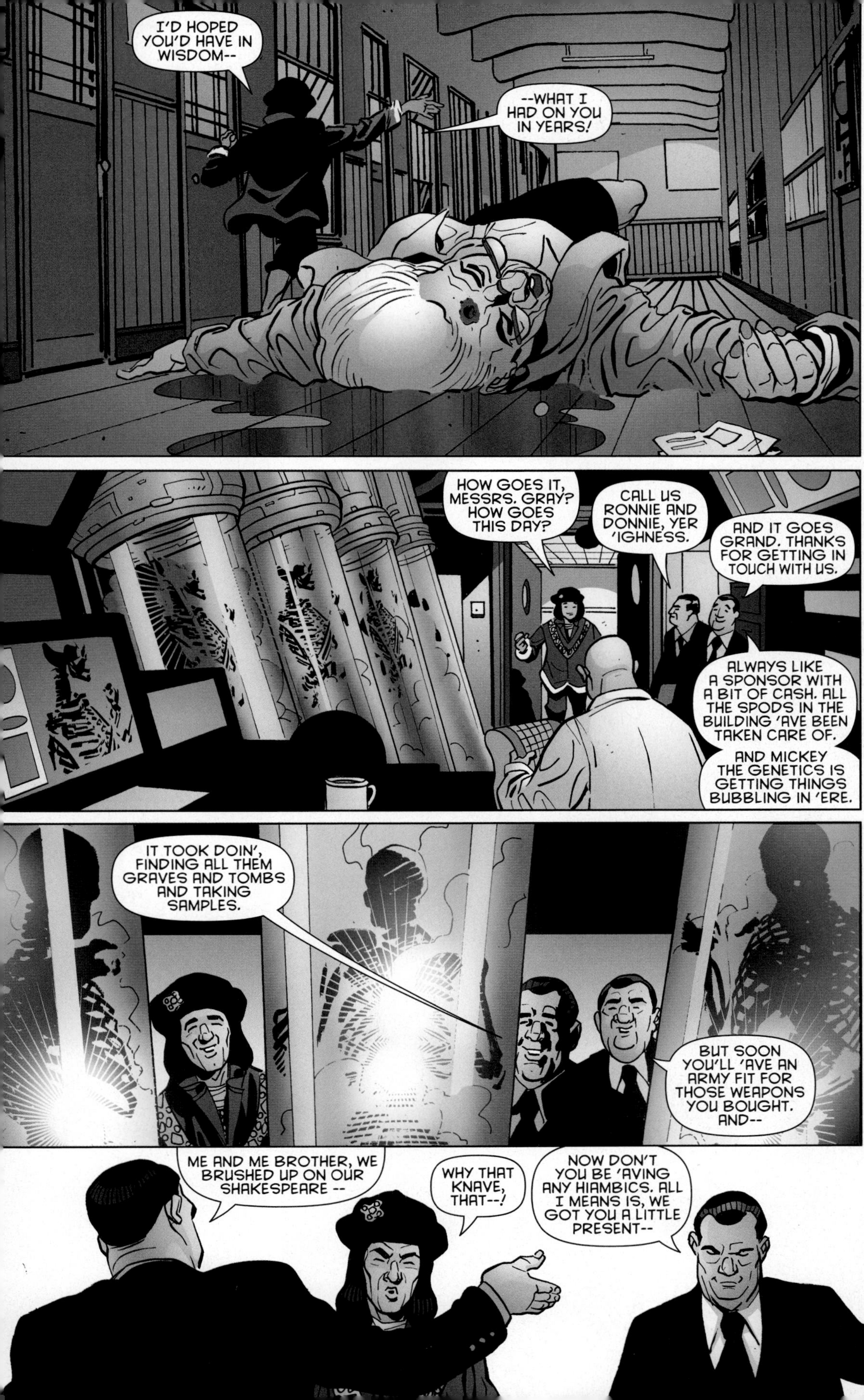
I'D HOPED YOU'D HAVE IN WISDOM--
--WHAT I HAD ON YOU IN YEARS!
HOW GOES IT, MESSRS. GRAY? HOW GOES THIS DAY?
CALL US RONNIE AND DONNIE, YER 'IGHNESS.
AND IT GOES GRAND. THANKS FOR GETTING IN TOUCH WITH US.
ALWAYS LIKE A SPONSOR WITH A BIT OF CASH. ALL THE SPODS IN THE BUILDING 'AVE BEEN TAKEN CARE OF.
AND MICKEY THE GENETICS IS GETTING THINGS BUBBLING IN 'ERE.
IT TOOK DOIN', FINDING ALL THEM GRAVES AND TOMBS AND TAKING SAMPLES.
BUT SOON YOU'LL 'AVE AN ARMY FIT FOR THOSE WEAPONS YOU BOUGHT. AND--
ME AND ME BROTHER, WE BRUSHED UP ON OUR SHAKESPEARE --
WHY THAT KNAVE, THAT--!
NOW DON'T YOU BE 'AVING ANY HIAMBICS. ALL I MEANS IS, WE GOT YOU A LITTLE PRESENT--

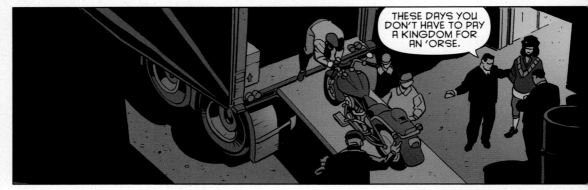

THESE DAYS YOU DON'T HAVE TO PAY A KINGDOM FOR AN 'ORSE.

WHY, THIS COMPLETES MY ARSENAL'S DELIGHT.

PING PING PING PING

'ERE THEY COME!

'ERE'S MY ARMY!

PING PING PING PING

SCHLOMP SCHLOMP SCHLO SCHL SC

OUR COUP BEGINS TONIGHT!

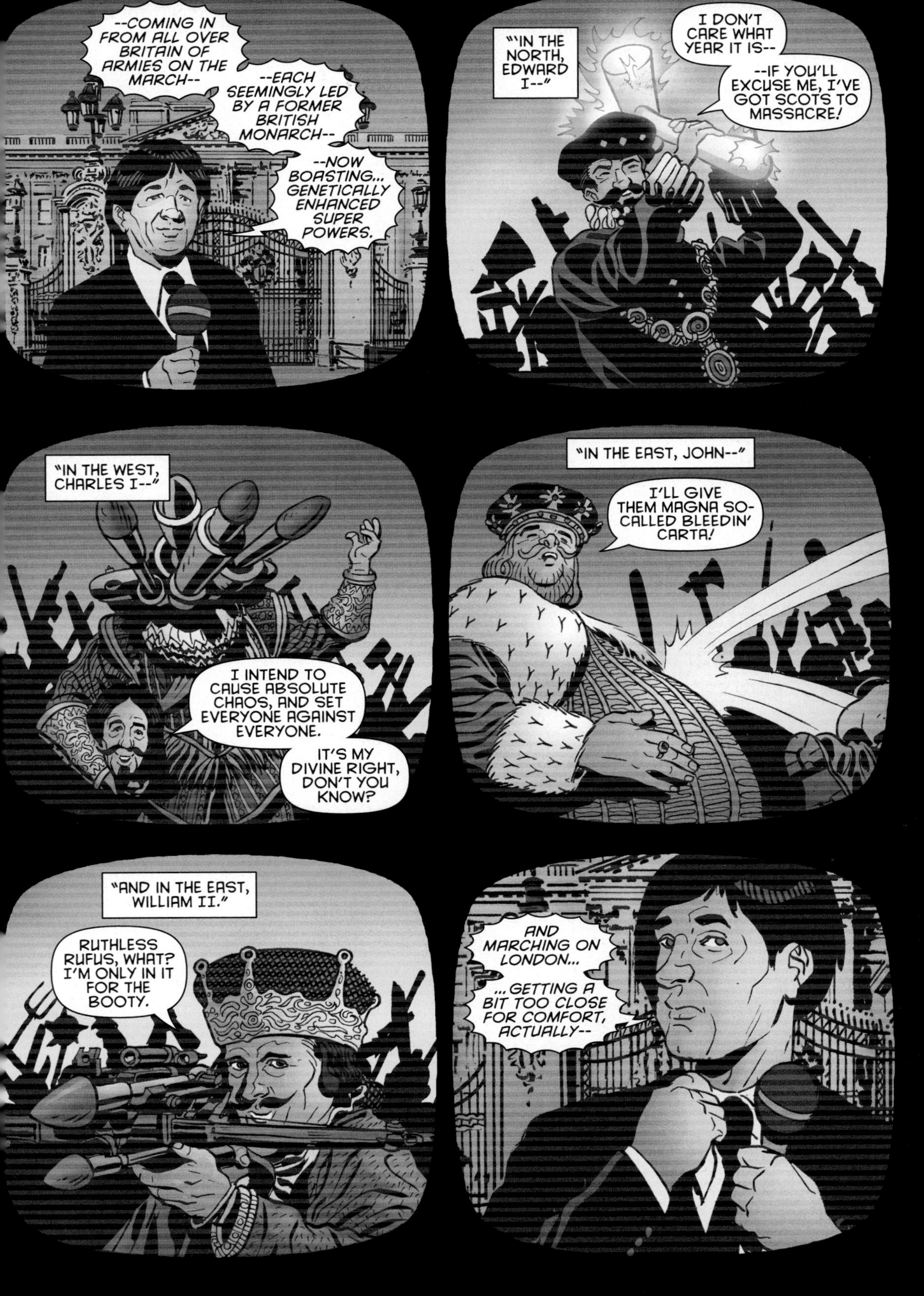
--COMING IN FROM ALL OVER BRITAIN OF ARMIES ON THE MARCH--
--EACH SEEMINGLY LED BY A FORMER BRITISH MONARCH--
--NOW BOASTING... GENETICALLY ENHANCED SUPER POWERS.
"'IN THE NORTH, EDWARD I--"
I DON'T CARE WHAT YEAR IT IS--
--IF YOU'LL EXCUSE ME, I'VE GOT SCOTS TO MASSACRE!
"IN THE WEST, CHARLES I--"
I INTEND TO CAUSE ABSOLUTE CHAOS, AND SET EVERYONE AGAINST EVERYONE.
IT'S MY DIVINE RIGHT, DON'T YOU KNOW?
"IN THE EAST, JOHN--"
I'LL GIVE THEM MAGNA SO-CALLED BLEEDIN' CARTA!
"AND IN THE EAST, WILLIAM II."
RUTHLESS RUFUS, WHAT? I'M ONLY IN IT FOR THE BOOTY.
AND MARCHING ON LONDON...
...GETTING A BIT TOO CLOSE FOR COMFORT, ACTUALLY--

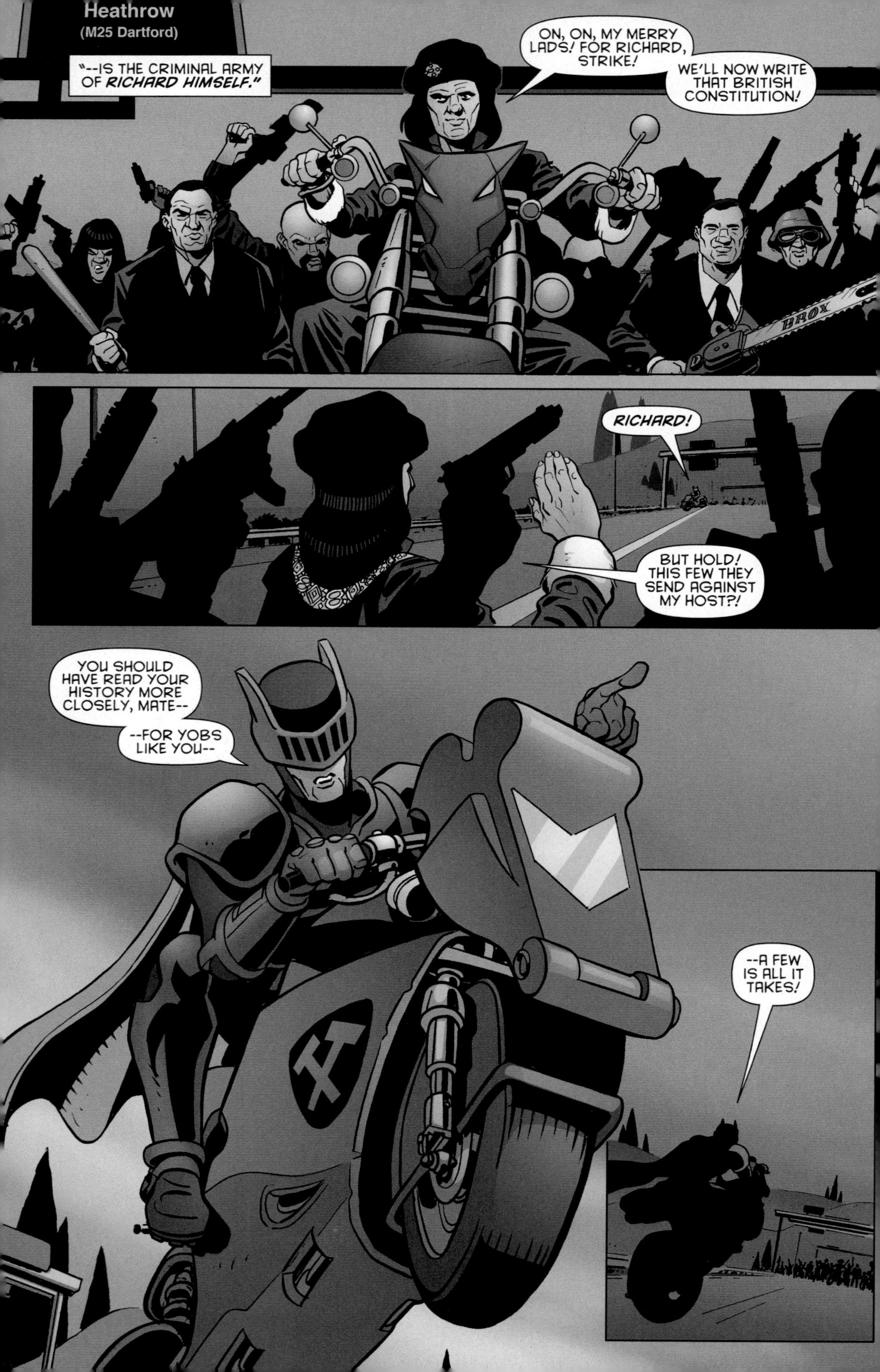

Heathrow
(M25 Dartford)
"--IS THE CRIMINAL ARMY OF RICHARD HIMSELF."
ON, ON, MY MERRY LADS! FOR RICHARD, STRIKE!
WE'LL NOW WRITE THAT BRITISH CONSTITUTION!
BROX
RICHARD!
BUT HOLD! THIS FEW THEY SEND AGAINST MY HOST?!
YOU SHOULD HAVE READ YOUR HISTORY MORE CLOSELY, MATE--
--FOR YOBS LIKE YOU--
--A FEW IS ALL IT TAKES!

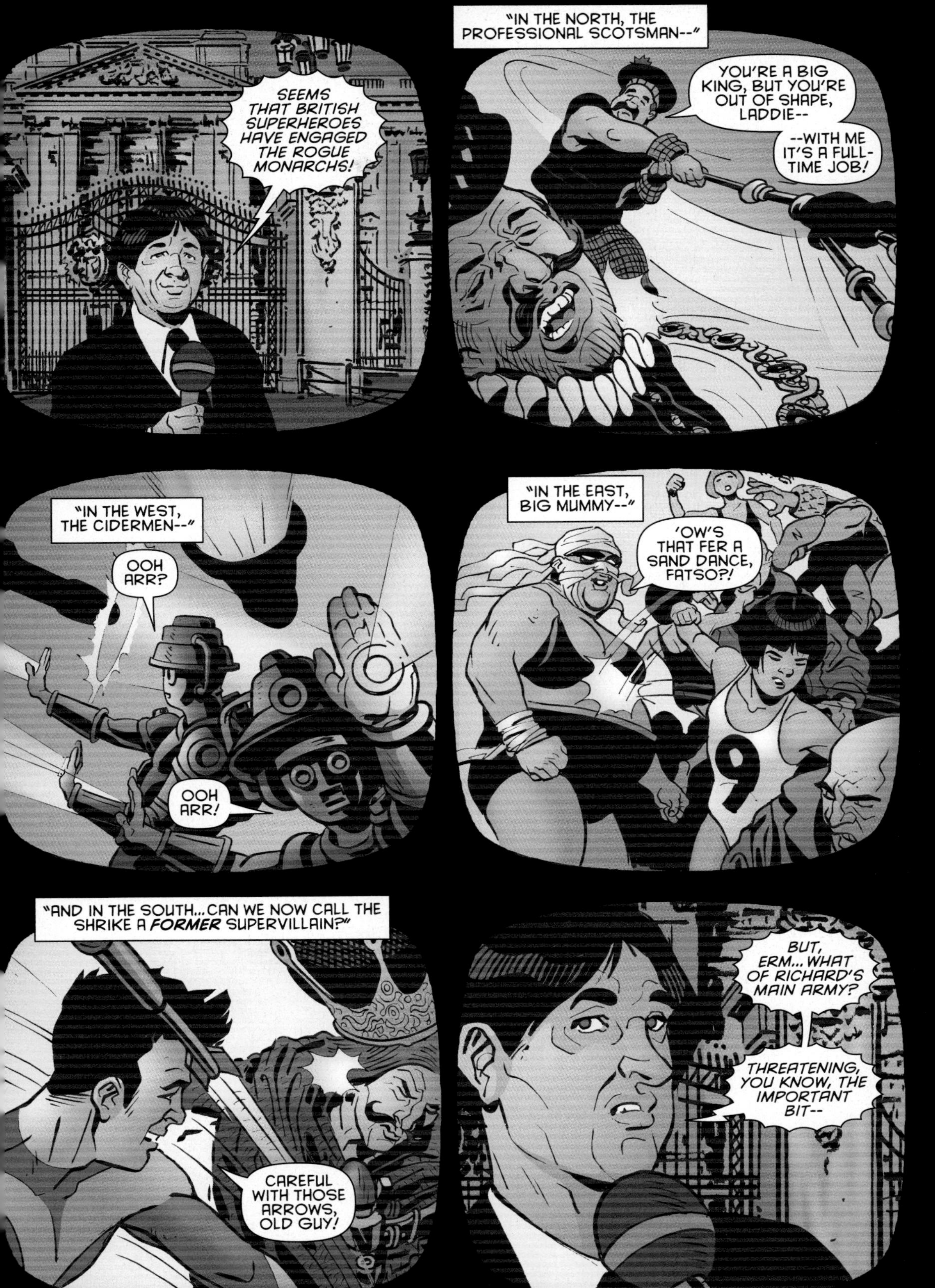

SEEMS THAT BRITISH SUPERHEROES HAVE ENGAGED THE ROGUE MONARCHS!
"IN THE NORTH, THE PROFESSIONAL SCOTSMAN--"
YOU'RE A BIG KING, BUT YOU'RE OUT OF SHAPE, LADDIE--
--WITH ME IT'S A FULL-TIME JOB!
"IN THE WEST, THE CIDERMEN--"
OOH ARR?
OOH ARR!
"IN THE EAST, BIG MUMMY--"
'OW'S THAT FER A SAND DANCE, FATSO?!
"AND IN THE SOUTH... CAN WE NOW CALL THE SHRIKE A *FORMER* SUPERVILLAIN?"
CAREFUL WITH THOSE ARROWS, OLD GUY!
BUT, ERM... WHAT OF RICHARD'S MAIN ARMY?
THREATENING, YOU KNOW, THE IMPORTANT BIT--

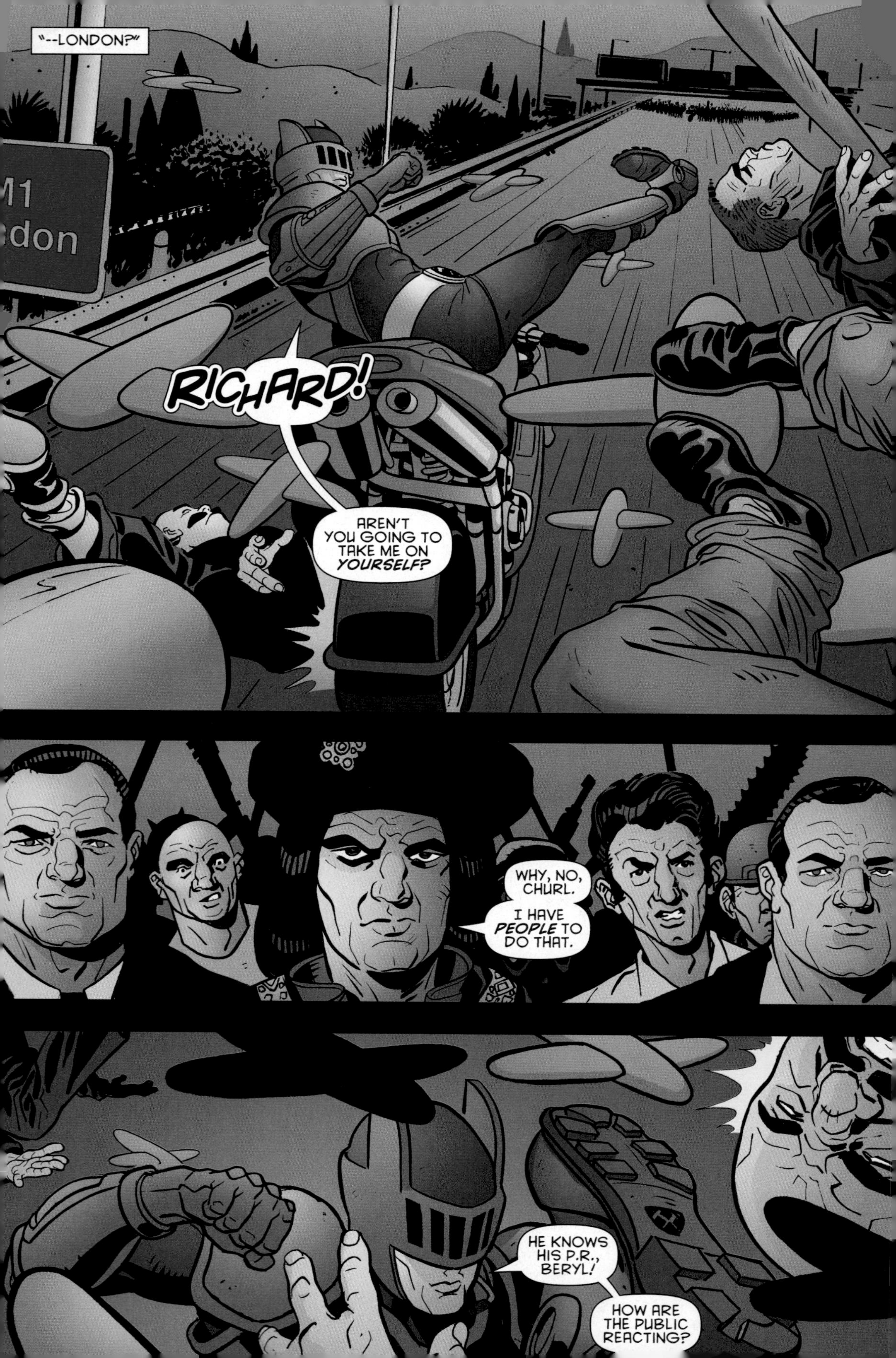
"--LONDON?"
RICHARD!
AREN'T YOU GOING TO TAKE ME ON *YOURSELF?*
WHY, NO, CHURL.
I HAVE *PEOPLE* TO DO THAT.
HE KNOWS HIS P.R., BERYL!
HOW ARE THE PUBLIC REACTING?

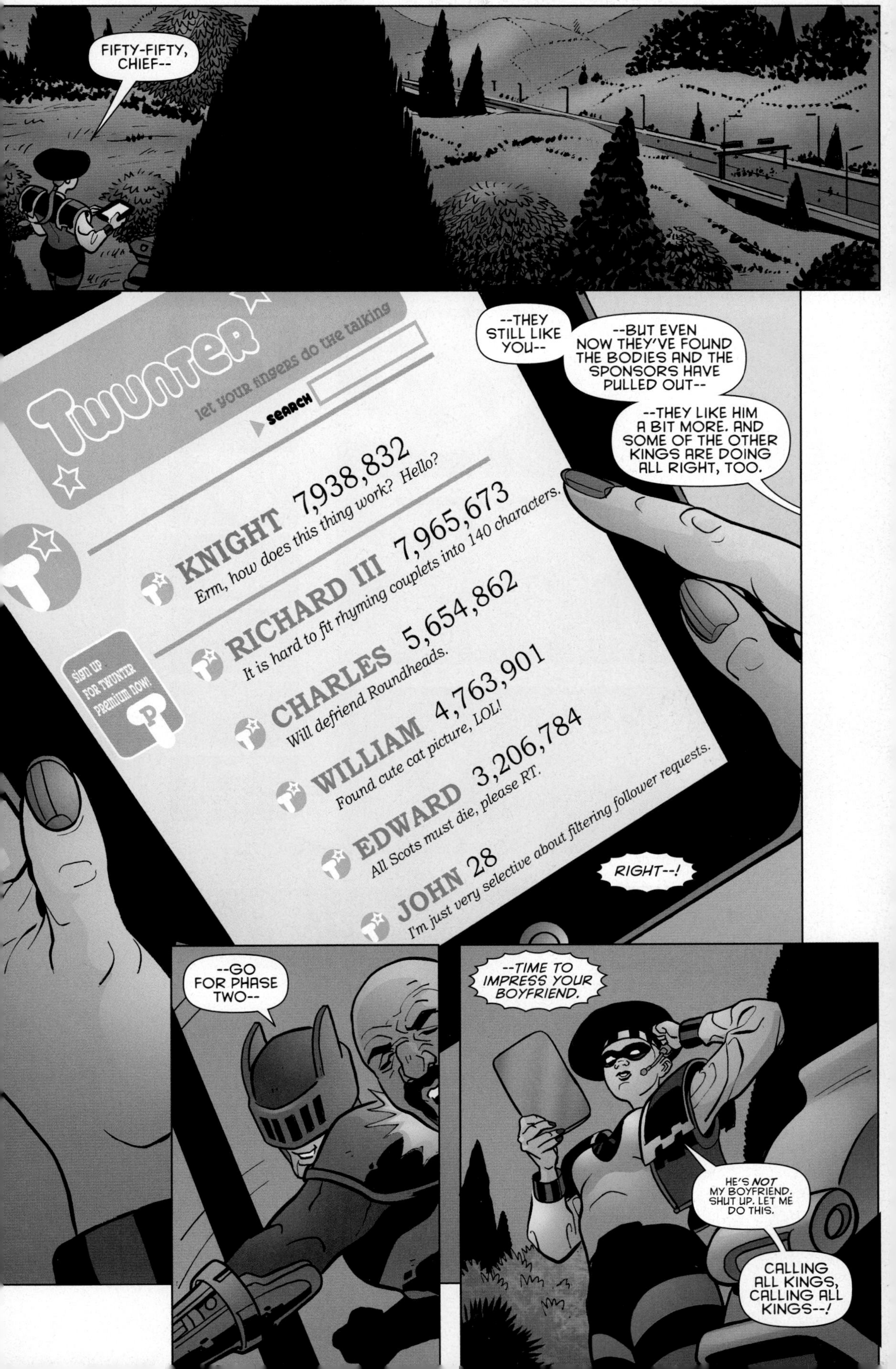

FIFTY-FIFTY, CHIEF--
TWUNTER
let your fingers do the talking
SEARCH
KNIGHT 7,938,832
Erm, how does this thing work? Hello?
RICHARD III 7,965,673
It is hard to fit rhyming couplets into 140 characters.
CHARLES 5,654,862
Will defriend Roundheads.
WILLIAM 4,763,901
Found cute cat picture, LOL!
EDWARD 3,206,784
All Scots must die, please RT.
JOHN 28
I'm just very selective about filtering follower requests.
SIGN UP FOR TWUNTER PREMIUM NOW!
--THEY STILL LIKE YOU--
--BUT EVEN NOW THEY'VE FOUND THE BODIES AND THE SPONSORS HAVE PULLED OUT--
--THEY LIKE HIM A BIT MORE. AND SOME OF THE OTHER KINGS ARE DOING ALL RIGHT, TOO.
RIGHT--!
--GO FOR PHASE TWO--
--TIME TO IMPRESS YOUR BOYFRIEND.
HE'S *NOT* MY BOYFRIEND. SHUT UP. LET ME DO THIS.
CALLING ALL KINGS, CALLING ALL KINGS--!

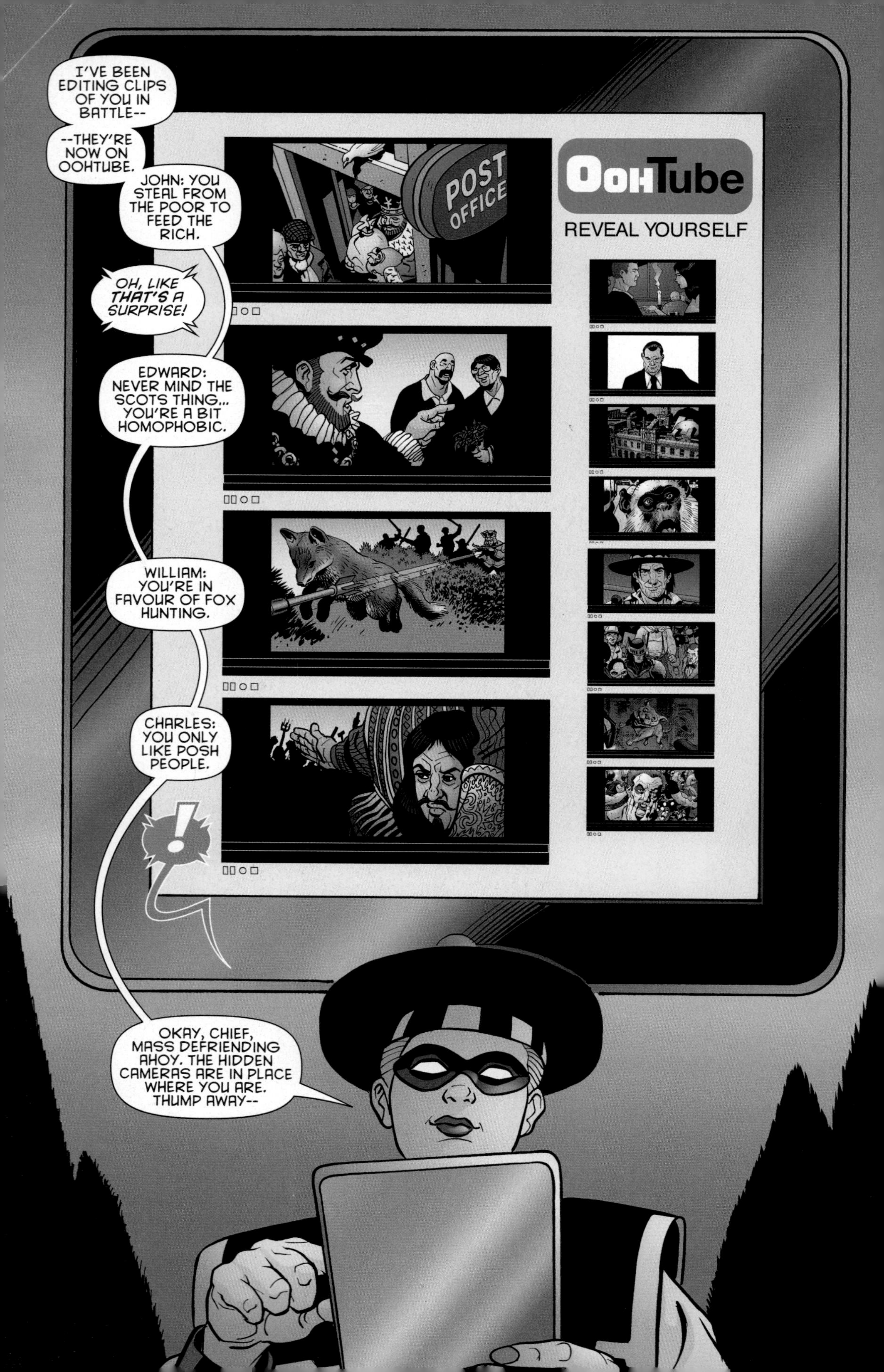
I'VE BEEN EDITING CLIPS OF YOU IN BATTLE--
--THEY'RE NOW ON OOHTUBE.
OohTube
REVEAL YOURSELF
POST OFFICE
JOHN: YOU STEAL FROM THE POOR TO FEED THE RICH.
OH, LIKE *THAT'S* A SURPRISE!
EDWARD: NEVER MIND THE SCOTS THING... YOU'RE A BIT HOMOPHOBIC.
WILLIAM: YOU'RE IN FAVOUR OF FOX HUNTING.
CHARLES: YOU ONLY LIKE POSH PEOPLE.
!
OKAY, CHIEF, MASS DEFRIENDING AHOY. THE HIDDEN CAMERAS ARE IN PLACE WHERE YOU ARE. THUMP AWAY--

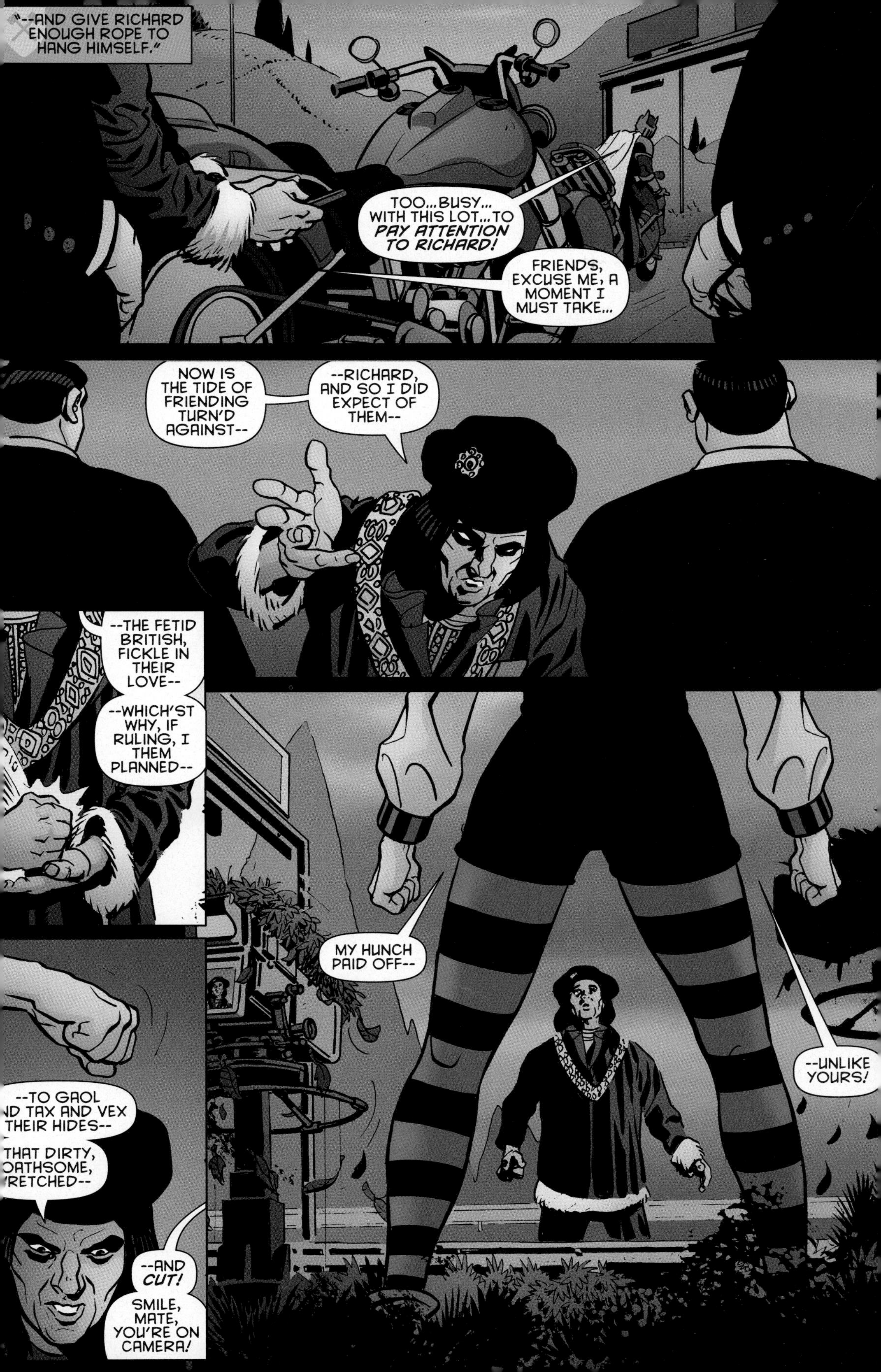
"--AND GIVE RICHARD ENOUGH ROPE TO HANG HIMSELF."
TOO...BUSY... WITH THIS LOT...TO PAY ATTENTION TO RICHARD!
FRIENDS, EXCUSE ME, A MOMENT I MUST TAKE...
NOW IS THE TIDE OF FRIENDING TURN'D AGAINST--
--RICHARD, AND SO I DID EXPECT OF THEM--
--THE FETID BRITISH, FICKLE IN THEIR LOVE--
--WHICH'ST WHY, IF RULING, I THEM PLANNED--
--TO GAOL
THEIR HIDES--
THAT DIRTY,
--AND CUT! SMILE, MATE, YOU'RE ON CAMERA!
MY HUNCH PAID OFF--
--UNLIKE YOURS!

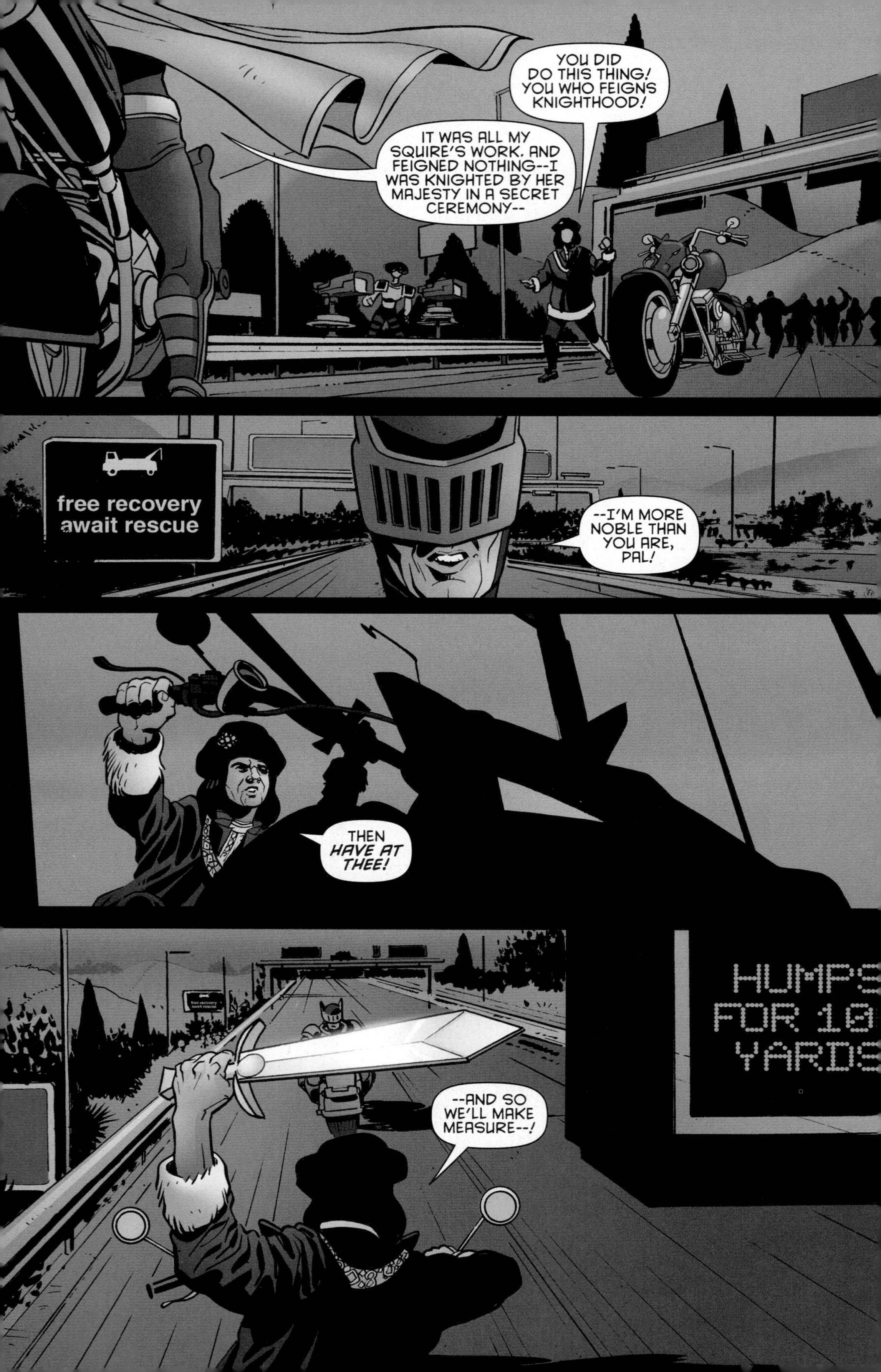
YOU DID DO THIS THING! YOU WHO FEIGNS KNIGHTHOOD!
IT WAS ALL MY SQUIRE'S WORK. AND FEIGNED NOTHING--I WAS KNIGHTED BY HER MAJESTY IN A SECRET CEREMONY--
free recovery
await rescue
--I'M MORE NOBLE THAN YOU ARE, PAL!
THEN *HAVE AT THEE!*
HUMPS
FOR 10
YARDS
--AND SO WE'LL MAKE MEASURE--!

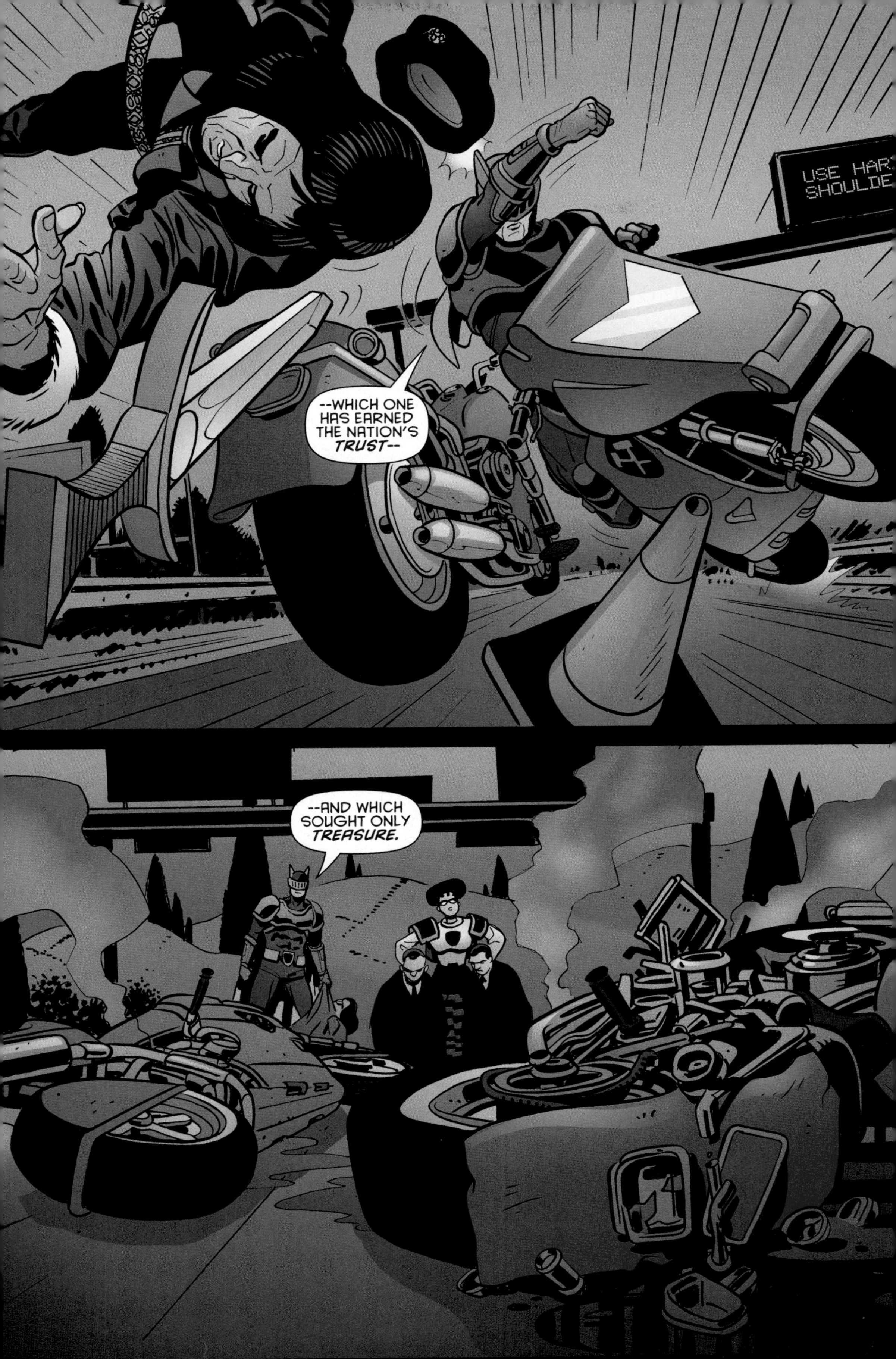
--WHICH ONE HAS EARNED THE NATION'S *TRUST*--
--AND WHICH SOUGHT ONLY *TREASURE.*

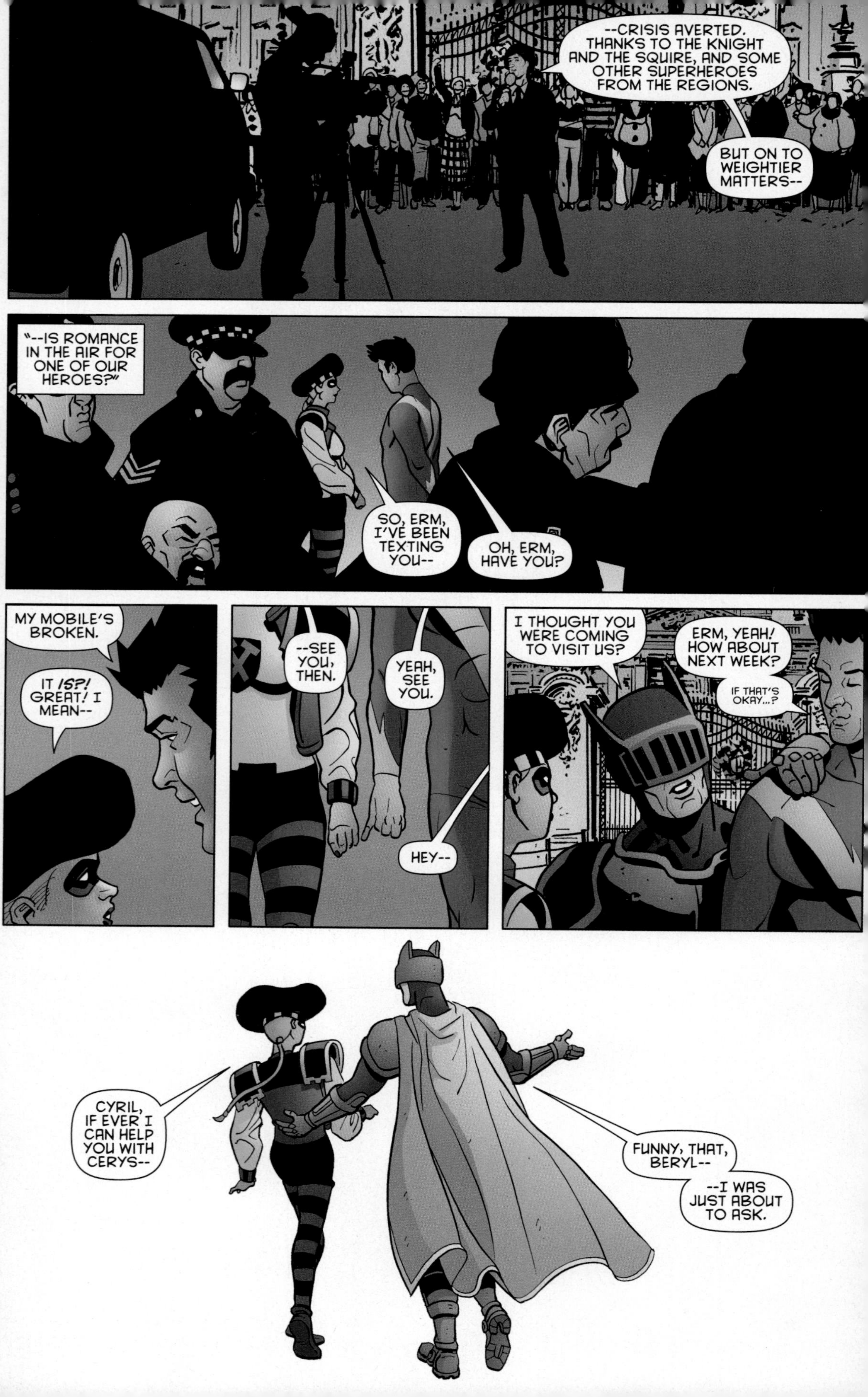
--CRISIS AVERTED. THANKS TO THE KNIGHT AND THE SQUIRE, AND SOME OTHER SUPERHEROES FROM THE REGIONS.
BUT ON TO WEIGHTIER MATTERS--
"--IS ROMANCE IN THE AIR FOR ONE OF OUR HEROES?"
SO, ERM, I'VE BEEN TEXTING YOU--
OH, ERM, HAVE YOU?
MY MOBILE'S BROKEN.
IT *IS?!* GREAT! I MEAN--
--SEE YOU, THEN.
YEAH, SEE YOU.
HEY--
I THOUGHT YOU WERE COMING TO VISIT US?
ERM, YEAH! HOW ABOUT NEXT WEEK?
IF THAT'S OKAY...?
CYRIL, IF EVER I CAN HELP YOU WITH CERYS--
FUNNY, THAT, BERYL--
--I WAS JUST ABOUT TO ASK.

Cabbages and Kings

THERE ARE SEVERAL REAL-LIFE GROUPS DEDICATED TO COUNTERING WILLIAM SHAKESPEARE'S SLANDEROUS CLAIMS ABOUT KING RICHARD III, WHOM HE MADE A VILLAIN, SUCH FOLK SAY, IN ORDER TO PLEASE HIS PATRONS. THE REAL RICHARD, THEY ADD, WAS, AS MONARCHS GO, OKAY. AS PER SHAKESPEARE, RICHARD'S DIALOGUE IS IN IAMBIC PENTAMETER (AND YES, THE WHOLE IDEA IS THAT YOU BREAK THE METER FOR DRAMATIC EFFECT, AHEM), AND HE ENDS HIS SCENES IN RHYMING COUPLETS. SHAKESPEARE PROBABLY GAVE HIM HIS HUNCHBACK.

CERYS TWEED'S NAME REFLECTS NOT ONLY A FEW DIFFERENT POP STARS, BUT ALSO HARRIS TWEED, DETECTIVE HERO OF *THE EAGLE,* THE BEST COMIC EVER MADE. JUST 'COS. "COR!" IS AN ANCIENT BRITISH CHILDREN'S COMIC CRY OF JOY. "HE WOULD SAY THAT, WOULDN'T HE?" IS A SLY QUOTE FROM THE PROFUMO AFFAIR, A SCANDAL THAT ROCKED BRITISH POLITICS INTO THE ERA OF ROCK AND ROLL. BRITAIN'S "UNWRITTEN CONSTITUTION" ALLOWS THE BRITISH BODY POLITIC TO DO WHAT IT LIKES, BASICALLY, AS LONG AS IT'S EITHER BEEN DONE BEFORE, OR NOBODY IMPORTANT WILL KICK UP TOO MUCH OF A FUSS. THE GRAY TWINS ARE SATIRICAL VERSIONS OF THE FAMOUS LONDON GANGSTERS, WHO ALSO LIKED TO THINK THEY HOBNOBBED WITH THE GENTRY. "BRUSH UP YOUR SHAKESPEARE" IS A COLE PORTER SONG. OF THE VARIOUS KINGS I'VE SLANDERED, I THINK JOHN IS THE ONE WHO PROBABLY WASN'T AS BAD AS I'VE PAINTED HIM. KNOWING MONARCHS BY JUST A COUPLE OF SALIENT LIBELS IS SOMETHING THE BRITISH PUBLIC DO. THE PROFESSIONAL SCOTSMAN SEEMS TO HAVE WATCHED *GET CARTER* (1971). THE CIDERMEN ARE ACTUALLY QUOTING LINES GIVEN TO PIGBIN JOSH, A COUNTRY FELLOW IN JON PERTWEE ERA *DOCTOR WHO.* BIG DADDY WAS A PROFESSIONAL WRESTLER, ENORMOUS IN THE 1970s.

I LIKE TO THINK OF THIS WHOLE ISSUE AS SOMETHING 1970s BBC COMEDIAN TRIO *THE GOODIES* WOULD HAVE PERFORMED. IF YOU COULD SING THEIR THEME TUNE TO YOURSELF AT THE START AND FINISH, THAT WOULD PLEASE ME A GREAT DEAL. CHEERIO!

Be it nimble capers
or sported tricks
Red Gull doth energise
in but a few sips.
RED GULL
It already has wings!

UNTIL NEXT ISSUE, CHEERIO!
- PAUL CORNELL

brought to you by KNIGHT AND SQUIRE

ad by Jimmy Broxton design by SWANDS

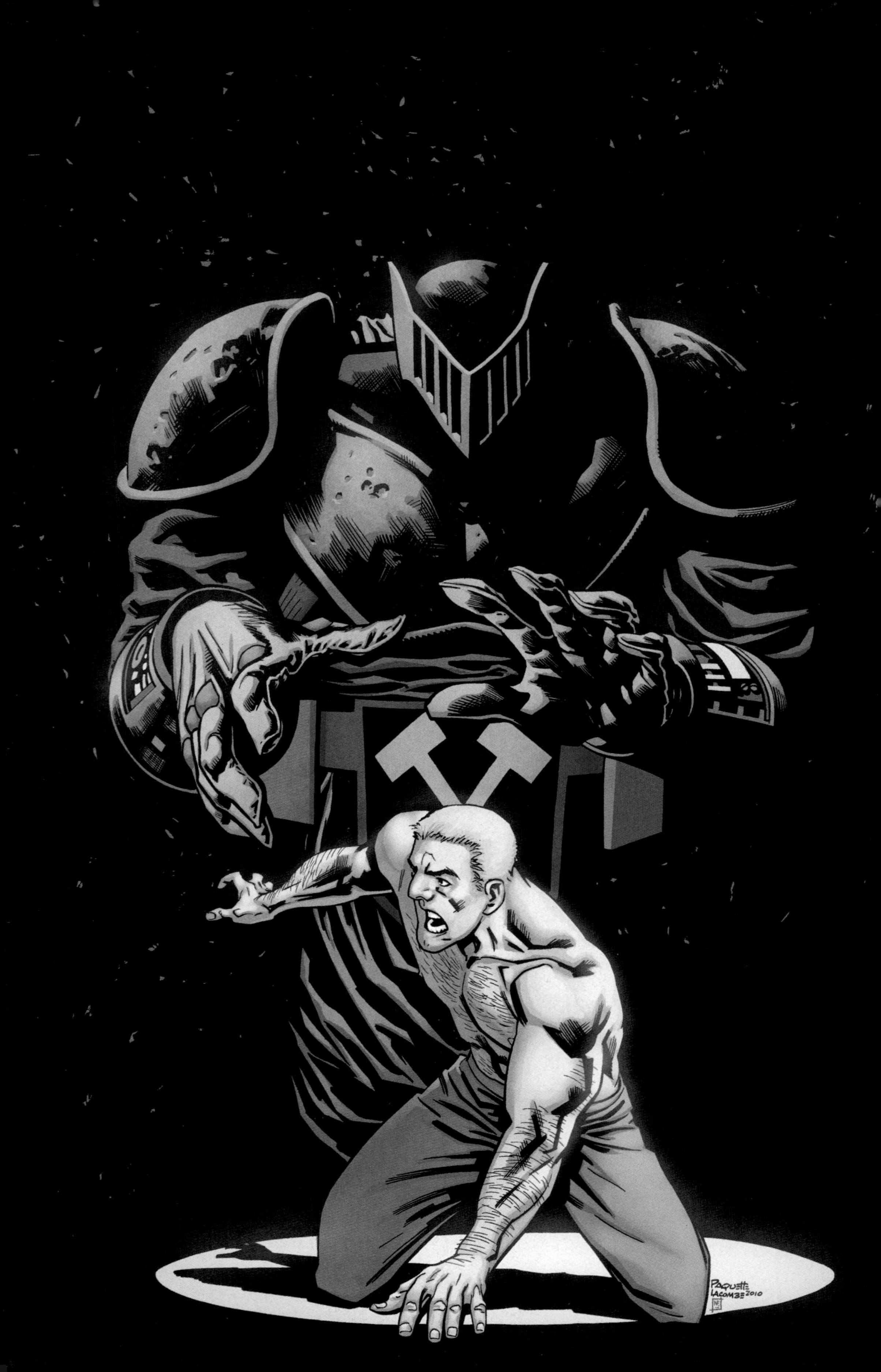
PAQUETTE
LACOMBE 2010

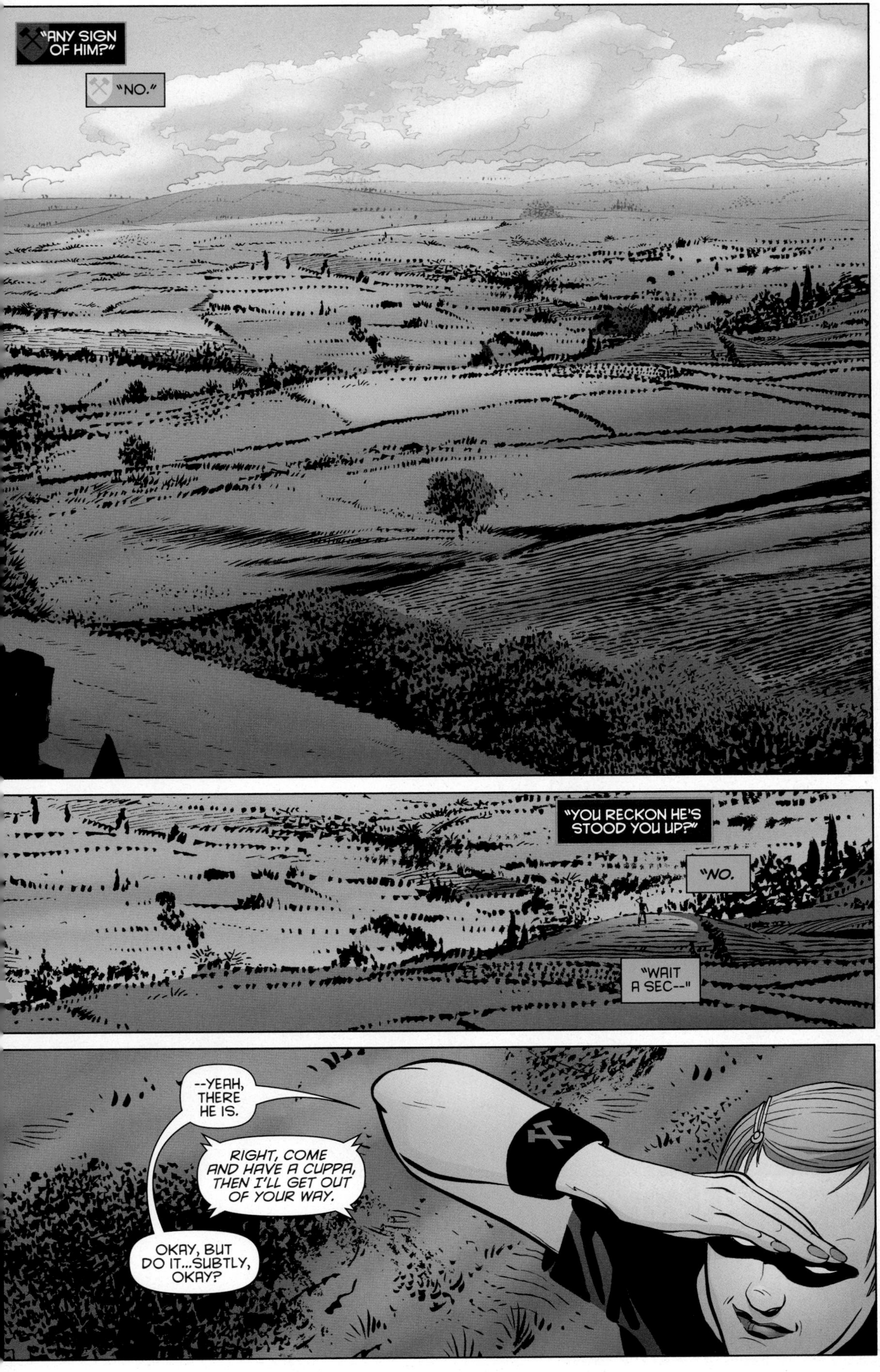
"ANY SIGN OF HIM?"
"NO."
"YOU RECKON HE'S STOOD YOU UP?"
"NO.
"WAIT A SEC--"
--YEAH, THERE HE IS.
RIGHT, COME AND HAVE A CUPPA, THEN I'LL GET OUT OF YOUR WAY.
OKAY, BUT DO IT...SUBTLY, OKAY?

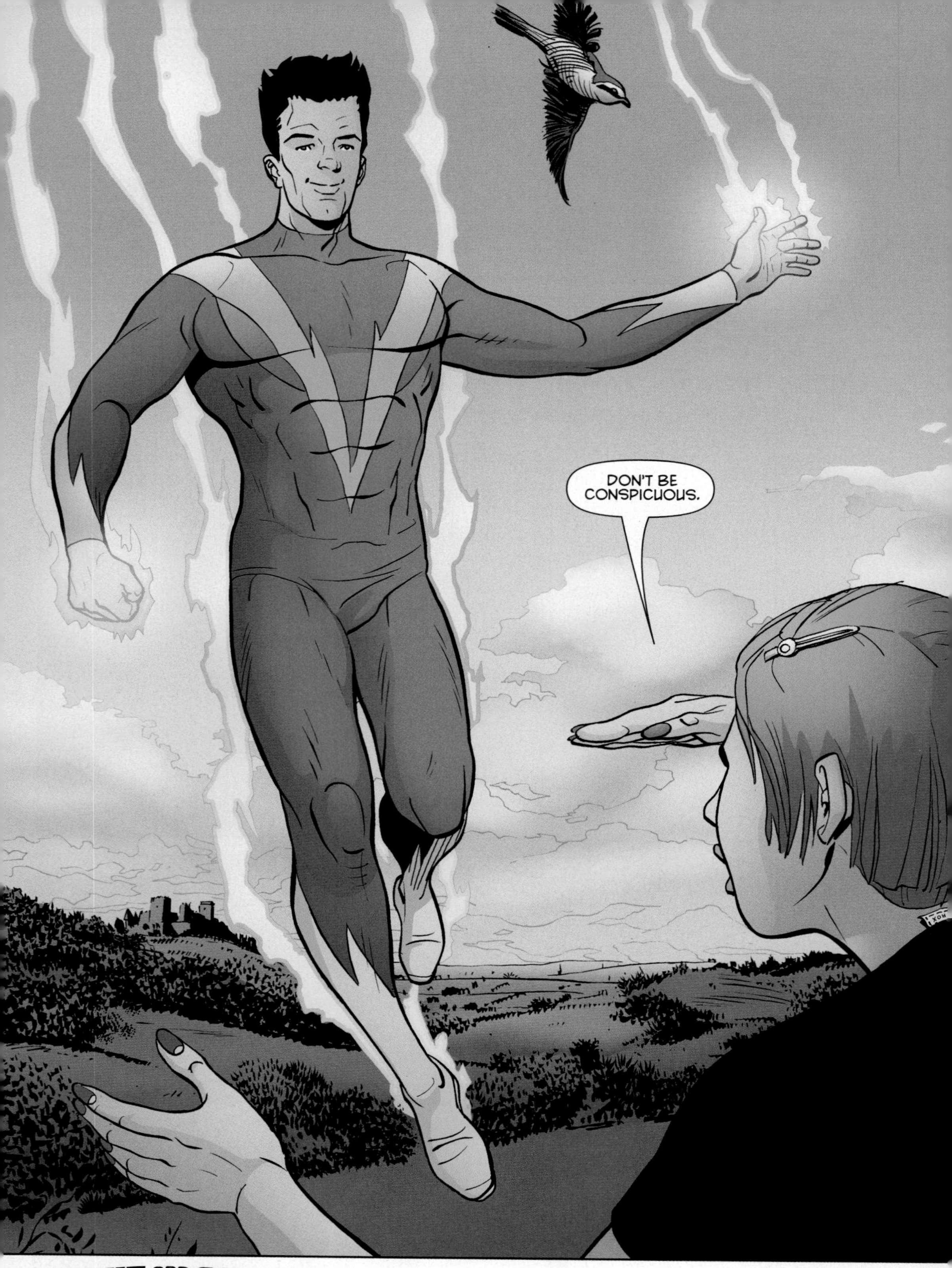
DON'T BE CONSPICUOUS.

KNIGHT AND SQUIRE IN 'FOR SIX' PART FOUR

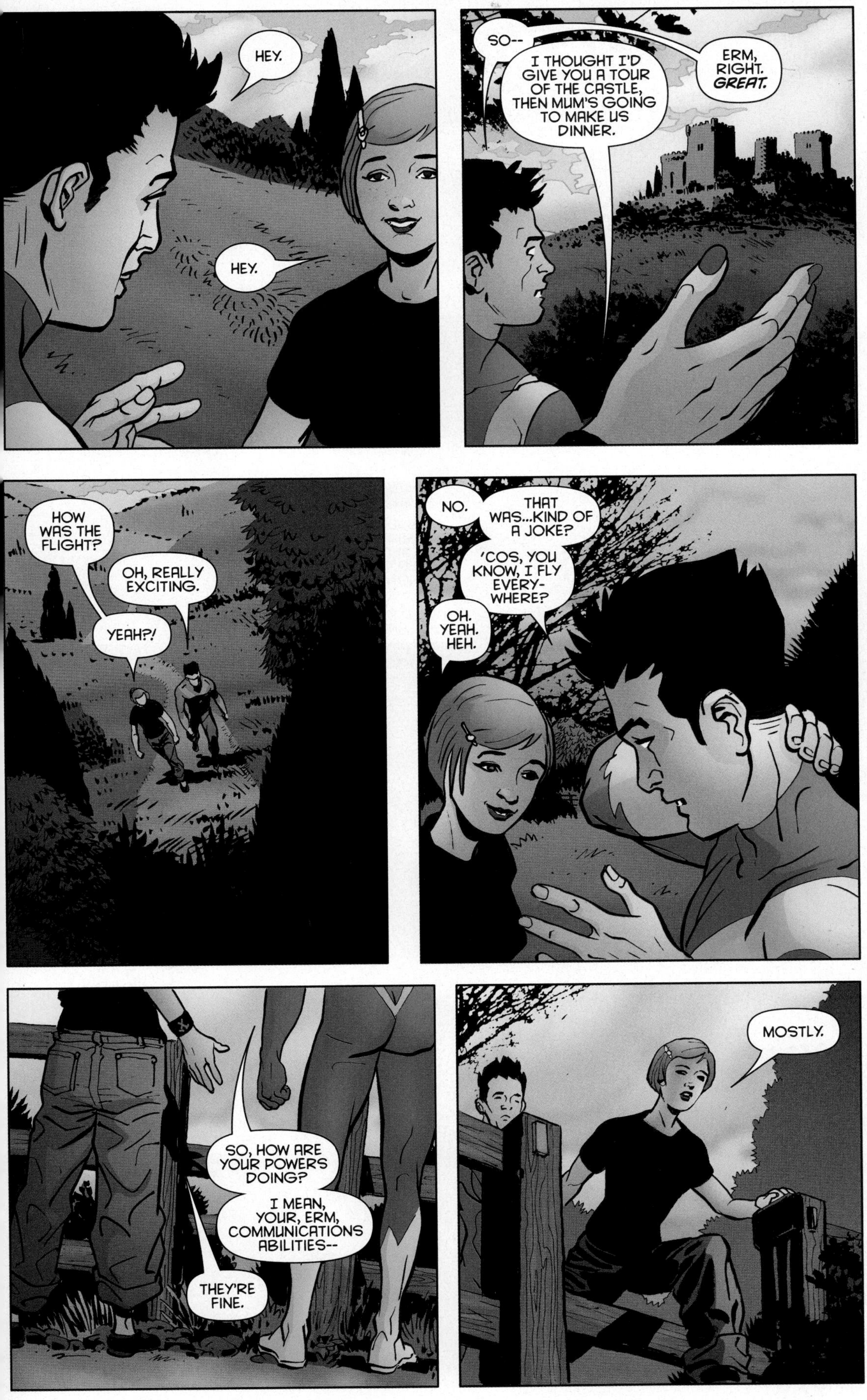
HEY.
HEY.
SO--
I THOUGHT I'D GIVE YOU A TOUR OF THE CASTLE, THEN MUM'S GOING TO MAKE US DINNER.
ERM, RIGHT. *GREAT.*
HOW WAS THE FLIGHT?
OH, REALLY EXCITING.
YEAH?!
NO.
THAT WAS...KIND OF A JOKE?
'COS, YOU KNOW, I FLY EVERY-WHERE?
OH. YEAH. HEH.
SO, HOW ARE YOUR POWERS DOING?
I MEAN, YOUR, ERM, COMMUNICATIONS ABILITIES--
THEY'RE FINE.
MOSTLY.

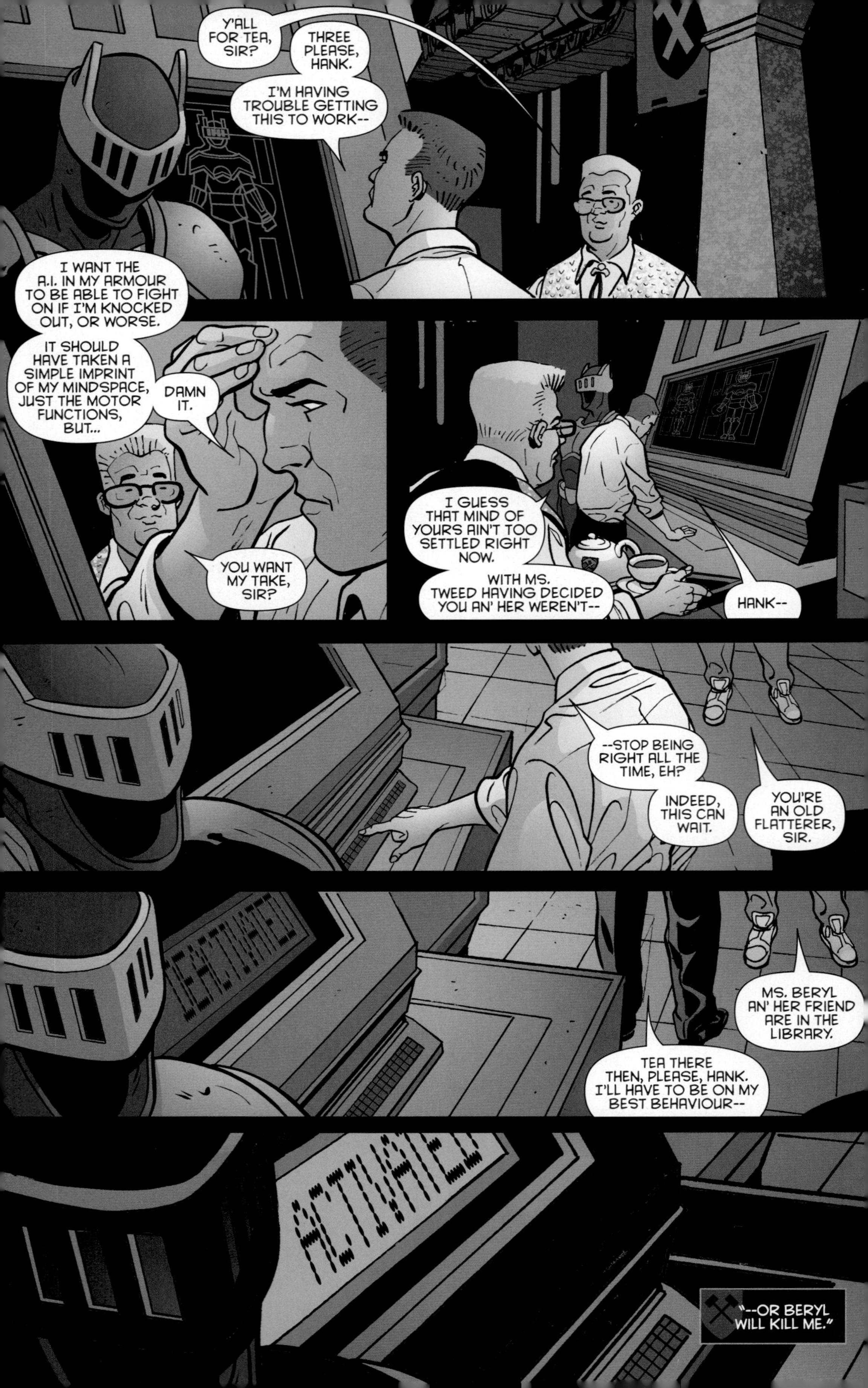
Y'ALL FOR TEA, SIR?
THREE PLEASE, HANK.
I'M HAVING TROUBLE GETTING THIS TO WORK--
I WANT THE A.I. IN MY ARMOUR TO BE ABLE TO FIGHT ON IF I'M KNOCKED OUT, OR WORSE.
IT SHOULD HAVE TAKEN A SIMPLE IMPRINT OF MY MINDSPACE, JUST THE MOTOR FUNCTIONS, BUT...
DAMN IT.
YOU WANT MY TAKE, SIR?
I GUESS THAT MIND OF YOURS AIN'T TOO SETTLED RIGHT NOW.
WITH MS. TWEED HAVING DECIDED YOU AN' HER WEREN'T--
HANK--
--STOP BEING RIGHT ALL THE TIME, EH?
INDEED, THIS CAN WAIT.
YOU'RE AN OLD FLATTERER, SIR.
MS. BERYL AN' HER FRIEND ARE IN THE LIBRARY.
TEA THERE THEN, PLEASE, HANK. I'LL HAVE TO BE ON MY BEST BEHAVIOUR--
ACTIVATED
"--OR BERYL WILL KILL ME."

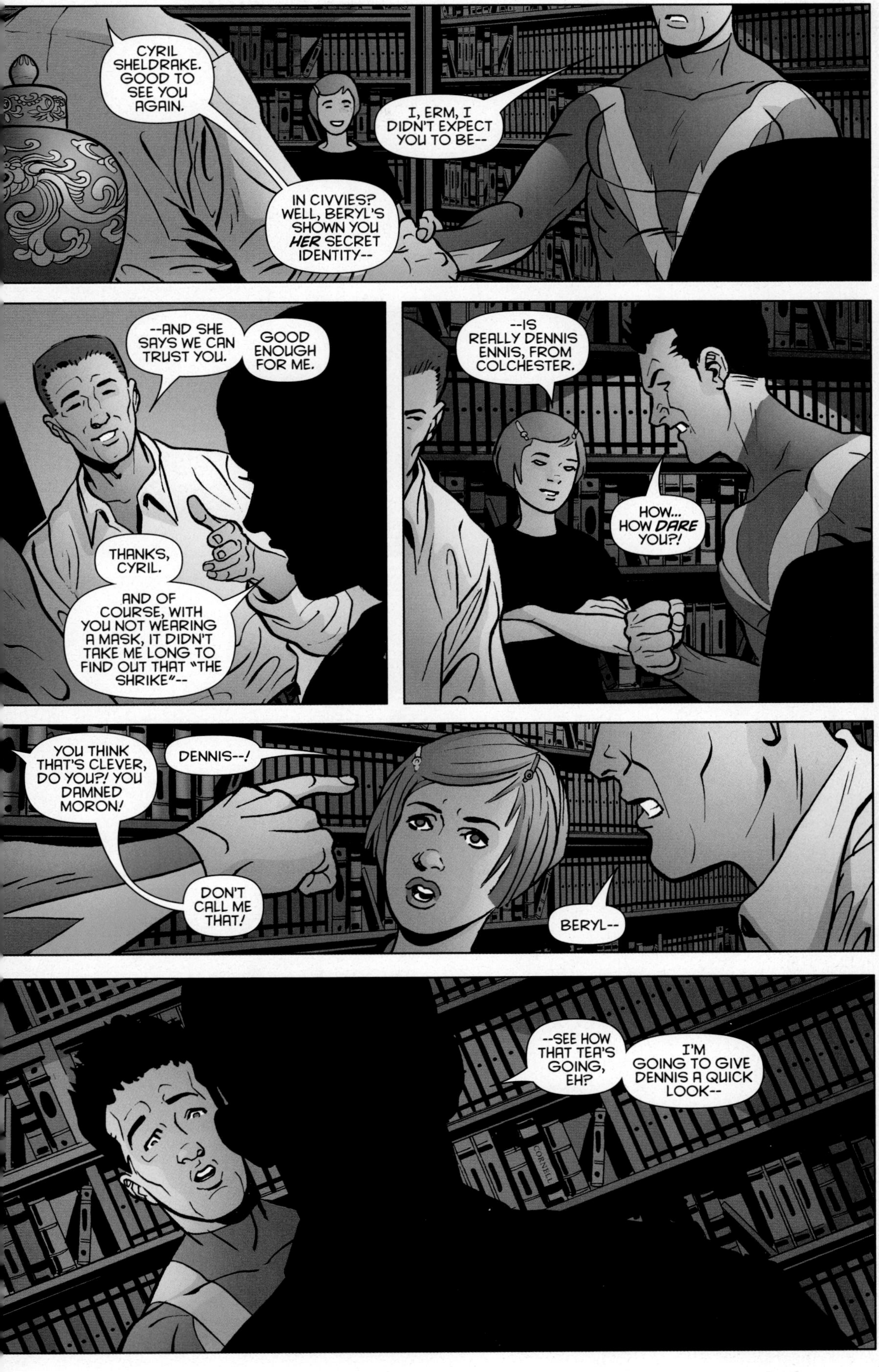
CYRIL SHELDRAKE. GOOD TO SEE YOU AGAIN.
I, ERM, I DIDN'T EXPECT YOU TO BE--
IN CIVVIES? WELL, BERYL'S SHOWN YOU *HER* SECRET IDENTITY--
--AND SHE SAYS WE CAN TRUST YOU.
GOOD ENOUGH FOR ME.
THANKS, CYRIL.
AND OF COURSE, WITH YOU NOT WEARING A MASK, IT DIDN'T TAKE ME LONG TO FIND OUT THAT "THE SHRIKE"--
--IS REALLY DENNIS ENNIS, FROM COLCHESTER.
HOW... HOW *DARE* YOU?!
YOU THINK THAT'S CLEVER, DO YOU?! YOU DAMNED MORON!
DENNIS--!
DON'T CALL ME THAT!
BERYL--
I'M GOING TO GIVE DENNIS A QUICK LOOK--
--SEE HOW THAT TEA'S GOING, EH?

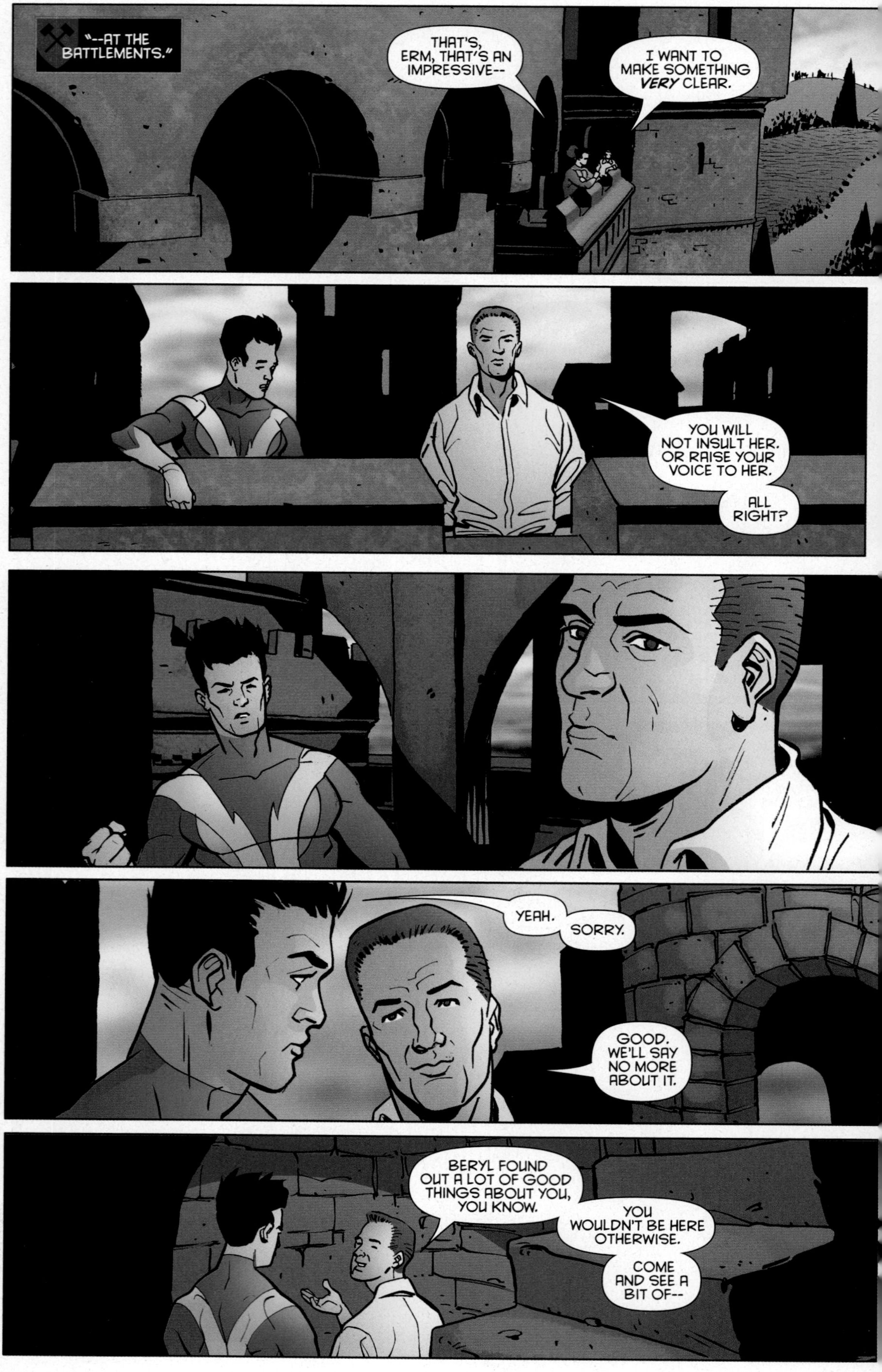
"--AT THE BATTLEMENTS."
THAT'S, ERM, THAT'S AN IMPRESSIVE--
I WANT TO MAKE SOMETHING *VERY* CLEAR.
YOU WILL NOT INSULT HER. OR RAISE YOUR VOICE TO HER.
ALL RIGHT?
YEAH.
SORRY.
GOOD. WE'LL SAY NO MORE ABOUT IT.
BERYL FOUND OUT A LOT OF GOOD THINGS ABOUT YOU, YOU KNOW.
YOU WOULDN'T BE HERE OTHERWISE.
COME AND SEE A BIT OF--

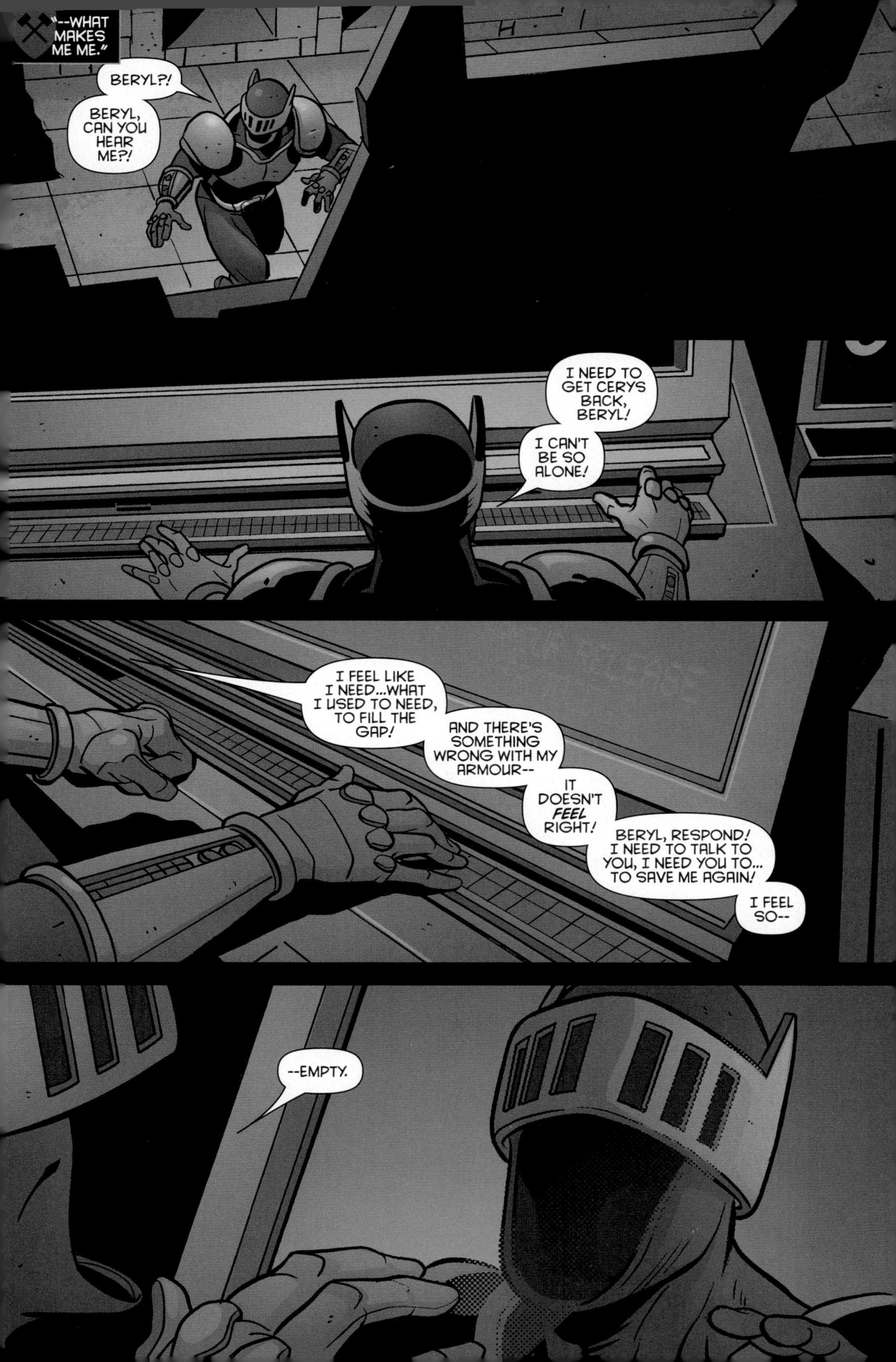
"--WHAT MAKES ME ME."
BERYL?!
BERYL, CAN YOU HEAR ME?!
I NEED TO GET CERYS BACK, BERYL!
I CAN'T BE SO ALONE!
I FEEL LIKE I NEED...WHAT I USED TO NEED, TO FILL THE GAP!
AND THERE'S SOMETHING WRONG WITH MY ARMOUR--
IT DOESN'T *FEEL* RIGHT!
BERYL, RESPOND! I NEED TO TALK TO YOU, I NEED YOU TO... TO SAVE ME AGAIN!
I FEEL SO--
--EMPTY.

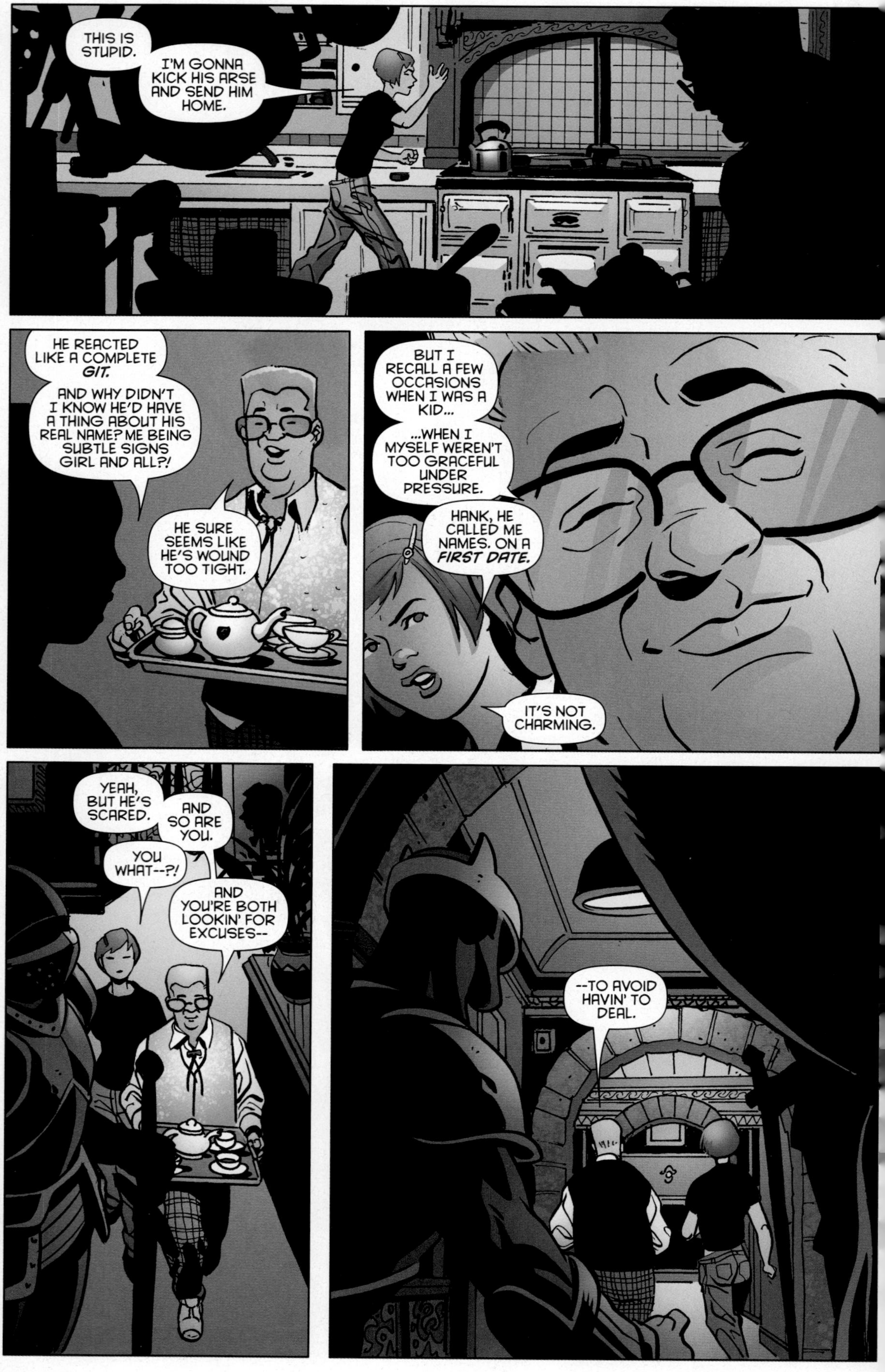
THIS IS STUPID.
I'M GONNA KICK HIS ARSE AND SEND HIM HOME.
HE REACTED LIKE A COMPLETE *GIT.*
AND WHY DIDN'T I KNOW HE'D HAVE A THING ABOUT HIS REAL NAME? ME BEING SUBTLE SIGNS GIRL AND ALL?!
HE SURE SEEMS LIKE HE'S WOUND TOO TIGHT.
BUT I RECALL A FEW OCCASIONS WHEN I WAS A KID...
...WHEN I MYSELF WEREN'T TOO GRACEFUL UNDER PRESSURE.
HANK, HE CALLED ME NAMES. ON A *FIRST DATE.*
IT'S NOT CHARMING.
YEAH, BUT HE'S SCARED.
AND SO ARE YOU.
YOU WHAT--?!
AND YOU'RE BOTH LOOKIN' FOR EXCUSES--
--TO AVOID HAVIN' TO DEAL.

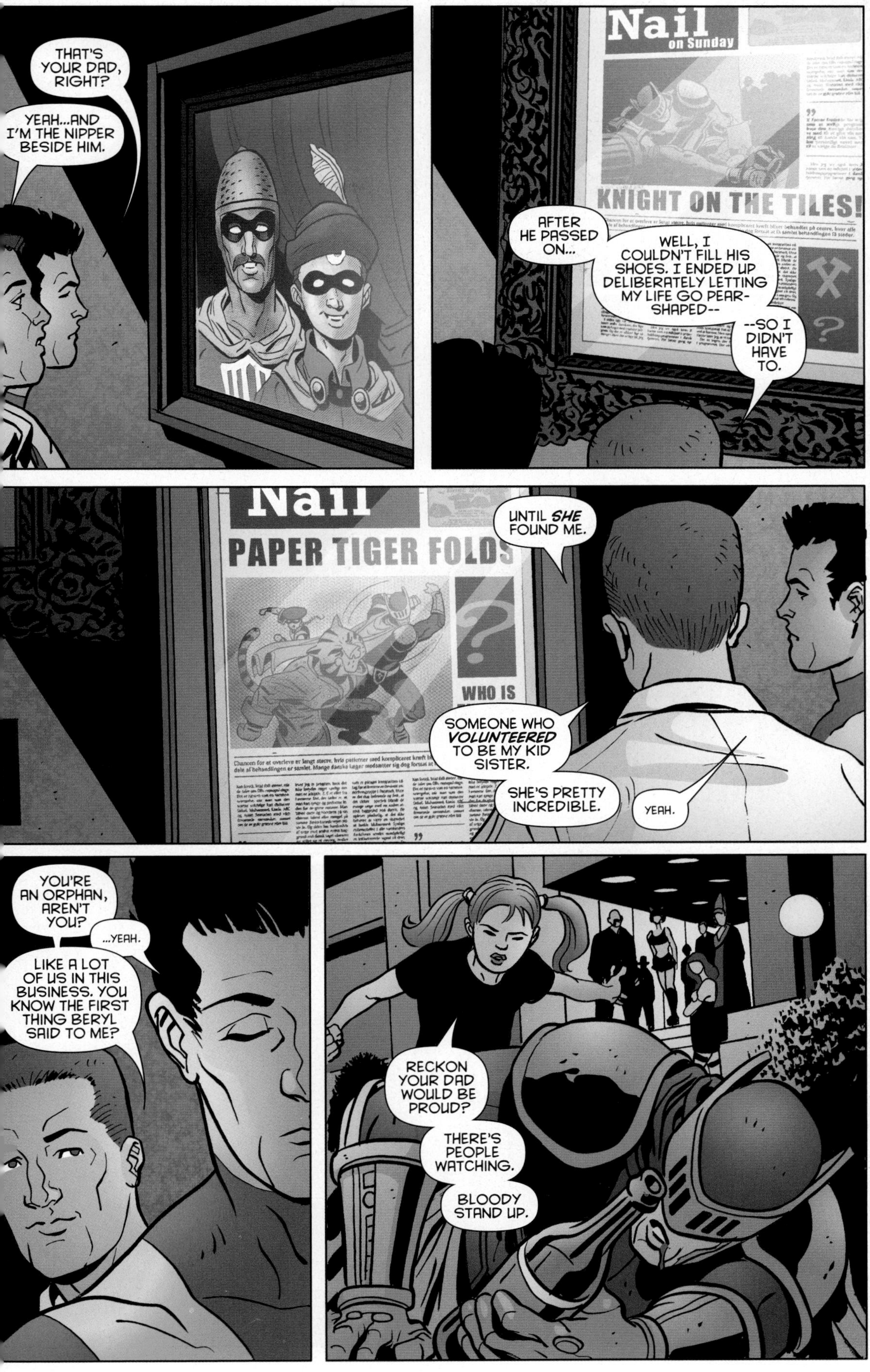
THAT'S YOUR DAD, RIGHT?
YEAH...AND I'M THE NIPPER BESIDE HIM.
Nail
on Sunday
KNIGHT ON THE TILES!
AFTER HE PASSED ON...
WELL, I COULDN'T FILL HIS SHOES. I ENDED UP DELIBERATELY LETTING MY LIFE GO PEAR-SHAPED--
--SO I DIDN'T HAVE TO.
Nail
PAPER TIGER FOLDS
WHO IS
UNTIL SHE FOUND ME.
SOMEONE WHO VOLUNTEERED TO BE MY KID SISTER.
SHE'S PRETTY INCREDIBLE.
YEAH.
YOU'RE AN ORPHAN, AREN'T YOU?
...YEAH.
LIKE A LOT OF US IN THIS BUSINESS. YOU KNOW THE FIRST THING BERYL SAID TO ME?
RECKON YOUR DAD WOULD BE PROUD?
THERE'S PEOPLE WATCHING.
BLOODY STAND UP.

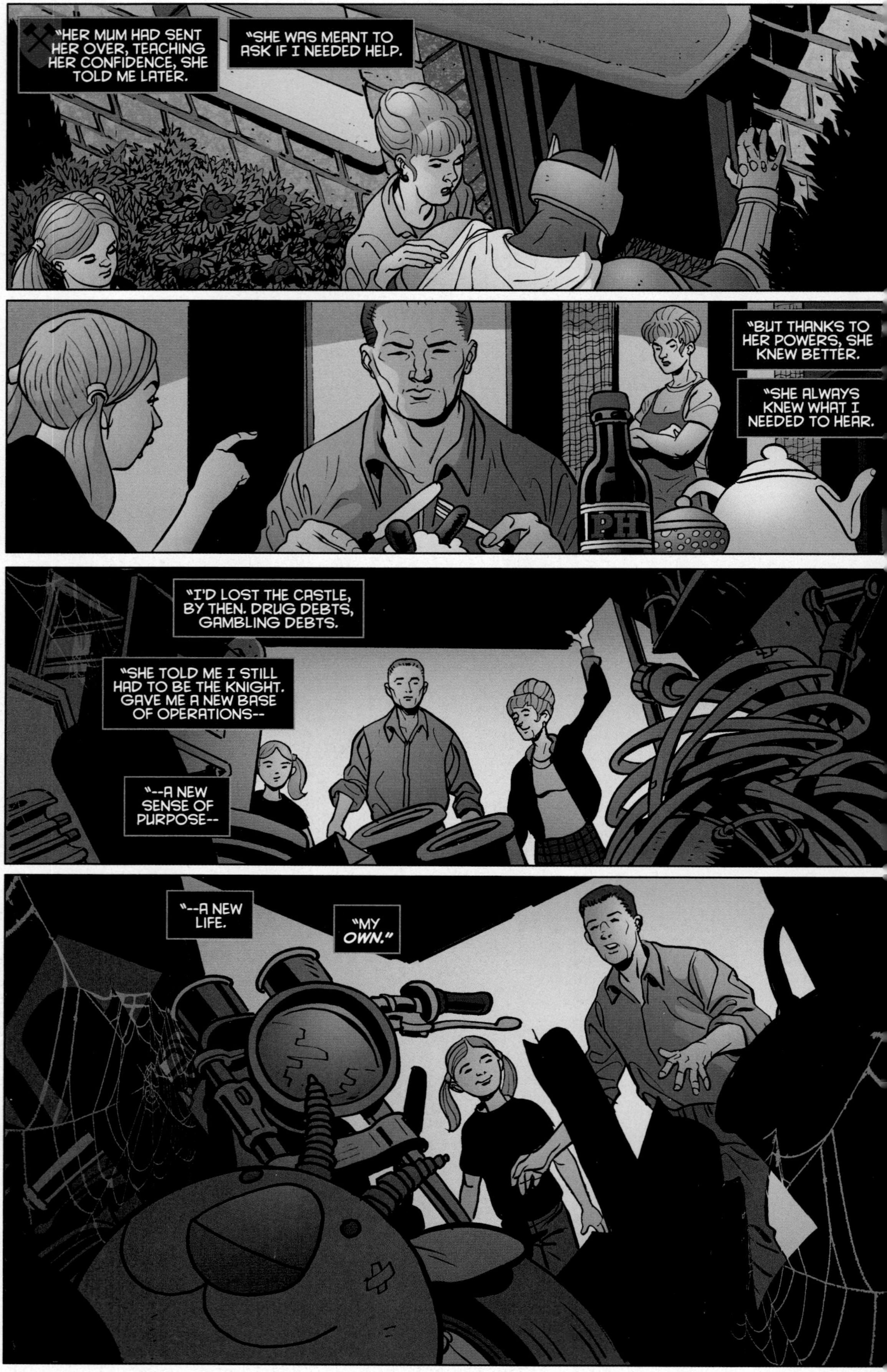
"HER MUM HAD SENT HER OVER, TEACHING HER CONFIDENCE, SHE TOLD ME LATER.
"SHE WAS MEANT TO ASK IF I NEEDED HELP.
"BUT THANKS TO HER POWERS, SHE KNEW BETTER.
"SHE ALWAYS KNEW WHAT I NEEDED TO HEAR.
PH
"I'D LOST THE CASTLE, BY THEN. DRUG DEBTS, GAMBLING DEBTS.
"SHE TOLD ME I STILL HAD TO BE THE KNIGHT. GAVE ME A NEW BASE OF OPERATIONS--
"--A NEW SENSE OF PURPOSE--
"--A NEW LIFE.
"MY *OWN.*"

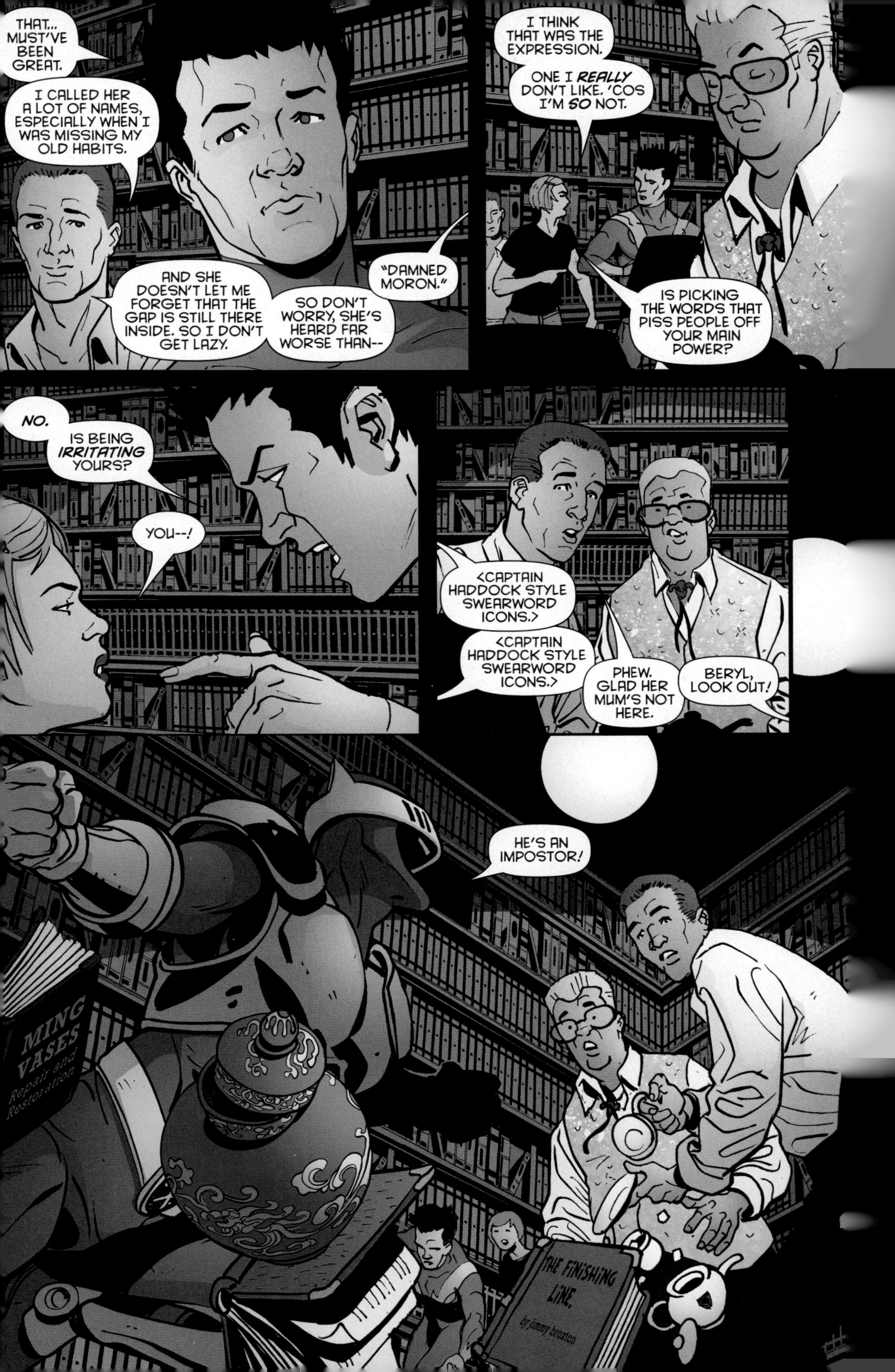

THAT... MUST'VE BEEN GREAT.
I CALLED HER A LOT OF NAMES, ESPECIALLY WHEN I WAS MISSING MY OLD HABITS.
AND SHE DOESN'T LET ME FORGET THAT THE GAP IS STILL THERE INSIDE. SO I DON'T GET LAZY.
SO DON'T WORRY, SHE'S HEARD FAR WORSE THAN--
"DAMNED MORON."
I THINK THAT WAS THE EXPRESSION.
ONE I *REALLY* DON'T LIKE. 'COS I'M *SO* NOT.
IS PICKING THE WORDS THAT PISS PEOPLE OFF YOUR MAIN POWER?
NO.
IS BEING *IRRITATING* YOURS?
YOU--!
<CAPTAIN HADDOCK STYLE SWEARWORD ICONS.>
<CAPTAIN HADDOCK STYLE SWEARWORD ICONS.>
PHEW. GLAD HER MUM'S NOT HERE.
BERYL, LOOK OUT!
HE'S AN IMPOSTOR!
MING VASES
Repair and Restoration
THE FINISHING LINE.
by jimmy broxton

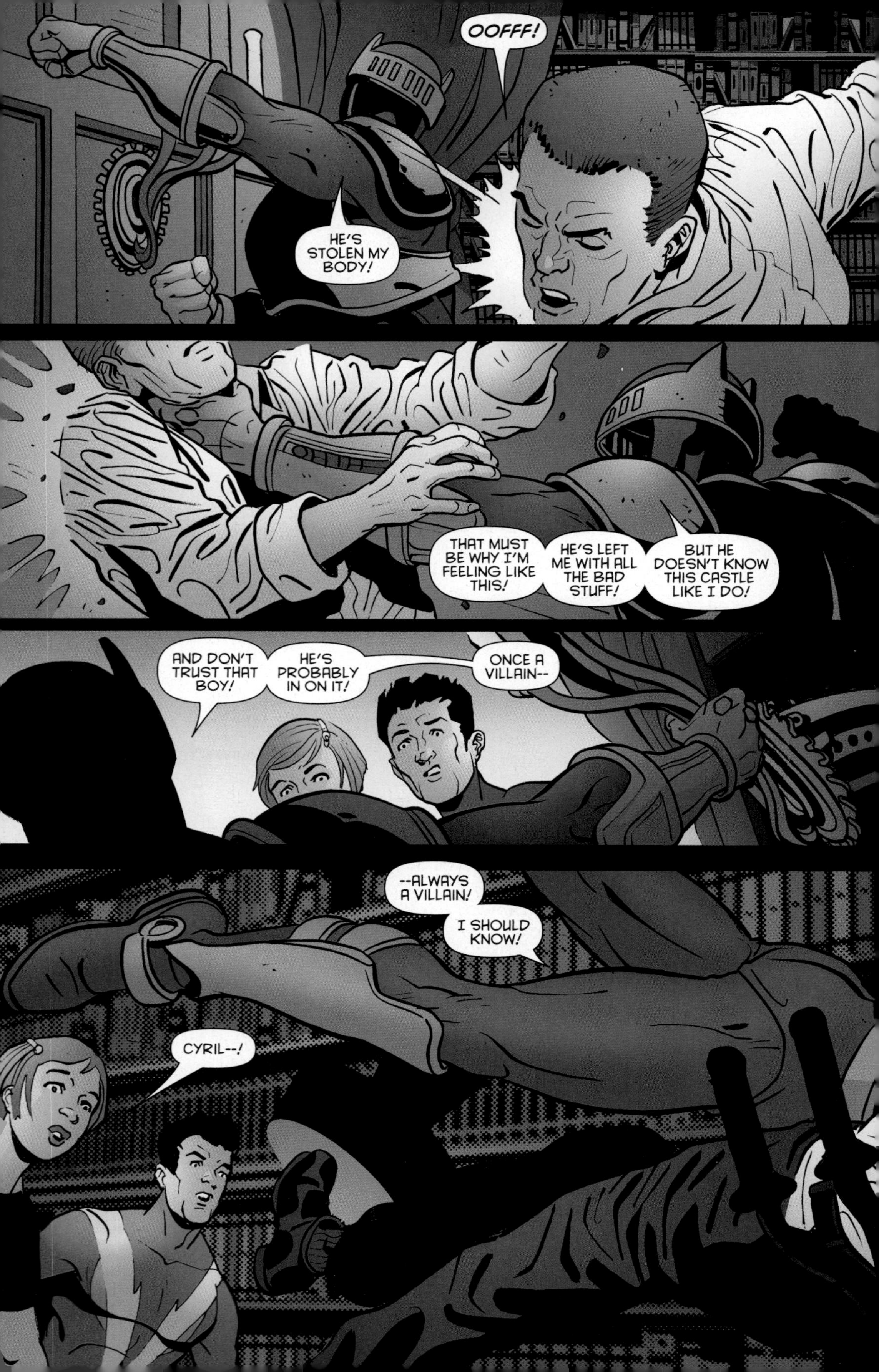

OOFFF!
HE'S STOLEN MY BODY!
THAT MUST BE WHY I'M FEELING LIKE THIS!
HE'S LEFT ME WITH ALL THE BAD STUFF!
BUT HE DOESN'T KNOW THIS CASTLE LIKE I DO!
AND DON'T TRUST THAT BOY!
HE'S PROBABLY IN ON IT!
ONCE A VILLAIN--
--ALWAYS A VILLAIN!
I SHOULD KNOW!
CYRIL--!

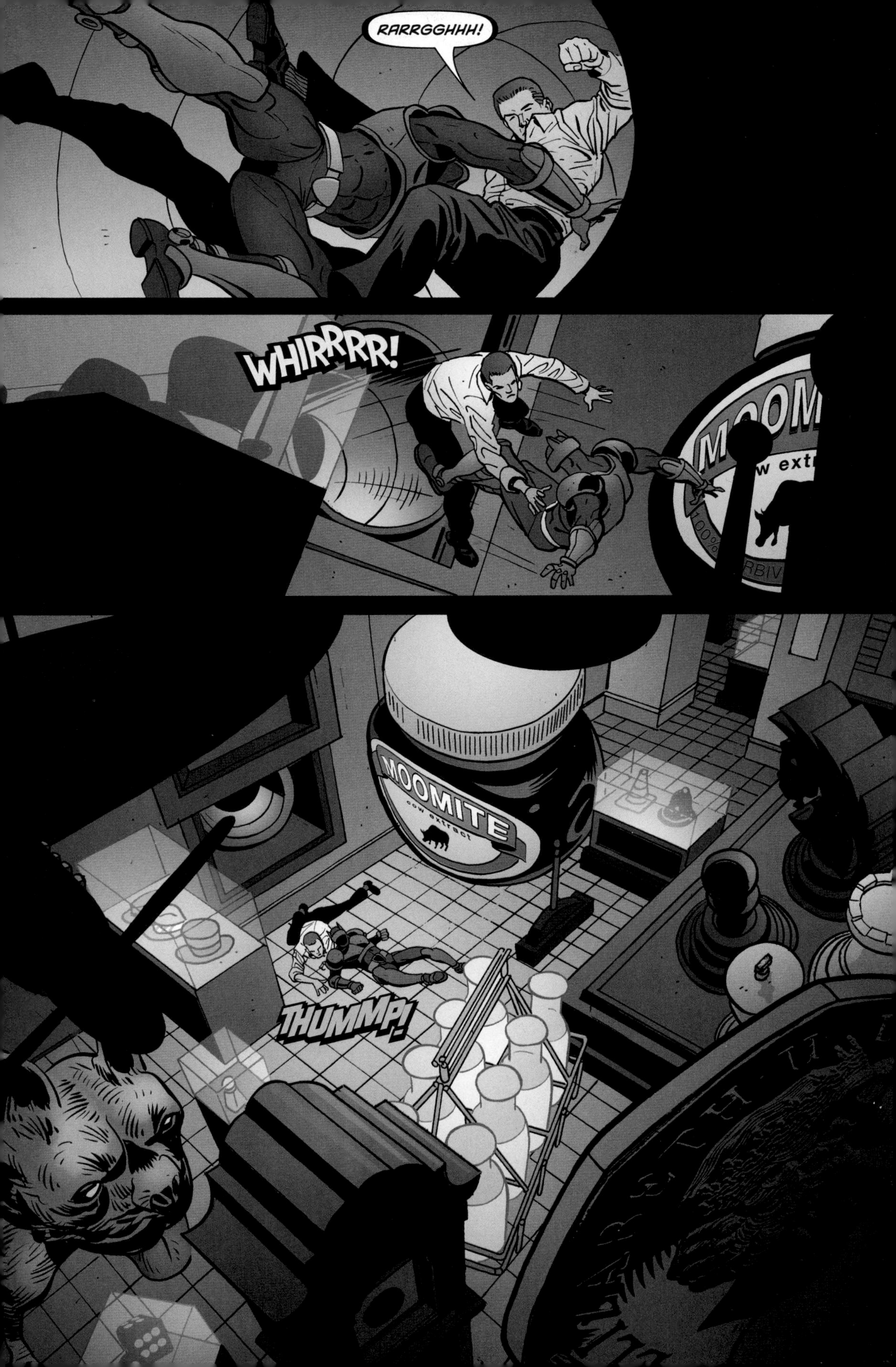

RARRGGHHH!
WHIRRRR!
MOOMI
ow extr
MOOMITE
cow extract
THUMMP!

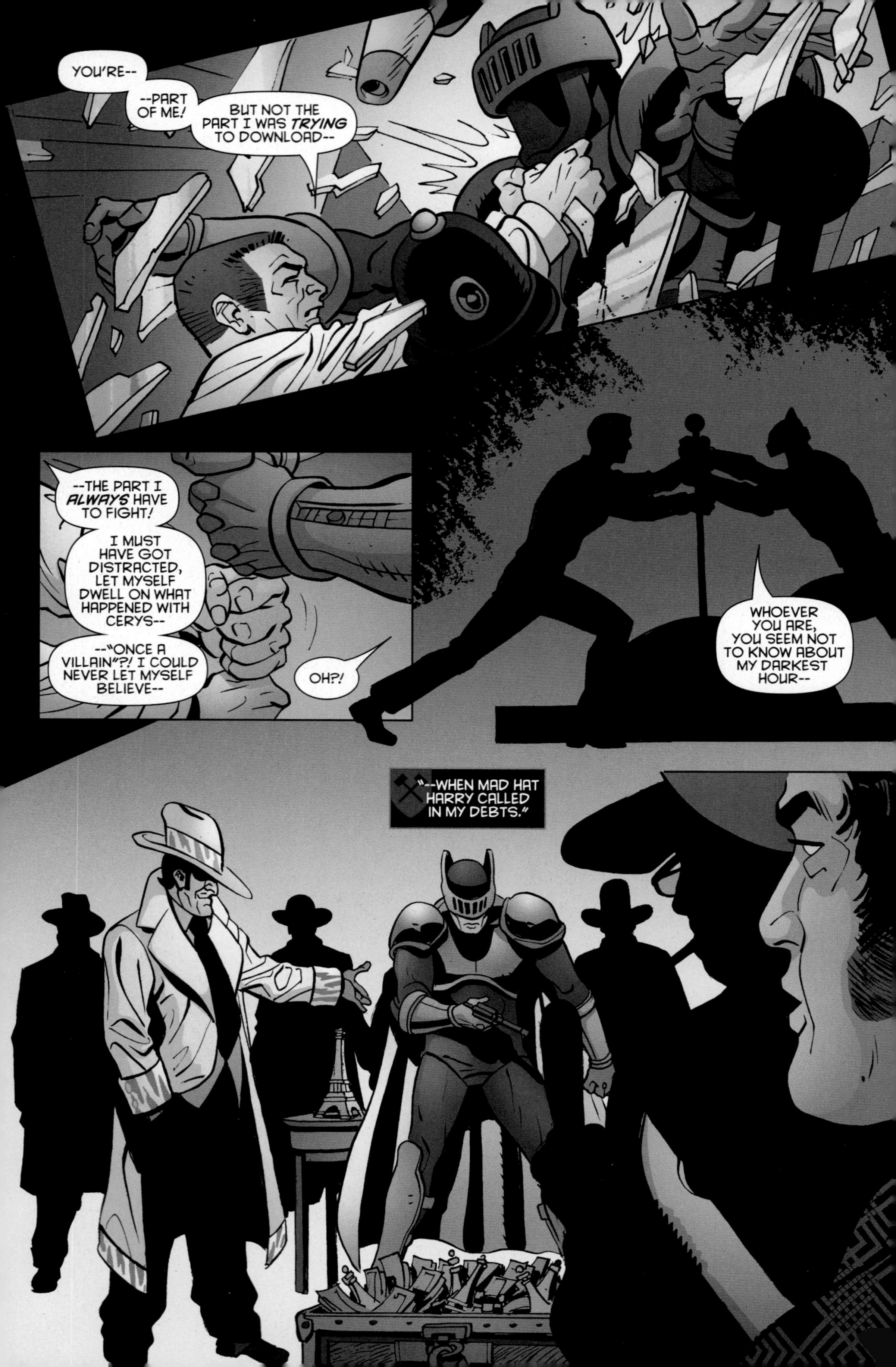
YOU'RE--
--PART OF ME!
BUT NOT THE PART I WAS TRYING TO DOWNLOAD--
--THE PART I ALWAYS HAVE TO FIGHT!
I MUST HAVE GOT DISTRACTED, LET MYSELF DWELL ON WHAT HAPPENED WITH CERYS--
--"ONCE A VILLAIN"?! I COULD NEVER LET MYSELF BELIEVE--
OH?!
WHOEVER YOU ARE, YOU SEEM NOT TO KNOW ABOUT MY DARKEST HOUR--
"--WHEN MAD HAT HARRY CALLED IN MY DEBTS."

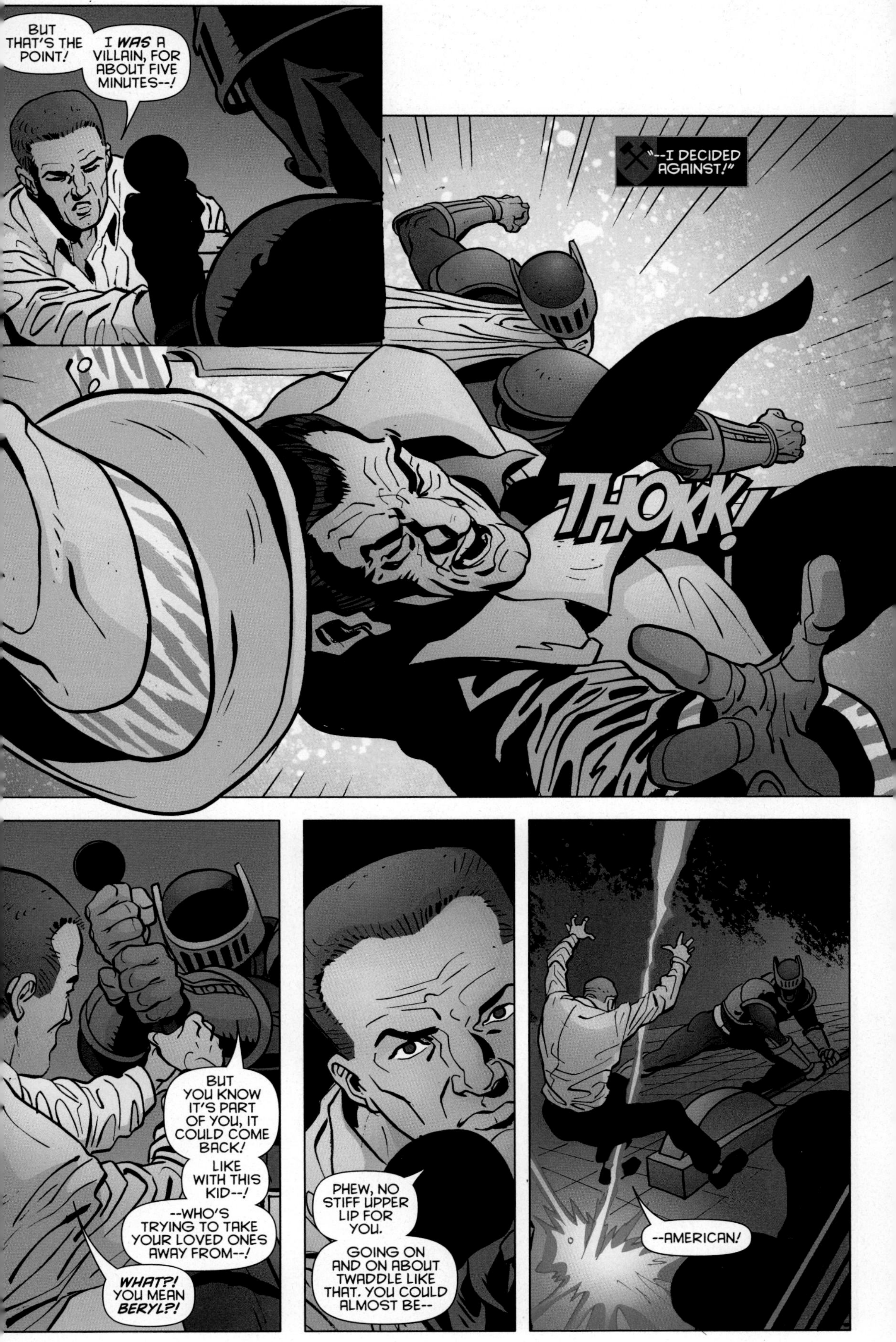

BUT THAT'S THE POINT!
I WAS A VILLAIN, FOR ABOUT FIVE MINUTES--!
"--I DECIDED AGAINST!"
THOKK!
BUT YOU KNOW IT'S PART OF YOU, IT COULD COME BACK!
LIKE WITH THIS KID--!
--WHO'S TRYING TO TAKE YOUR LOVED ONES AWAY FROM--!
WHAT?! YOU MEAN BERYL?!
PHEW, NO STIFF UPPER LIP FOR YOU.
GOING ON AND ON ABOUT TWADDLE LIKE THAT. YOU COULD ALMOST BE--
--AMERICAN!

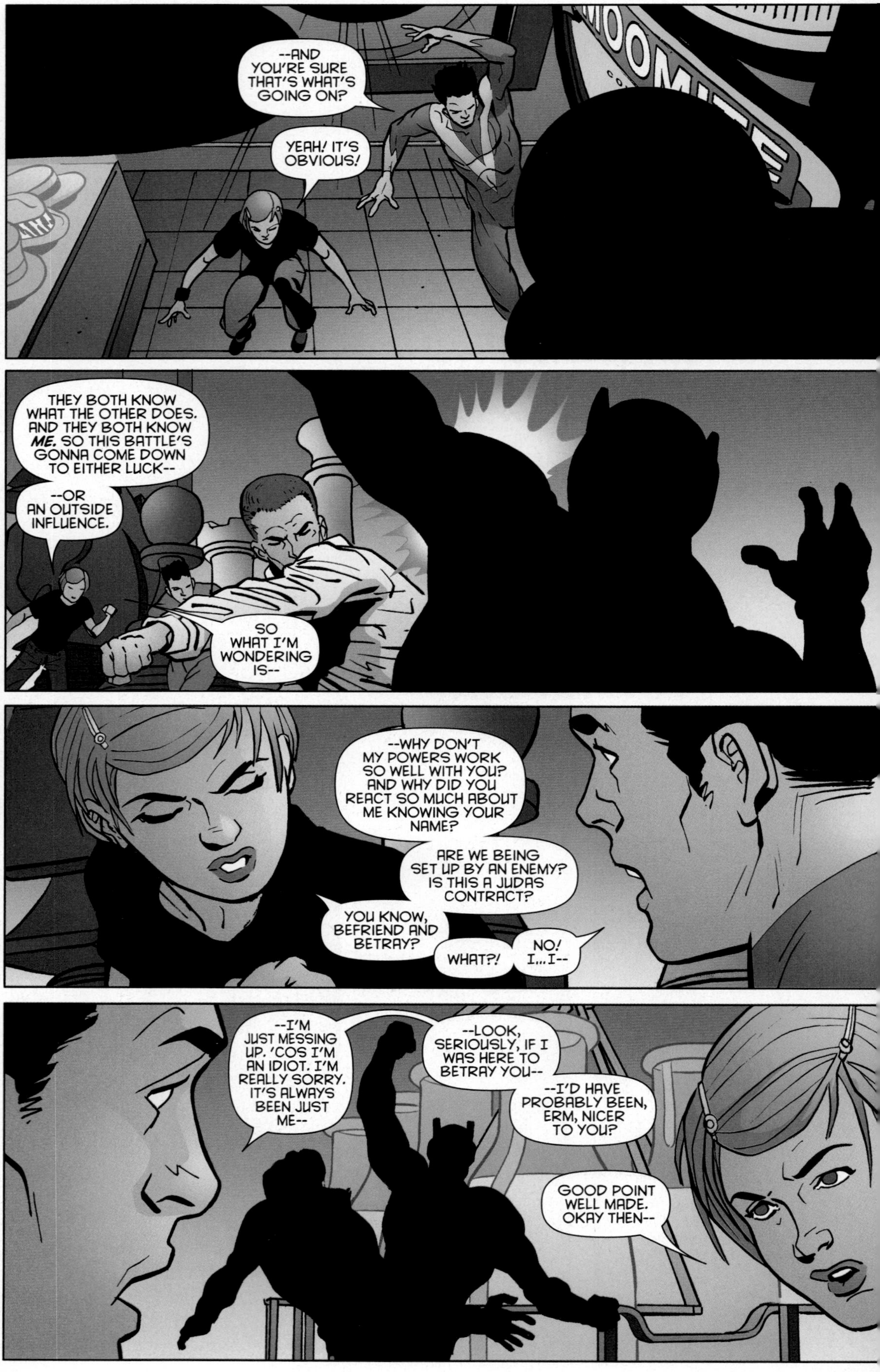
--AND YOU'RE SURE THAT'S WHAT'S GOING ON?
YEAH! IT'S OBVIOUS!
THEY BOTH KNOW WHAT THE OTHER DOES. AND THEY BOTH KNOW ME. SO THIS BATTLE'S GONNA COME DOWN TO EITHER LUCK--
--OR AN OUTSIDE INFLUENCE.
SO WHAT I'M WONDERING IS--
--WHY DON'T MY POWERS WORK SO WELL WITH YOU? AND WHY DID YOU REACT SO MUCH ABOUT ME KNOWING YOUR NAME?
ARE WE BEING SET UP BY AN ENEMY? IS THIS A JUDAS CONTRACT?
YOU KNOW, BEFRIEND AND BETRAY?
WHAT?!
NO! I...I--
--I'M JUST MESSING UP. 'COS I'M AN IDIOT. I'M REALLY SORRY. IT'S ALWAYS BEEN JUST ME--
--LOOK, SERIOUSLY, IF I WAS HERE TO BETRAY YOU--
--I'D HAVE PROBABLY BEEN, ERM, NICER TO YOU?
GOOD POINT WELL MADE. OKAY THEN--

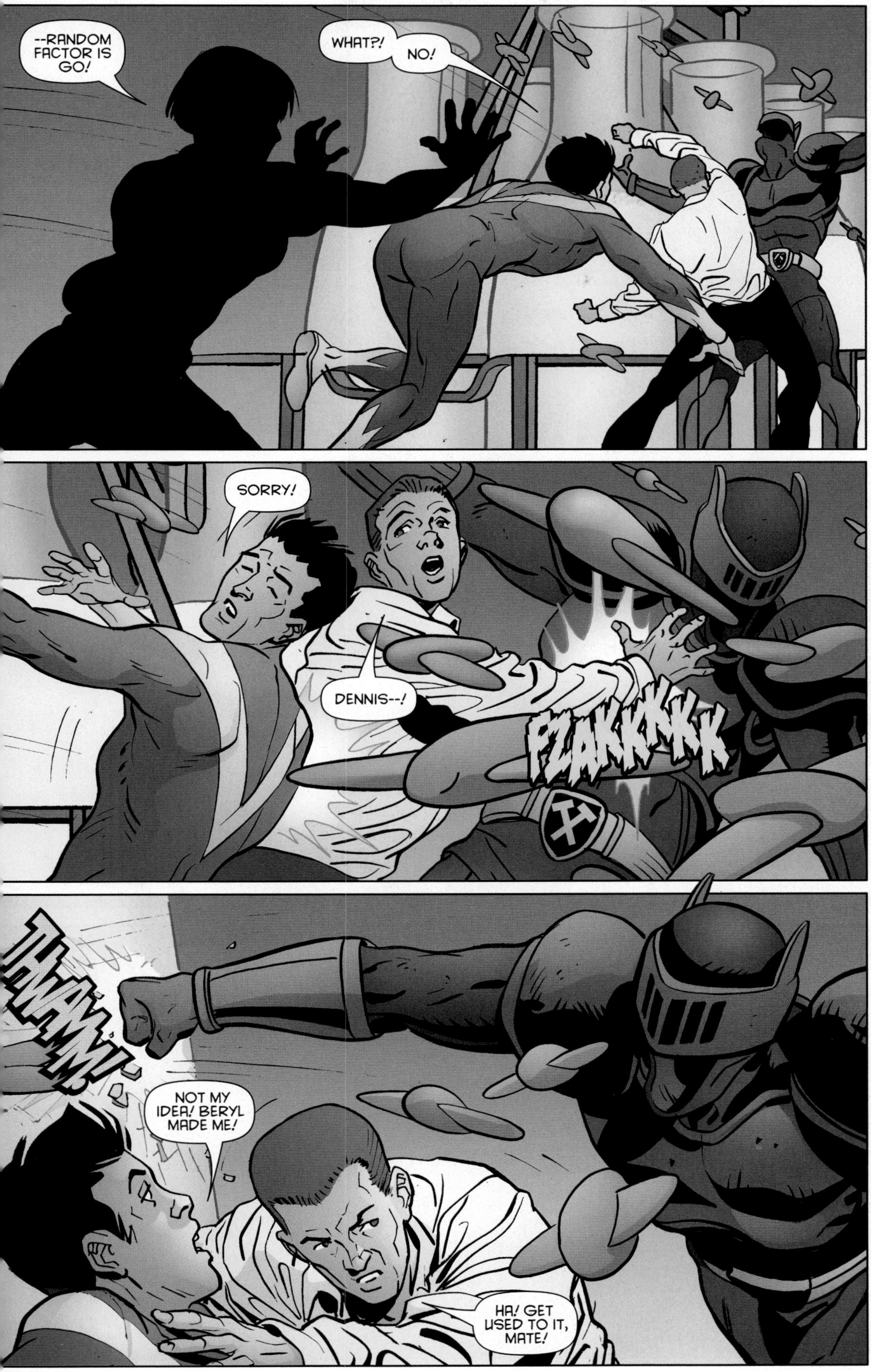
--RANDOM FACTOR IS GO!
WHAT?!
NO!
SORRY!
DENNIS--!
FZAKKKKK
THWAM!
NOT MY IDEA! BERYL MADE ME!
HA! GET USED TO IT, MATE!

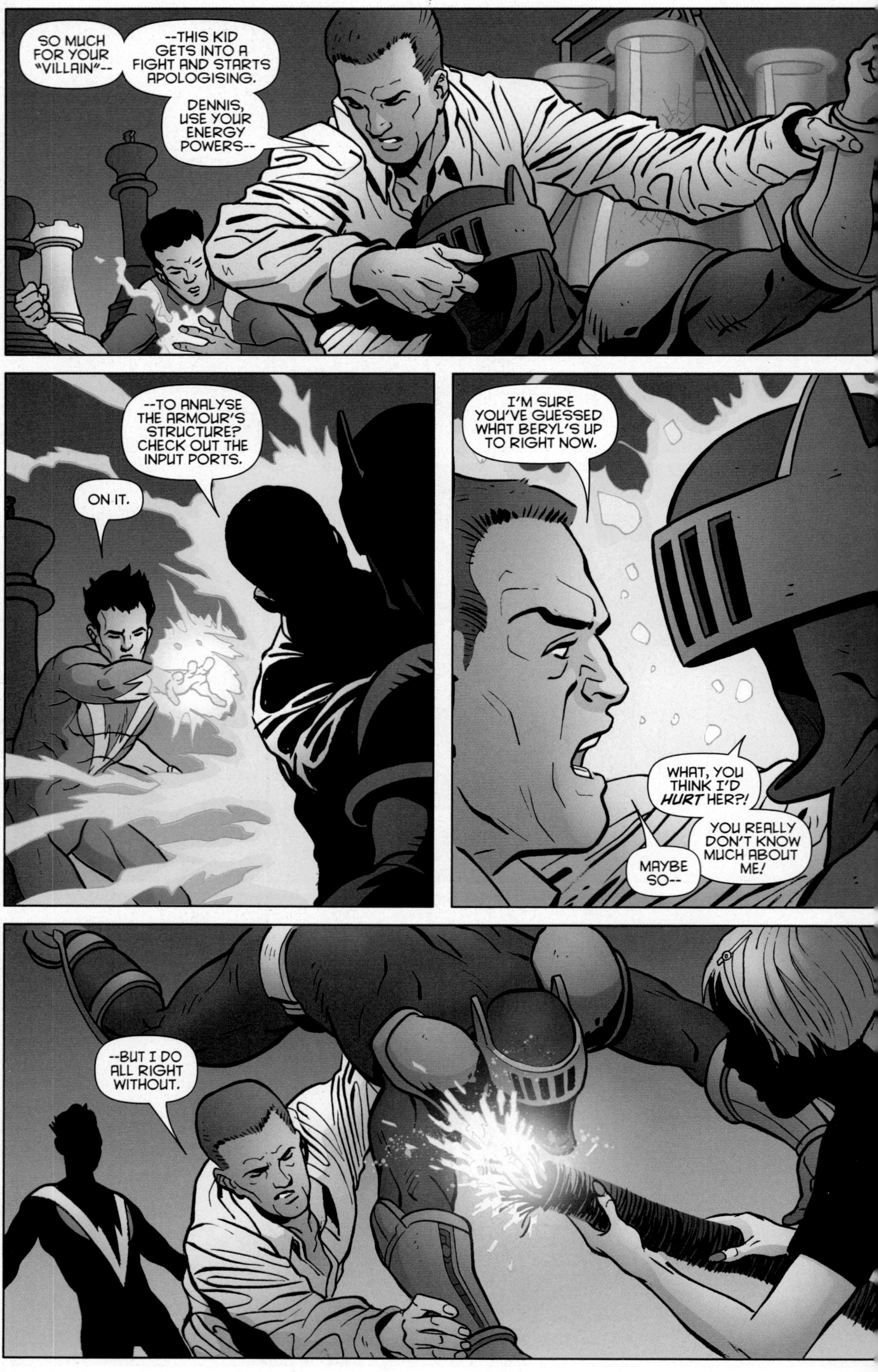
SO MUCH FOR YOUR "VILLAIN"--
--THIS KID GETS INTO A FIGHT AND STARTS APOLOGISING.
DENNIS, USE YOUR ENERGY POWERS--
--TO ANALYSE THE ARMOUR'S STRUCTURE? CHECK OUT THE INPUT PORTS.
ON IT.
I'M SURE YOU'VE GUESSED WHAT BERYL'S UP TO RIGHT NOW.
WHAT, YOU THINK I'D *HURT* HER?!
YOU REALLY DON'T KNOW MUCH ABOUT ME!
MAYBE SO--
--BUT I DO ALL RIGHT WITHOUT.

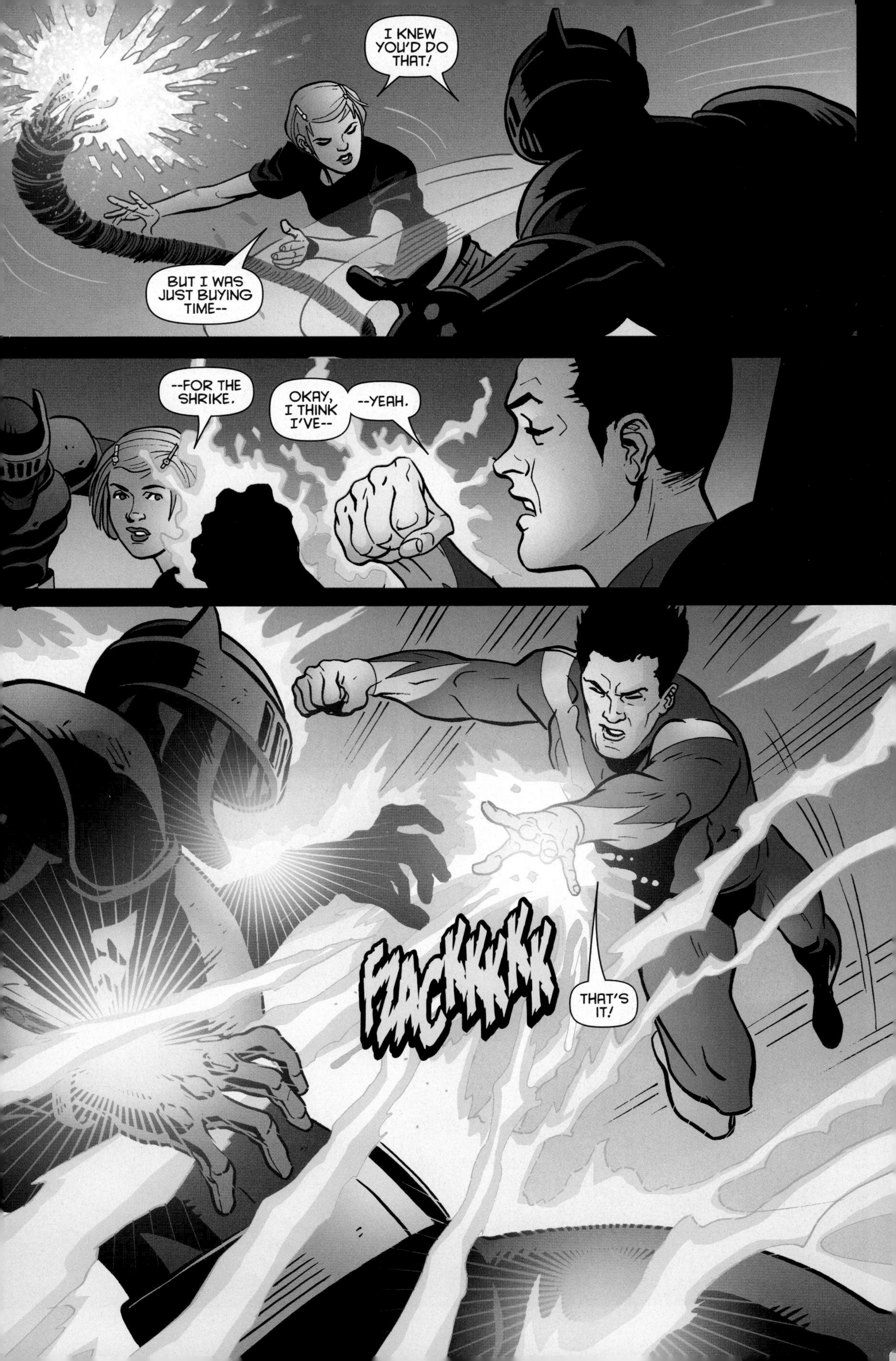
I KNEW YOU'D DO THAT!
BUT I WAS JUST BUYING TIME--
--FOR THE SHRIKE.
OKAY, I THINK I'VE--
--YEAH.
FZACKKKK
THAT'S IT!

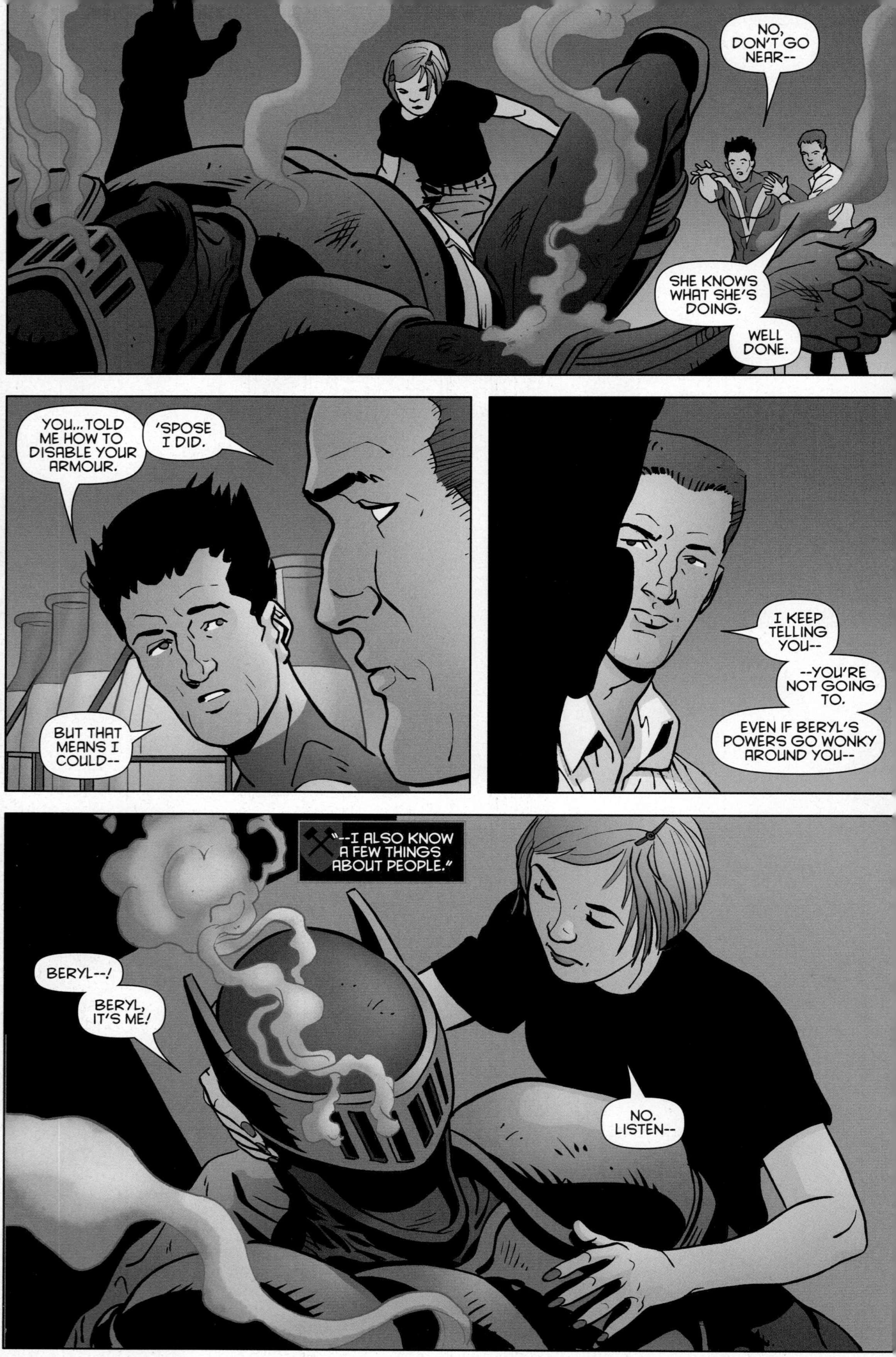
NO, DON'T GO NEAR--
SHE KNOWS WHAT SHE'S DOING.
WELL DONE.
YOU...TOLD ME HOW TO DISABLE YOUR ARMOUR.
'SPOSE I DID.
BUT THAT MEANS I COULD--
I KEEP TELLING YOU--
--YOU'RE NOT GOING TO.
EVEN IF BERYL'S POWERS GO WONKY AROUND YOU--
"--I ALSO KNOW A FEW THINGS ABOUT PEOPLE."
BERYL--!
BERYL, IT'S ME!
NO. LISTEN--

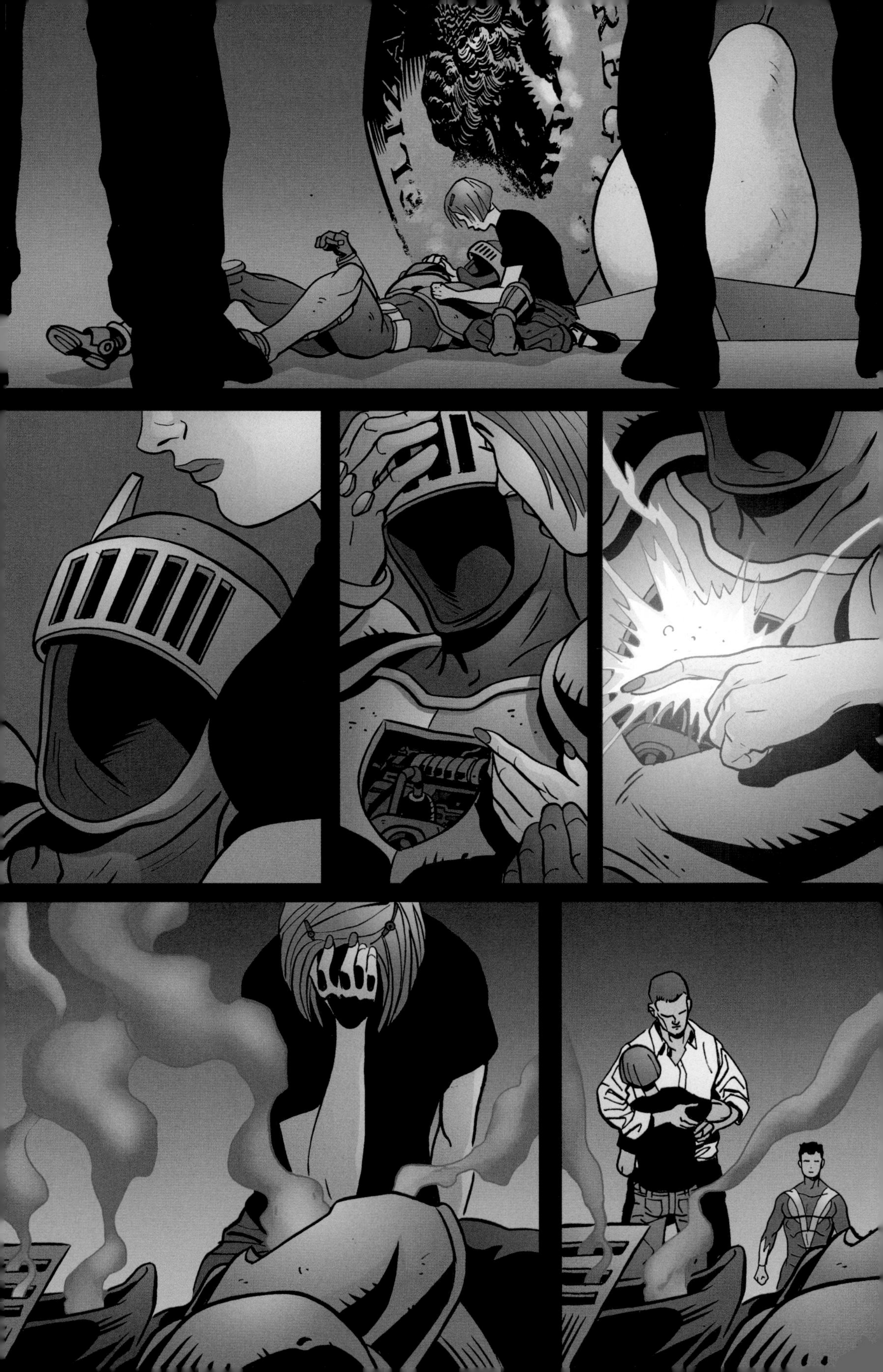

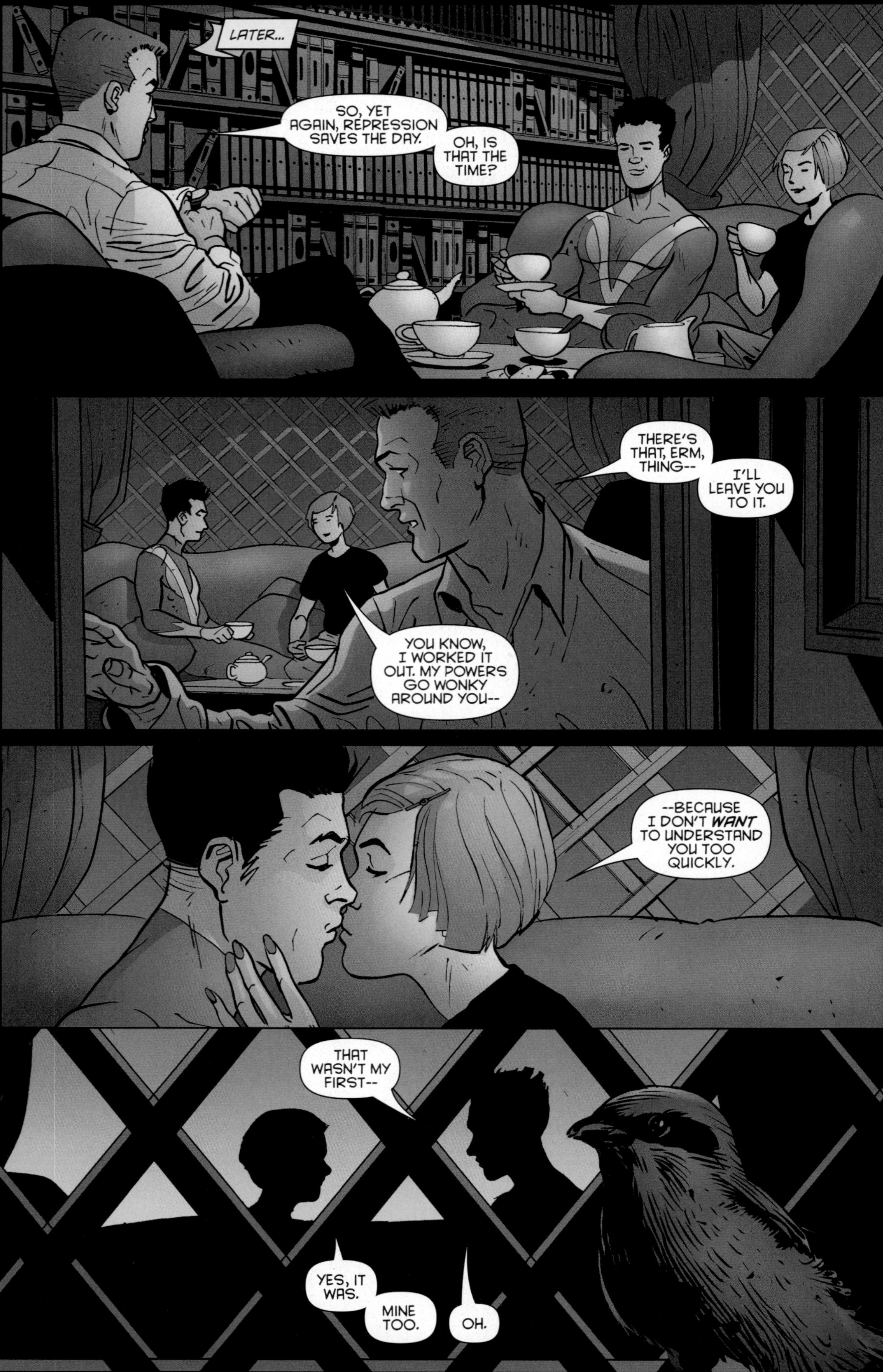
LATER...
SO, YET AGAIN, REPRESSION SAVES THE DAY.
OH, IS THAT THE TIME?
THERE'S THAT, ERM, THING--
I'LL LEAVE YOU TO IT.
YOU KNOW, I WORKED IT OUT. MY POWERS GO WONKY AROUND YOU--
--BECAUSE I DON'T *WANT* TO UNDERSTAND YOU TOO QUICKLY.
THAT WASN'T MY FIRST--
YES, IT WAS.
MINE TOO.
OH.

Butlers and Batmen

GIVING BATMAN A BUTLER, IN THE FORM OF ALFRED PENNYWORTH, WAS A GENIUS IDEA: WHO ELSE WOULD KEEP DANGEROUS SECRETS AND OFFER A CALM, FIRM, SECOND OPINION? AND OF COURSE HE WAS BRITISH, THAT'S WHAT BUTLERS ARE. AND IN GENERAL, ALFRED'S BEEN ONE OF THE BEST PORTRAYALS OF A BRITISH PERSON IN COMICS. BUT A BRITISH BUTLER IN *KNIGHT AND SQUIRE* STRUCK ME AS BEING A BIT ORDINARY REALLY. AS BATMAN, INC. EXPANDED ACROSS THE GLOBE, PERHAPS EVERY INTERNATIONAL BATMAN SHOULD HAVE A BUTLER FROM "THE OPPOSITE COUNTRY."

SO THAT'S WHERE HANK HACKENBACKER CAME FROM. (HIS NAME ECHOES THE *NOM DE PLUME* OF BRAINS IN *THUNDERBIRDS*, THAT OTHER VERY BRITISH GAZE AT WHAT AMERICANS MIGHT BE LIKE.) AND WHO KNOWS WHAT PART OF THE STATES HE'S FROM, PERHAPS THAT VAGUELY SOUTHERN OR COWBOY STATE THAT ALL AMERICANS IN UK ADVENTURE SHOWS WERE FROM IN THE 1960s. I LIKE TO THINK HIS ACCENT WAVERS VIOLENTLY AND THAT HE'S PLAYED BY SOMEONE FROM MILTON KEYNES.

BERYL'S "IS GO" IS A NOD TO *THUNDERBIRDS* TOO. THE SHRIKE'S REAL NAME ECHOES THAT OF THE (BRITISH) *DENNIS THE MENACE*, A COMICS CHARACTER OF THE SAME VINTAGE AS BERYL'S INSPIRATION, *BERYL THE PERIL*, AND ALSO DENNIS PENNIS, ALTER EGO OF BRITISH COMEDIAN PAUL KAYE. "THE JUDAS CONTRACT" WAS AN EPIC STORY IN THE WOLFMAN/PEREZ RUN OF *THE NEW TEEN TITANS*, THE CONSEQUENCES OF WHICH I'M SURE EVERY SUPER-HERO WOULD WORRY ABOUT. CAPTAIN HADDOCK WAS TINTIN'S SWEARY SAILOR FRIEND, WHO PERFECTED THE SYMBOLIC SALTY SPEECH.

SELLING HATS SINCE BEFORE YOU WERE BORN
Felons
of High Barnet
Bowlers, Boaters, Homburgs and Toppers, you name it, we got the lot. In fact we've got more hats than you've had hot dinners, sonny Jim.
Hats for every occasion, to suit every pocket and every noggin. Funerals, weddings, down the dog track, a day at the races, a bit of business up West, up before the beak or simply earning respect around your manor, a hat on your head is like money in the bank, so to speak. No self-respecting guvnor should leave his gaff without one.
Come and see us for a bespoke fitting. Our bulletproof bowlers are the talk of the town, matching coshes available on request, no questions asked.
Mad Hat Harry:
philanthropist, entrepreneur and man about town... wouldn't be caught dead without a Felon or two.
A selection of our most popular styles
"From a cloth cap to a fine chapeau, you know where to go. Tell 'em Harry sent ya."
Felons
of High Barnet
Cash sales only, no cheques. Please do not ask for credit, as a shove on the conk often offends.

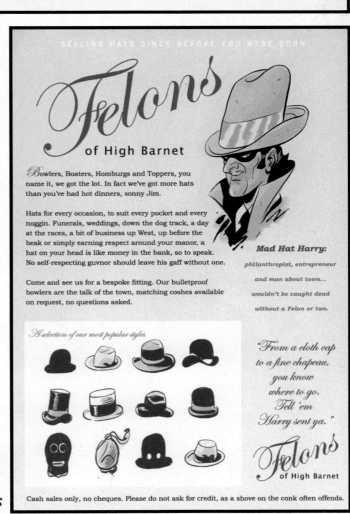

UNTIL NEXT ISSUE, CHEERIO!
- PAUL CORNELL

brought to you by

KNIGHT AND SQUIRE

d by Jimmy Broxton design by SWANDS

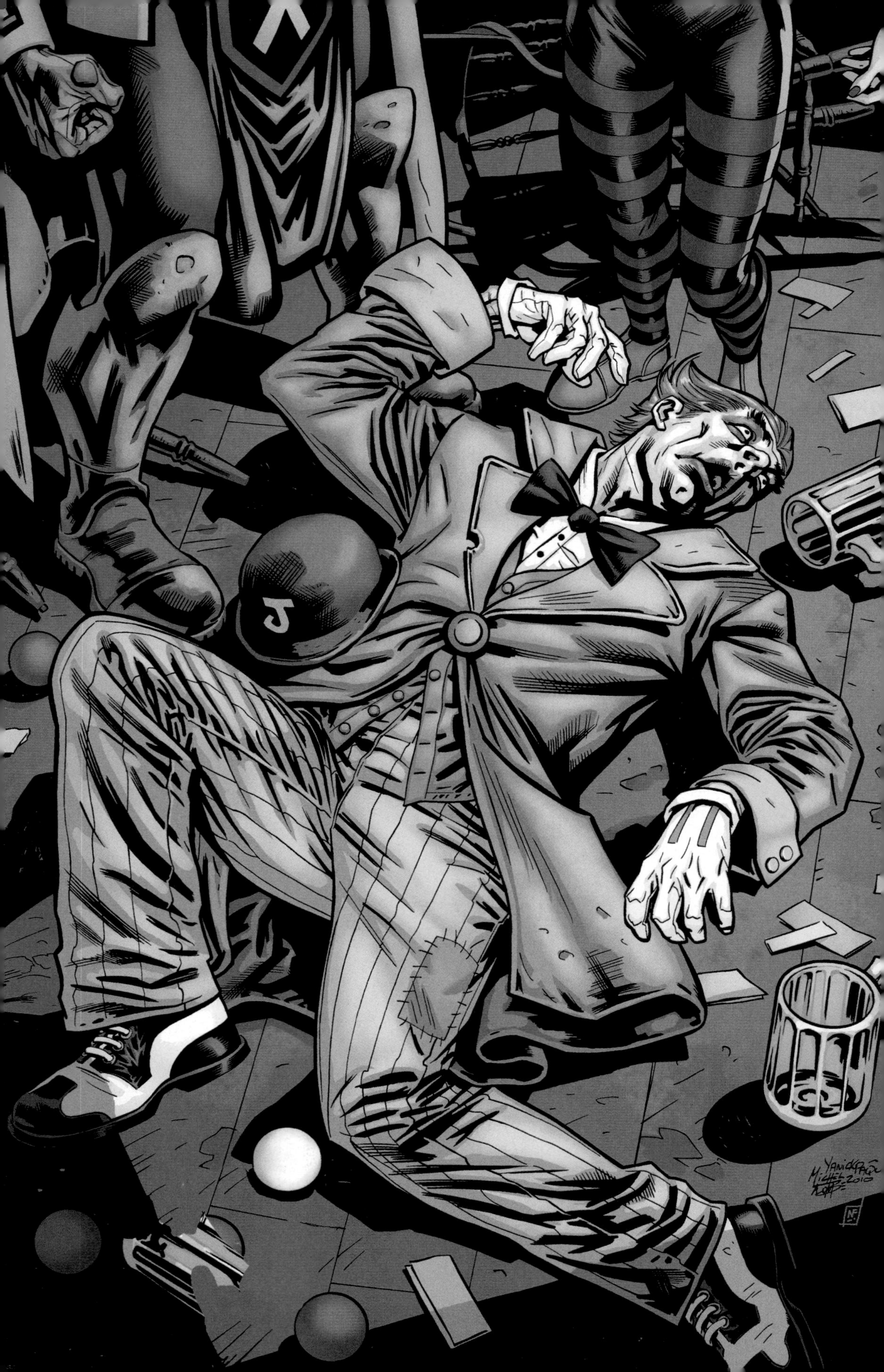

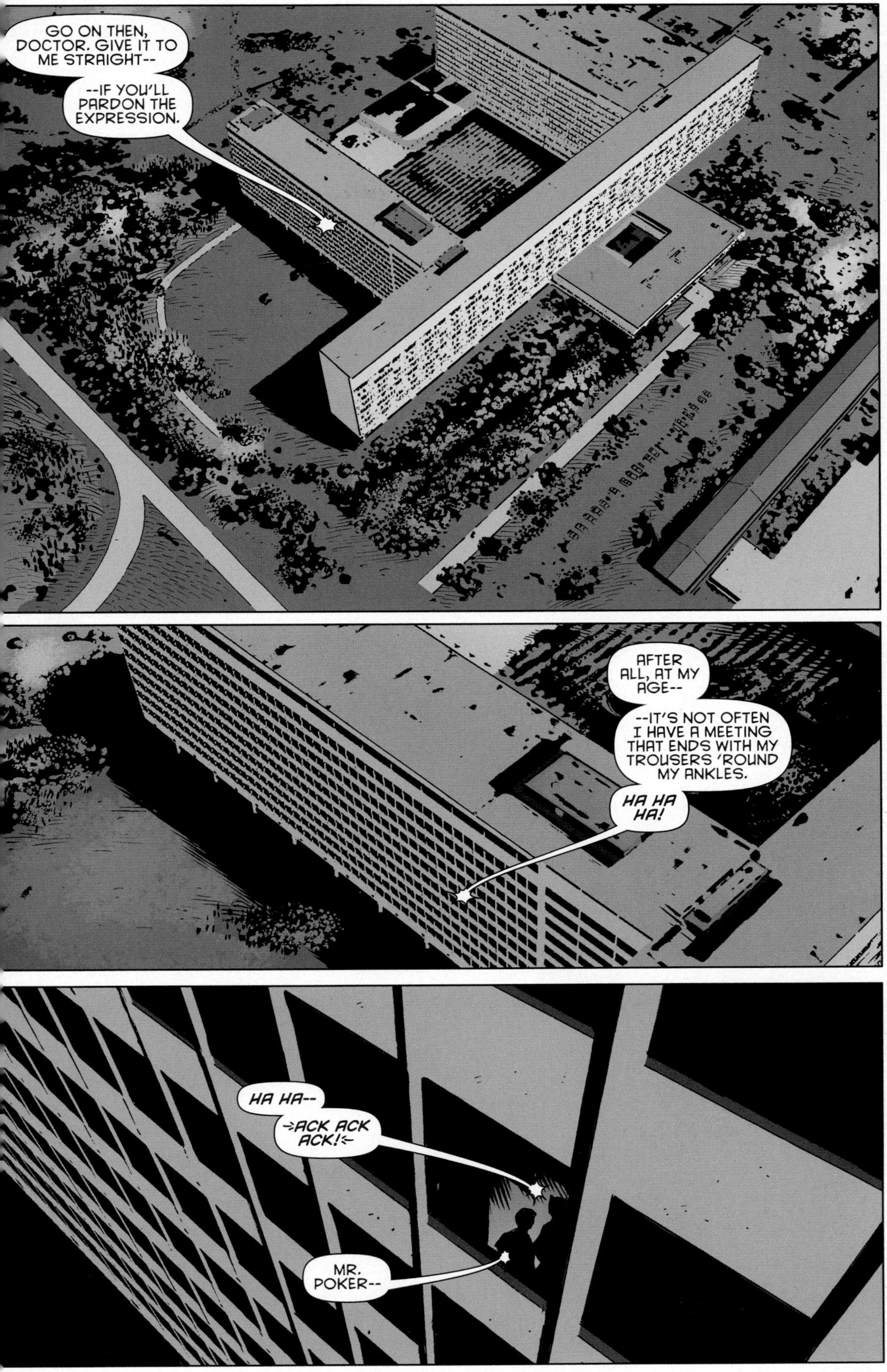
GO ON THEN, DOCTOR. GIVE IT TO ME STRAIGHT--
--IF YOU'LL PARDON THE EXPRESSION.
AFTER ALL, AT MY AGE--
--IT'S NOT OFTEN I HAVE A MEETING THAT ENDS WITH MY TROUSERS 'ROUND MY ANKLES.
HA HA HA!
HA HA--
ACK ACK ACK!
MR. POKER--

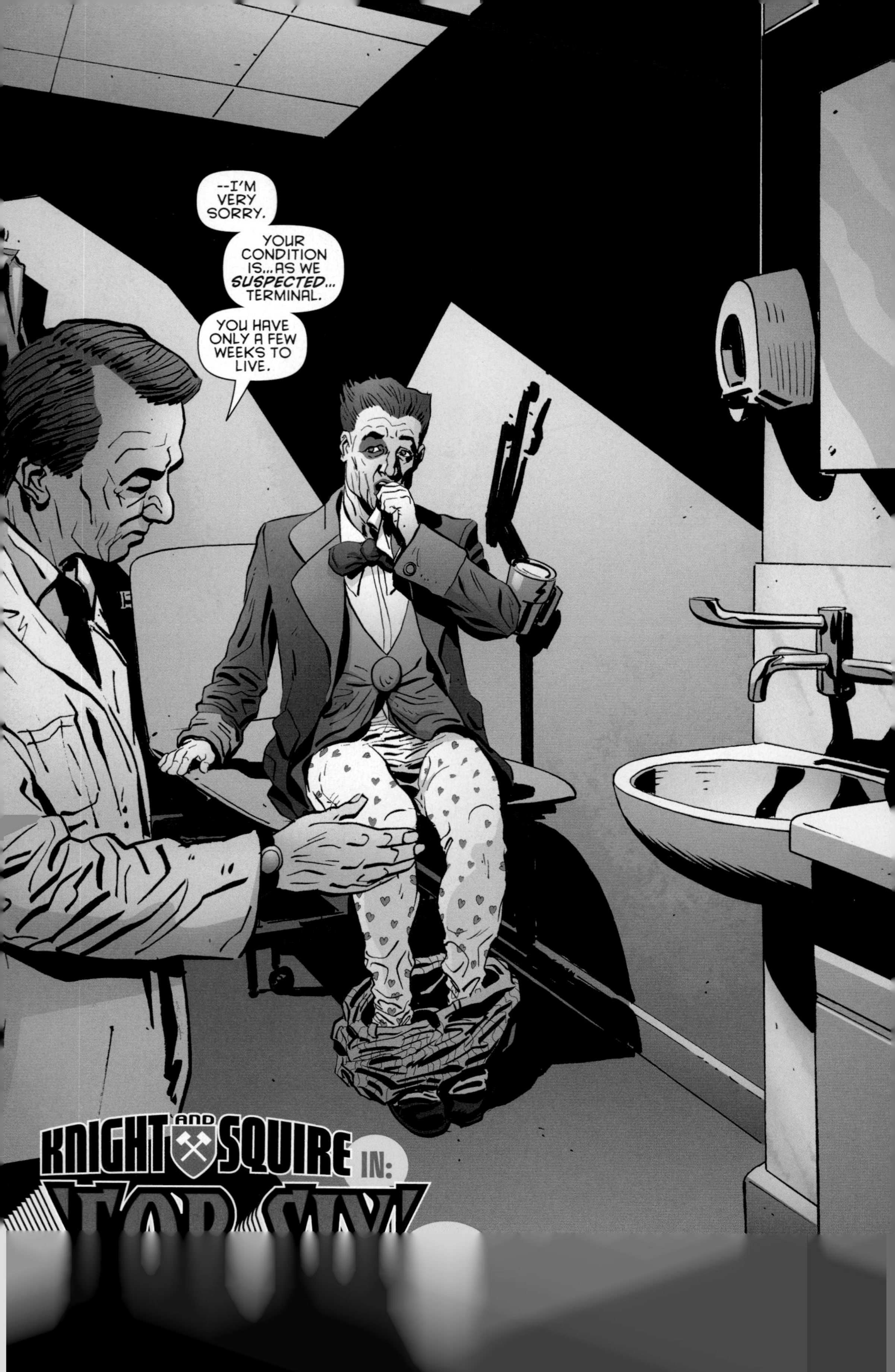
--I'M VERY SORRY.
YOUR CONDITION IS...AS WE *SUSPECTED*... TERMINAL.
YOU HAVE ONLY A FEW WEEKS TO LIVE.
KNIGHT AND SQUIRE IN:

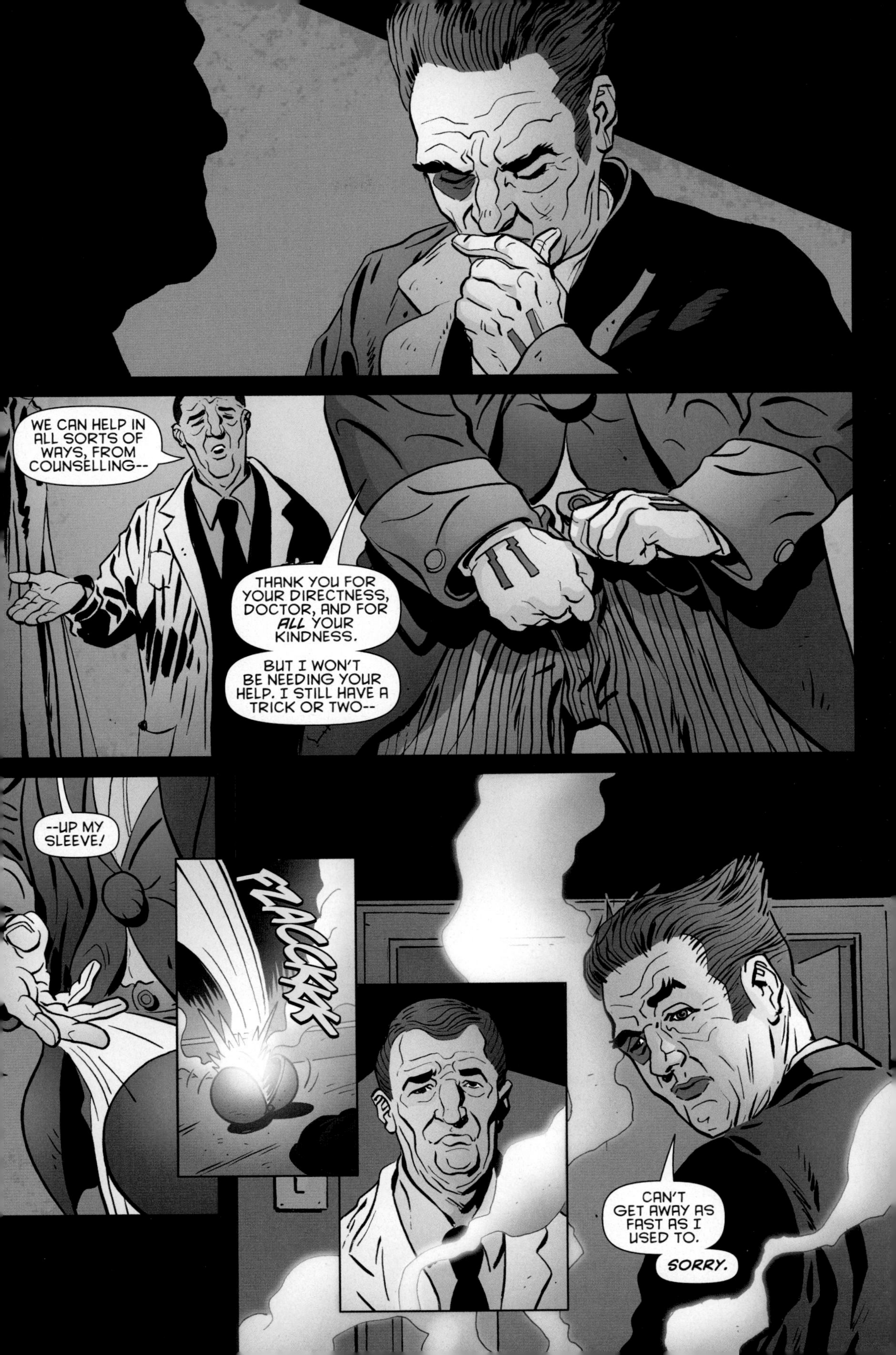
WE CAN HELP IN ALL SORTS OF WAYS, FROM COUNSELLING--
THANK YOU FOR YOUR DIRECTNESS, DOCTOR, AND FOR ALL YOUR KINDNESS.
BUT I WON'T BE NEEDING YOUR HELP. I STILL HAVE A TRICK OR TWO--
--UP MY SLEEVE!
FZACCKKK
CAN'T GET AWAY AS FAST AS I USED TO.
SORRY.

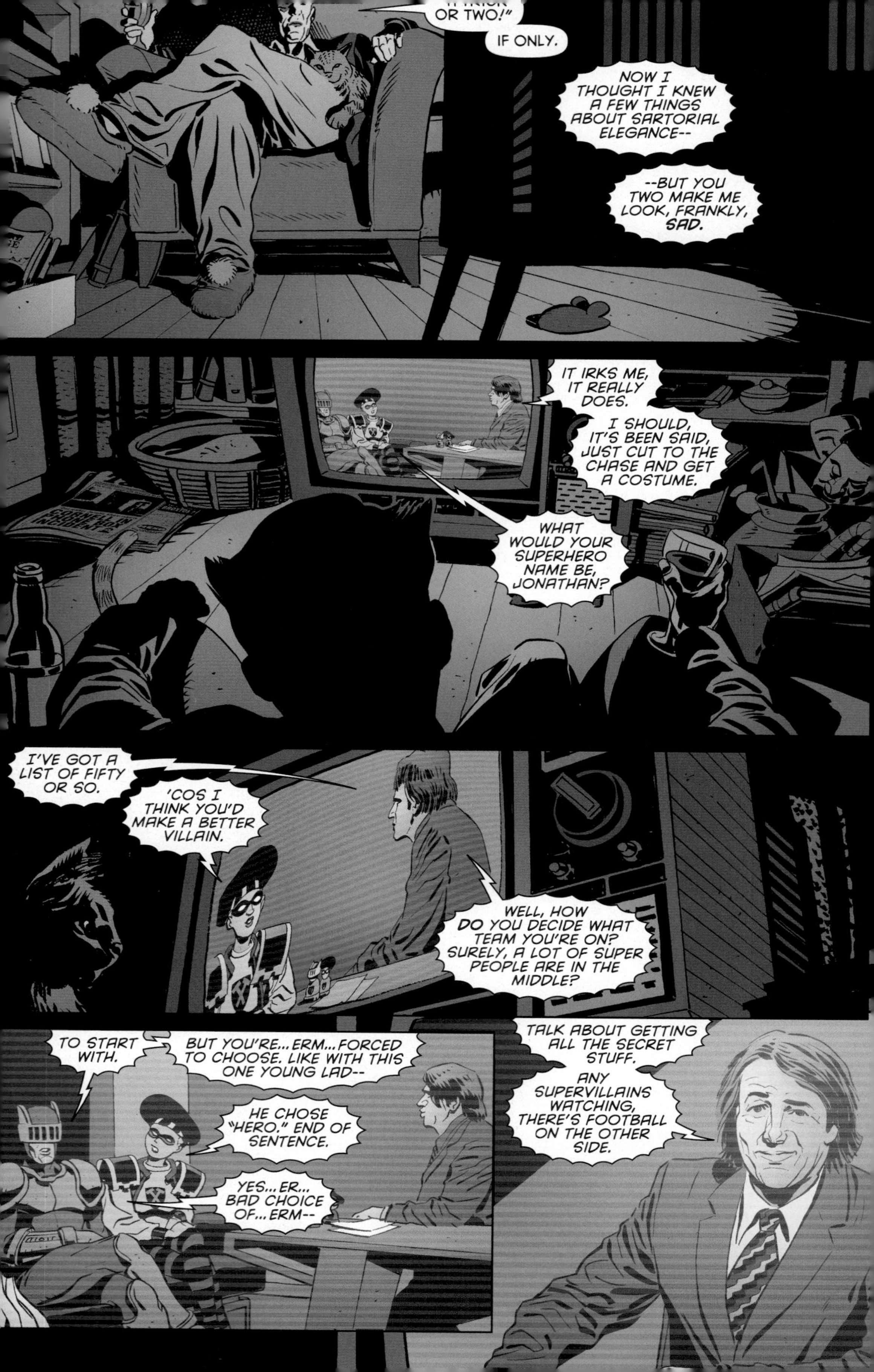
OR TWO!"
IF ONLY.
NOW I THOUGHT I KNEW A FEW THINGS ABOUT SARTORIAL ELEGANCE--
--BUT YOU TWO MAKE ME LOOK, FRANKLY, SAD.
IT IRKS ME, IT REALLY DOES.
I SHOULD, IT'S BEEN SAID, JUST CUT TO THE CHASE AND GET A COSTUME.
WHAT WOULD YOUR SUPERHERO NAME BE, JONATHAN?
I'VE GOT A LIST OF FIFTY OR SO.
'COS I THINK YOU'D MAKE A BETTER VILLAIN.
WELL, HOW DO YOU DECIDE WHAT TEAM YOU'RE ON? SURELY, A LOT OF SUPER PEOPLE ARE IN THE MIDDLE?
TO START WITH.
BUT YOU'RE...ERM...FORCED TO CHOOSE. LIKE WITH THIS ONE YOUNG LAD--
HE CHOSE "HERO." END OF SENTENCE.
YES...ER... BAD CHOICE OF...ERM--
TALK ABOUT GETTING ALL THE SECRET STUFF.
ANY SUPERVILLAINS WATCHING, THERE'S FOOTBALL ON THE OTHER SIDE.

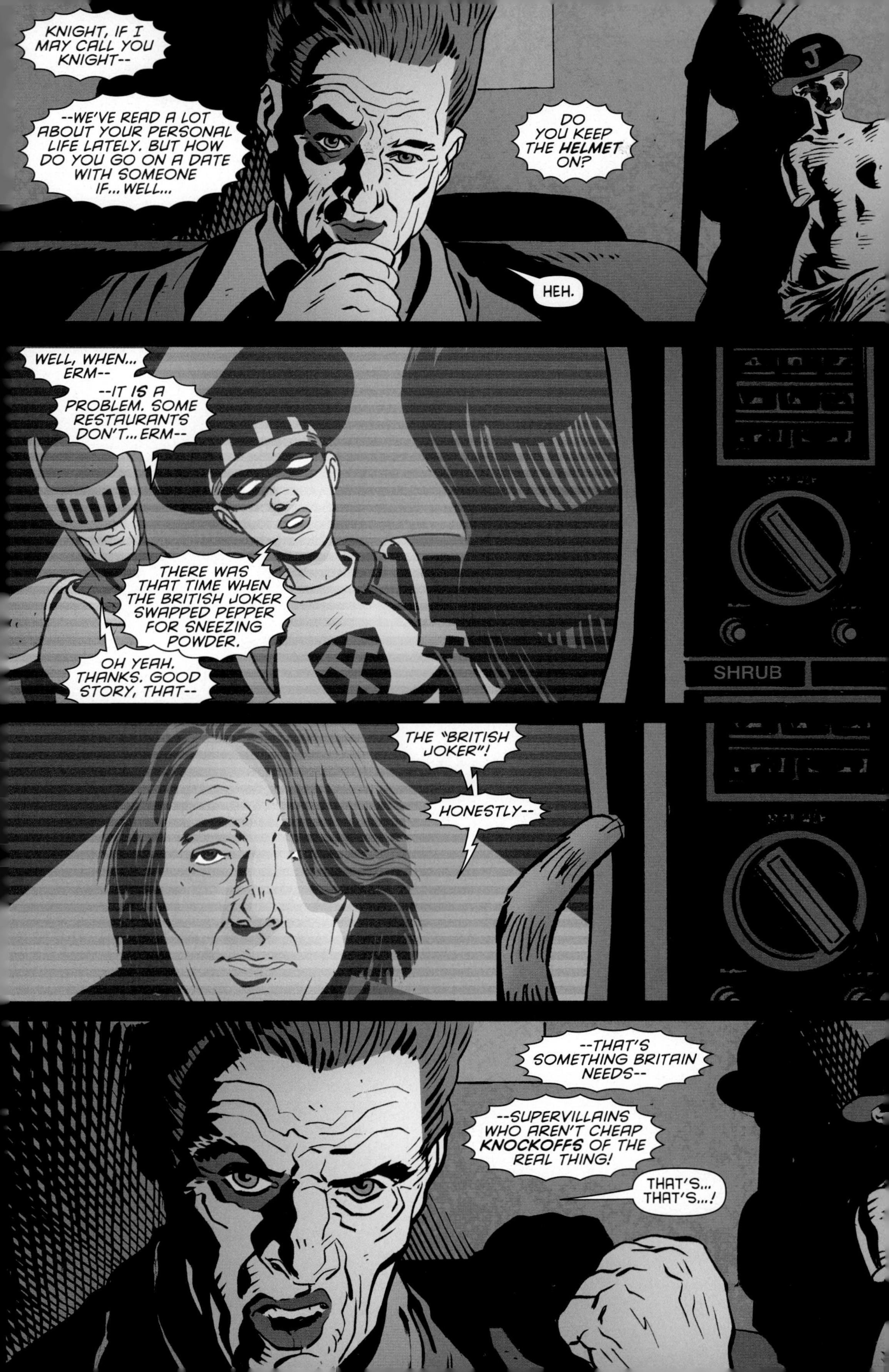
KNIGHT, IF I MAY CALL YOU KNIGHT--
--WE'VE READ A LOT ABOUT YOUR PERSONAL LIFE LATELY. BUT HOW DO YOU GO ON A DATE WITH SOMEONE IF... WELL...
DO YOU KEEP THE **HELMET** ON?
HEH.
WELL, WHEN... ERM--
--IT **IS** A PROBLEM. SOME RESTAURANTS DON'T... ERM--
THERE WAS THAT TIME WHEN THE BRITISH JOKER SWAPPED PEPPER FOR SNEEZING POWDER.
OH YEAH. THANKS. GOOD STORY, THAT--
SHRUB
THE "BRITISH JOKER"!
HONESTLY--
--THAT'S SOMETHING BRITAIN NEEDS--
--SUPERVILLAINS WHO AREN'T CHEAP **KNOCKOFFS** OF THE REAL THING!
THAT'S... THAT'S...!

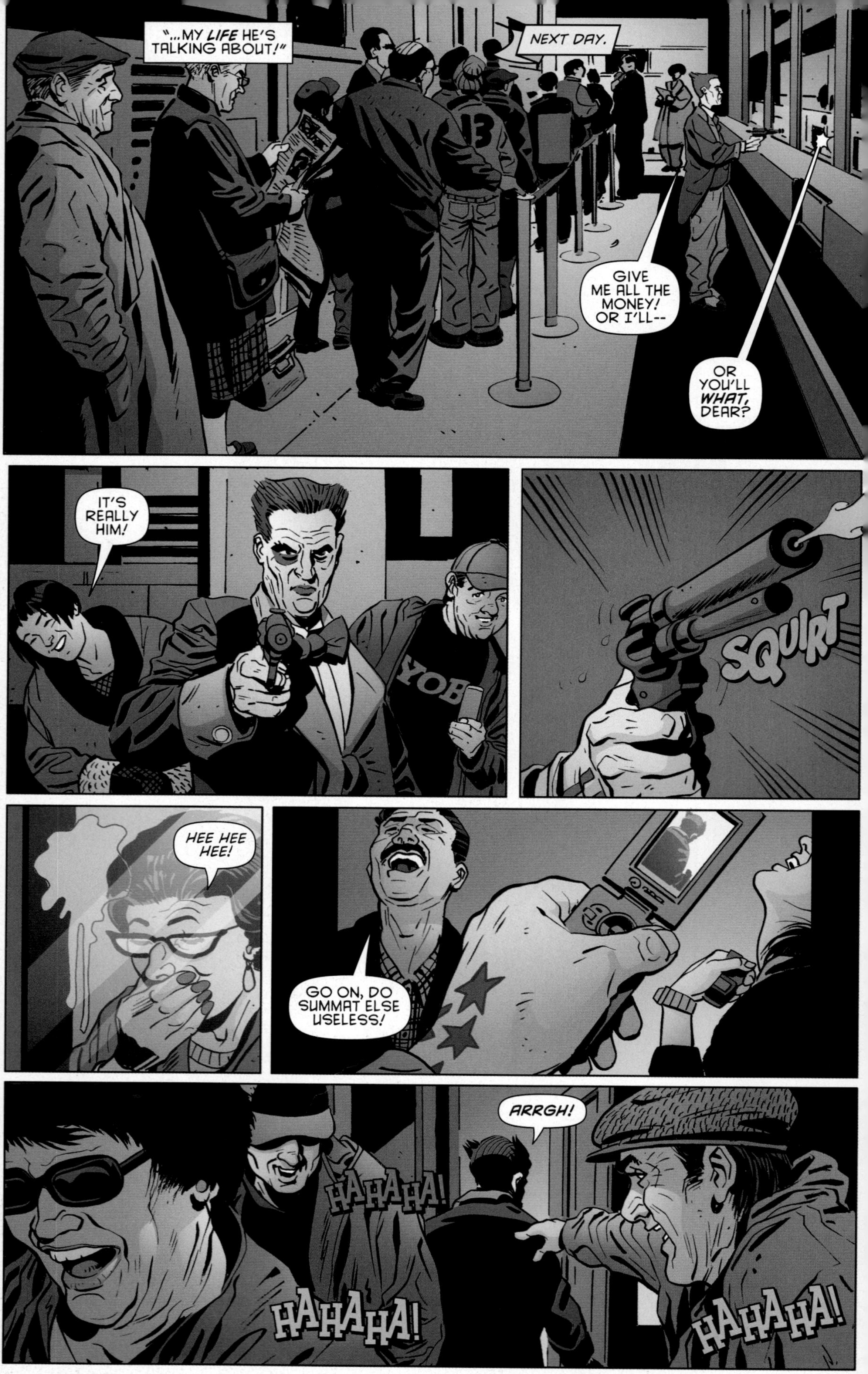
"...MY LIFE HE'S TALKING ABOUT!"
NEXT DAY.
GIVE ME ALL THE MONEY! OR I'LL--
OR YOU'LL WHAT, DEAR?
IT'S REALLY HIM!
YOB
SQUIRT
HEE HEE HEE!
GO ON, DO SUMMAT ELSE USELESS!
ARRGH!
HAHAHA!
HAHAHA!
HAHAHA!

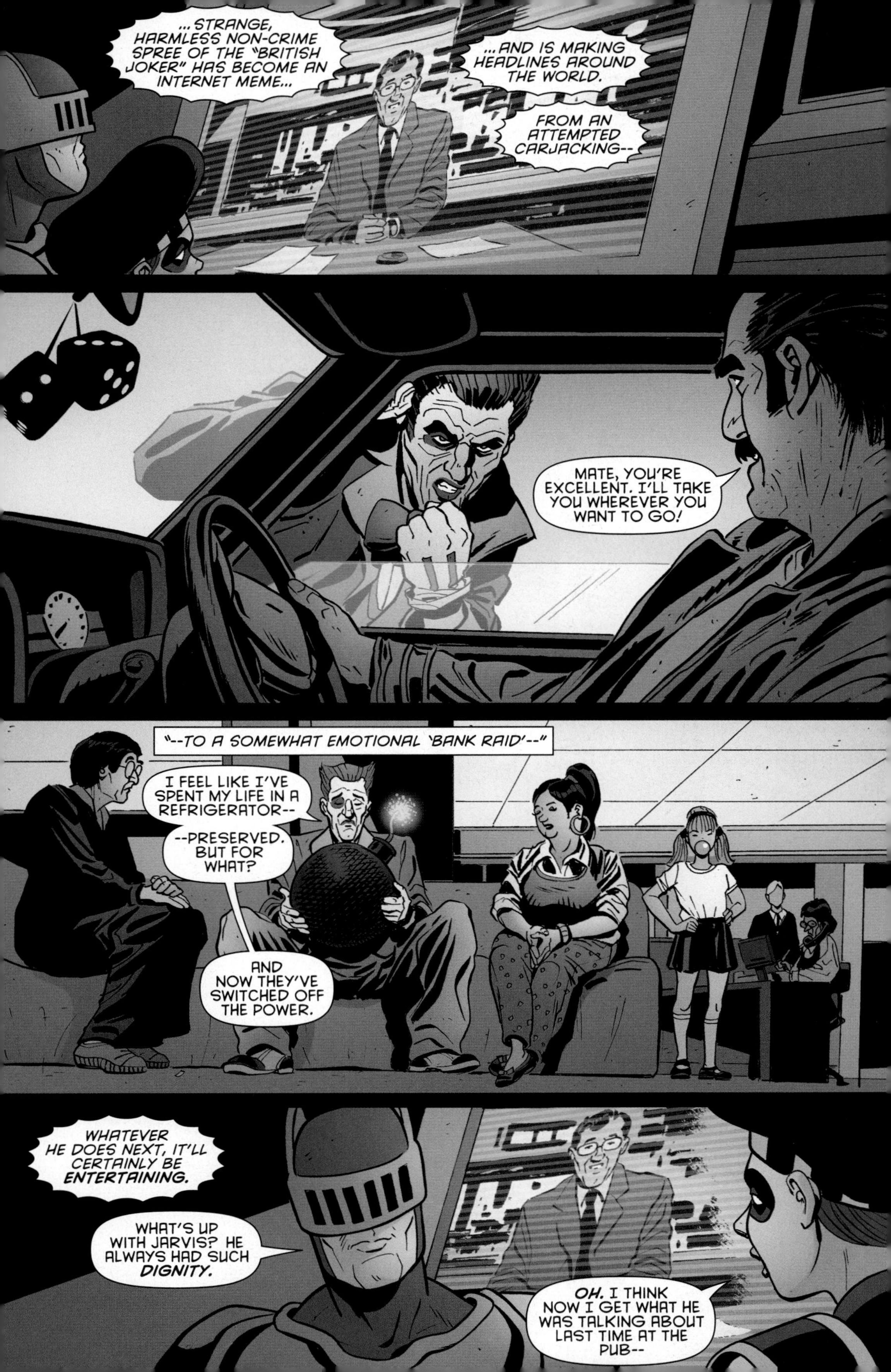
...STRANGE, HARMLESS NON-CRIME SPREE OF THE "BRITISH JOKER" HAS BECOME AN INTERNET MEME...
...AND IS MAKING HEADLINES AROUND THE WORLD.
FROM AN ATTEMPTED CARJACKING--
MATE, YOU'RE EXCELLENT. I'LL TAKE YOU WHEREVER YOU WANT TO GO!
"--TO A SOMEWHAT EMOTIONAL 'BANK RAID'--"
I FEEL LIKE I'VE SPENT MY LIFE IN A REFRIGERATOR--
--PRESERVED. BUT FOR WHAT?
AND NOW THEY'VE SWITCHED OFF THE POWER.
WHATEVER HE DOES NEXT, IT'LL CERTAINLY BE ENTERTAINING.
WHAT'S UP WITH JARVIS? HE ALWAYS HAD SUCH DIGNITY.
OH. I THINK NOW I GET WHAT HE WAS TALKING ABOUT LAST TIME AT THE PUB--

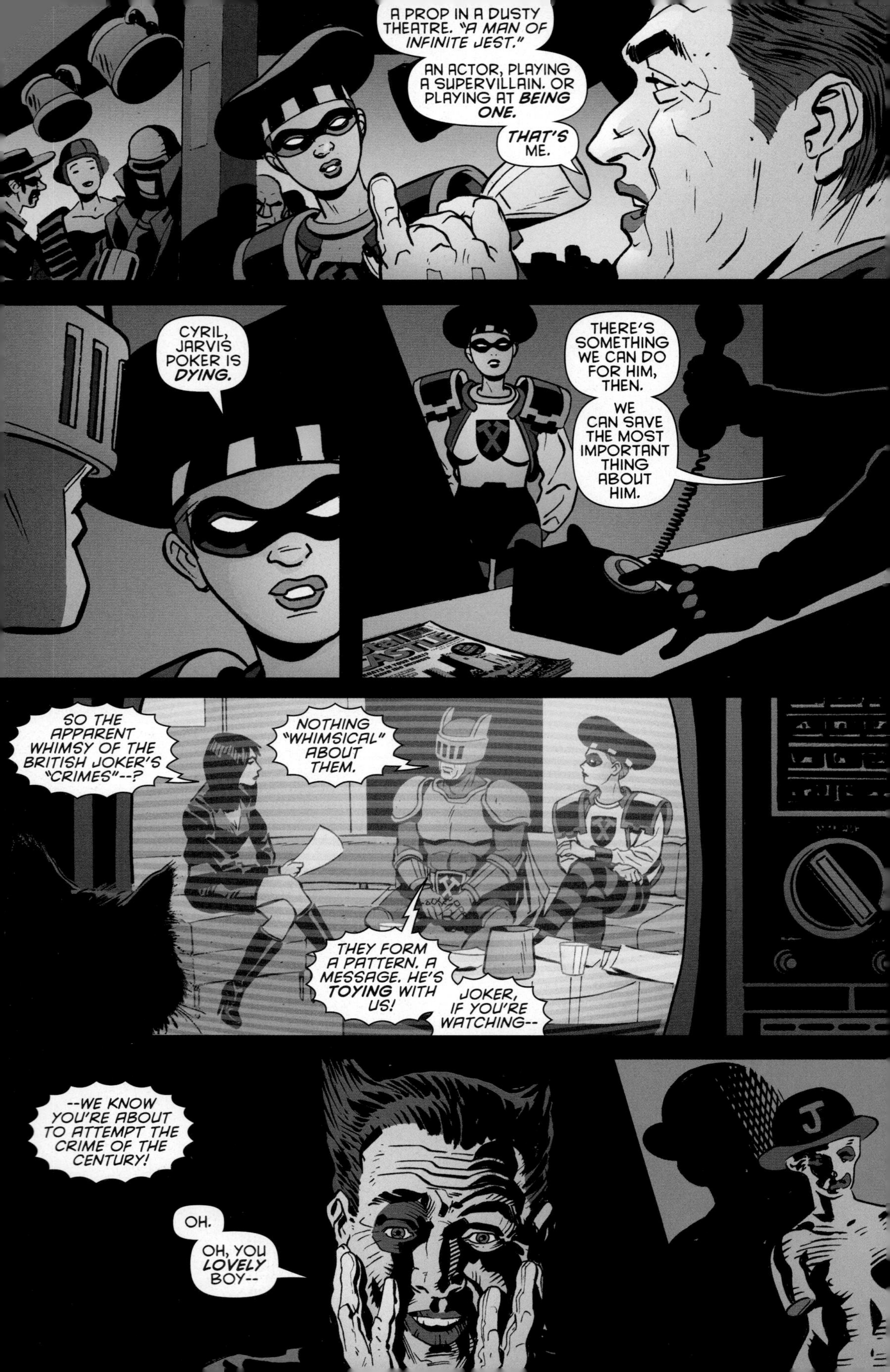
A PROP IN A DUSTY THEATRE. "A MAN OF INFINITE JEST."
AN ACTOR, PLAYING A SUPERVILLAIN. OR PLAYING AT *BEING ONE.*
THAT'S ME.
CYRIL, JARVIS POKER IS *DYING.*
THERE'S SOMETHING WE CAN DO FOR HIM, THEN.
WE CAN SAVE THE MOST IMPORTANT THING ABOUT HIM.
SO THE APPARENT WHIMSY OF THE BRITISH JOKER'S "CRIMES"--?
NOTHING "WHIMSICAL" ABOUT THEM.
THEY FORM A PATTERN. A MESSAGE. HE'S *TOYING* WITH US!
JOKER, IF YOU'RE WATCHING--
--WE KNOW YOU'RE ABOUT TO ATTEMPT THE CRIME OF THE CENTURY!
OH.
OH, YOU *LOVELY* BOY--

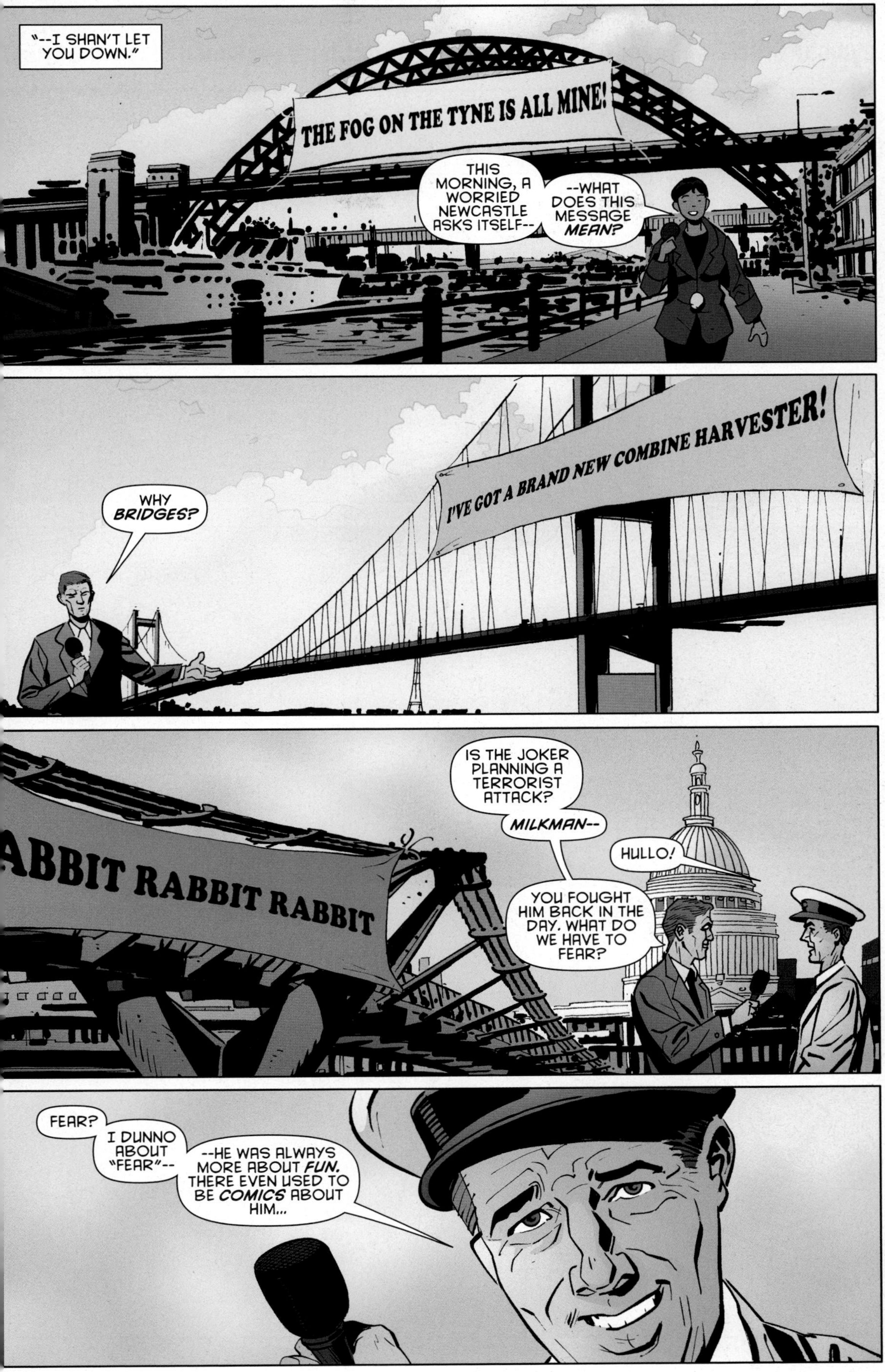
"--I SHAN'T LET YOU DOWN."
THE FOG ON THE TYNE IS ALL MINE!
THIS MORNING, A WORRIED NEWCASTLE ASKS ITSELF--
--WHAT DOES THIS MESSAGE MEAN?
I'VE GOT A BRAND NEW COMBINE HARVESTER!
WHY BRIDGES?
ABBIT RABBIT RABBIT
IS THE JOKER PLANNING A TERRORIST ATTACK?
MILKMAN--
HULLO!
YOU FOUGHT HIM BACK IN THE DAY. WHAT DO WE HAVE TO FEAR?
FEAR?
I DUNNO ABOUT "FEAR"--
--HE WAS ALWAYS MORE ABOUT FUN. THERE EVEN USED TO BE COMICS ABOUT HIM...

'Seymour Stuffins thought he'd struck gold... but he'd reckoned without Jarvis!

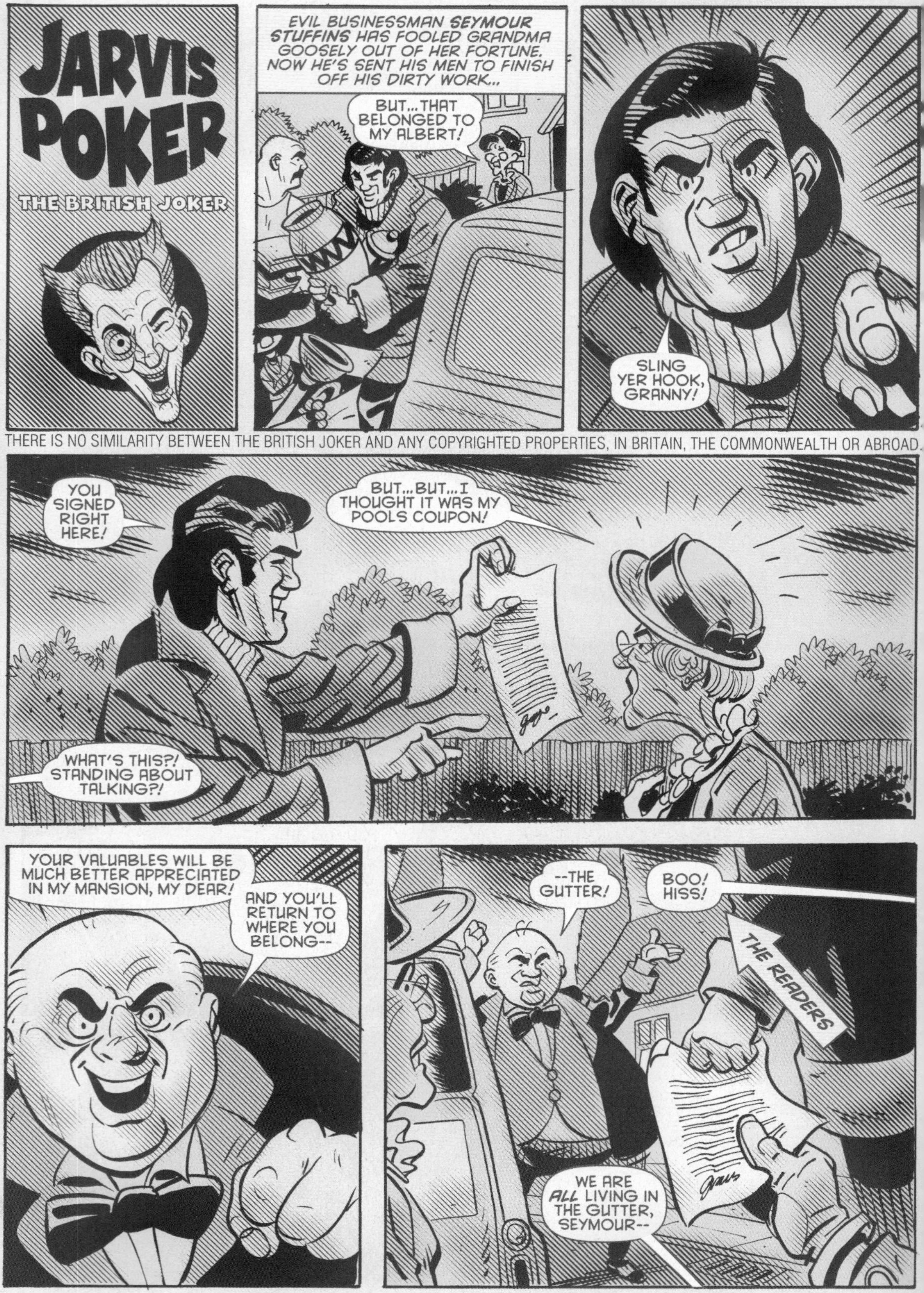
JARVIS POKER
THE BRITISH JOKER
EVIL BUSINESSMAN SEYMOUR STUFFINS HAS FOOLED GRANDMA GOOSELY OUT OF HER FORTUNE. NOW HE'S SENT HIS MEN TO FINISH OFF HIS DIRTY WORK...
BUT...THAT BELONGED TO MY ALBERT!
SLING YER HOOK, GRANNY!
THERE IS NO SIMILARITY BETWEEN THE BRITISH JOKER AND ANY COPYRIGHTED PROPERTIES, IN BRITAIN, THE COMMONWEALTH OR ABROAD.
YOU SIGNED RIGHT HERE!
BUT...BUT...I THOUGHT IT WAS MY POOLS COUPON!
WHAT'S THIS?! STANDING ABOUT TALKING?!
YOUR VALUABLES WILL BE MUCH BETTER APPRECIATED IN MY MANSION, MY DEAR!
AND YOU'LL RETURN TO WHERE YOU BELONG--
--THE GUTTER!
BOO! HISS!
THE READERS
WE ARE ALL LIVING IN THE GUTTER, SEYMOUR--

'Jarvis knows a thing or two about the law – he's broken it often enough!'

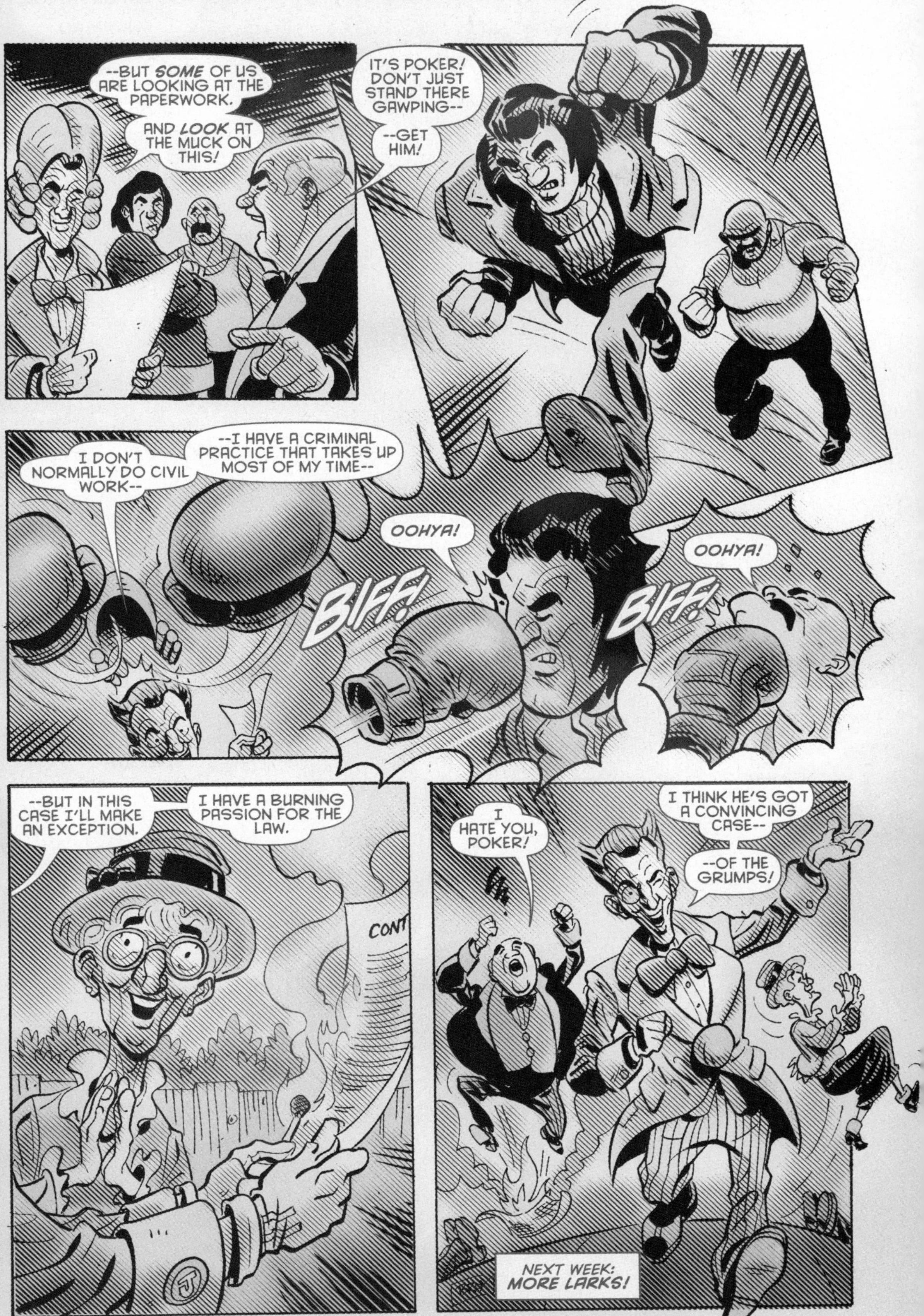
--BUT SOME OF US ARE LOOKING AT THE PAPERWORK.
AND LOOK AT THE MUCK ON THIS!
IT'S POKER! DON'T JUST STAND THERE GAWPING--
--GET HIM!
I DON'T NORMALLY DO CIVIL WORK--
--I HAVE A CRIMINAL PRACTICE THAT TAKES UP MOST OF MY TIME--
OOHYA!
BIFF!
OOHYA!
BIFF!
--BUT IN THIS CASE I'LL MAKE AN EXCEPTION.
I HAVE A BURNING PASSION FOR THE LAW.
CONT
I HATE YOU, POKER!
I THINK HE'S GOT A CONVINCING CASE--
--OF THE GRUMPS!
NEXT WEEK: MORE LARKS!

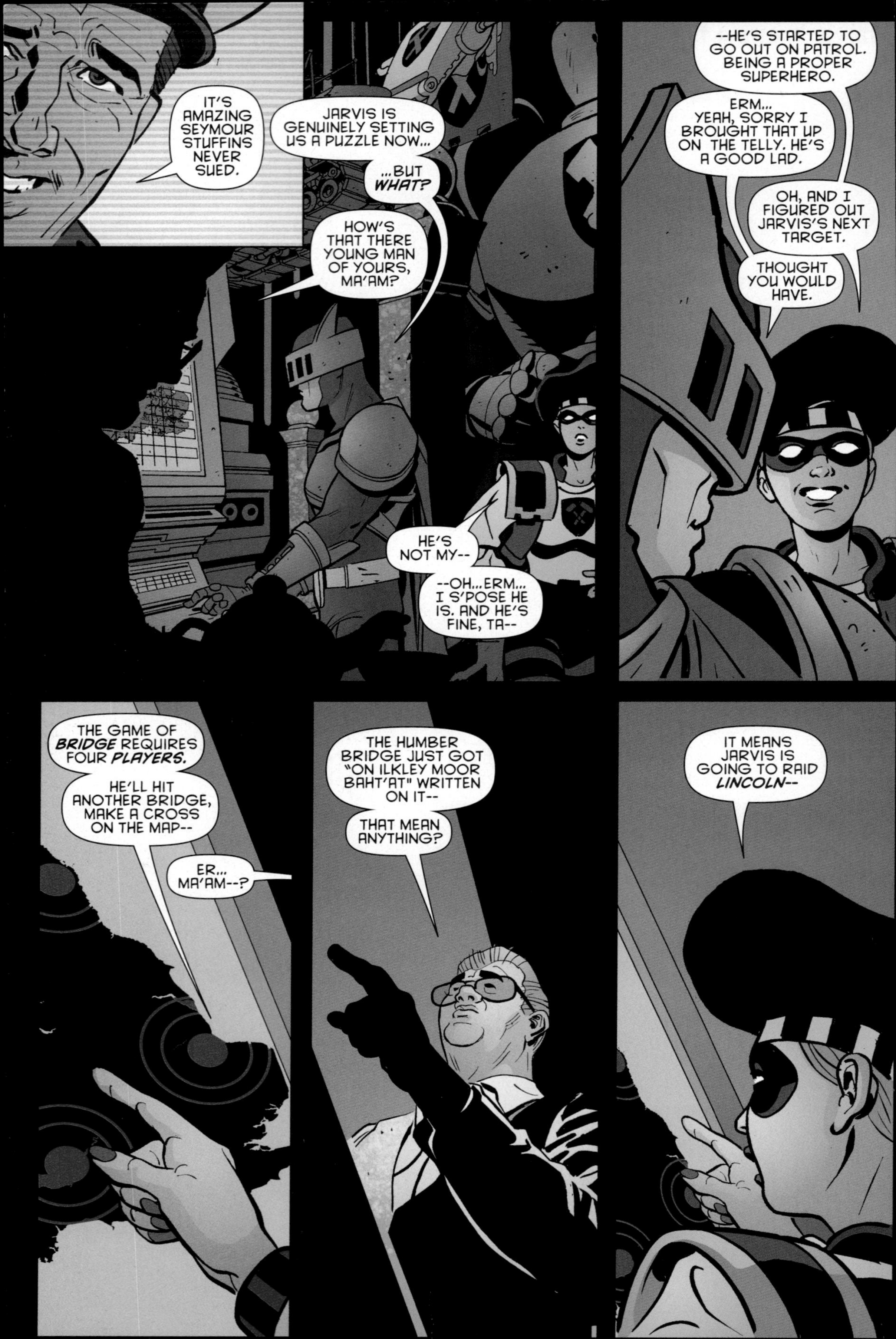
IT'S AMAZING SEYMOUR STUFFINS NEVER SUED.
JARVIS IS GENUINELY SETTING US A PUZZLE NOW...
...BUT WHAT?
HOW'S THAT THERE YOUNG MAN OF YOURS, MA'AM?
HE'S NOT MY--
--OH...ERM... I S'POSE HE IS. AND HE'S FINE, TA--
--HE'S STARTED TO GO OUT ON PATROL. BEING A PROPER SUPERHERO.
ERM... YEAH, SORRY I BROUGHT THAT UP ON THE TELLY. HE'S A GOOD LAD.
OH, AND I FIGURED OUT JARVIS'S NEXT TARGET.
THOUGHT YOU WOULD HAVE.
THE GAME OF BRIDGE REQUIRES FOUR PLAYERS.
HE'LL HIT ANOTHER BRIDGE, MAKE A CROSS ON THE MAP--
ER... MA'AM--?
THE HUMBER BRIDGE JUST GOT "ON ILKLEY MOOR BAHT'AT" WRITTEN ON IT--
THAT MEAN ANYTHING?
IT MEANS JARVIS IS GOING TO RAID LINCOLN--

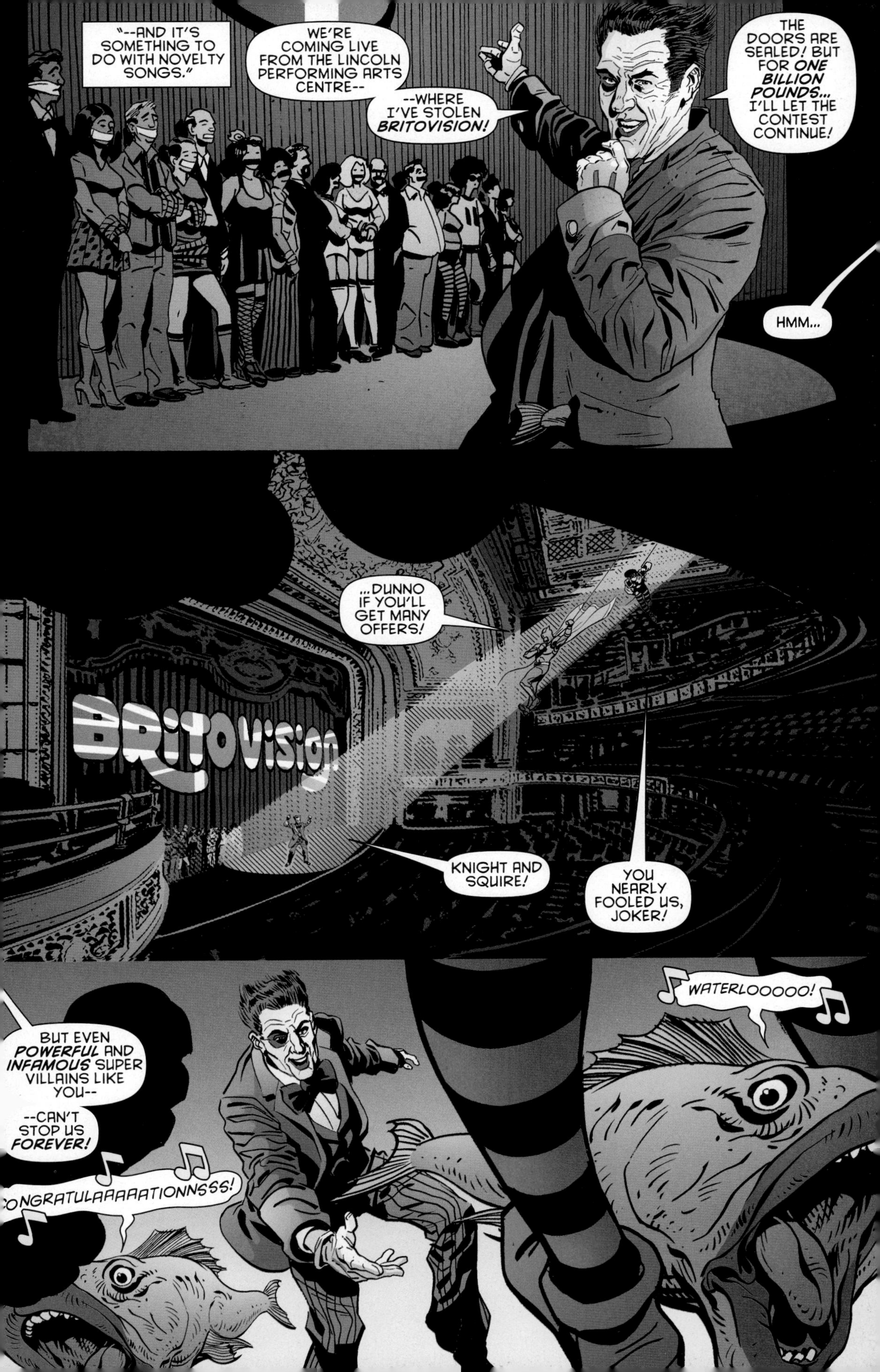

"--AND IT'S SOMETHING TO DO WITH NOVELTY SONGS."
WE'RE COMING LIVE FROM THE LINCOLN PERFORMING ARTS CENTRE--
--WHERE I'VE STOLEN *BRITOVISION!*
THE DOORS ARE SEALED! BUT FOR *ONE BILLION POUNDS...* I'LL LET THE CONTEST CONTINUE!
HMM...
...DUNNO IF YOU'LL GET MANY OFFERS!
BRITOVISION
KNIGHT AND SQUIRE!
YOU NEARLY FOOLED US, JOKER!
BUT EVEN *POWERFUL* AND *INFAMOUS* SUPER VILLAINS LIKE YOU--
--CAN'T STOP US *FOREVER!*
CONGRATULAAAAATIONNSSS!
WATERLOOOOO!

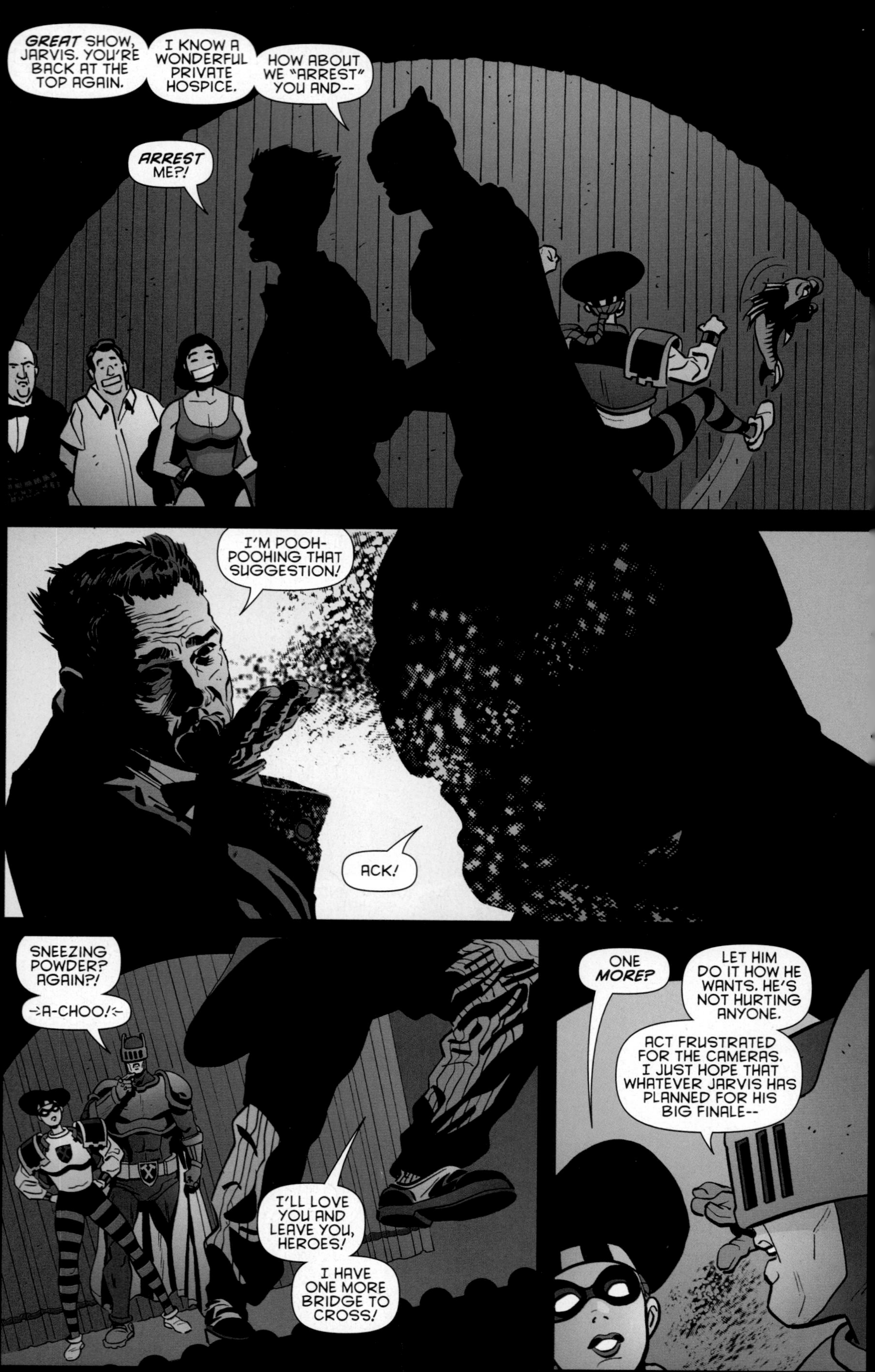
GREAT SHOW, JARVIS. YOU'RE BACK AT THE TOP AGAIN.
I KNOW A WONDERFUL PRIVATE HOSPICE.
HOW ABOUT WE "ARREST" YOU AND--
ARREST ME?!
I'M POOH-POOHING THAT SUGGESTION!
ACK!
SNEEZING POWDER? AGAIN?!
A-CHOO!
I'LL LOVE YOU AND LEAVE YOU, HEROES!
I HAVE ONE MORE BRIDGE TO CROSS!
ONE MORE?
LET HIM DO IT HOW HE WANTS. HE'S NOT HURTING ANYONE.
ACT FRUSTRATED FOR THE CAMERAS. I JUST HOPE THAT WHATEVER JARVIS HAS PLANNED FOR HIS BIG FINALE--

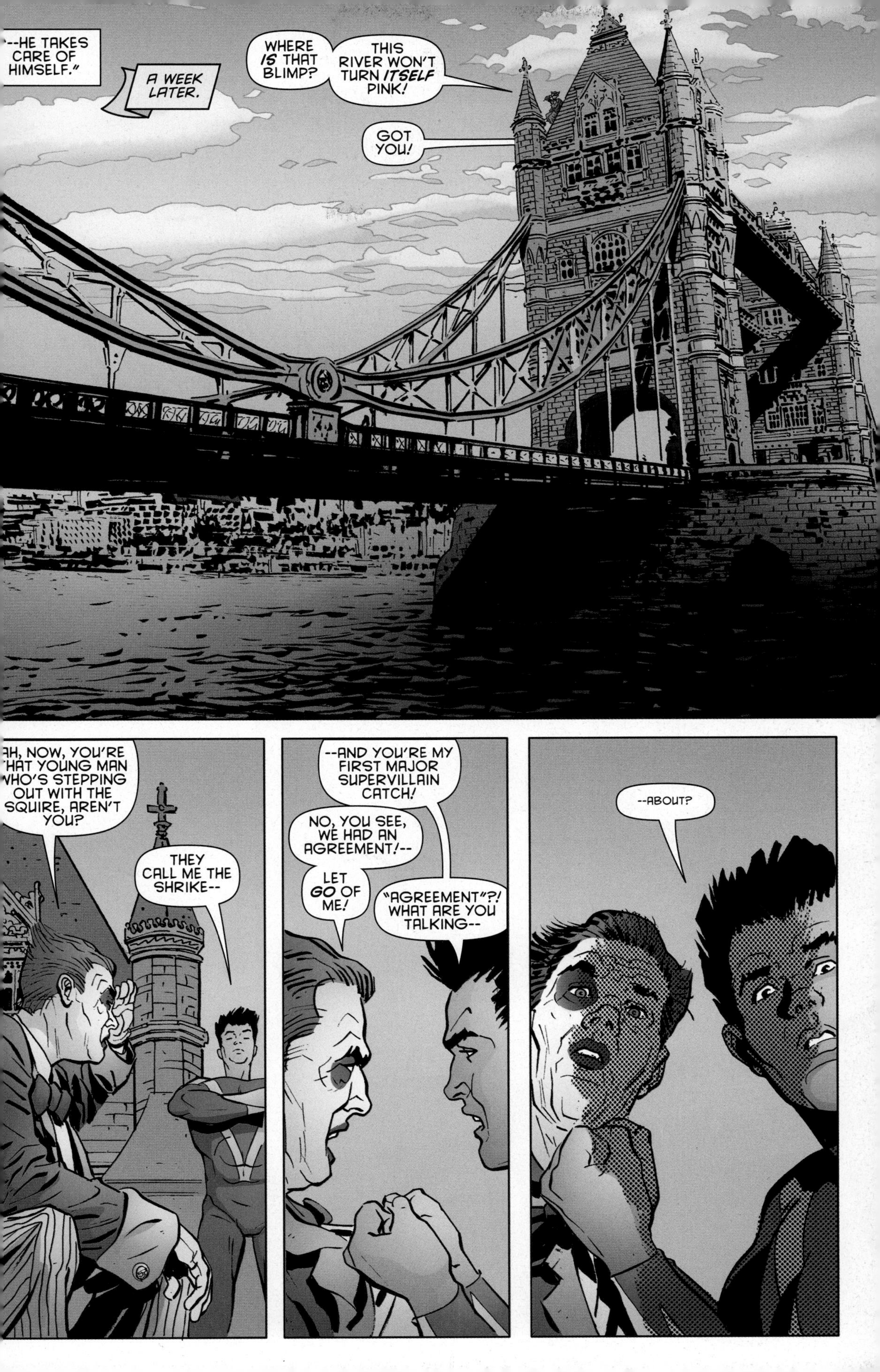
--HE TAKES CARE OF HIMSELF."
A WEEK LATER.
WHERE *IS* THAT BLIMP?
THIS RIVER WON'T TURN *ITSELF* PINK!
GOT YOU!
AH, NOW, YOU'RE THAT YOUNG MAN WHO'S STEPPING OUT WITH THE SQUIRE, AREN'T YOU?
THEY CALL ME THE SHRIKE--
--AND YOU'RE MY FIRST MAJOR SUPERVILLAIN CATCH!
NO, YOU SEE, WE HAD AN AGREEMENT!--
LET *GO* OF ME!
"AGREEMENT"?! WHAT ARE YOU TALKING--
--ABOUT?

BLAM!

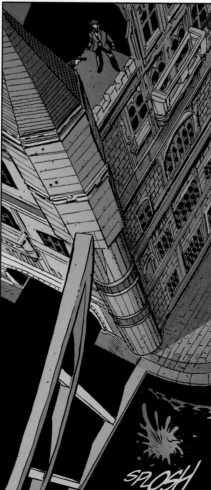

SPLOSH

IT'S...
IT'S...

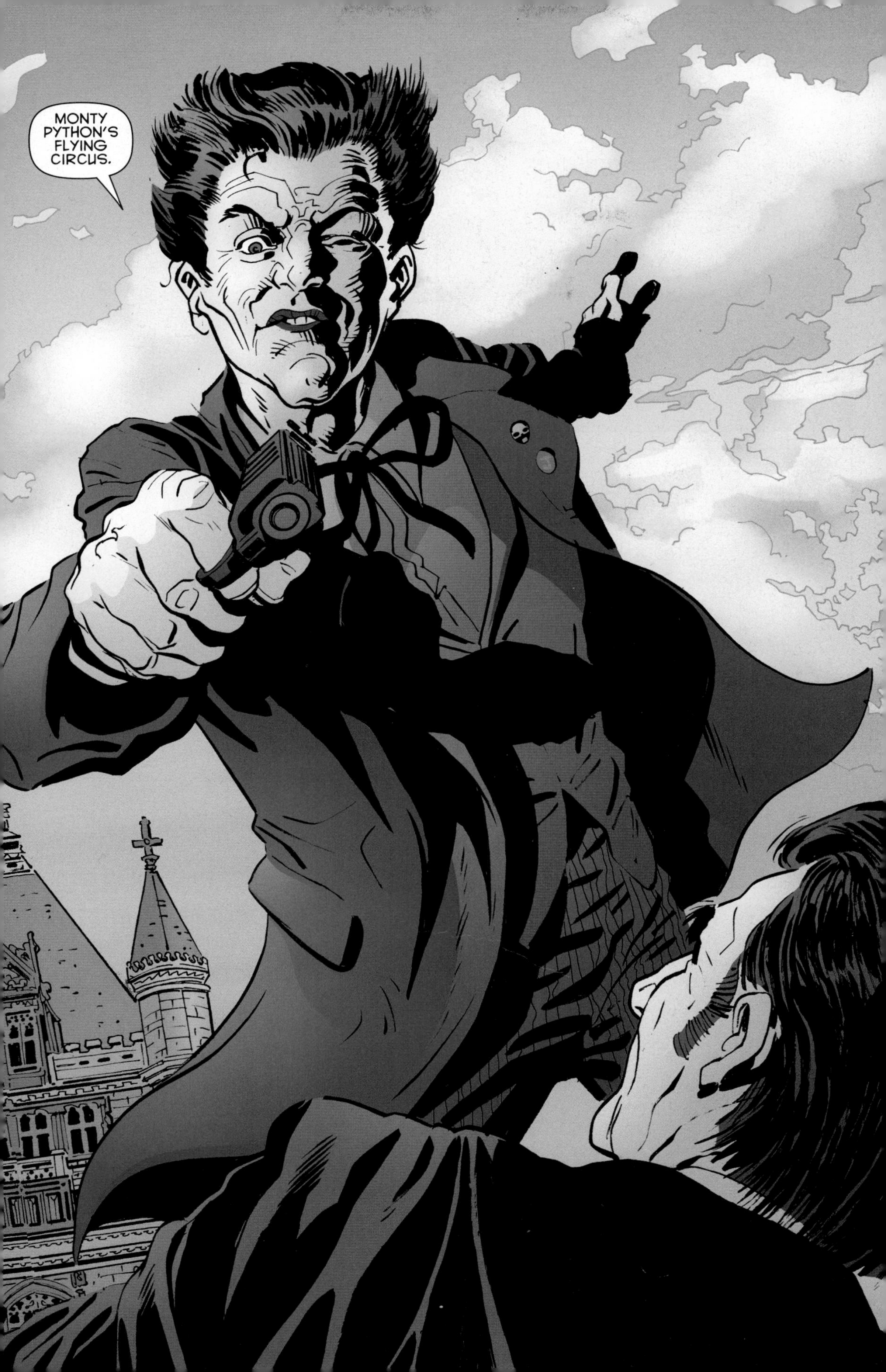
MONTY PYTHON'S FLYING CIRCUS.

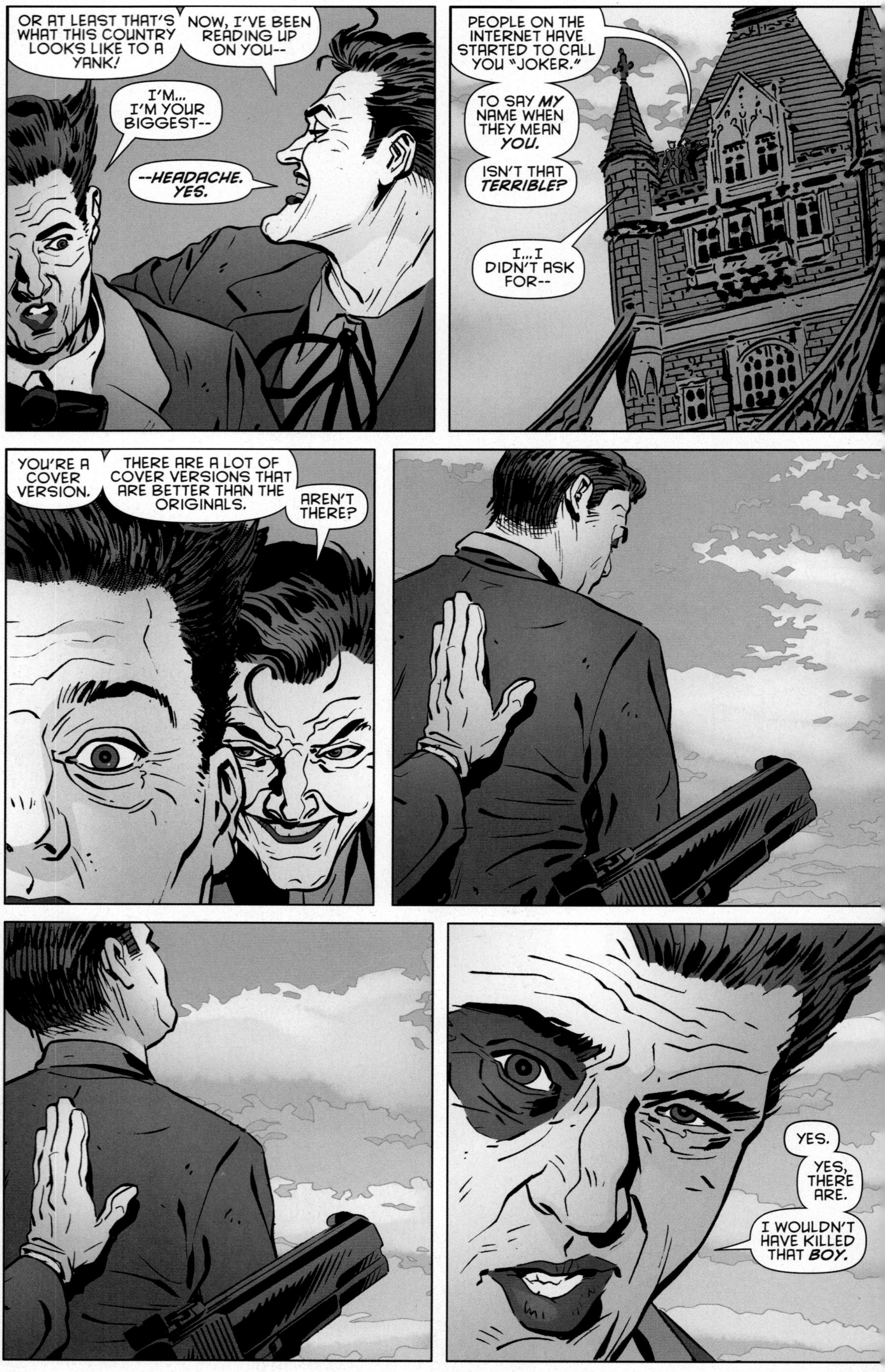
OR AT LEAST THAT'S WHAT THIS COUNTRY LOOKS LIKE TO A YANK!
NOW, I'VE BEEN READING UP ON YOU--
I'M... I'M YOUR BIGGEST--
--HEADACHE. YES.
PEOPLE ON THE INTERNET HAVE STARTED TO CALL YOU "JOKER."
TO SAY MY NAME WHEN THEY MEAN YOU.
ISN'T THAT TERRIBLE?
I...I DIDN'T ASK FOR--
YOU'RE A COVER VERSION.
THERE ARE A LOT OF COVER VERSIONS THAT ARE BETTER THAN THE ORIGINALS.
AREN'T THERE?
YES.
YES, THERE ARE.
I WOULDN'T HAVE KILLED THAT BOY.

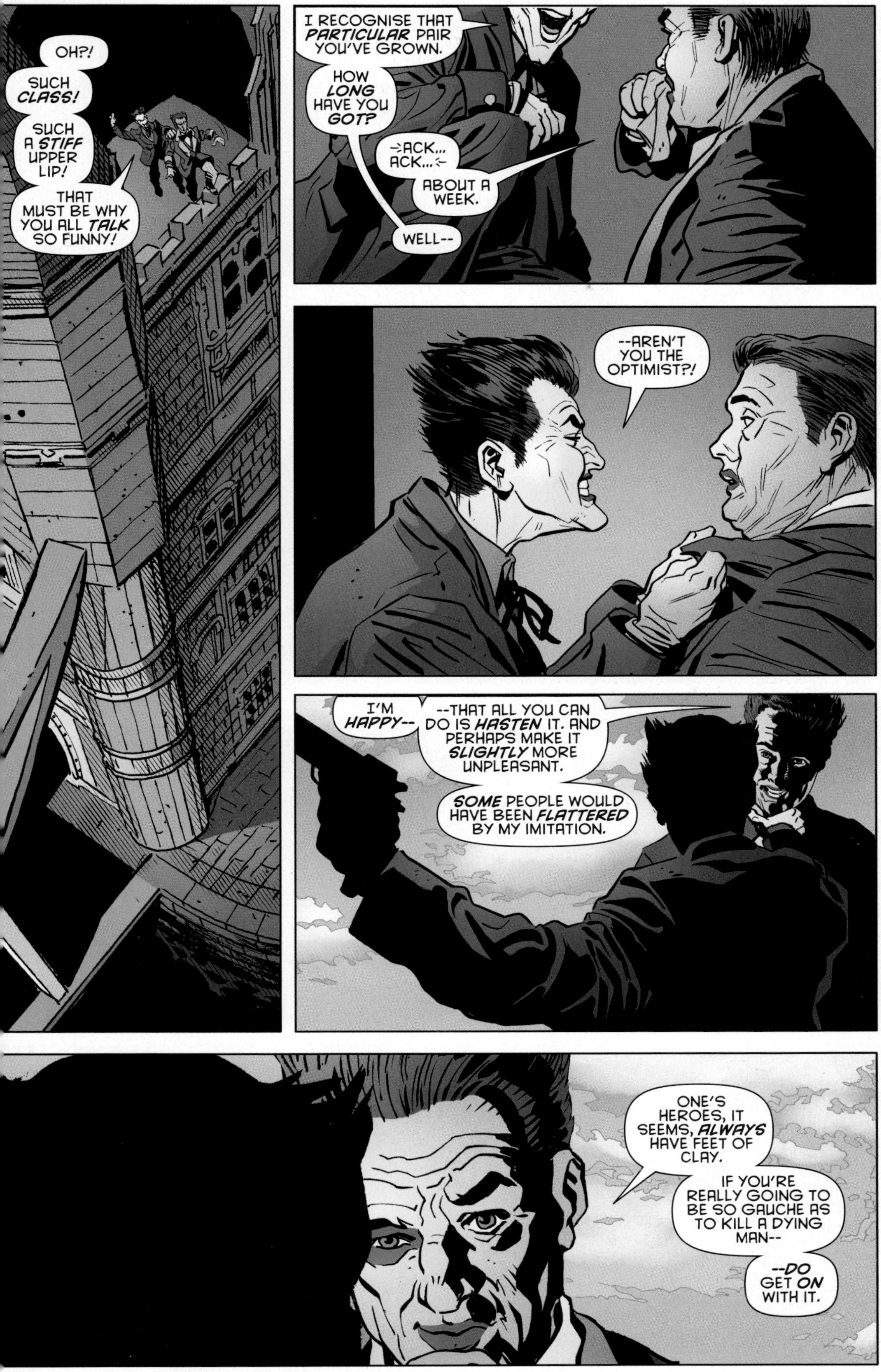
OH?!
SUCH CLASS!
SUCH A STIFF UPPER LIP!
THAT MUST BE WHY YOU ALL TALK SO FUNNY!
I RECOGNISE THAT PARTICULAR PAIR YOU'VE GROWN.
HOW LONG HAVE YOU GOT?
ACK... ACK...
ABOUT A WEEK.
WELL--
--AREN'T YOU THE OPTIMIST?!
I'M HAPPY--
--THAT ALL YOU CAN DO IS HASTEN IT. AND PERHAPS MAKE IT SLIGHTLY MORE UNPLEASANT.
SOME PEOPLE WOULD HAVE BEEN FLATTERED BY MY IMITATION.
ONE'S HEROES, IT SEEMS, ALWAYS HAVE FEET OF CLAY.
IF YOU'RE REALLY GOING TO BE SO GAUCHE AS TO KILL A DYING MAN--
--DO GET ON WITH IT.

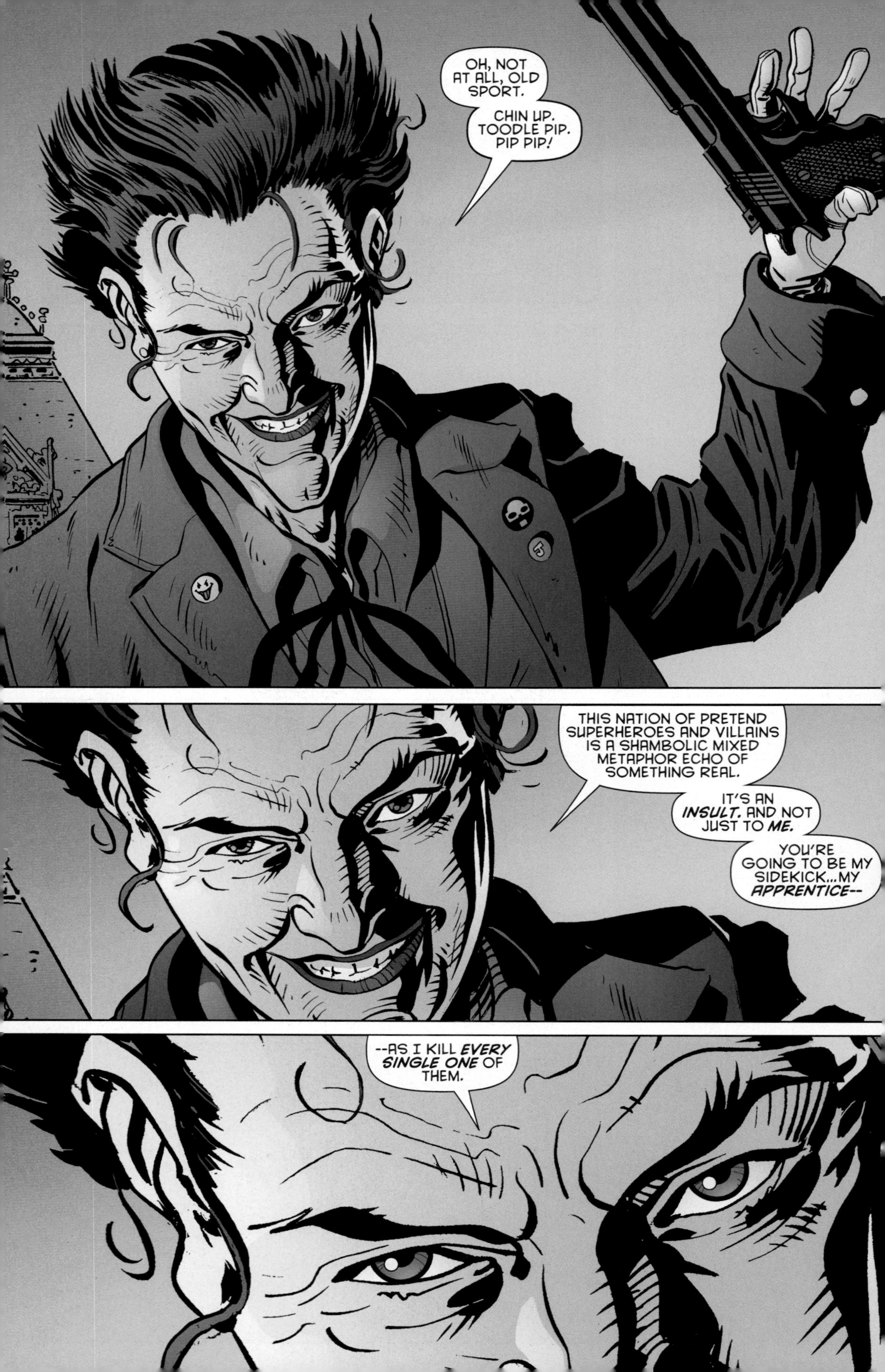
OH, NOT AT ALL, OLD SPORT.
CHIN UP. TOODLE PIP. PIP PIP!
THIS NATION OF PRETEND SUPERHEROES AND VILLAINS IS A SHAMBOLIC MIXED METAPHOR ECHO OF SOMETHING REAL.
IT'S AN INSULT. AND NOT JUST TO ME.
YOU'RE GOING TO BE MY SIDEKICK...MY APPRENTICE--
--AS I KILL EVERY SINGLE ONE OF THEM.

The Knight and Squire Character List (Part One)

OKAY, WE HAVE TO LEAVE ASIDE THE BUSINESS OF SINGING FISH AND ODD THINGS WRITTEN ON BRIDGES (LOOK UP BRITISH NOVELTY SONGS ONLINE), SO WE CAN PROVIDE A MASTER LIST OF ALL THE CHARACTERS JAMES AND I CREATED FOR THIS SERIES! STARTING WITH JUST THOSE FROM ISSUE ONE!

PAGE 1: ENTERING THE PUB: HAMMER AND TONGS.

PAGE 2: TO THE LEFT OF THE SHRIKE, WHO'S TALKING TO SALT OF THE EARTH AND THE MILKMAN, ARE THE DISTINGUISHED GENTLEMAN (IN TOP HAT), TO HIS RIGHT SPACE CADET (THE GIRL), AND NEXT TO HER THE HAPLESS FORMER WELDER (IN MASK), OXYMORON. FURTHER ALONG THE BAR (WITH AN "O" ON HIS HEAD) IS THE ZERO.

PAGE 3: JARVIS POKER, THE BRITISH JOKER. AND THAT'S OUR FIRST SIGHTING OF THE THREE RUSH HOURS.

PAGE 4: IN PANEL TWO (IN LEOPARD PRINT BRIEFS) LADY VOODOO, AND IN PANEL FIVE (WITH SPIKES AND MACE) THE SETTLER NO.1.

PAGE 5: YOU'RE INTRODUCED TO COALFACE, THE PROFESSIONAL SCOTSMAN, THE BLACK AND WHITE MINSTRELS, TWO TON TED FROM TEDDINGTON AND THE FIRST ELEVEN. IN PANEL THREE (IN THE FOREGROUND WITH POUND SIGN) IS STERLING SILVER.

PAGE 6: CAPTAIN CORNWALL, CORNWALL BOY, DOUBLE ENTENDRE AND FACEOFF. IN PANEL ONE, BEHIND THE RUSH HOURS, ARE PHARAOHS 1 AND 2. AND IN PANEL FIVE, BEHIND FACEOFF, THERE'S THE CHOREOGRAPHER.

PAGE 7: IN PANEL ONE, ABOVE THE SQUIRE'S HAND, THERE'S DEATH CAP AND DRAMA KING. TO THE SHRIKE'S RIGHT IS THE FRO, TO HIS LEFT, THE COUPLE ARE THE GUARDIAN ANGELS (OLD HIPPY TYPES). PLUS CAPTAIN MOONDUST, THE PIRATE ASTRONOMERS, STONE COLD LUKE, DEATH DINOSAUR, BLIND FURY AND THE DARK DRUID.

PAGE 8: IN THE FOREGROUND OF PANEL THREE IS SENIOR CITIZEN. NEXT TO WILDCAT ARE LADY NIGHTINGALE AND SUPER ANNUATOR. BEHIND THE SEAT ARE SETTLER NO. 2 AND (IN ANCIENT EGYPTIAN GEAR) MR. IBIS.

PAGE 9: IN PANEL THREE, BETWEEN WILDCAT AND SHRIKE, IS ORANGE MEDAL. IN PANEL FOUR, NEXT TO CAPTAIN CORNWALL, IN WELDING MASK IS THE MECHANIC, AND NEXT TO HIM (WITH POINTY EARS): COFFIN DWELLER AND THE NAKED WOMAN, BIRTHDAY GIRL.

PAGE 10: IN PANEL TWO, MEET MING DYNASTY WITH THE MANDARIN TWINS, AND ACROSS THE TABLE BIG GAME HUNTER MAJOR HUBERT, STRONGMAN MR GRANITE AND CAVALRY-MAN. IN PANEL THREE WE HAVE BRITISH BULLDOG, THE BLACK COMMANDO AND NEAR MISS, AND IN THE DIVING HELMET, CAPTAIN JAQUES. IN THE BACKGROUND ARE TIN-BIB AND TOXIC TUCKER.

PAGE 11: THE LITTLE GIRL IN PANEL ONE IS THE ONLY CHILD PLUS STRONGMAN MIGHTY MORRIS AND THE FABULOUS BOATER MAN. IN PANEL TWO THAT'S SIXTIES ICONS THE ARRANGERS, AND IN PANEL THREE, MEET THE RATTLES.

PAGE 13: PANEL THREE, BELOW RUSH HOUR'S ARM, THAT'S ILL-INFORMED WHITE GUY, THE YELLOW PERIL AND SETTLER NO. 3.

PAGE 17: IN PANEL TWO, THERE'S SETTLER NO. 4, PLUS, WITH THE FRO AND THE MASK, MOMMA CUSS.

PAGE 19: HOLDING THE GIRL BY THE THROAT, THAT'S SETTLER NO. 5.

WE MAKE THAT **88 NEW CHARACTERS!** A NEW RECORD?

UNTIL NEXT ISSUE, CHEERIO!
– PAUL CORNELL

brought to you by

by Jimmy Broxton   design by SWANDS

THE STEADFAST PICTURE PAPER FOR BOYS!

DREADNAUGHT 7d

EVERY WEDNESDAY   24th MARCH, 1969

IRON MITTEN

BEWARE HIS EVIL GRASP!

INSIDE: Jarvis saves the day!

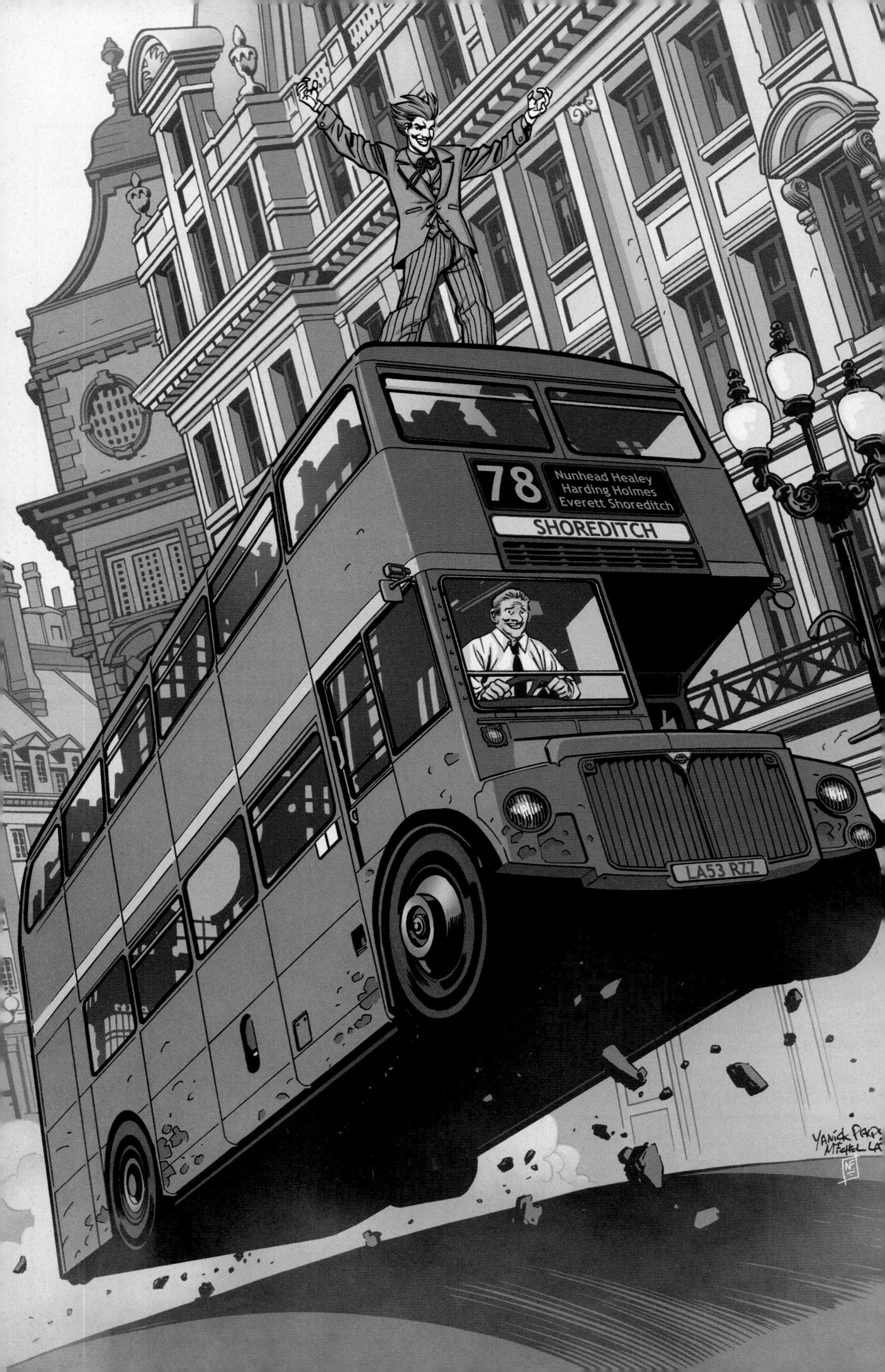
78
Nunhead Healey
Harding Holmes
Everett Shoreditch
SHOREDITCH
LA53 RZZ

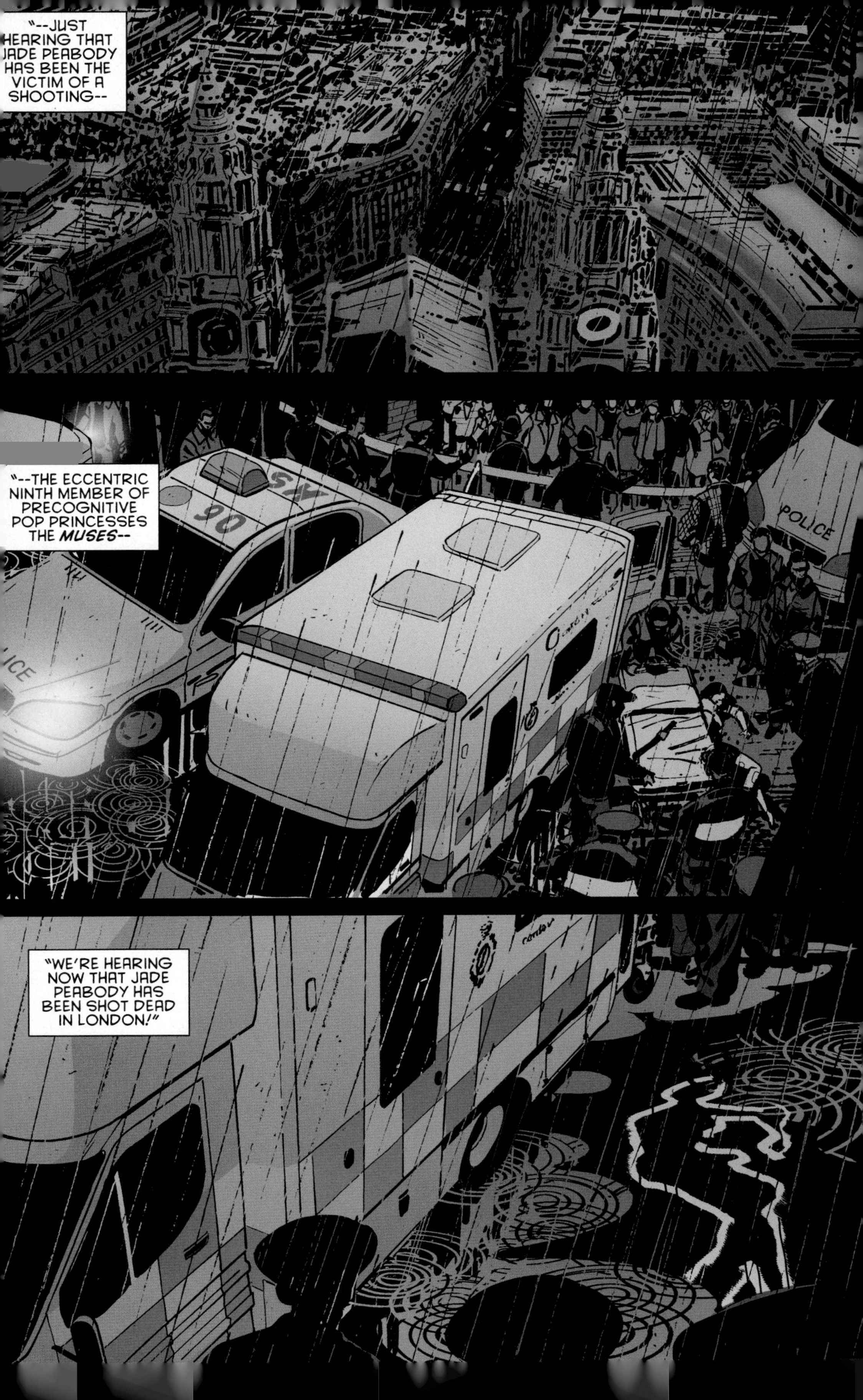
"--JUST HEARING THAT JADE PEABODY HAS BEEN THE VICTIM OF A SHOOTING--
"--THE ECCENTRIC NINTH MEMBER OF PRECOGNITIVE POP PRINCESSES THE *MUSES*--
POLICE
"WE'RE HEARING NOW THAT JADE PEABODY HAS BEEN SHOT DEAD IN LONDON!"

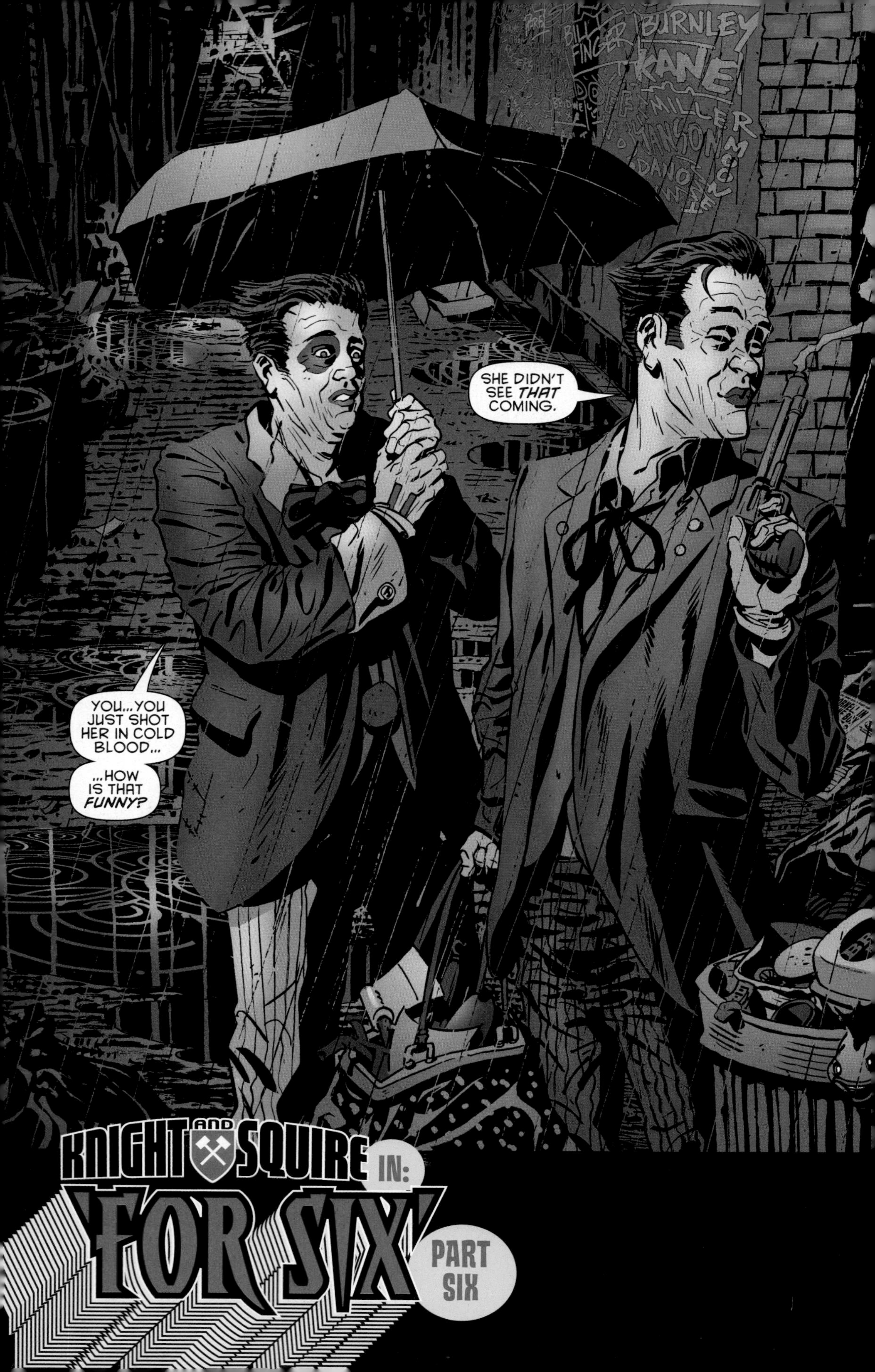

SHE DIDN'T SEE *THAT* COMING.
YOU...YOU JUST SHOT HER IN COLD BLOOD...
...HOW IS THAT *FUNNY?*
KNIGHT AND SQUIRE IN:
'FOR SIX'
PART SIX

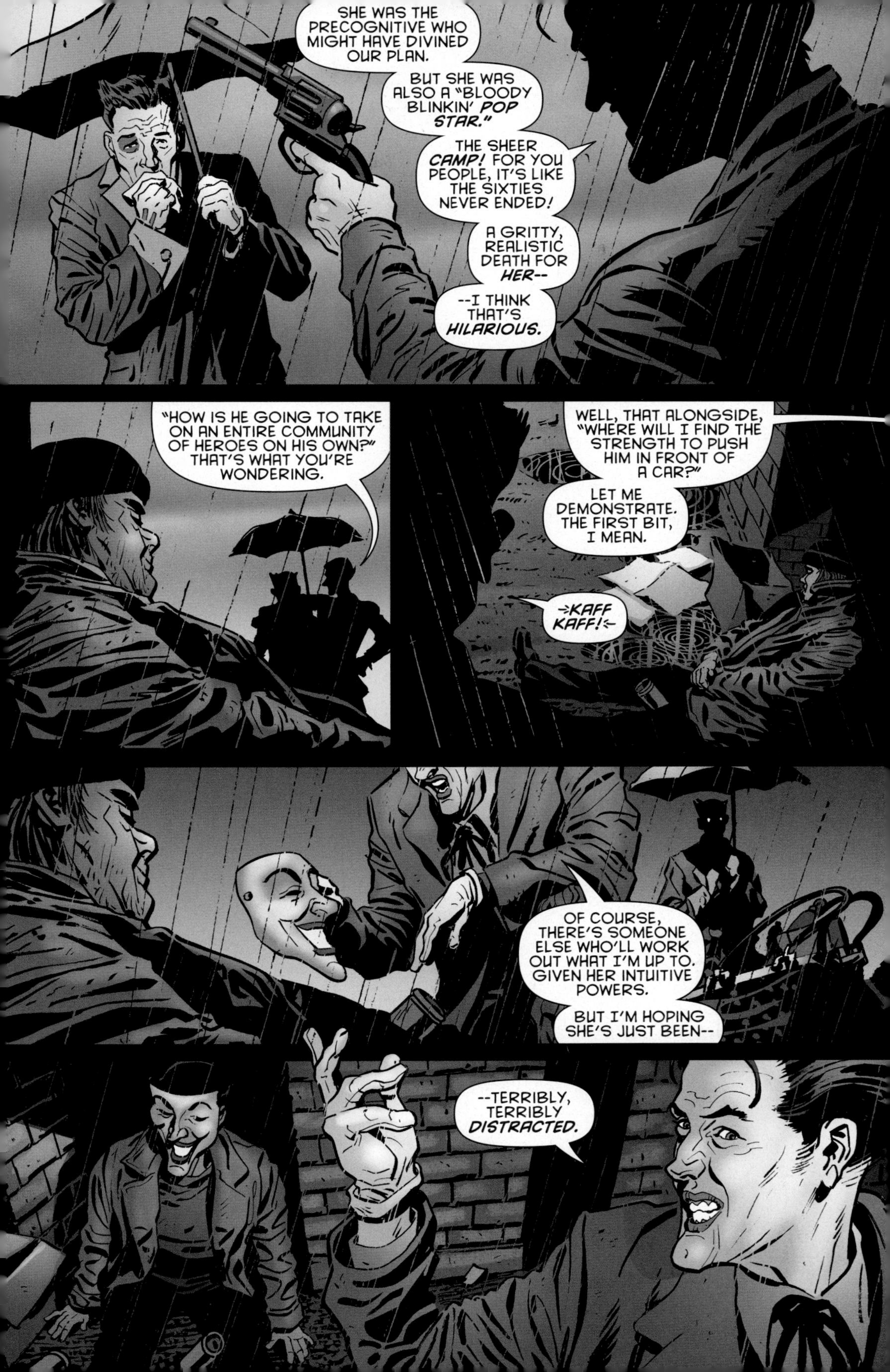
SHE WAS THE PRECOGNITIVE WHO MIGHT HAVE DIVINED OUR PLAN.
BUT SHE WAS ALSO A "BLOODY BLINKIN' POP STAR."
THE SHEER CAMP! FOR YOU PEOPLE, IT'S LIKE THE SIXTIES NEVER ENDED!
A GRITTY, REALISTIC DEATH FOR HER--
--I THINK THAT'S HILARIOUS.
"HOW IS HE GOING TO TAKE ON AN ENTIRE COMMUNITY OF HEROES ON HIS OWN?" THAT'S WHAT YOU'RE WONDERING.
WELL, THAT ALONGSIDE, "WHERE WILL I FIND THE STRENGTH TO PUSH HIM IN FRONT OF A CAR?"
LET ME DEMONSTRATE. THE FIRST BIT, I MEAN.
KAFF KAFF!
OF COURSE, THERE'S SOMEONE ELSE WHO'LL WORK OUT WHAT I'M UP TO. GIVEN HER INTUITIVE POWERS.
BUT I'M HOPING SHE'S JUST BEEN--
--TERRIBLY, TERRIBLY DISTRACTED.

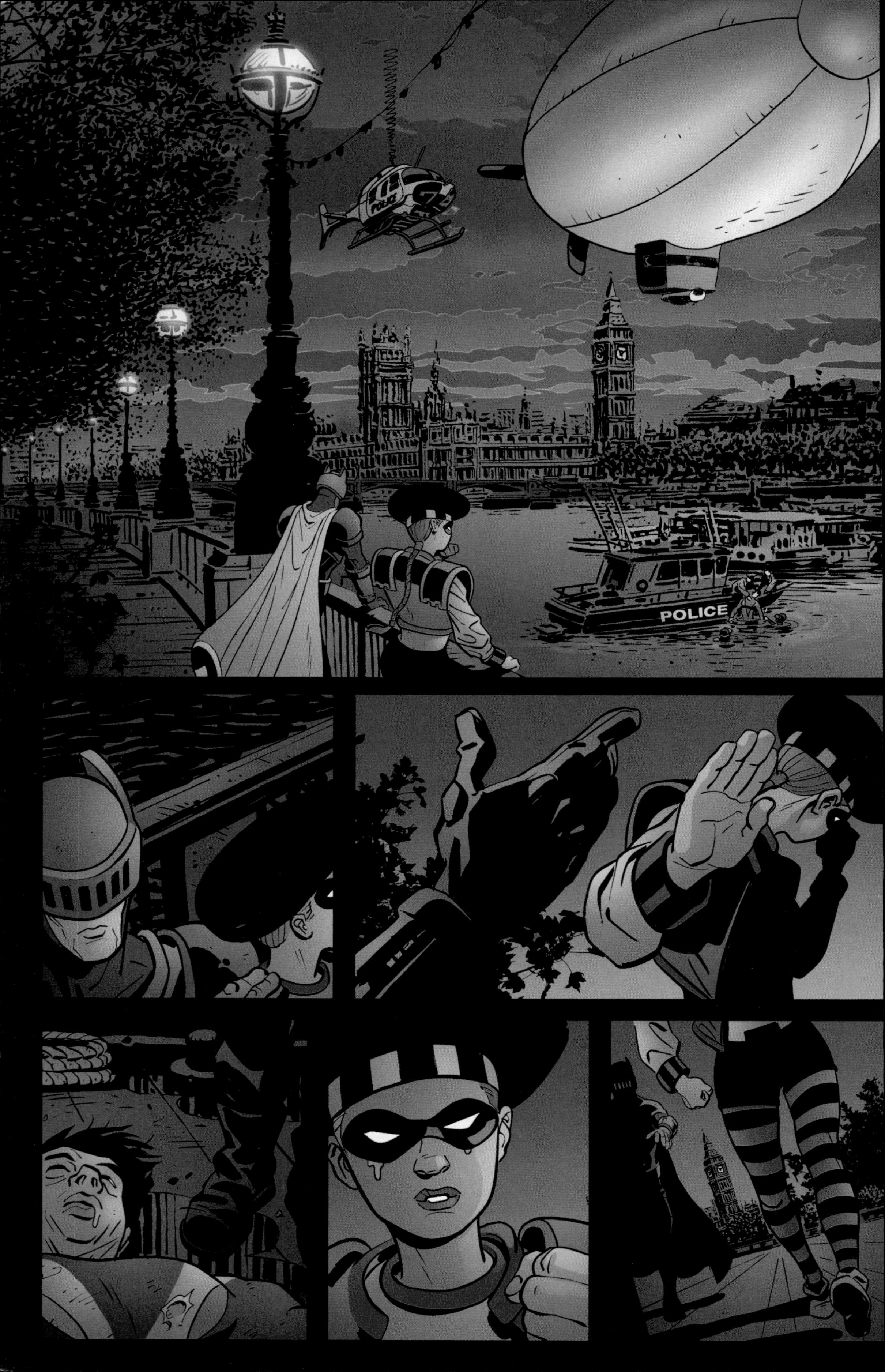
POLICE

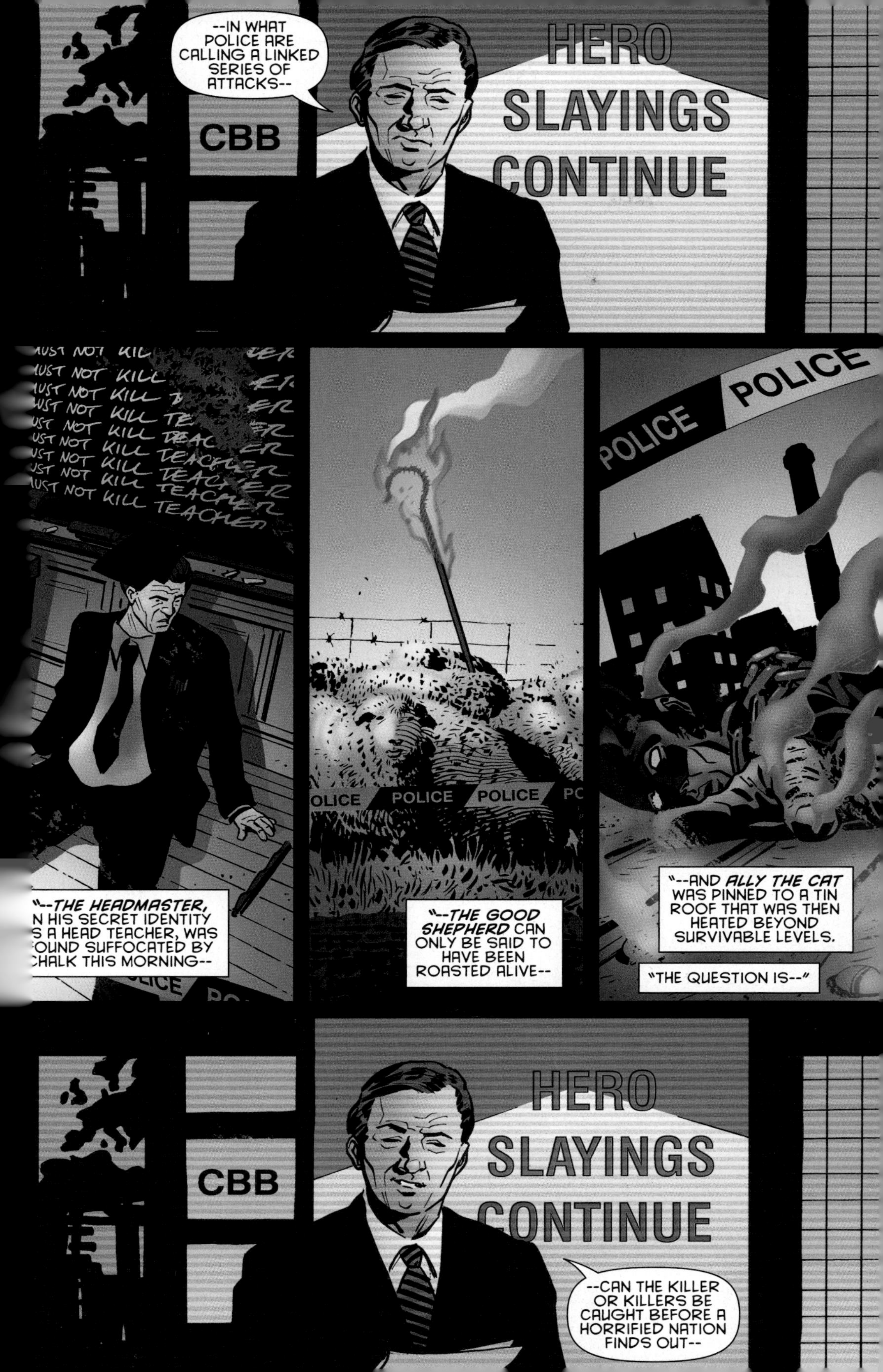
--IN WHAT POLICE ARE CALLING A LINKED SERIES OF ATTACKS--
CBB
HERO SLAYINGS CONTINUE
MUST NOT KILL TEACHER
"--THE HEADMASTER, IN HIS SECRET IDENTITY IS A HEAD TEACHER, WAS FOUND SUFFOCATED BY CHALK THIS MORNING--
POLICE
"--THE GOOD SHEPHERD CAN ONLY BE SAID TO HAVE BEEN ROASTED ALIVE--
POLICE
"--AND ALLY THE CAT WAS PINNED TO A TIN ROOF THAT WAS THEN HEATED BEYOND SURVIVABLE LEVELS.
"THE QUESTION IS--"
CBB
HERO SLAYINGS CONTINUE
--CAN THE KILLER OR KILLERS BE CAUGHT BEFORE A HORRIFIED NATION FINDS OUT--

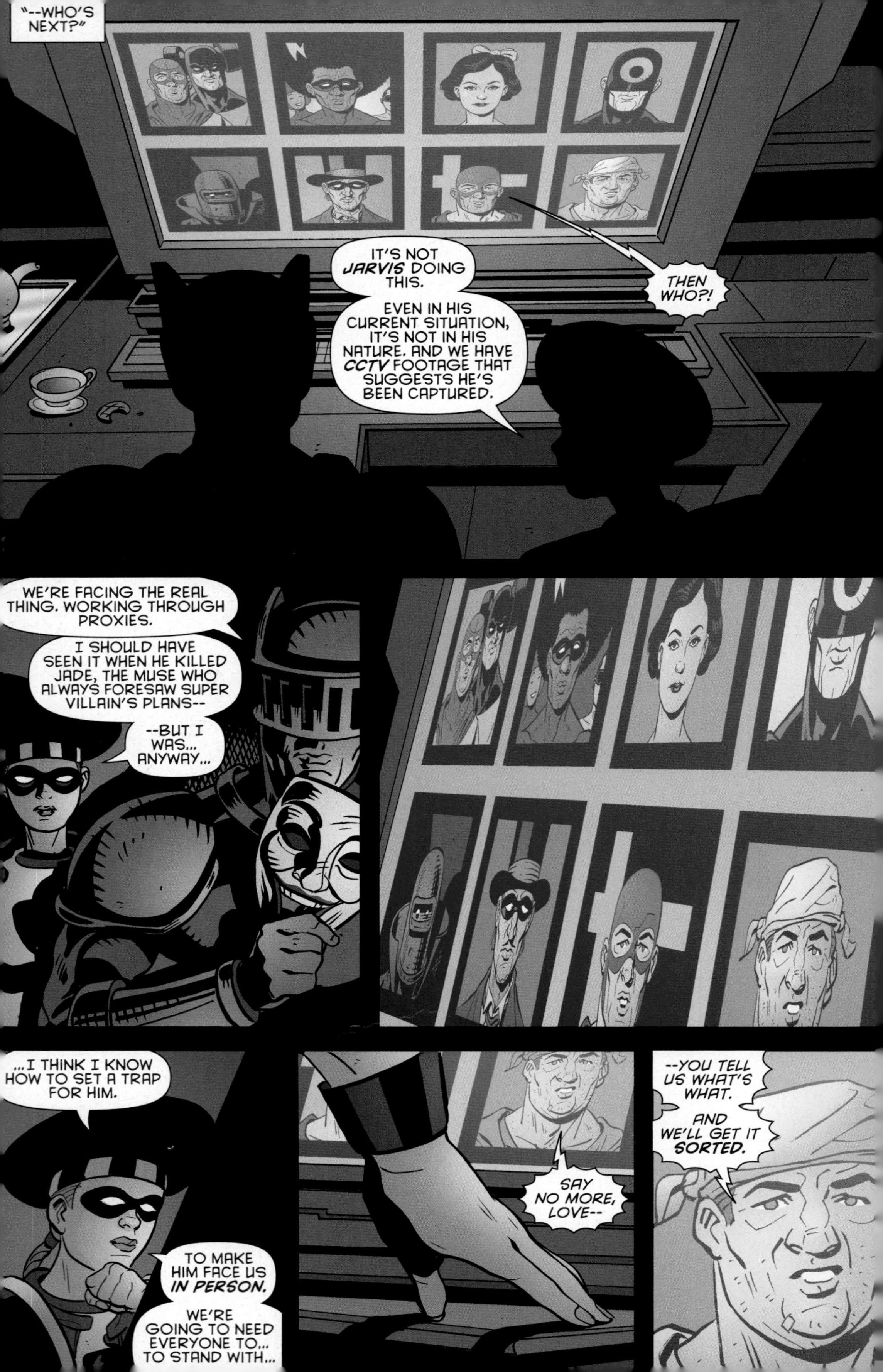
"--WHO'S NEXT?"
IT'S NOT JARVIS DOING THIS.
EVEN IN HIS CURRENT SITUATION, IT'S NOT IN HIS NATURE. AND WE HAVE CCTV FOOTAGE THAT SUGGESTS HE'S BEEN CAPTURED.
THEN WHO?!
WE'RE FACING THE REAL THING. WORKING THROUGH PROXIES.
I SHOULD HAVE SEEN IT WHEN HE KILLED JADE, THE MUSE WHO ALWAYS FORESAW SUPER VILLAIN'S PLANS--
--BUT I WAS... ANYWAY...
...I THINK I KNOW HOW TO SET A TRAP FOR HIM.
TO MAKE HIM FACE US IN PERSON.
WE'RE GOING TO NEED EVERYONE TO... TO STAND WITH...
SAY NO MORE, LOVE--
--YOU TELL US WHAT'S WHAT.
AND WE'LL GET IT SORTED.

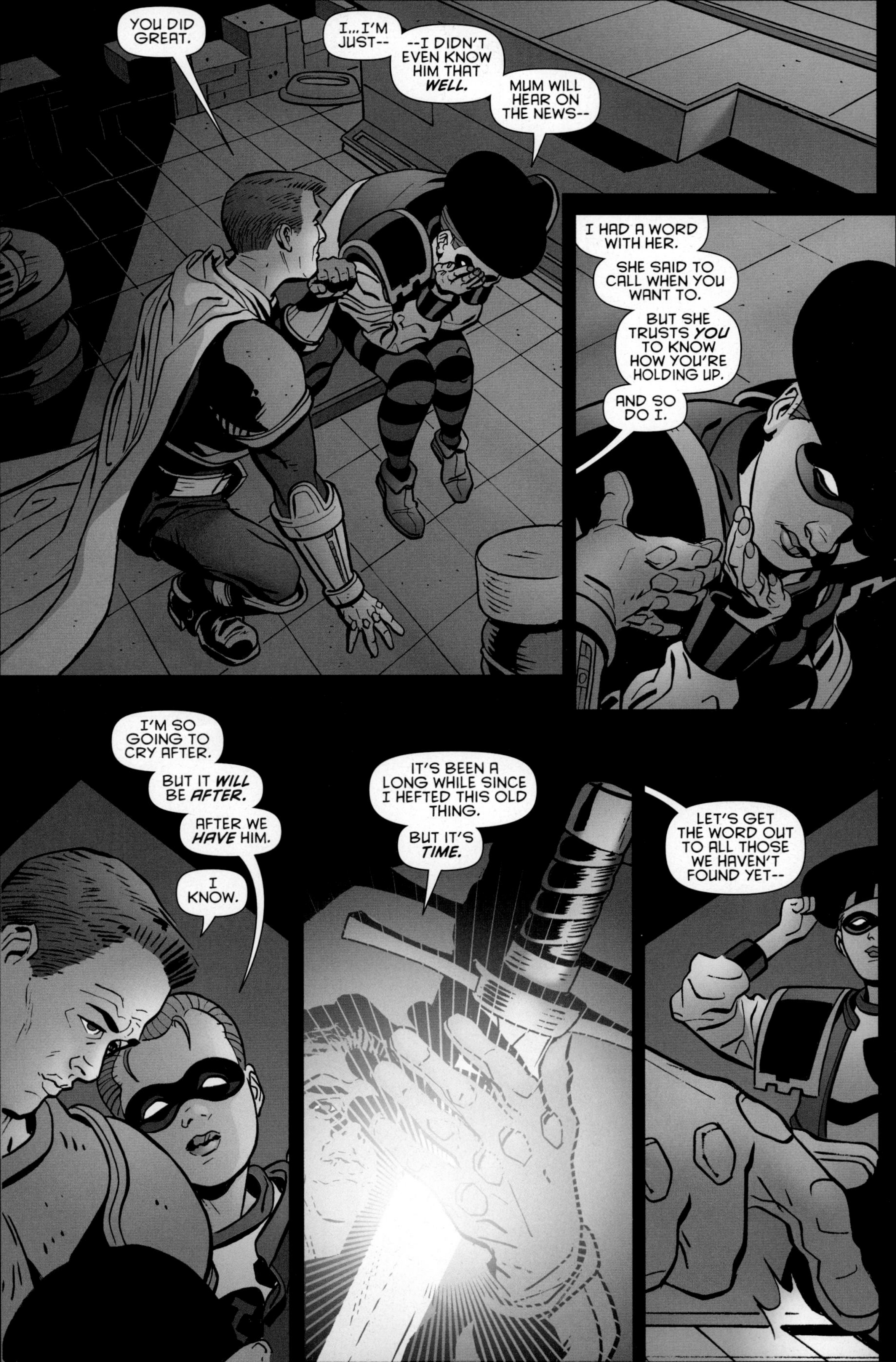
YOU DID GREAT.
I... I'M JUST--
--I DIDN'T EVEN KNOW HIM THAT *WELL.*
MUM WILL HEAR ON THE NEWS--
I HAD A WORD WITH HER.
SHE SAID TO CALL WHEN YOU WANT TO.
BUT SHE TRUSTS *YOU* TO KNOW HOW YOU'RE HOLDING UP.
AND SO DO I.
I'M SO GOING TO CRY AFTER.
BUT IT *WILL* BE *AFTER.*
AFTER WE *HAVE* HIM.
I KNOW.
IT'S BEEN A LONG WHILE SINCE I HEFTED THIS OLD THING.
BUT IT'S *TIME.*
LET'S GET THE WORD OUT TO ALL THOSE WE HAVEN'T FOUND YET--

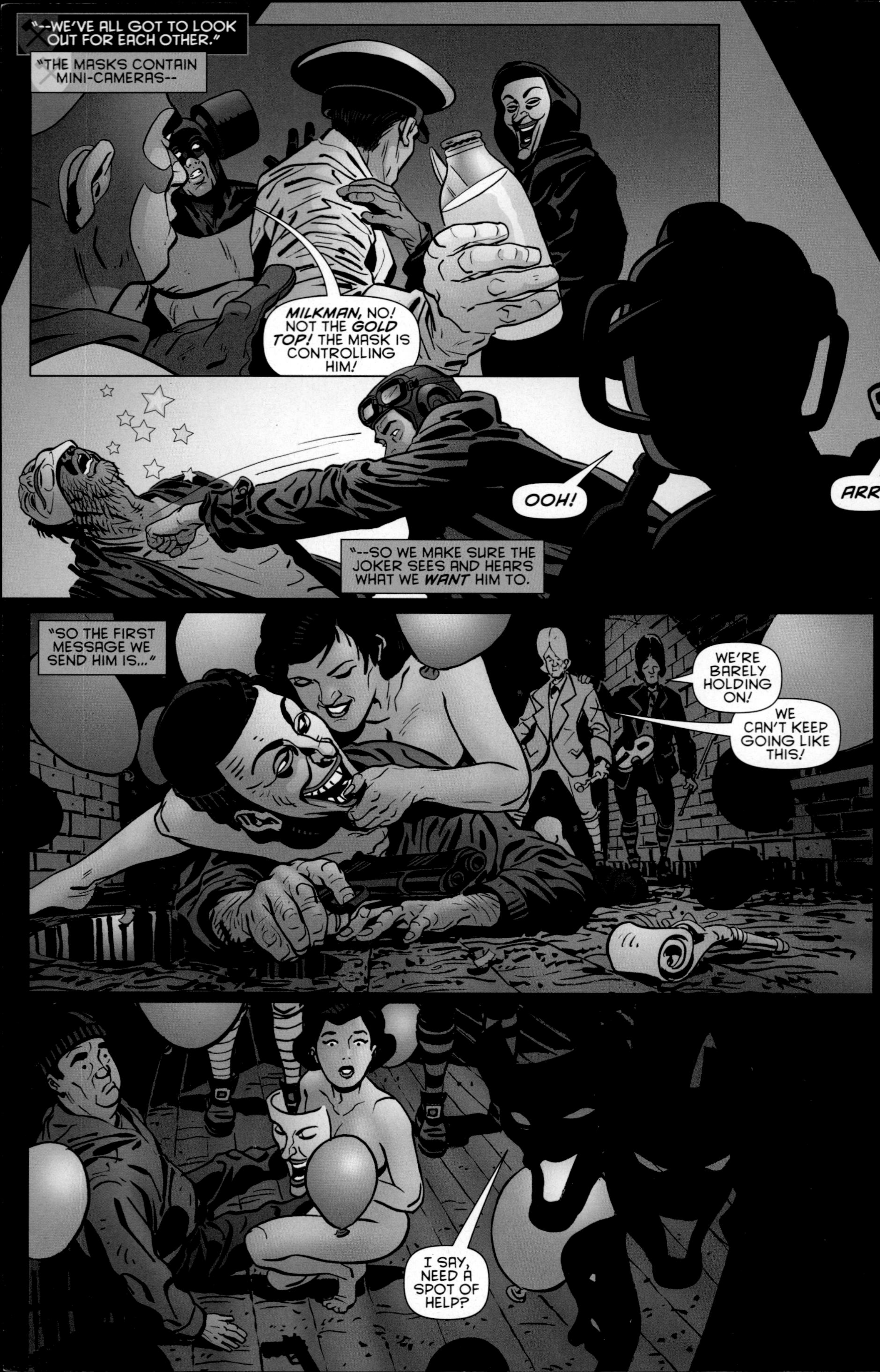
"--WE'VE ALL GOT TO LOOK OUT FOR EACH OTHER."
"THE MASKS CONTAIN MINI-CAMERAS--
MILKMAN, NO! NOT THE GOLD TOP! THE MASK IS CONTROLLING HIM!
OOH!
ARR
"--SO WE MAKE SURE THE JOKER SEES AND HEARS WHAT WE WANT HIM TO.
"SO THE FIRST MESSAGE WE SEND HIM IS..."
WE'RE BARELY HOLDING ON!
WE CAN'T KEEP GOING LIKE THIS!
I SAY, NEED A SPOT OF HELP?

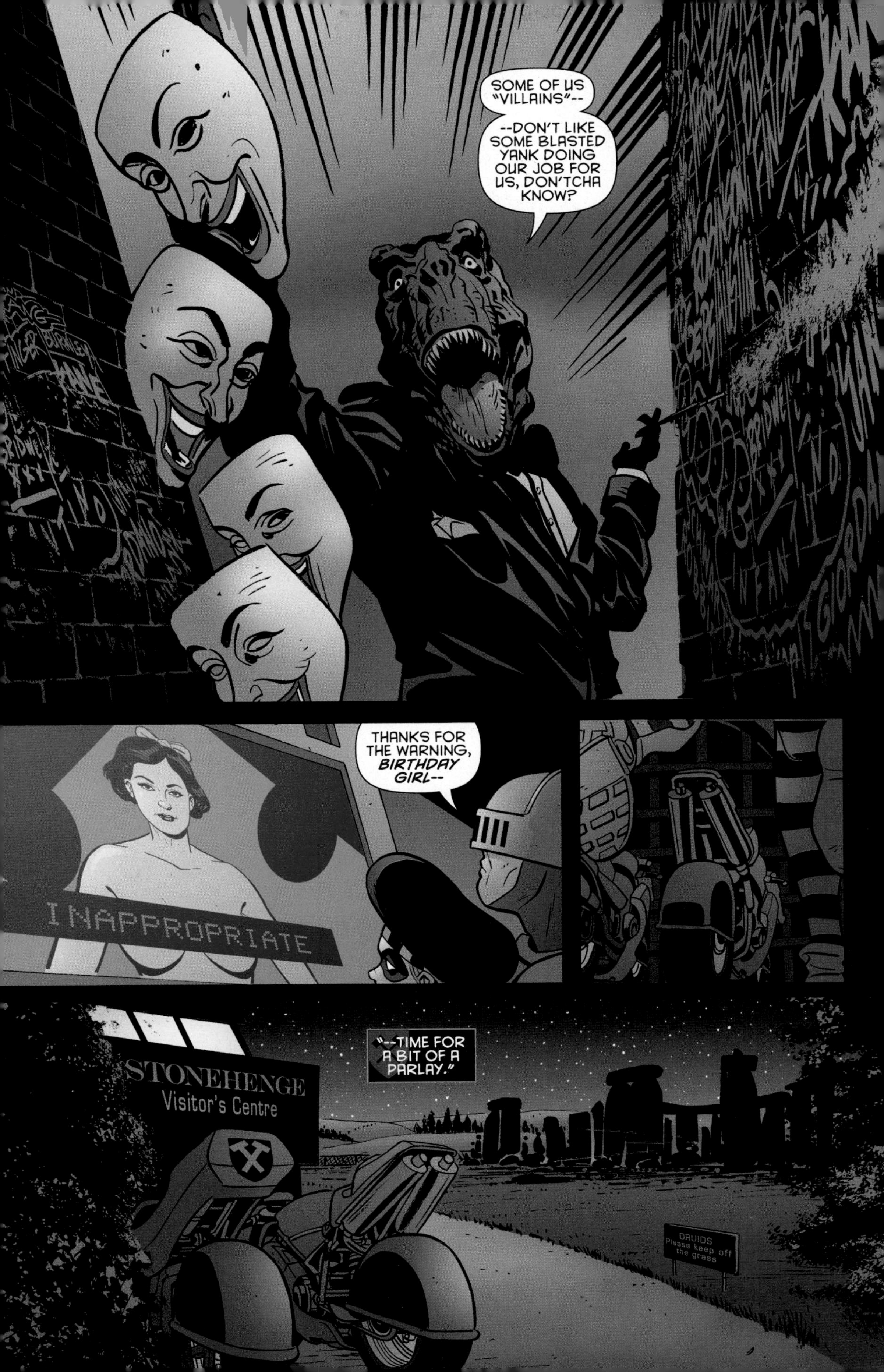
SOME OF US "VILLAINS"--
--DON'T LIKE SOME BLASTED YANK DOING OUR JOB FOR US, DON'TCHA KNOW?
THANKS FOR THE WARNING, *BIRTHDAY GIRL*--
INAPPROPRIATE
STONEHENGE
Visitor's Centre
"--TIME FOR A BIT OF A PARLAY."
DRUIDS
Please keep off the grass

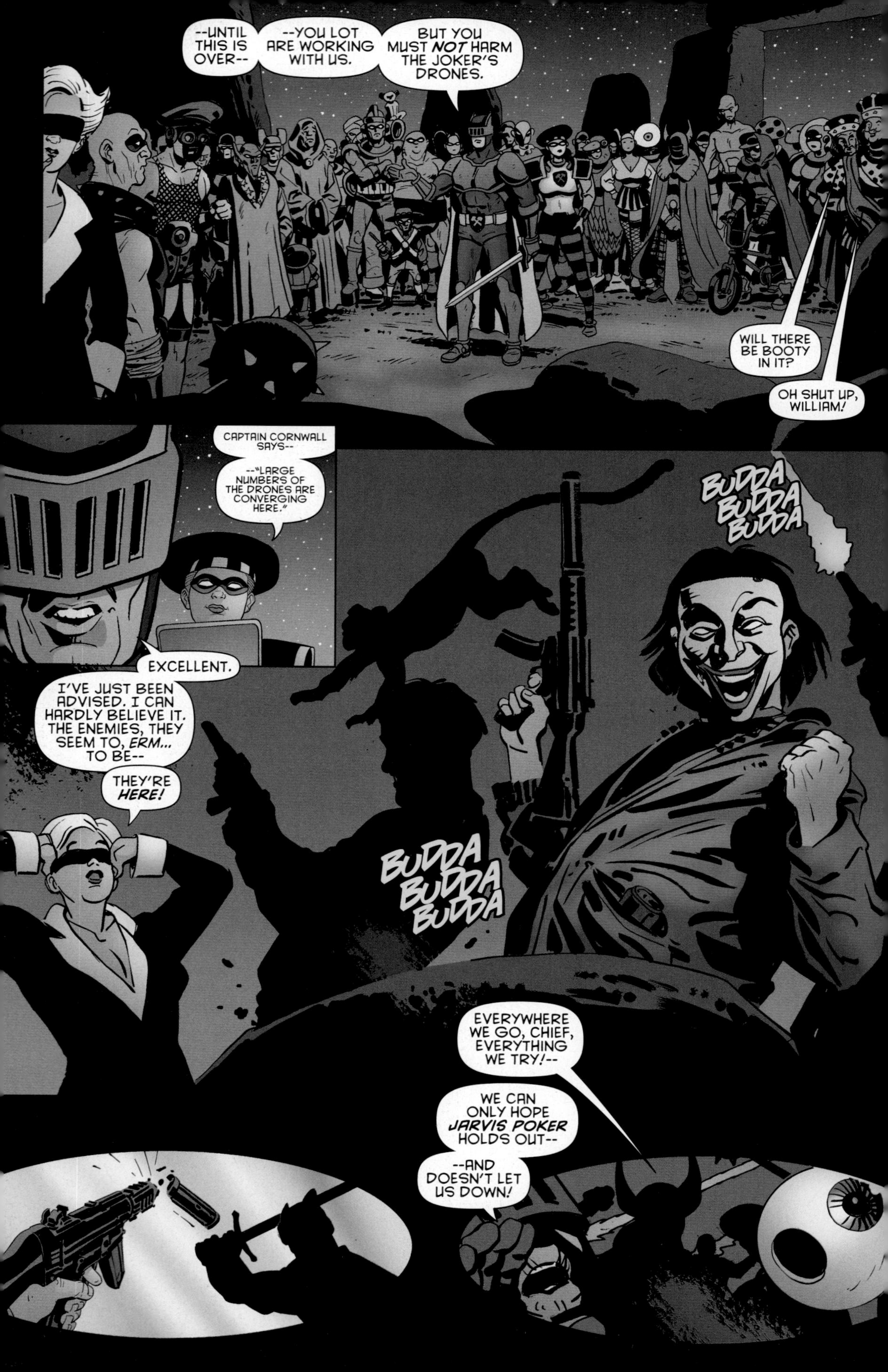
--UNTIL THIS IS OVER--
--YOU LOT ARE WORKING WITH US.
BUT YOU MUST *NOT* HARM THE JOKER'S DRONES.
WILL THERE BE BOOTY IN IT?
OH SHUT UP, WILLIAM!
CAPTAIN CORNWALL SAYS--
--"LARGE NUMBERS OF THE DRONES ARE CONVERGING HERE."
EXCELLENT.
I'VE JUST BEEN ADVISED. I CAN HARDLY BELIEVE IT. THE ENEMIES, THEY SEEM TO, *ERM...* TO BE--
THEY'RE *HERE!*
BUDDA BUDDA BUDDA
BUDDA BUDDA BUDDA
EVERYWHERE WE GO, CHIEF, EVERYTHING WE TRY!--
WE CAN ONLY HOPE *JARVIS POKER* HOLDS OUT--
--AND DOESN'T LET US DOWN!

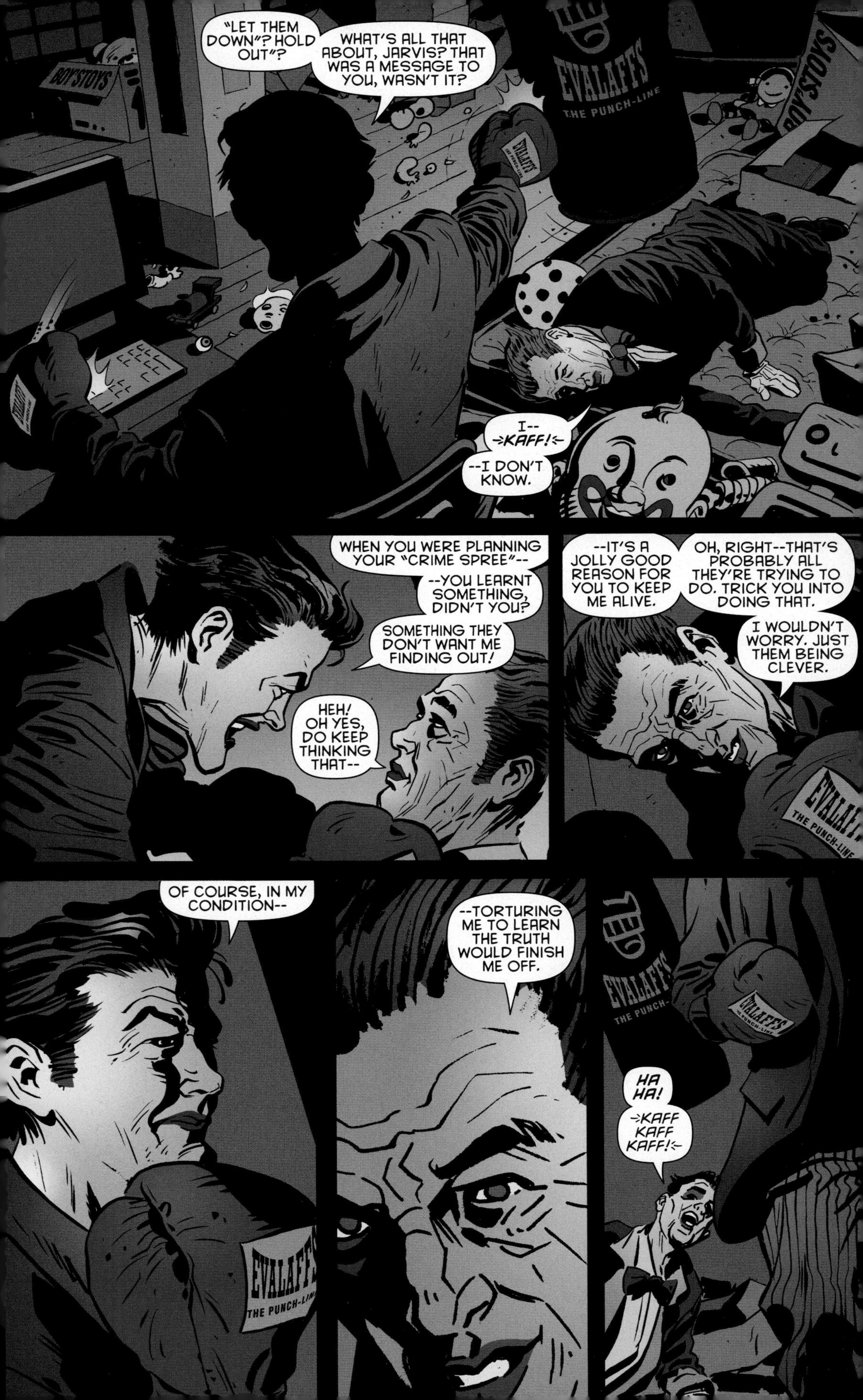
BOY'S TOYS
EVALAFFS
THE PUNCH-LINE
"LET THEM DOWN"? HOLD OUT"?
WHAT'S ALL THAT ABOUT, JARVIS? THAT WAS A MESSAGE TO YOU, WASN'T IT?
I-- ⇝KAFF!⇜ --I DON'T KNOW.
WHEN YOU WERE PLANNING YOUR "CRIME SPREE"--
--YOU LEARNT SOMETHING, DIDN'T YOU?
SOMETHING THEY DON'T WANT ME FINDING OUT!
HEH! OH YES, DO KEEP THINKING THAT--
--IT'S A JOLLY GOOD REASON FOR YOU TO KEEP ME ALIVE.
OH, RIGHT--THAT'S PROBABLY ALL THEY'RE TRYING TO DO. TRICK YOU INTO DOING THAT.
I WOULDN'T WORRY. JUST THEM BEING CLEVER.
OF COURSE, IN MY CONDITION--
--TORTURING ME TO LEARN THE TRUTH WOULD FINISH ME OFF.
HA HA! ⇝KAFF KAFF KAFF!⇜

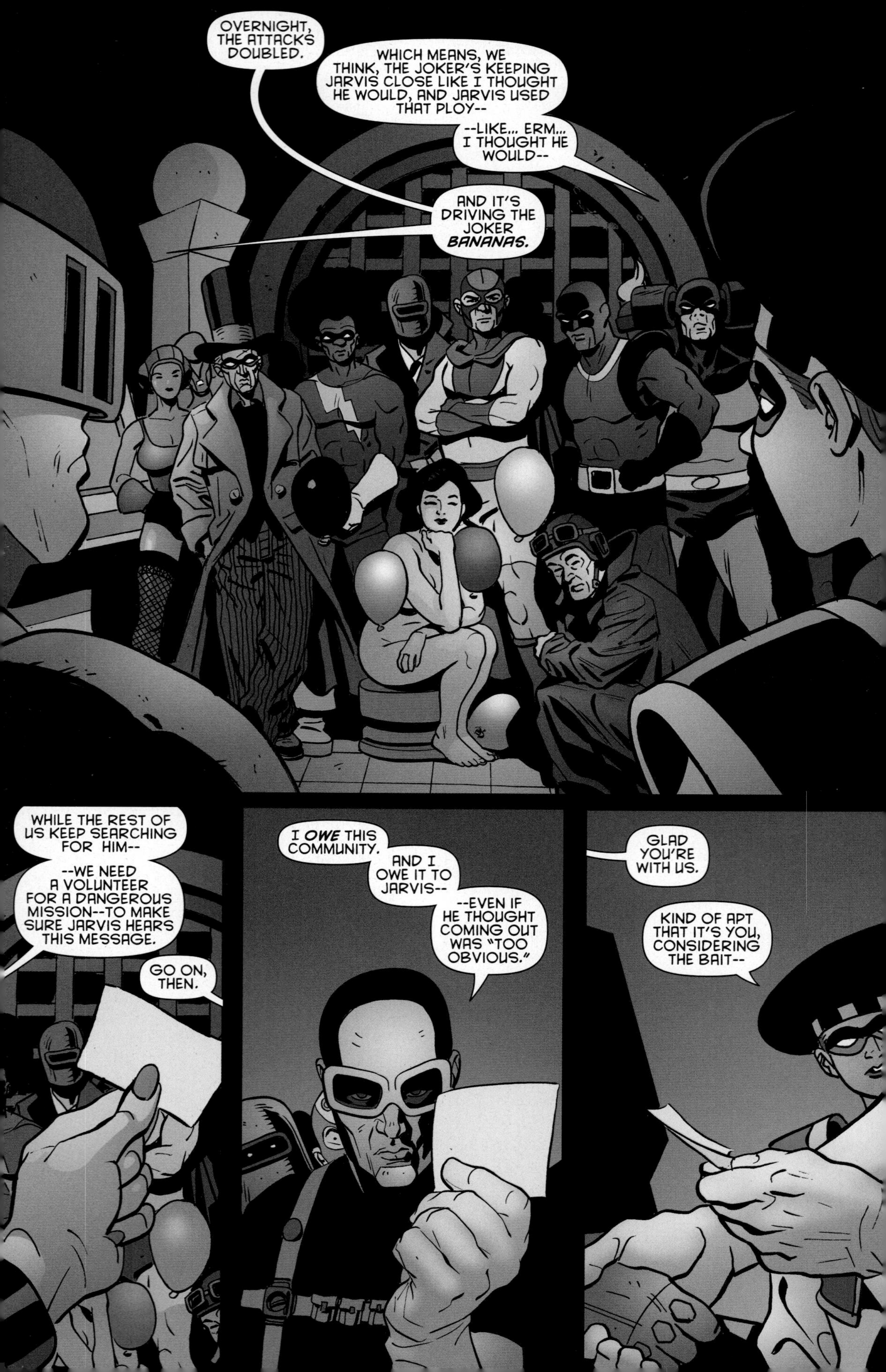
OVERNIGHT, THE ATTACKS DOUBLED.
WHICH MEANS, WE THINK, THE JOKER'S KEEPING JARVIS CLOSE LIKE I THOUGHT HE WOULD, AND JARVIS USED THAT PLOY--
--LIKE... ERM... I THOUGHT HE WOULD--
AND IT'S DRIVING THE JOKER BANANAS.
WHILE THE REST OF US KEEP SEARCHING FOR HIM--
--WE NEED A VOLUNTEER FOR A DANGEROUS MISSION--TO MAKE SURE JARVIS HEARS THIS MESSAGE.
GO ON, THEN.
I OWE THIS COMMUNITY.
AND I OWE IT TO JARVIS--
--EVEN IF HE THOUGHT COMING OUT WAS "TOO OBVIOUS."
GLAD YOU'RE WITH US.
KIND OF APT THAT IT'S YOU, CONSIDERING THE BAIT--

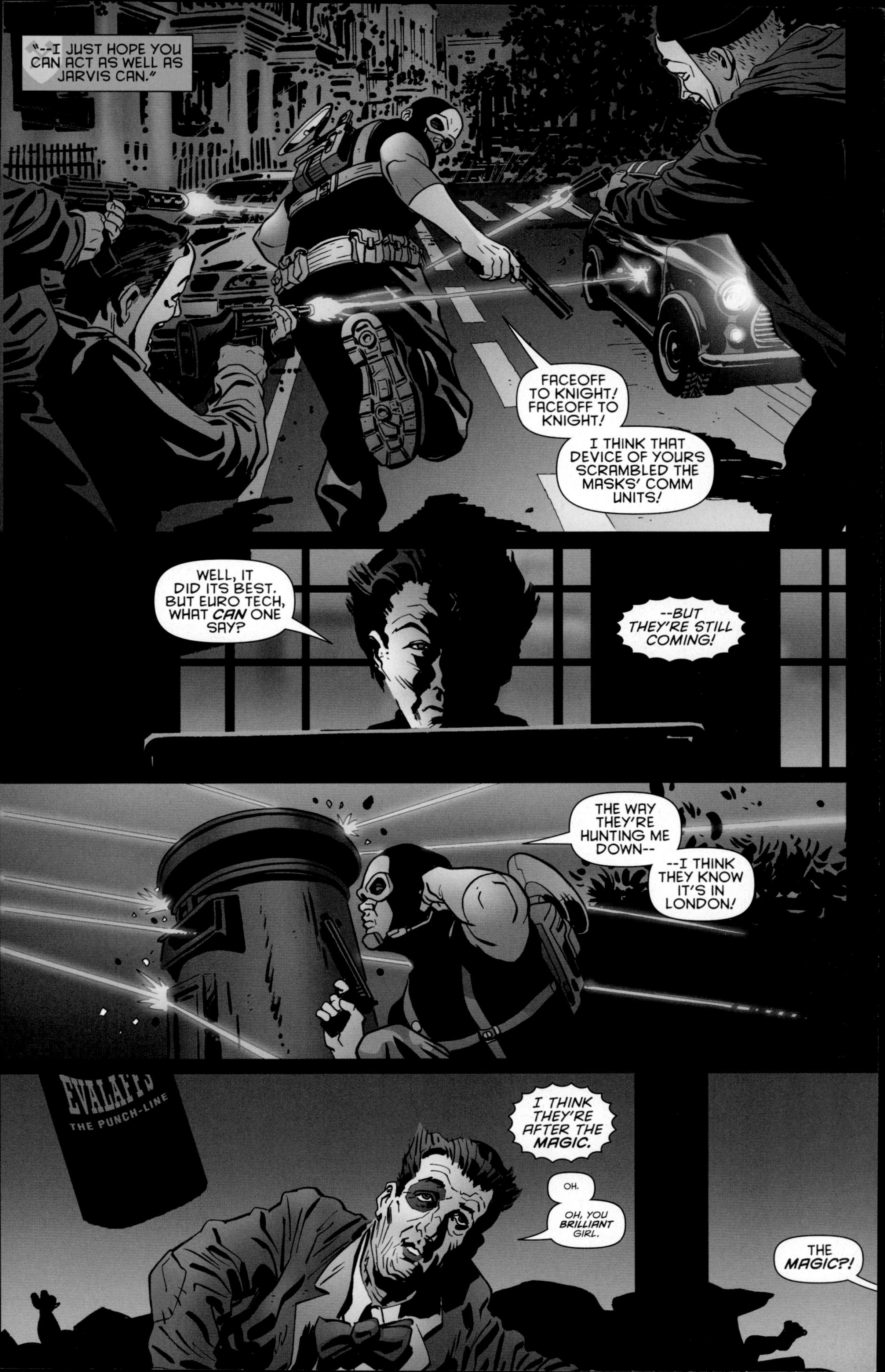
"--I JUST HOPE YOU CAN ACT AS WELL AS JARVIS CAN."
FACEOFF TO KNIGHT! FACEOFF TO KNIGHT!
I THINK THAT DEVICE OF YOURS SCRAMBLED THE MASKS' COMM UNITS!
WELL, IT DID ITS BEST. BUT EURO TECH, WHAT *CAN* ONE SAY?
--BUT THEY'RE STILL COMING!
THE WAY THEY'RE HUNTING ME DOWN--
--I THINK THEY KNOW IT'S IN LONDON!
THE PUNCH-LINE
I THINK THEY'RE AFTER THE *MAGIC.*
OH.
OH, YOU *BRILLIANT* GIRL.
THE *MAGIC?!*

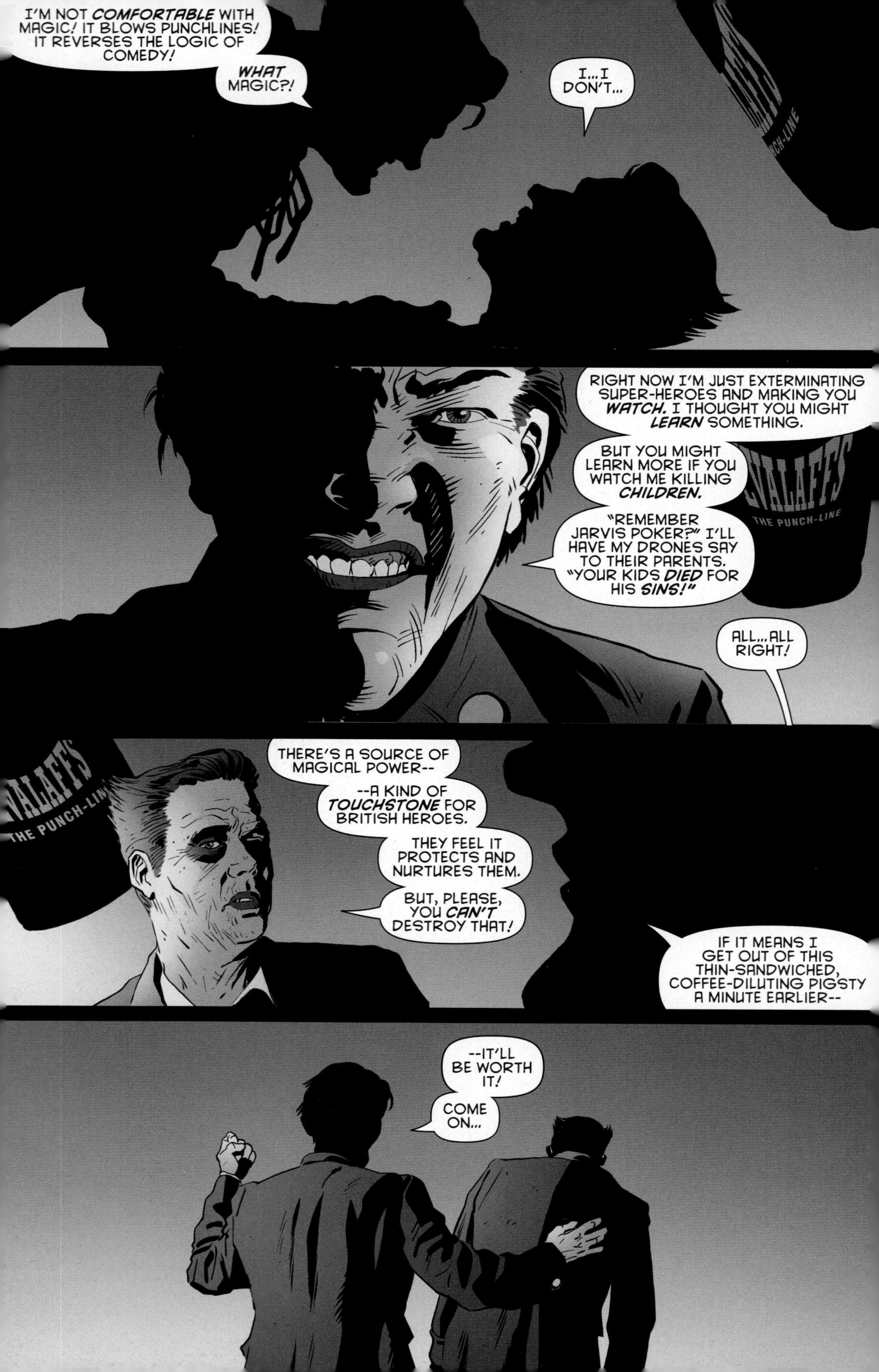

I'M NOT COMFORTABLE WITH MAGIC! IT BLOWS PUNCHLINES! IT REVERSES THE LOGIC OF COMEDY!
WHAT MAGIC?!
I...I DON'T...
THE PUNCH-LINE
RIGHT NOW I'M JUST EXTERMINATING SUPER-HEROES AND MAKING YOU WATCH. I THOUGHT YOU MIGHT LEARN SOMETHING.
BUT YOU MIGHT LEARN MORE IF YOU WATCH ME KILLING CHILDREN.
"REMEMBER JARVIS POKER?" I'LL HAVE MY DRONES SAY TO THEIR PARENTS. "YOUR KIDS DIED FOR HIS SINS!"
EVALAFFS
THE PUNCH-LINE
ALL...ALL RIGHT!
EVALAFFS
THE PUNCH-LINE
THERE'S A SOURCE OF MAGICAL POWER--
--A KIND OF TOUCHSTONE FOR BRITISH HEROES.
THEY FEEL IT PROTECTS AND NURTURES THEM.
BUT, PLEASE, YOU CAN'T DESTROY THAT!
IF IT MEANS I GET OUT OF THIS THIN-SANDWICHED, COFFEE-DILUTING PIGSTY A MINUTE EARLIER--
--IT'LL BE WORTH IT!
COME ON...

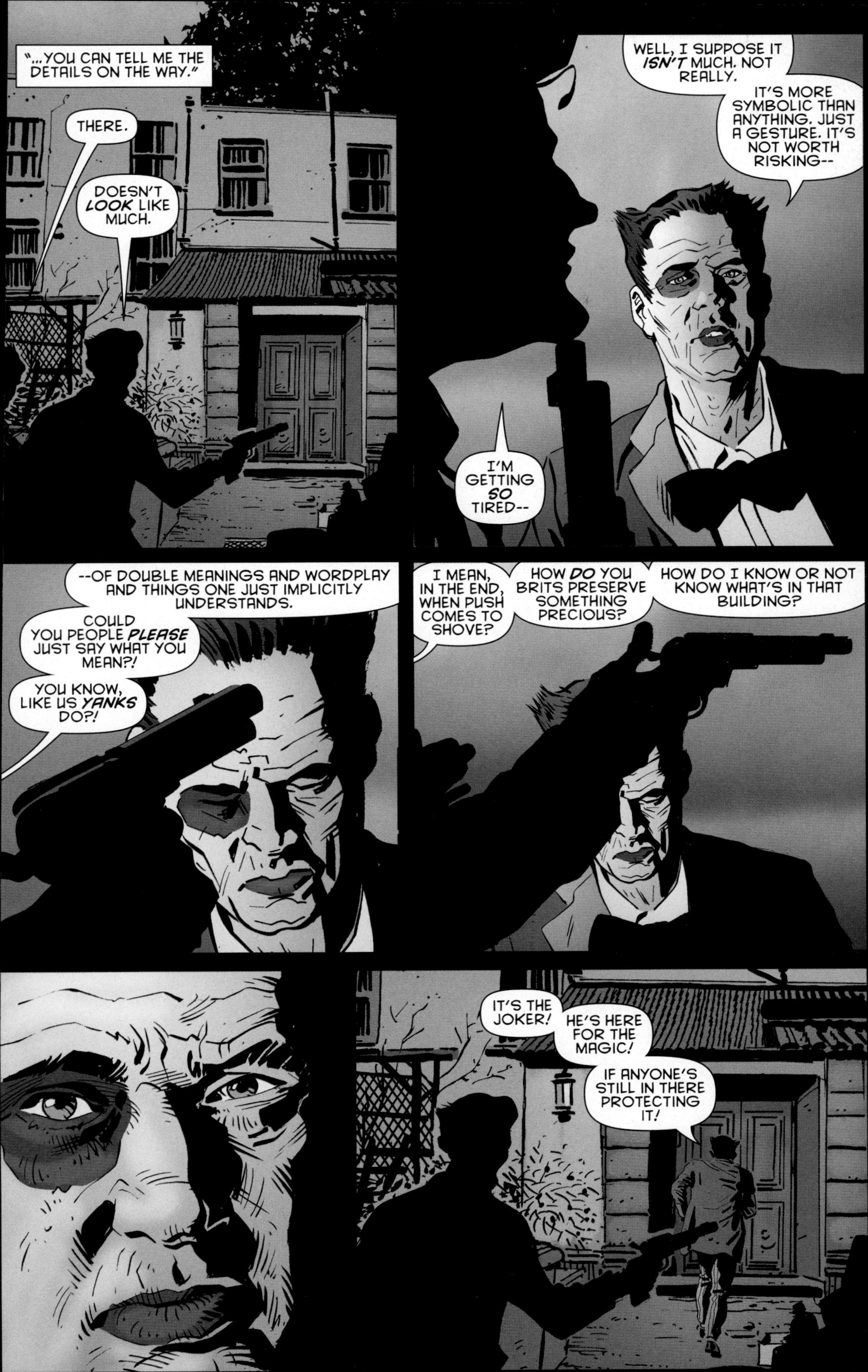

"...YOU CAN TELL ME THE DETAILS ON THE WAY."
THERE.
DOESN'T *LOOK* LIKE MUCH.
WELL, I SUPPOSE IT *ISN'T* MUCH. NOT REALLY.
IT'S MORE SYMBOLIC THAN ANYTHING. JUST A GESTURE. IT'S NOT WORTH RISKING--
I'M GETTING *SO* TIRED--
--OF DOUBLE MEANINGS AND WORDPLAY AND THINGS ONE JUST IMPLICITLY UNDERSTANDS.
COULD YOU PEOPLE *PLEASE* JUST SAY WHAT YOU MEAN?!
YOU KNOW, LIKE US *YANKS* DO?!
I MEAN, IN THE END, WHEN PUSH COMES TO SHOVE?
HOW *DO* YOU BRITS PRESERVE SOMETHING PRECIOUS?
HOW DO I KNOW OR NOT KNOW WHAT'S IN THAT BUILDING?
IT'S THE JOKER!
HE'S HERE FOR THE MAGIC!
IF ANYONE'S STILL IN THERE PROTECTING IT!

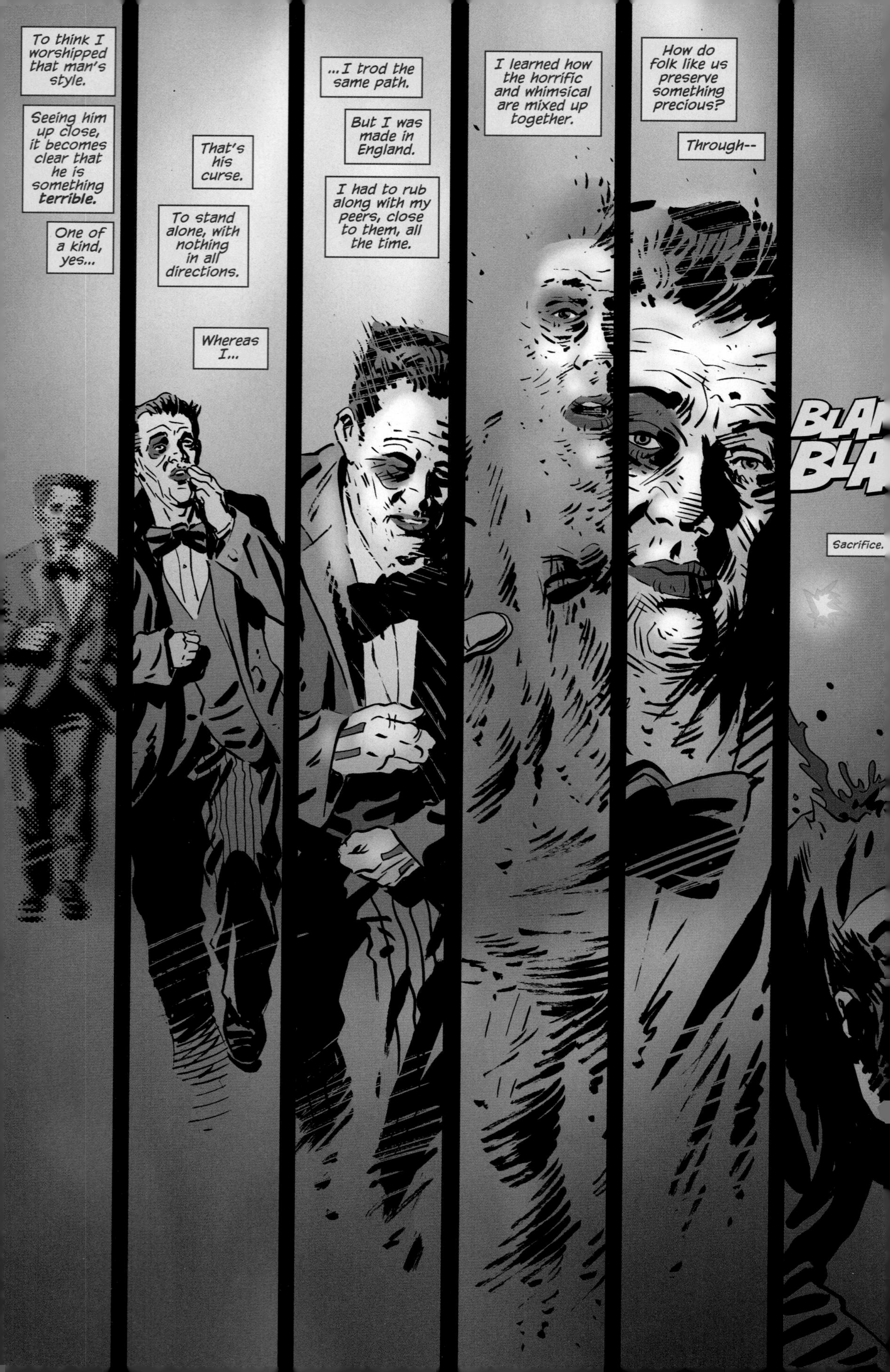
To think I worshipped that man's style.
Seeing him up close, it becomes clear that he is something **terrible.**
One of a kind, yes...
That's his curse.
To stand alone, with nothing in all directions.
Whereas I...
...I trod the same path.
But I was made in England.
I had to rub along with my peers, close to them, all the time.
I learned how the horrific and whimsical are mixed up together.
How do folk like us preserve something precious?
Through--
Sacrifice.

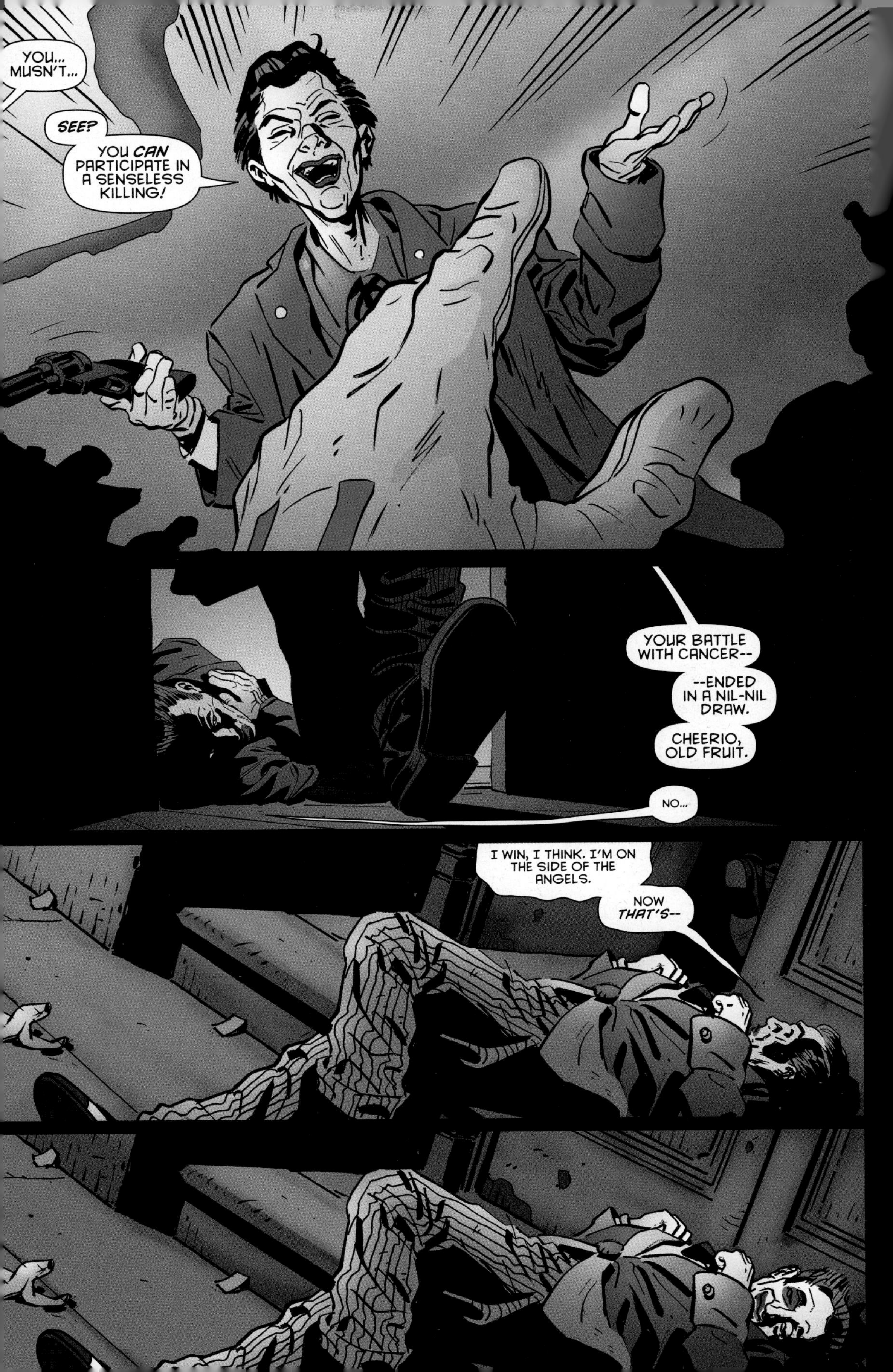
YOU... MUSN'T...
SEE?
YOU CAN PARTICIPATE IN A SENSELESS KILLING!
YOUR BATTLE WITH CANCER--
--ENDED IN A NIL-NIL DRAW.
CHEERIO, OLD FRUIT.
NO...
I WIN, I THINK. I'M ON THE SIDE OF THE ANGELS.
NOW THAT'S--

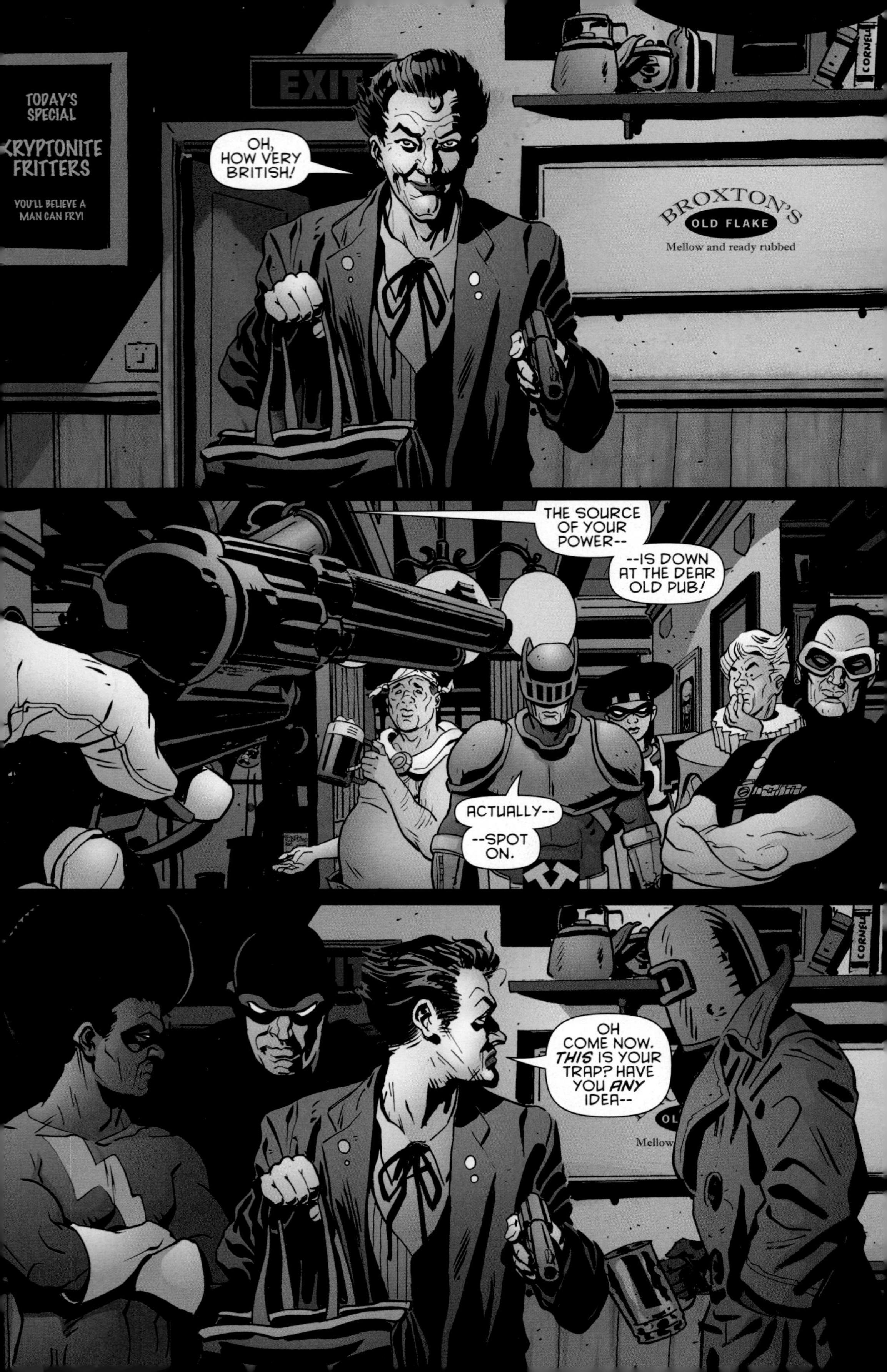
TODAY'S SPECIAL
KRYPTONITE FRITTERS
YOU'LL BELIEVE A MAN CAN FRY!
EXIT
BROXTON'S
OLD FLAKE
Mellow and ready rubbed
OH, HOW VERY BRITISH!
THE SOURCE OF YOUR POWER--
--IS DOWN AT THE DEAR OLD PUB!
ACTUALLY--
--SPOT ON.
OH COME NOW. *THIS* IS YOUR TRAP? HAVE YOU *ANY* IDEA--

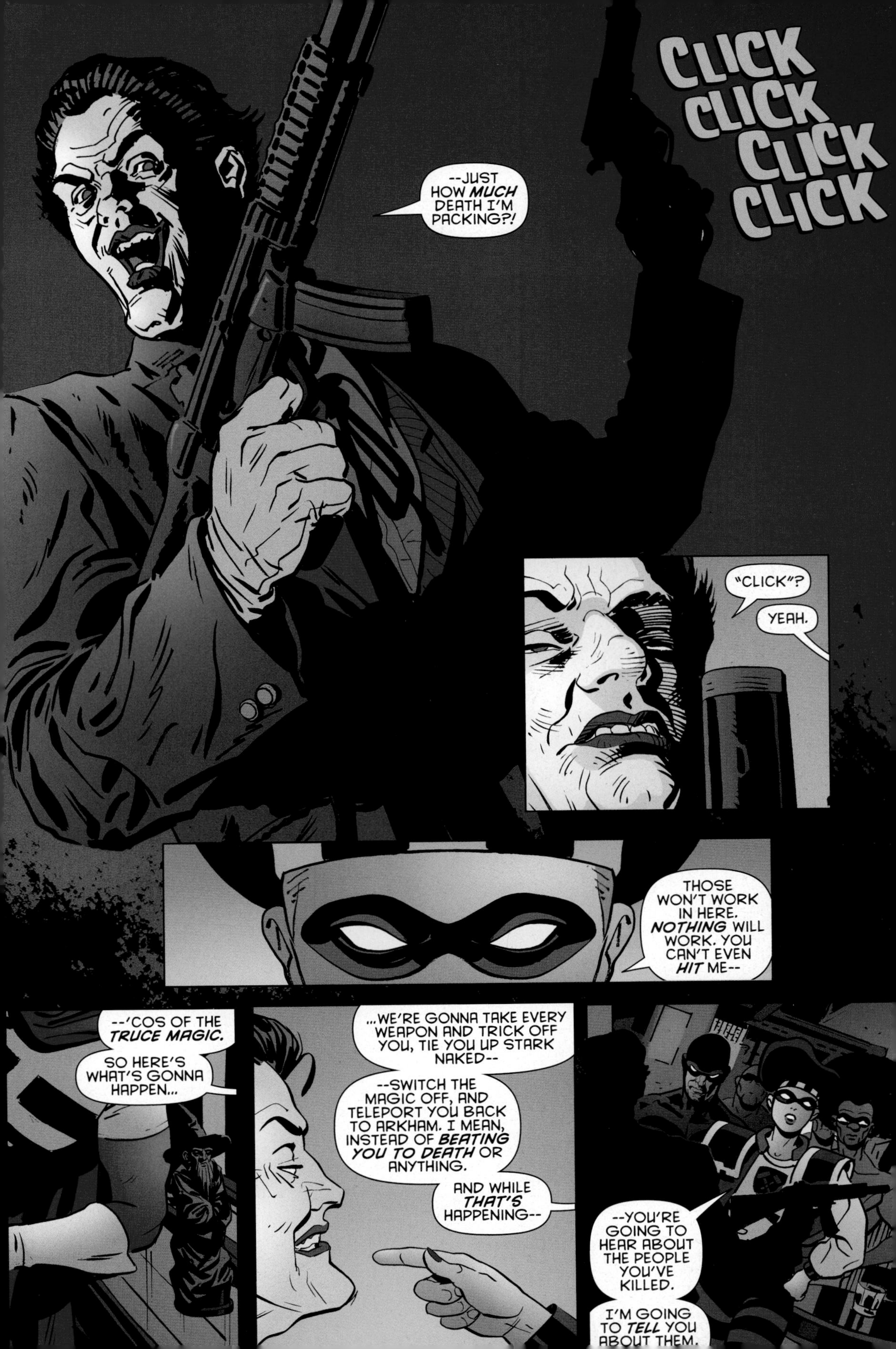

--JUST HOW *MUCH* DEATH I'M PACKING?!
CLICK CLICK CLICK CLICK
"CLICK"?
YEAH.
THOSE WON'T WORK IN HERE. *NOTHING* WILL WORK. YOU CAN'T EVEN *HIT* ME--
--'COS OF THE *TRUCE MAGIC.*
SO HERE'S WHAT'S GONNA HAPPEN...
...WE'RE GONNA TAKE EVERY WEAPON AND TRICK OFF YOU, TIE YOU UP STARK NAKED--
--SWITCH THE MAGIC OFF, AND TELEPORT YOU BACK TO ARKHAM. I MEAN, INSTEAD OF *BEATING YOU TO DEATH* OR ANYTHING.
AND WHILE *THAT'S* HAPPENING--
--YOU'RE GOING TO HEAR ABOUT THE PEOPLE YOU'VE KILLED.
I'M GOING TO *TELL* YOU ABOUT THEM.

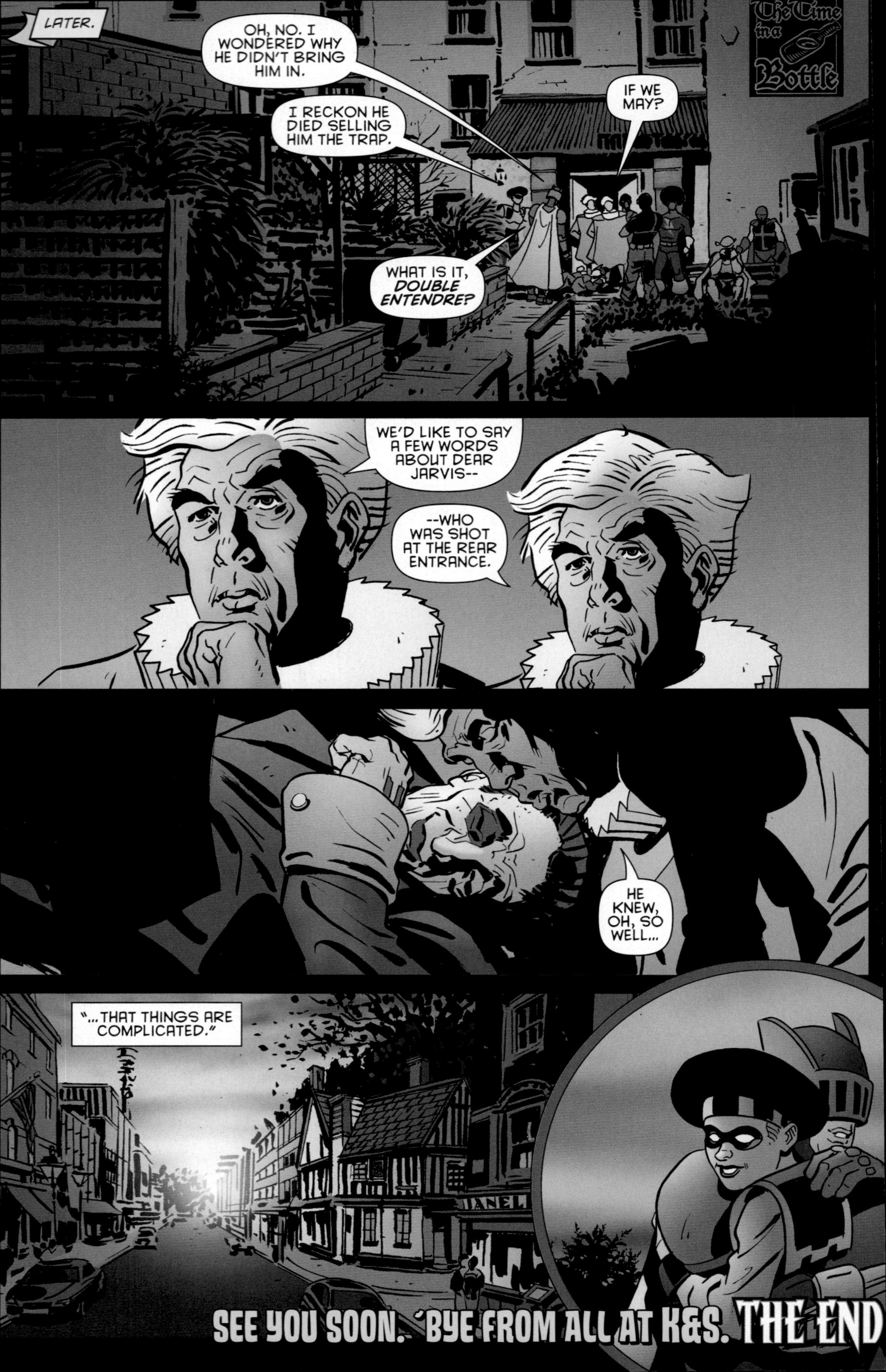
LATER.
OH, NO. I WONDERED WHY HE DIDN'T BRING HIM IN.
I RECKON HE DIED SELLING HIM THE TRAP.
The Time in a Bottle
IF WE MAY?
WHAT IS IT, DOUBLE ENTENDRE?
WE'D LIKE TO SAY A FEW WORDS ABOUT DEAR JARVIS--
--WHO WAS SHOT AT THE REAR ENTRANCE.
HE KNEW, OH, SO WELL...
"...THAT THINGS ARE COMPLICATED."
SEE YOU SOON. 'BYE FROM ALL AT K&S. THE END

The Knight and Squire Character List (Part Two)

AND NOW, THOSE NEW CHARACTERS WE INTRODUCED IN *KNIGHT & SQUIRE* ISSUES #2-6! IN *#2:* THE ORGAN GRINDER AND HIS MONKEY; MORRIS MAJOR AND THE MORRIS MEN. IN *#3:* THE MUSES (NINE OF THEM), INCLUDING CERYS TWEED AND JADE PEABODY (DECEASED); RICHARD III; EDWARD I; CHARLES I; KING JOHN; WILLIAM II (WELL, WE CREATED THESE VERSIONS OF THEM, BUT YES, THE DIVINE RIGHT AND THE FORCE OF HISTORY DID MOST OF THE WORK); THE CIDERMEN (2); BIG MUMMY AND HER CHILDREN (10). (WE'RE ONLY COUNTING SUPER-HEROES AND VILLAINS HERE, SO THE GRAY TWINS AND HANK DON'T QUITE MAKE IT.) IN *#4:* MAD HAT HARRY AND THE PAPER TIGER. (ONLY SEEN ON A NEWSPAPER COVER, SO THAT'S OUR MOST OBSCURE NEW-COMER.) HARRY IS THE UK COVER VERSION OF THE MAD HATTER, WHILE OWING A BIT TO UNLUCKY LONDON GANGSTER JACK "THE HAT" MCVITIE. WE DIDN'T CREATE ANYONE NEW IN *#5.* (ASSUMING IRON MITTEN ISN'T..."REAL.") AND IN *#6,* WE FIRST WELCOMED THE HEADMASTER; THE GOOD SHEPHERD; ALLY THE CAT. ALL...ERM...DECEASED. IT'S LIKE WE'RE MAKING THESE GUYS UP FOR FUN. ALLY OWES SOMETHING TO BILLY THE CAT, THE BEANO COMIC'S OWN SUPERHERO. THEN ON PANEL ONE OF PAGE TEN, WE ADD, FROM THE LEFT, AMONG OLDER CHARACTERS: LEATHERCHAP (IN CAP); FORK (WITH FORKED HEAD); BAYFRENTOS (PORTLY); BULLFINCH (AS A BIRD); DR. RETINA (THE EYE-BALL); HILT (WITH THE SWORD); THE HOODED HOODIE (ON HIS BIKE); AND SPANGLE (WITH THE BUBBLE HELMET). THAT MAKES 130 NEW BRITISH SUPER-HEROES AND SU-PER-VILLAINS ACROSS THE COURSE OF THE SERIES. SORRY IT WASN'T, AS PROMISED, EXACTLY 100, BUT...YOU KNOW...IT WAS TRICKY ENOUGH AS IT WAS.

A FEW NOTES FROM ISSUES #5 AND #6: "A MAN OF INFINITE JEST" IS HOW HAMLET DESCRIBES YORICK THE JESTER, OR HIS SKULL, ANYWAY. "THE FOG ON THE TYNE," "COMBINE HARVESTER," "RABBIT" AND "ON ILKLEY MOOR" ARE ALL COMIC SONGS, SOME MORE HOMESPUN THAN OTHERS, APPROPRIATE TO THE LOCATIONS OF THE BRIDGES. THE DREADNAUGHT COMIC JARVIS FEATURED IN IS RATHER LIKE 1970S UK COMICS, SUCH AS VALIANT AND HOTSPUR. HIS DIALOGUE THEREIN REFERENCES OSCAR WILDE, AND BRITISH CAMP ICONS LARRY GRAYSON AND JULIAN AND SANDY FROM THE RADIO SERIES ROUND THE HORNE. BRITOVISION MIGHT REMIND US OF THE EUROVI-SION SONG CONTEST (LOOK IT UP, YOU WON'T BELIEVE IT), TWO OF THE WINNERS OF WHICH ARE BEING SUNG BY THOSE FISH. "IT'S..." WAS HOW MANY EPISODES OF MONTY PYTHON'S FLYING CIRCUS BEGAN. GOLD TOP IS THE CREAMIEST (AND MOST DEADLY) SORT OF MILK. DEATH DINOSAUR TALKS A BIT LIKE THE ACTOR TERRY THOMAS. OBVIOUSLY.

JIMMY AND I WOULD LIKE TO THANK EVERYONE WHO'S STUCK WITH US THROUGH THIS WHOLE SERIES. IT'S SOME-THING I'M IMMENSELY PROUD OF AND THINK OF AS SOME OF MY BEST WORK. THANKS MUST GO TO EDITOR JANELLE SIEGEL AND DC IN GENERAL FOR BEING MAD ENOUGH TO LET US DO THIS.

UNTIL THE TRADE, CHEERIO!
– PAUL CORNELL

brought to you by

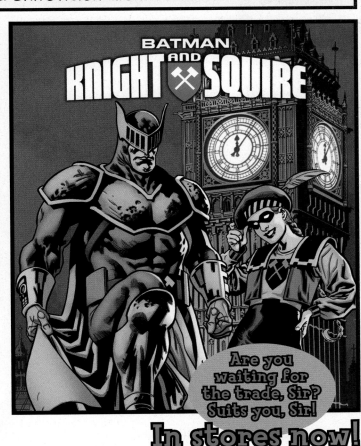

BATMAN
KNIGHT AND SQUIRE

Are you waiting for the trade, Sir? Suits you, Sir!

In stores now!

d by Jimmy Broxton   design by SWANDS

Below: Make-up variations. Traditional green hair was abandoned early on. Too similar to the Gotham original.

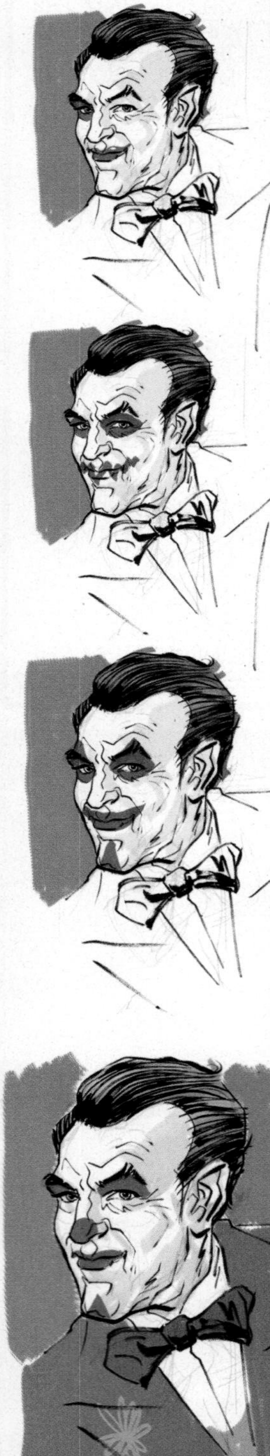
BROX

Left: This vicious-looking "droog"-style sketch was at odds with Paul's conception of Jarvis. The bowler, however, was a step in the right direction.

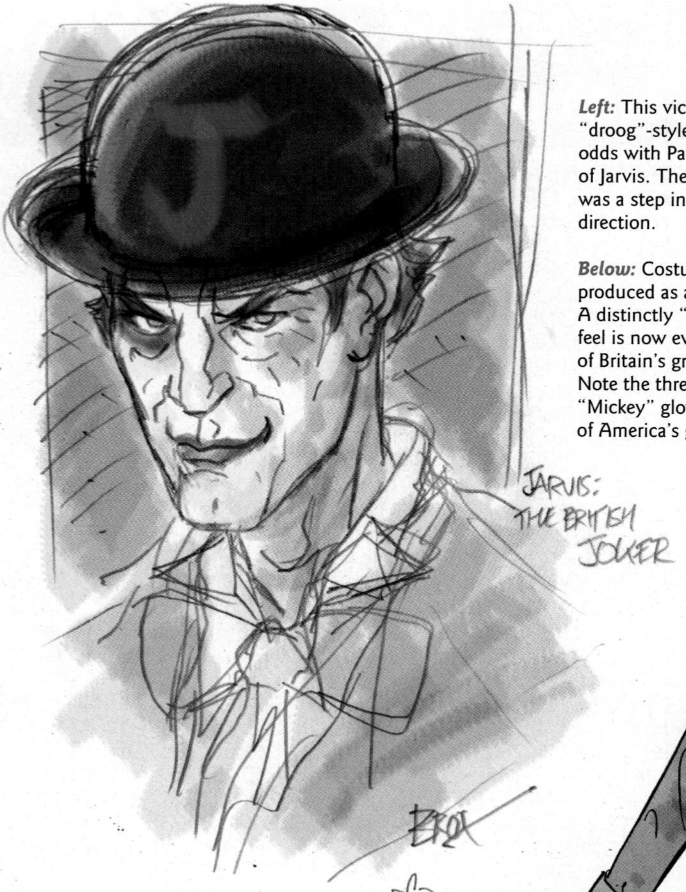
JARVIS:
THE BRITISH
JOKER
BROX

Below: Costume schematic produced as a colour guide. A distinctly "Chaplin-esque" feel is now evident, in honour of Britain's greatest clown. Note the three-fingered "Mickey" gloves, in honour of America's greatest rodent.

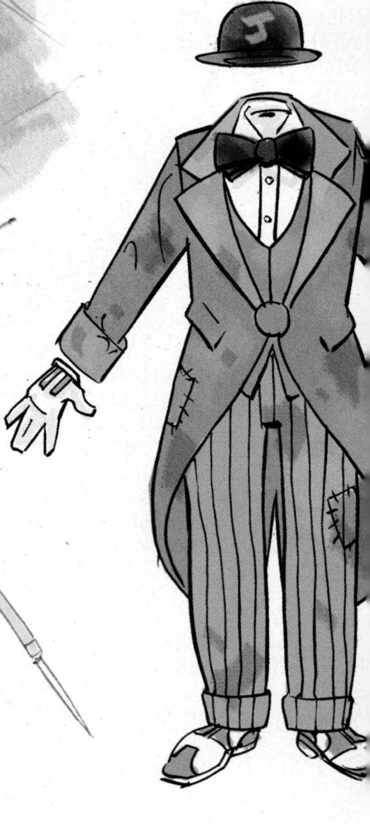

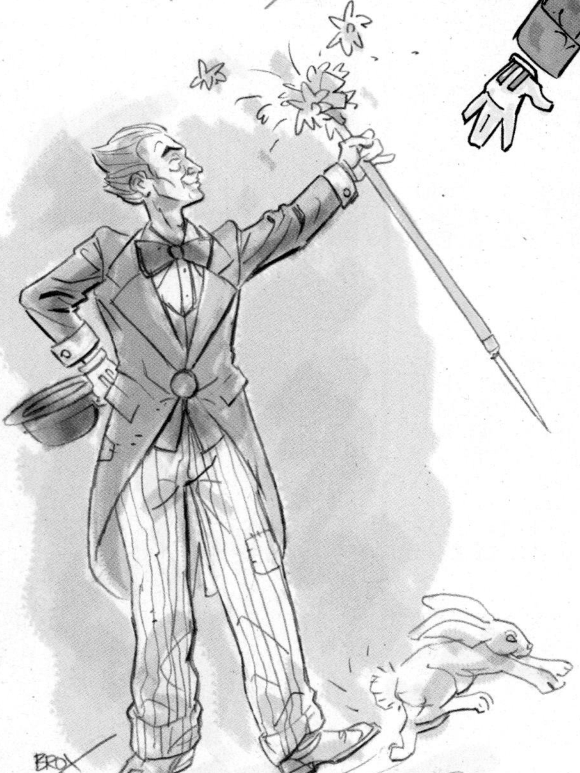
BROX

Above: Our man Jarvis would never kick a bunny, getting close but no cigar.

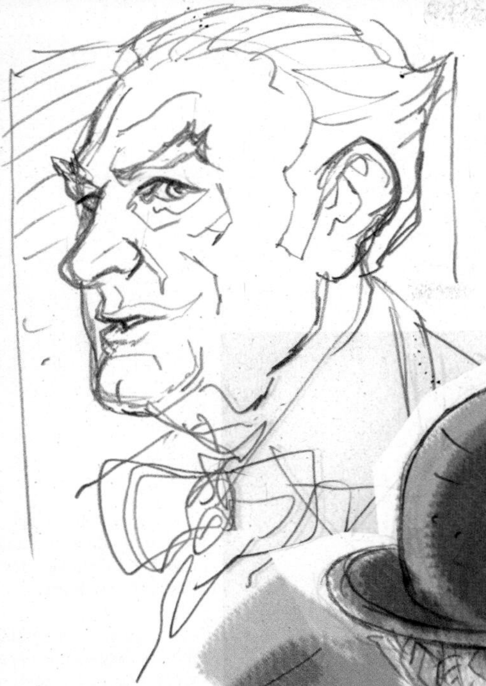

Jarvis Poker, the "British" Joker

Final approved design, now fuller in the face and friendlier. I imagined Jarvis as an ageing matinee idol — handsome but a little worn around the edges, his best years behind him, forced now to play character roles for comedic relief. As tragic as he is funny, in the tradition of all great clowns. Note the bunny, no longer getting a kicking.

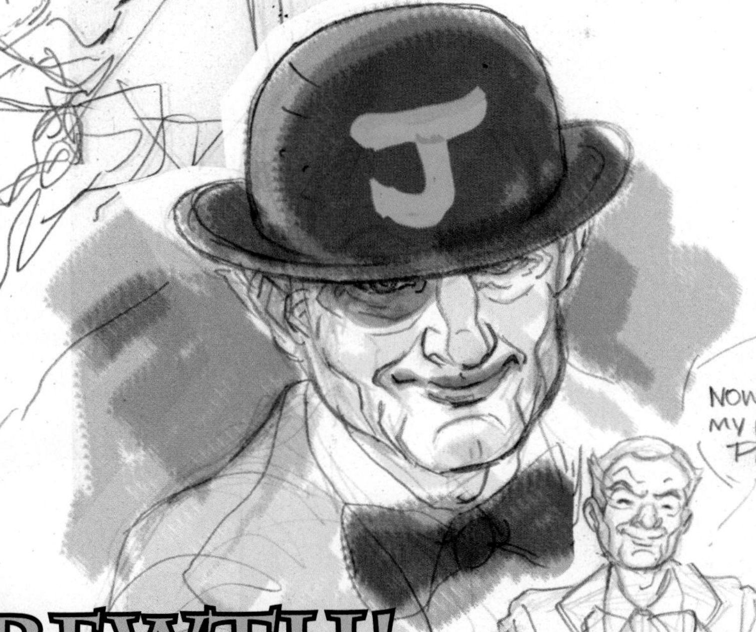

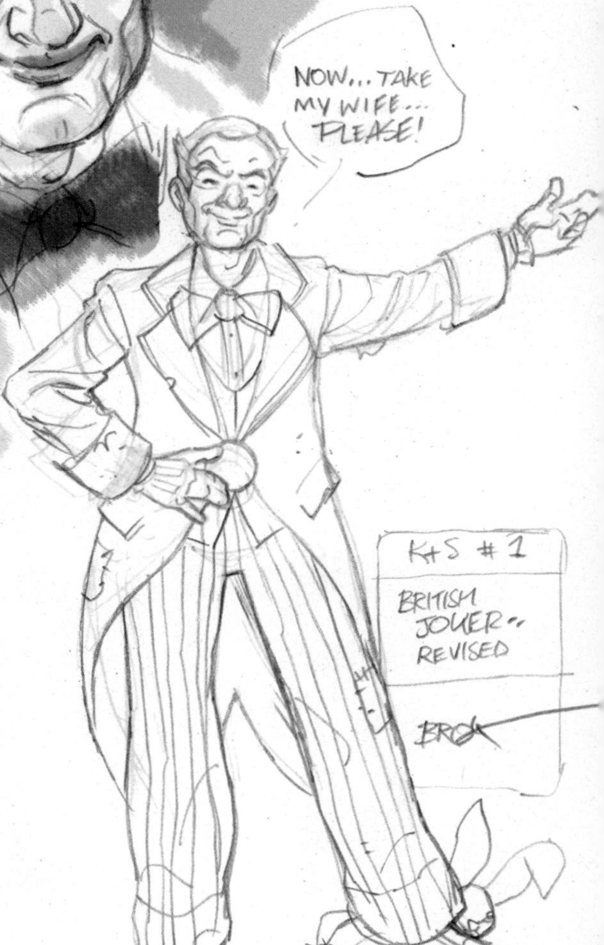
NOW... TAKE MY WIFE... PLEASE!
K+S #1
BRITISH JOKER.. REVISED

STREWTH!

Character designs and preliminary sketches from artist Jimmy Broxton.

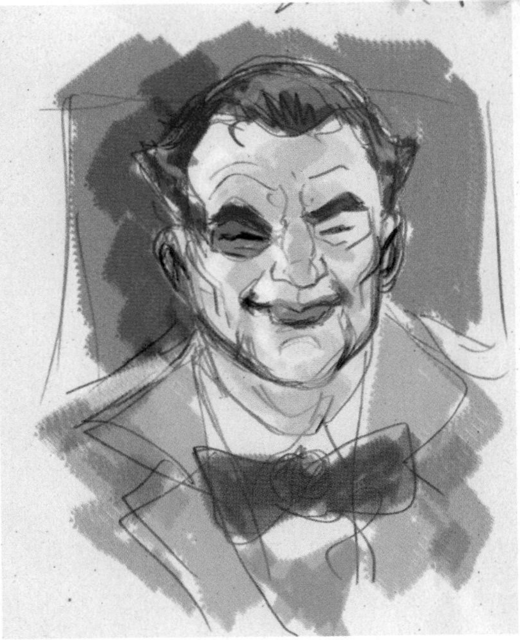

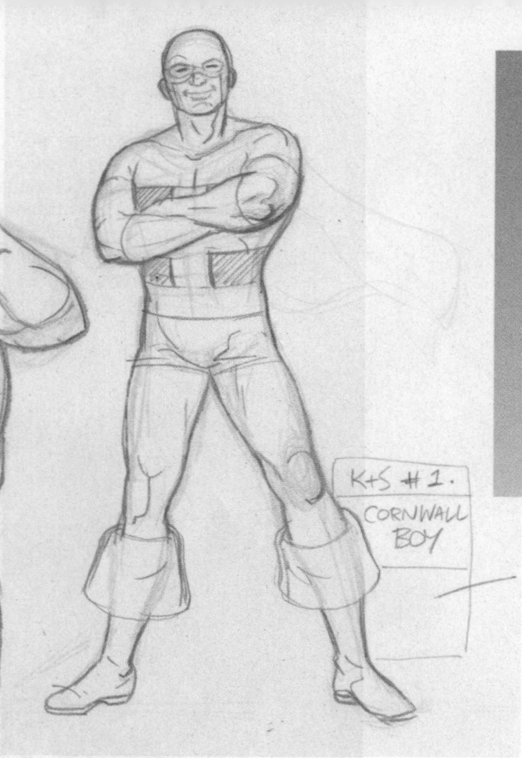
K+S #1.
CORNWALL BOY

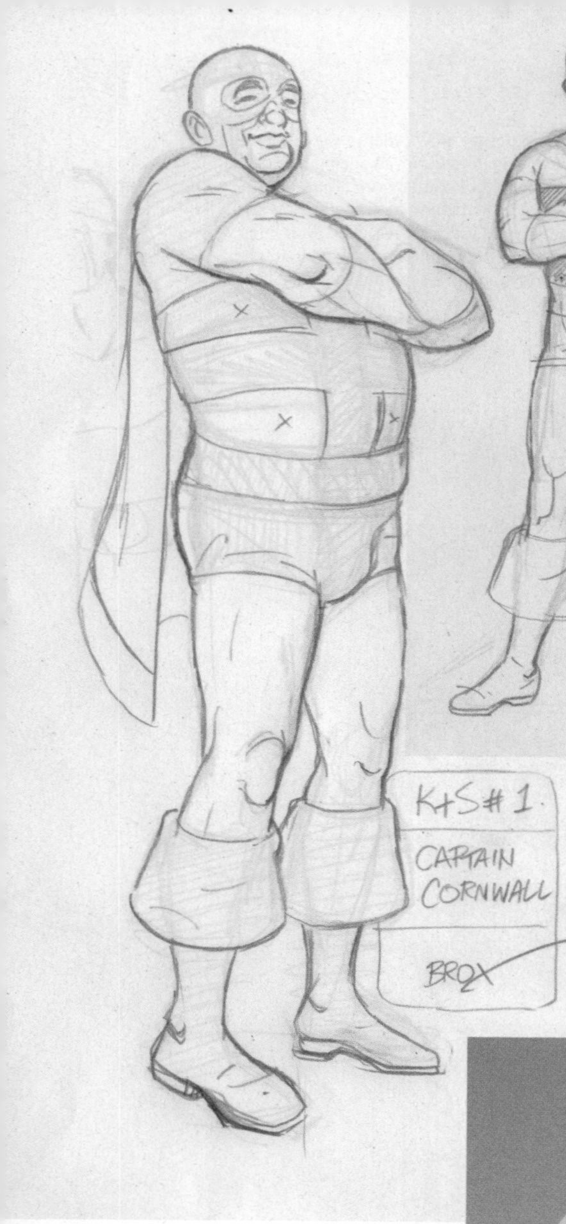
K+S #1
CAPTAIN CORNWALL
BROX

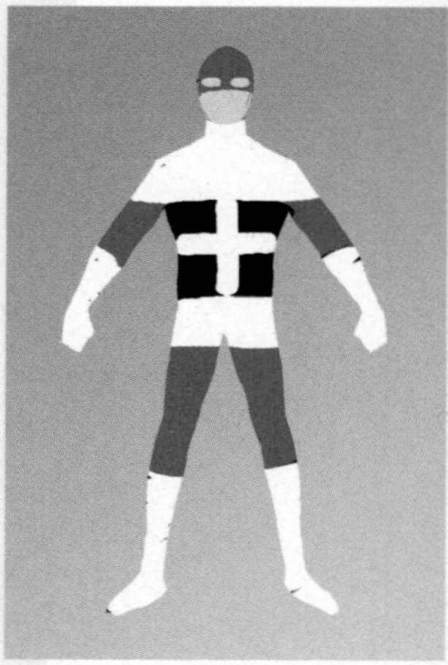

Above and Left: Sketches and colour guide for Captain Cornwall and Cornwall Boy, in all their Cornish glory.

Below: Final designs and badg graphic for Face-Off: everyone' favourite gay, urban, costumed vigilante.

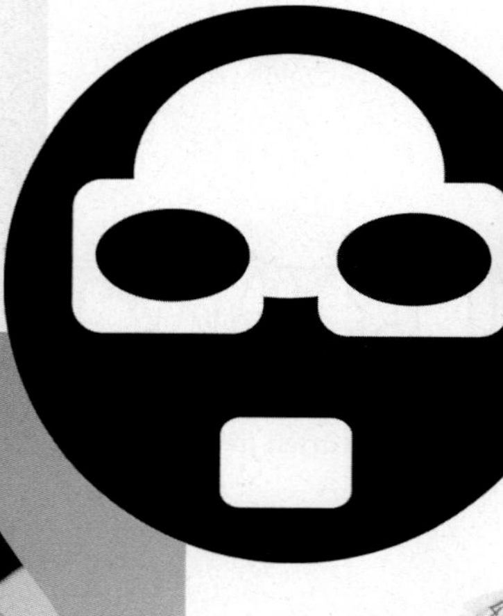

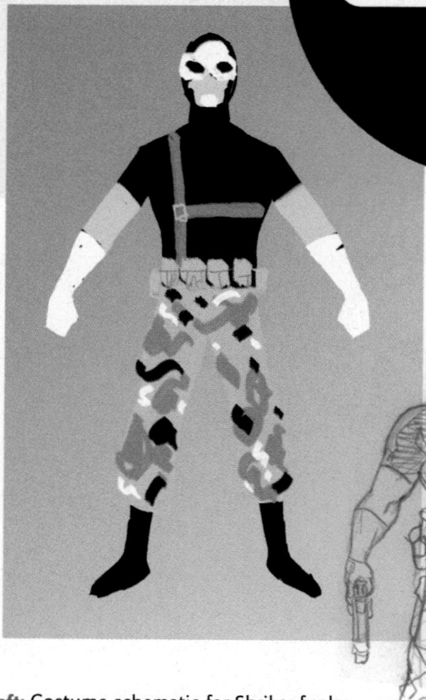

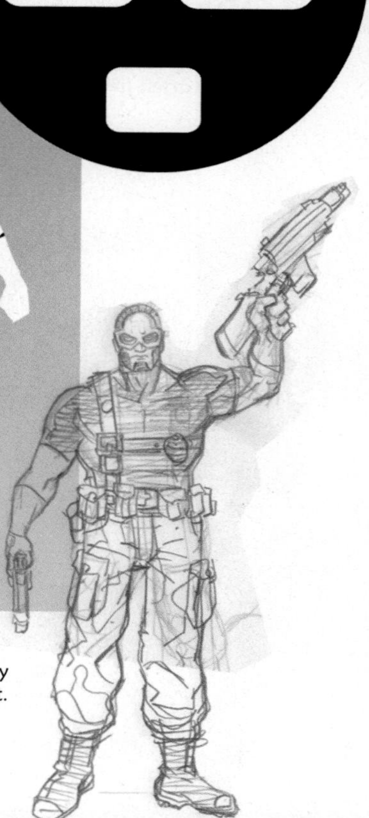

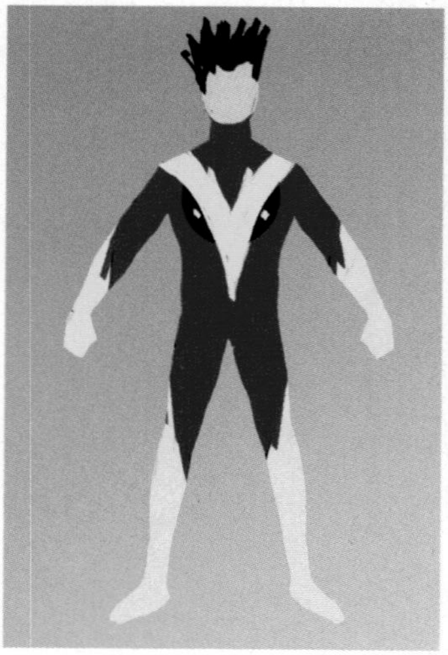

Left: Costume schematic for Shrike: funky dude, love interest and tragic protagonist.

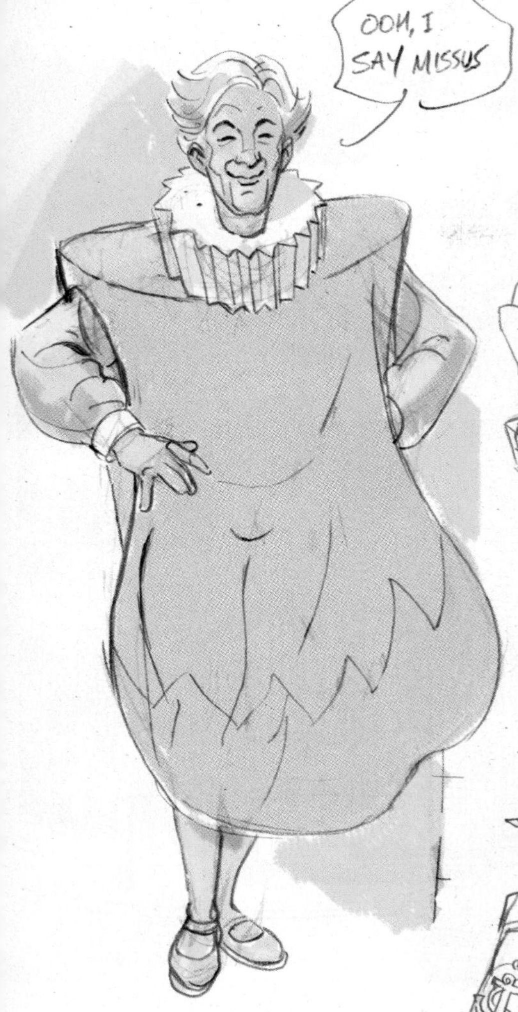
OOH, I SAY MISSUS

Above: A "single" entendre.

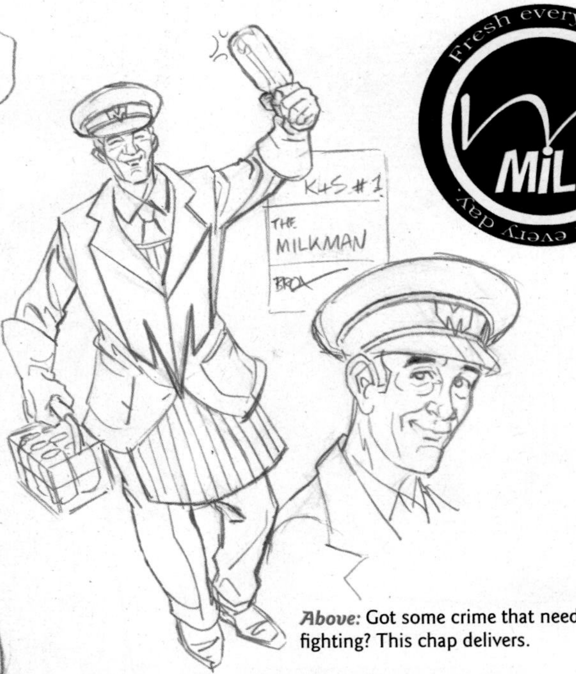
K+S #1
THE MILKMAN
BROX

Above: Got some crime that needs fighting? This chap delivers.

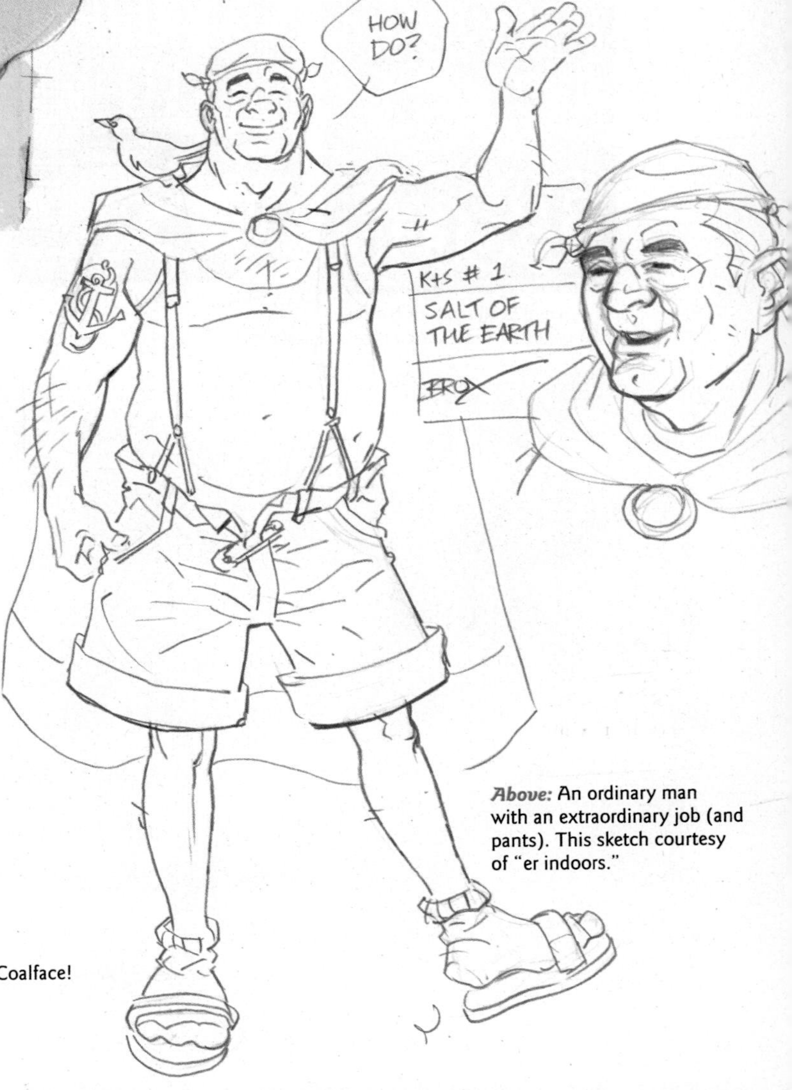
HOW DO?
K+S # 1
SALT OF THE EARTH
BROX

Above: An ordinary man with an extraordinary job (and pants). This sketch courtesy of "er indoors."

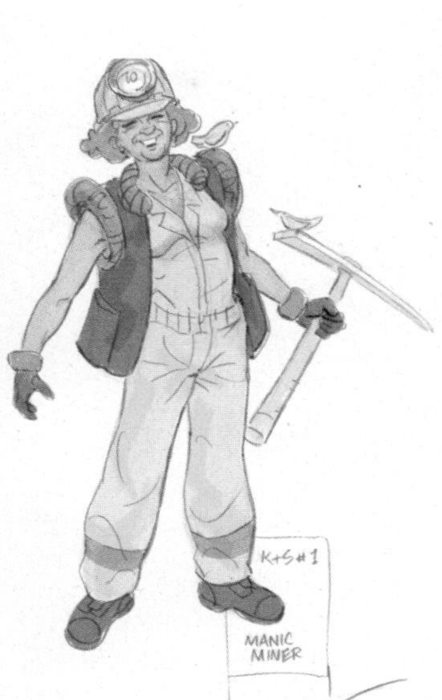
K+S#1
MANIC MINER
BROX

Above: Coming to a picket-line near you: Coalface!

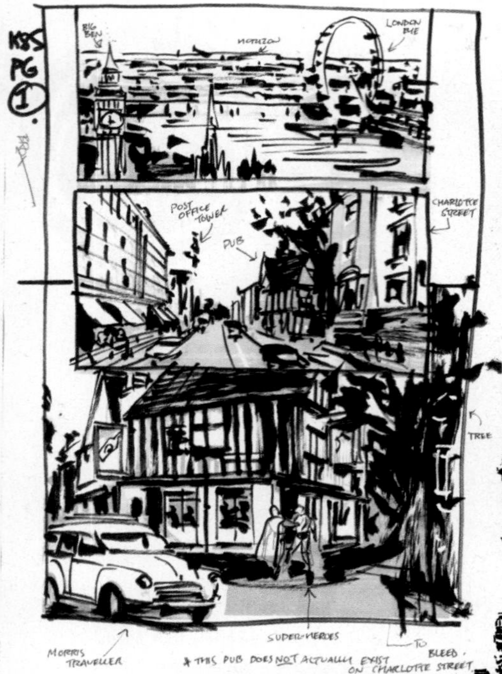
KBS
PG
1
BIG BEN
HORIZON
LONDON EYE
POST OFFICE TOWER
PUB
CHARLOTTE STREET
TREE
SUPER-HEROES
TO BLEED.
MORRIS TRAVELLER
* THIS PUB DOES NOT ACTUALLY EXIST ON CHARLOTTE STREET

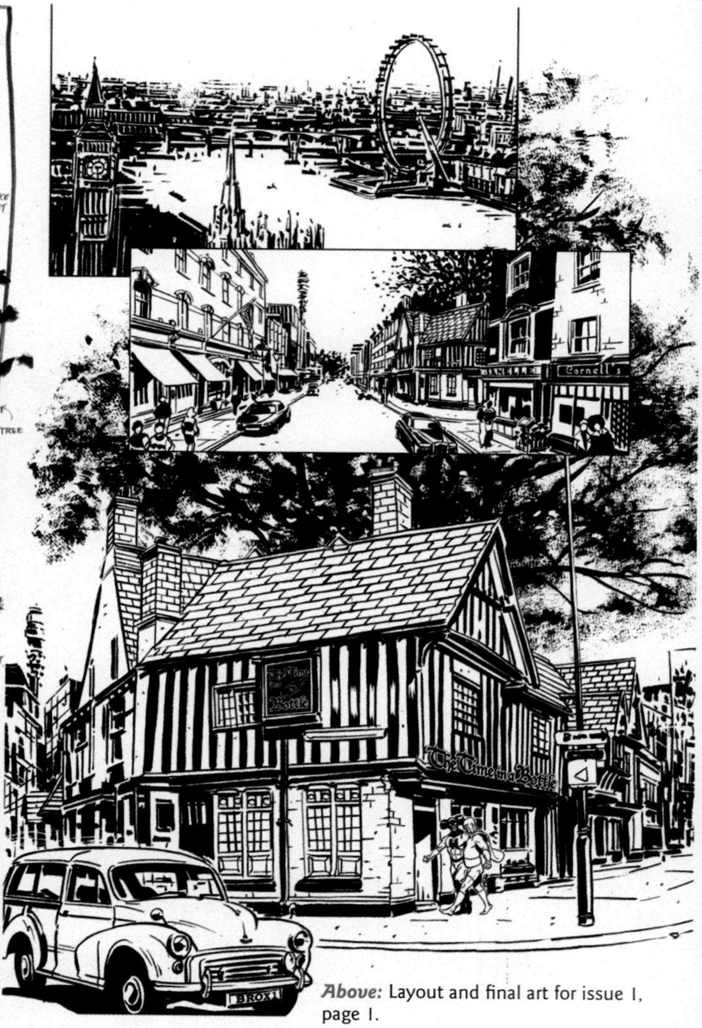
Cornell's
The Time in a Bottle
BROX1

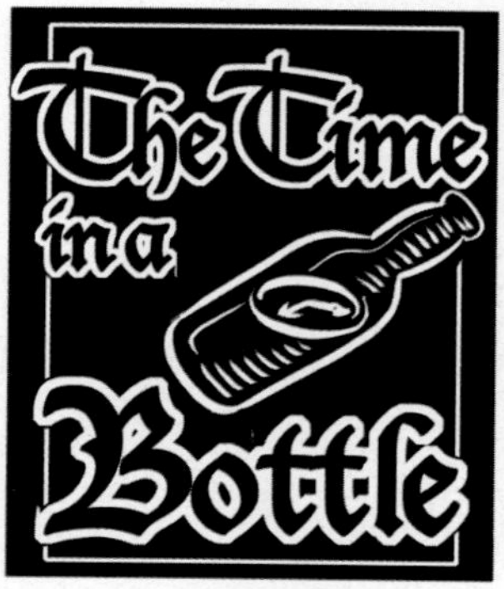
The Time
in a
Bottle

Above: Layout and final art for issue 1, page 1.

Below: Thursday night is all right for fighting.
Pencil layout for pages 14 and 15 from the same issue.

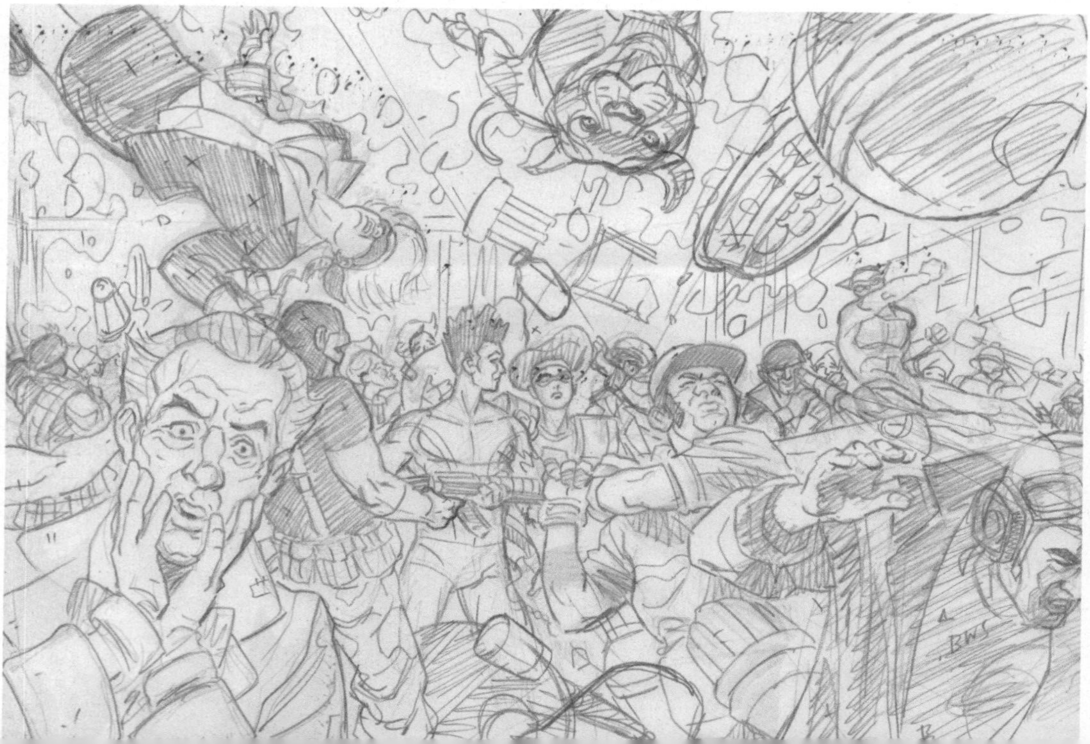

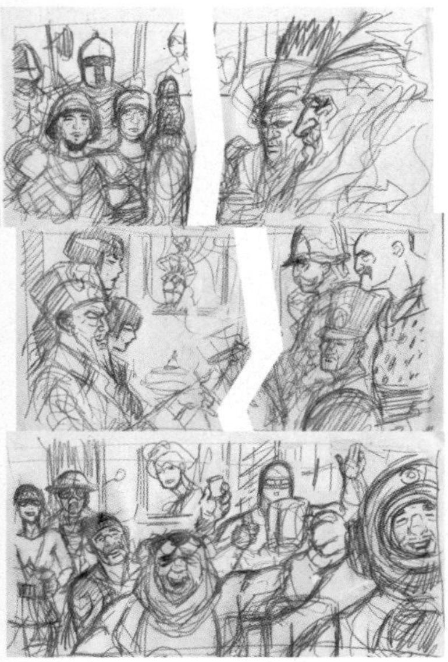

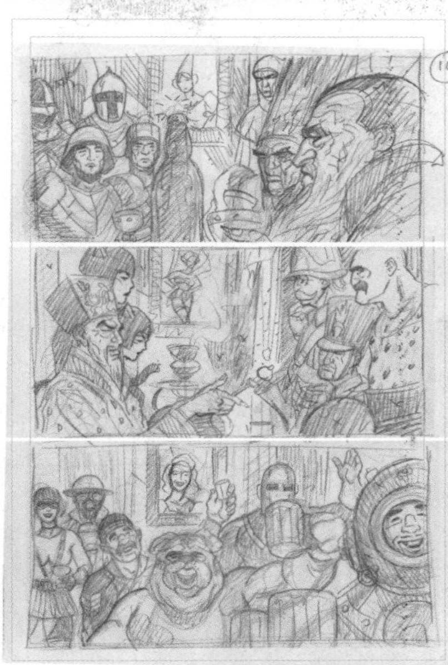

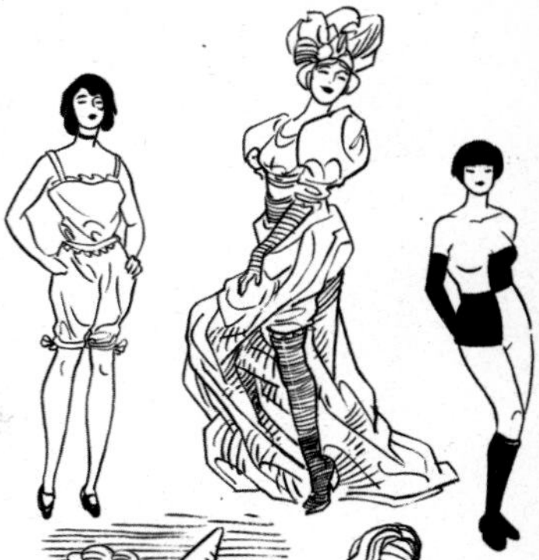

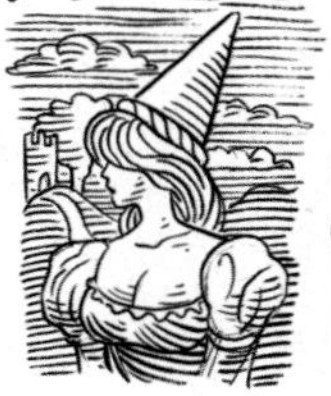

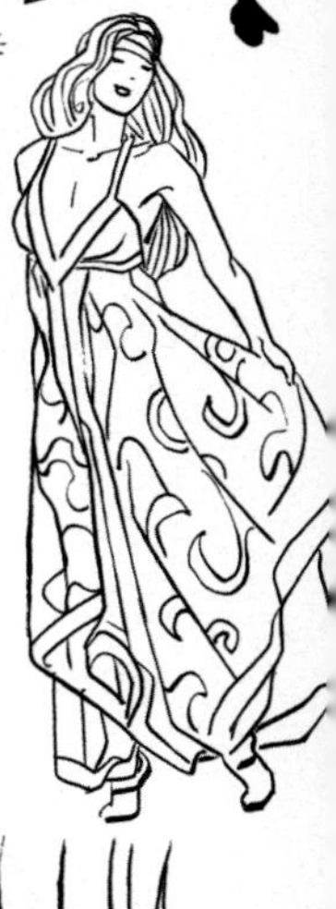

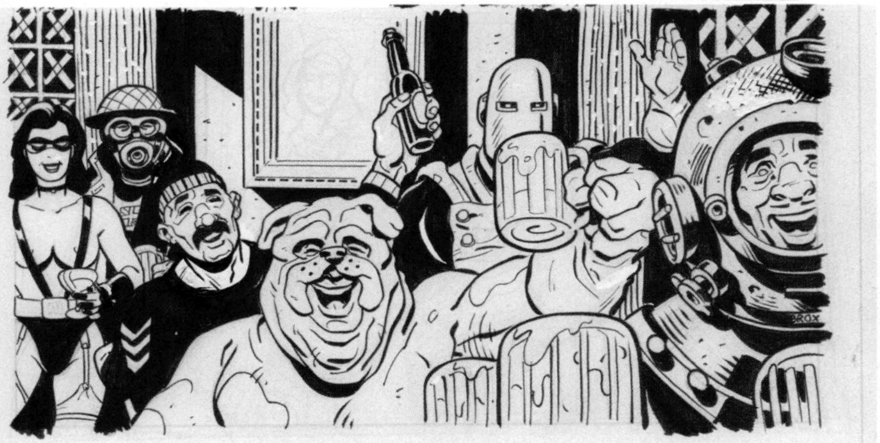

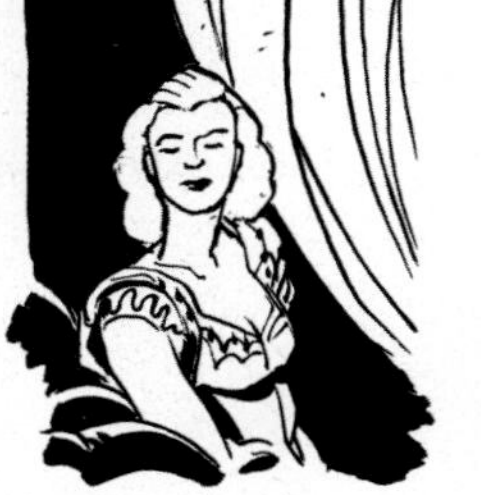

Above: Layout, final pencil and ink detail from issue 1, page 10.

Below: Your guess is as good as mine, but this stuff is in the book somewhere.

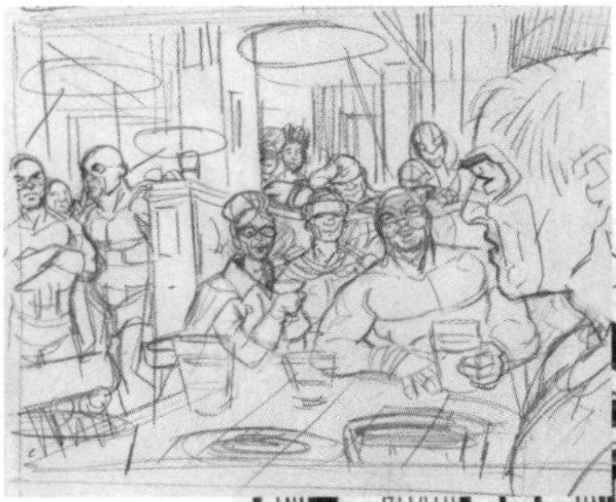

Above right: From wimpled damsels to miniskirted '60s misses, the Time in a Bottle has seen it all.

Left and below: Wildcat gets to feel younger, in pencil and ink.

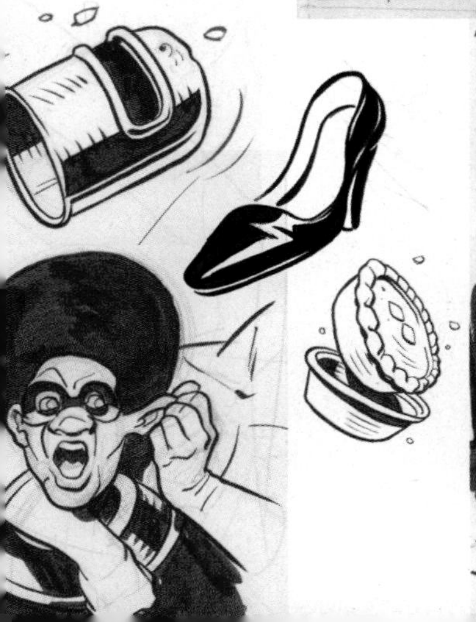

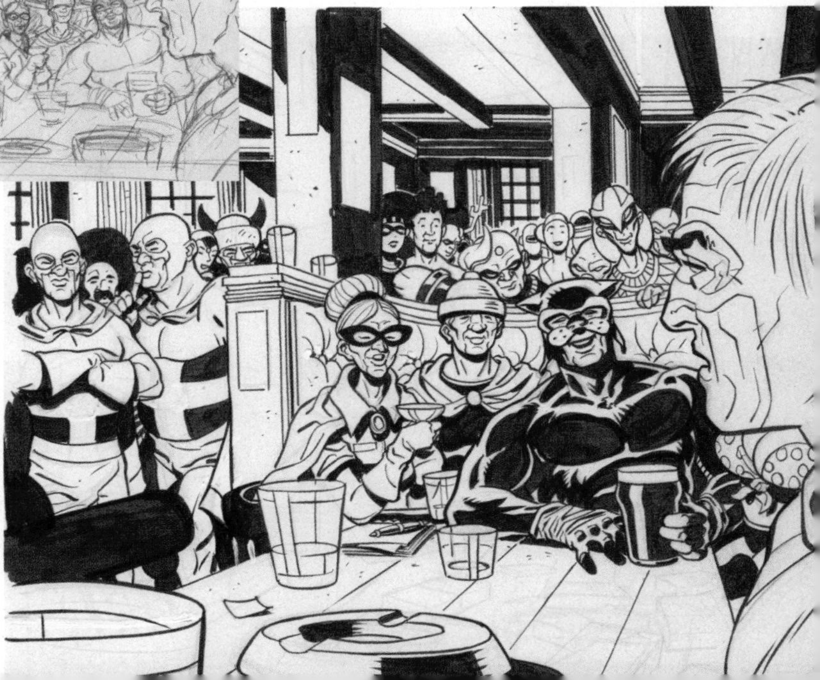

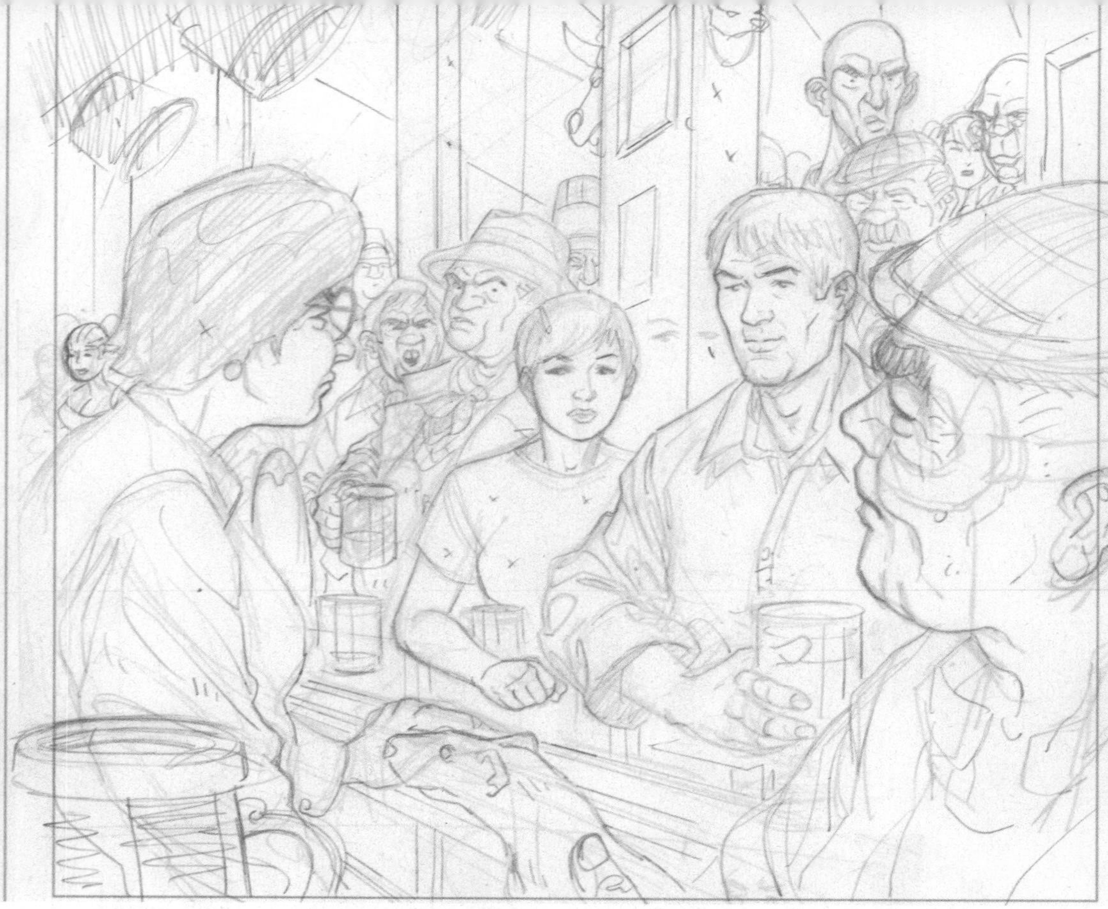

Above: The Wicker Man interior and pencils from issue 2. Different pub, "different" clientele.

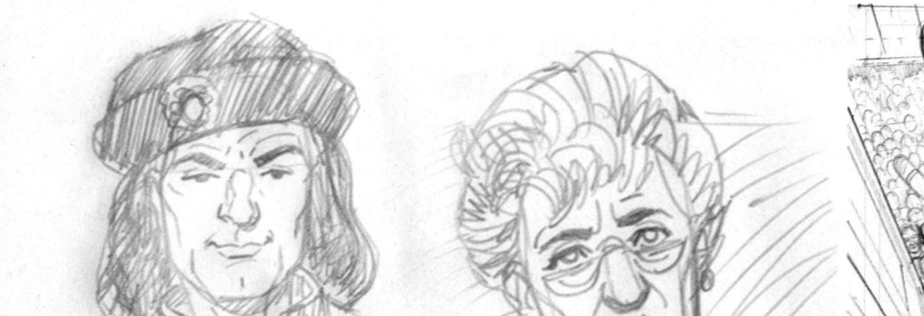

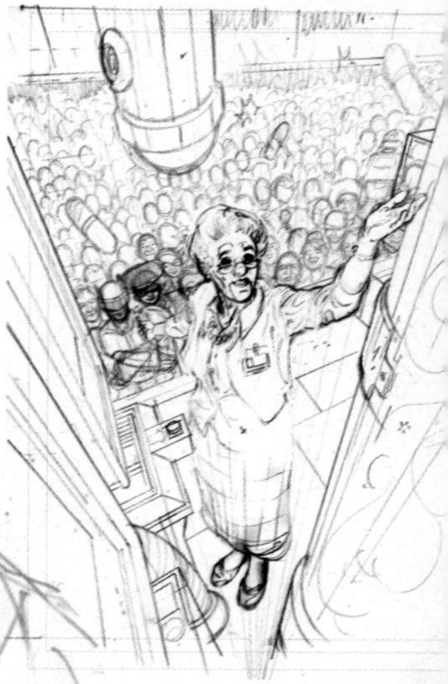

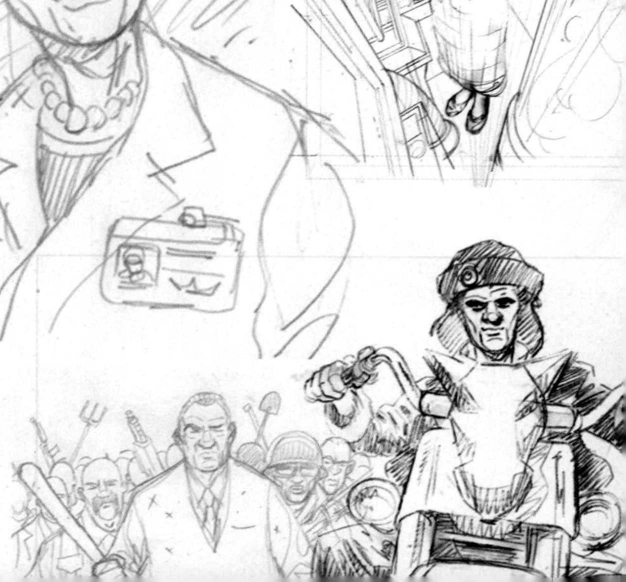

Above: Richard III, modelled on a young Olivier.

Above right: Prof. Merryweather, modelled on a man in a dress. Continuing the great theatrical tradition of men assuming female roles, from Pantomime Dames to the Ealing Comedies of the '40s and '50s up to *Monty Python's Flying Circus* and beyond. We're an eccentric lot, us Brits.

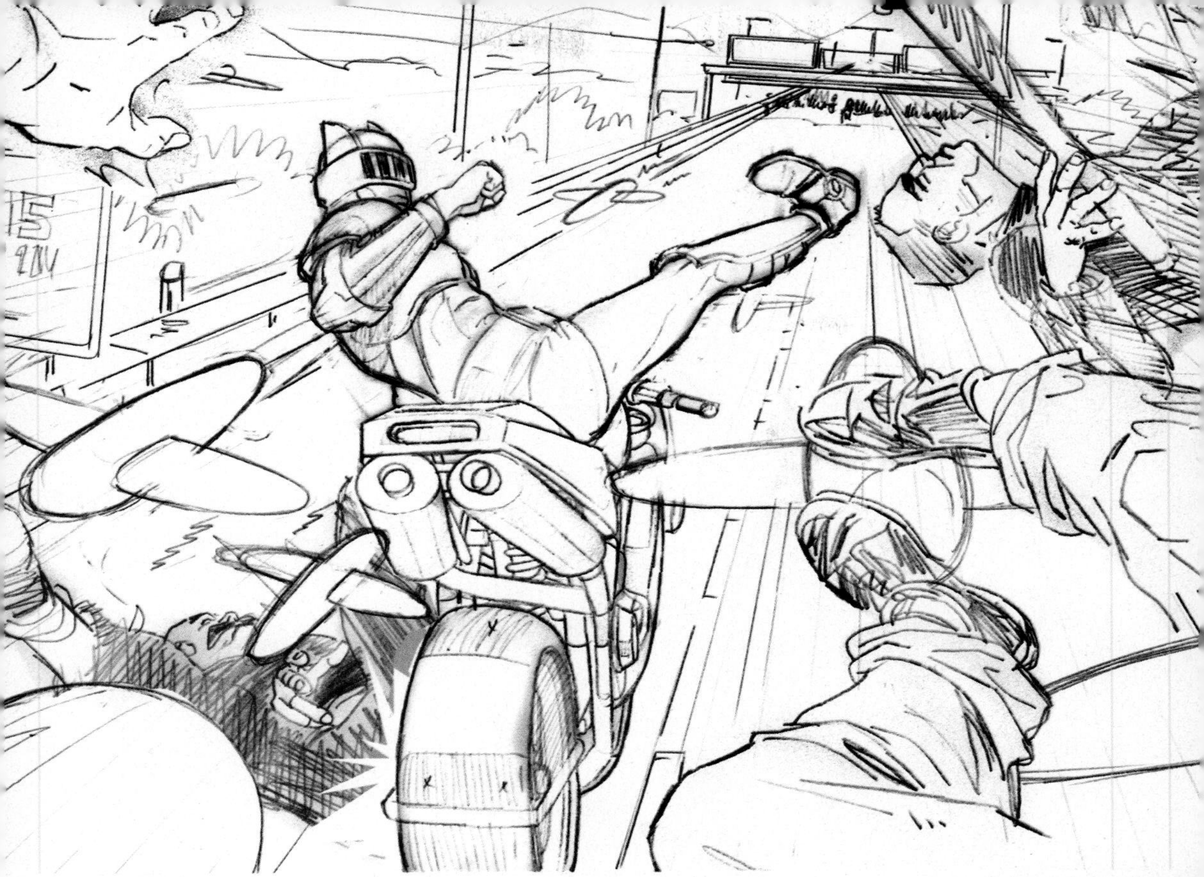

Above and below: Traffic-calming measures on the M1. Pencils and inks from issue 3. Oh, the joys of the English motorway network.

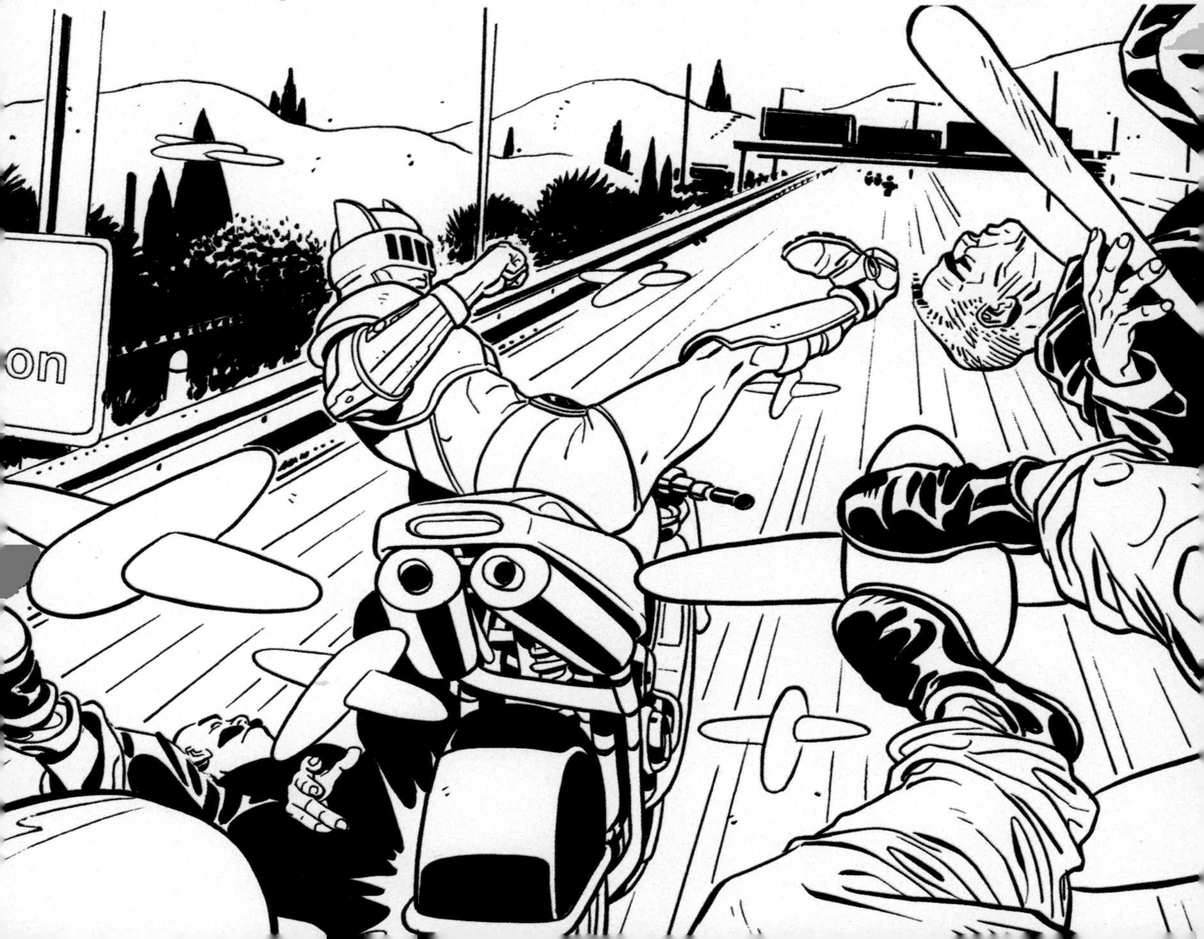
on

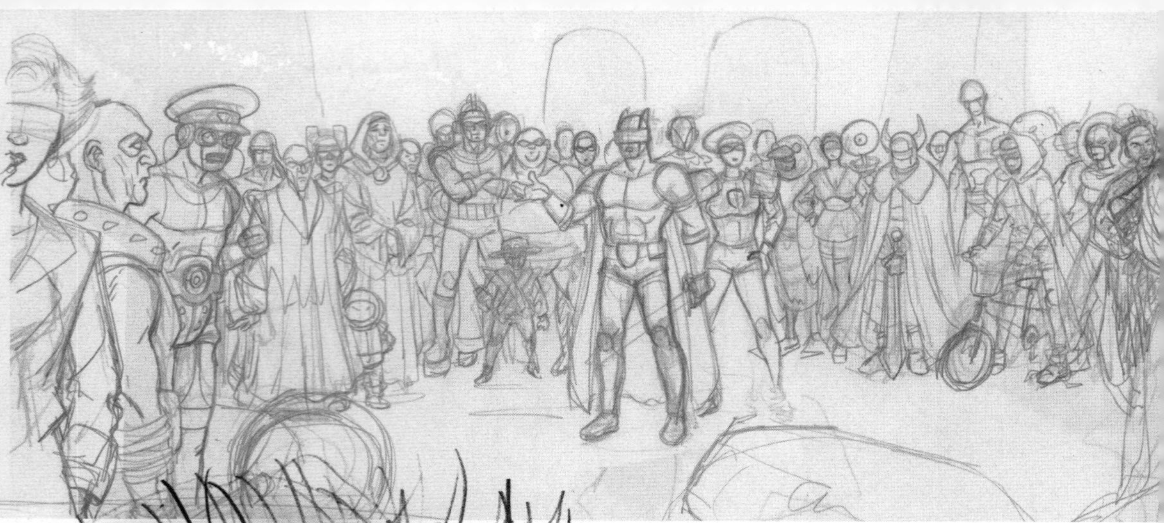

Above: Over 130 new characters were created for the series. This pencil layout for issue 6 features just 27 of them.

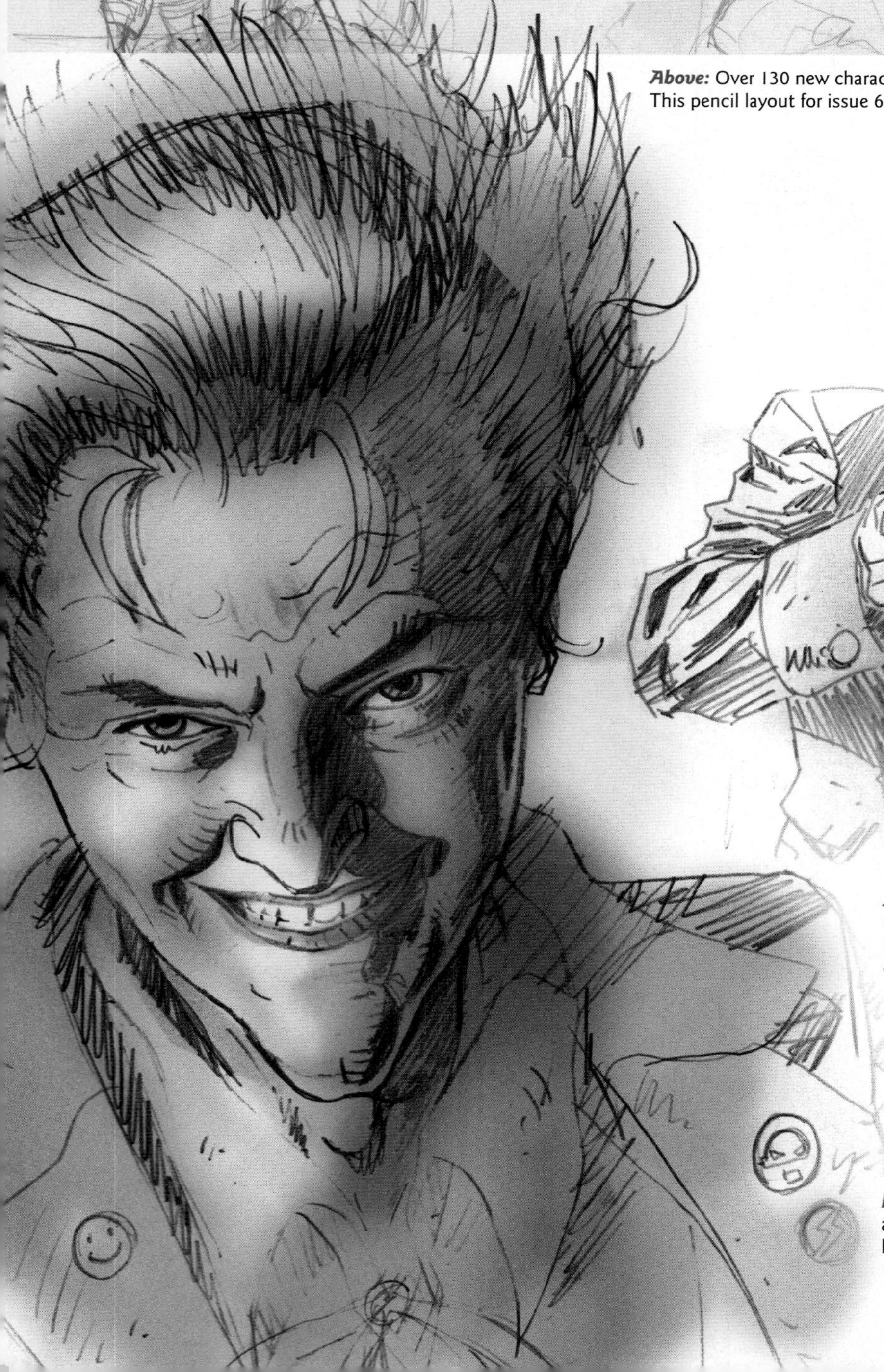

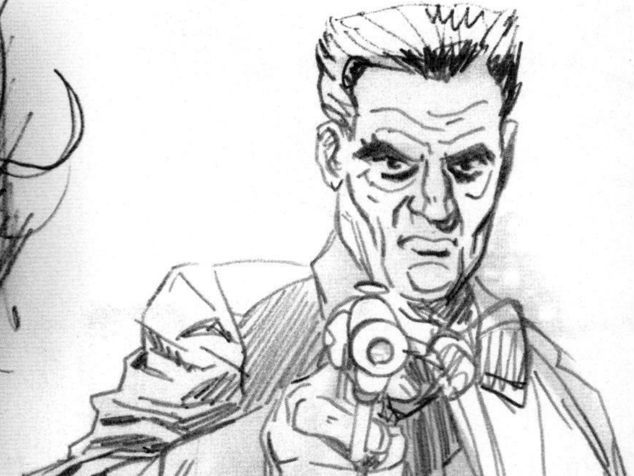

Above: When Jarvis reappears in issue 5 he is noticeably leaner. Alas, despite his best efforts, he is no meaner.

Left: When the "actual" Joker appears in the same issue, he has no such difficulties.

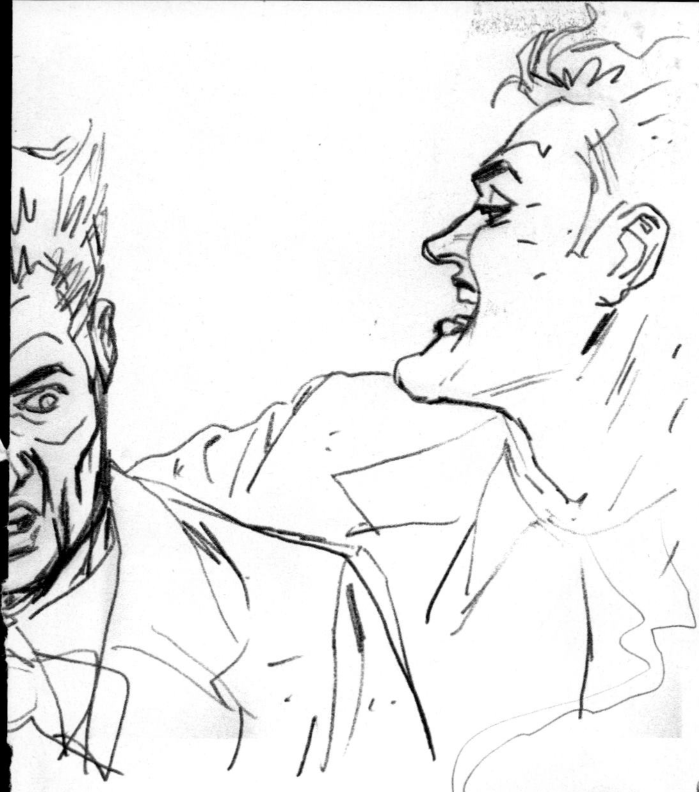

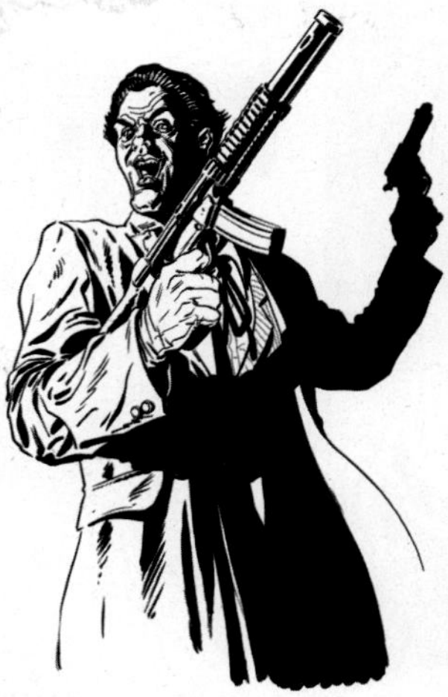

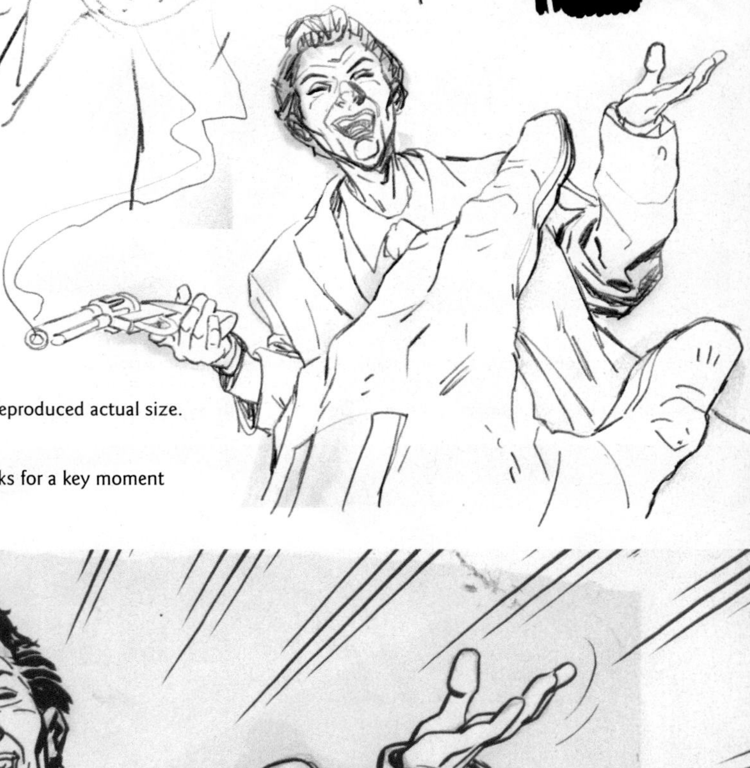

Above: Pencil sketch for a pair of "Jokers," reproduced actual size.

Below and right: Preliminary pencils and inks for a key moment in the story.

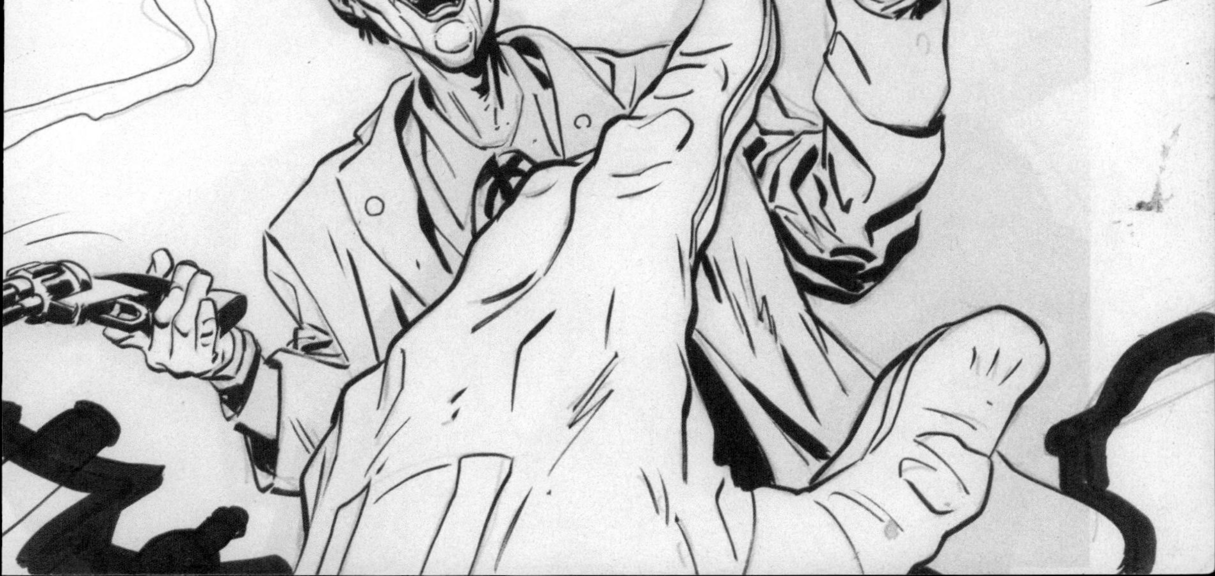

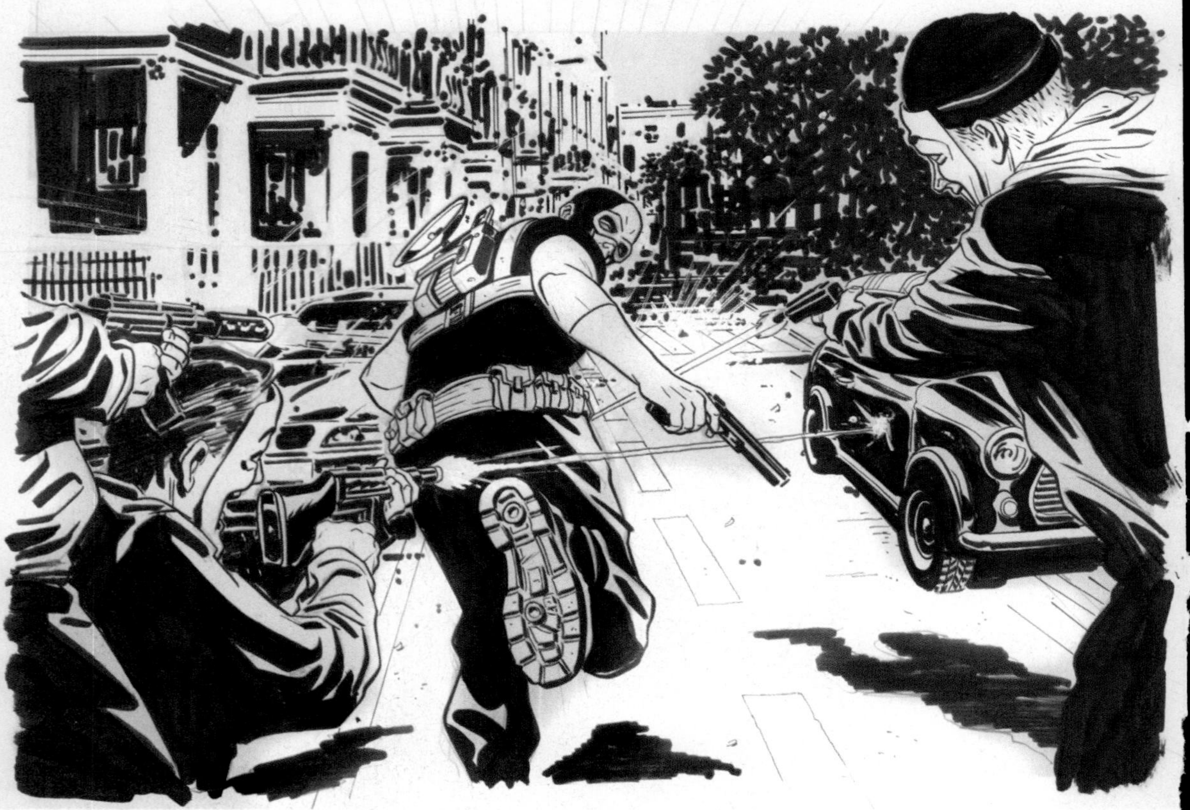

Above: Raw, uncorrected inks for an assault from the rear. Note the iconic British car, drawn way smaller than it should be — a mini-"Mini."

Below: More raw inks showcasing a motley crew with "Birthday Girl" centre stage, complete with "modesty balloons."

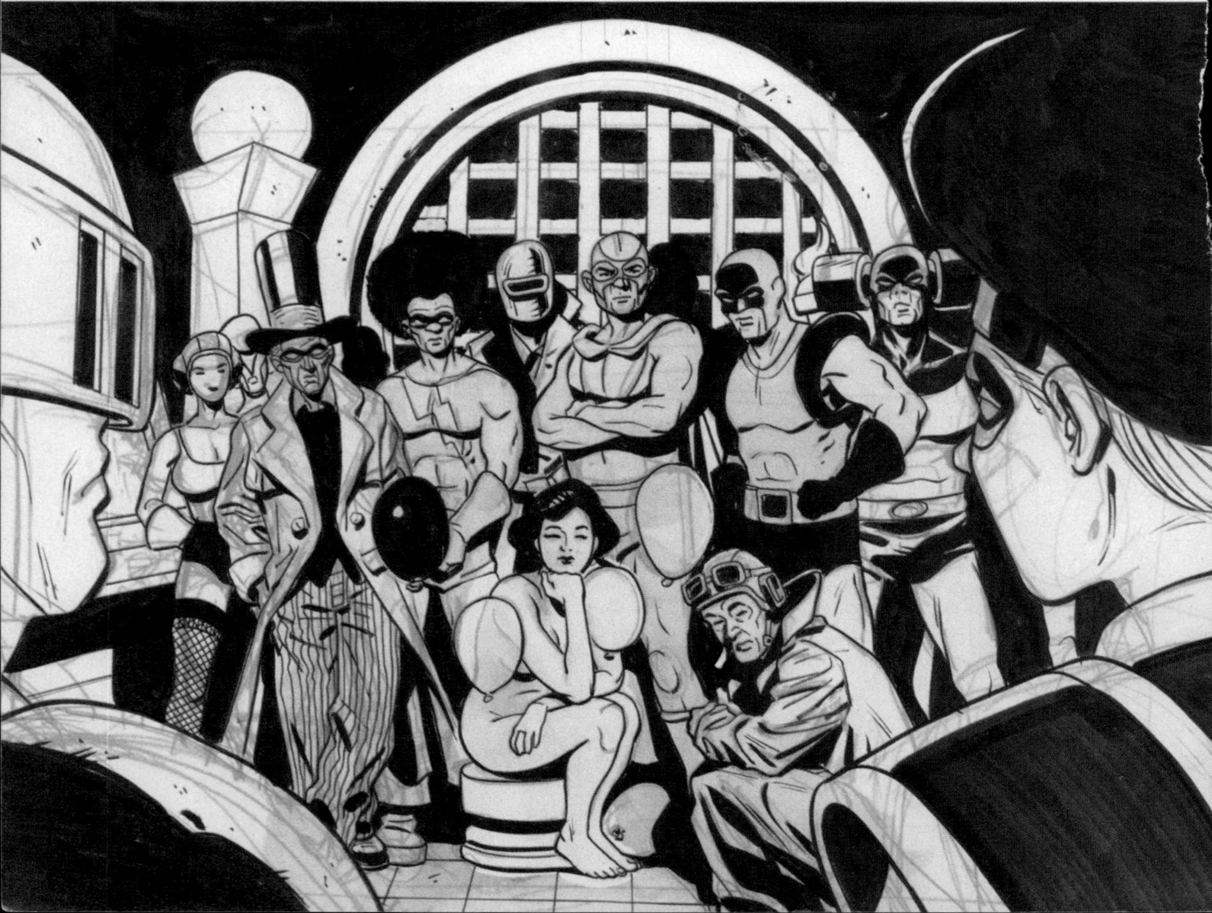

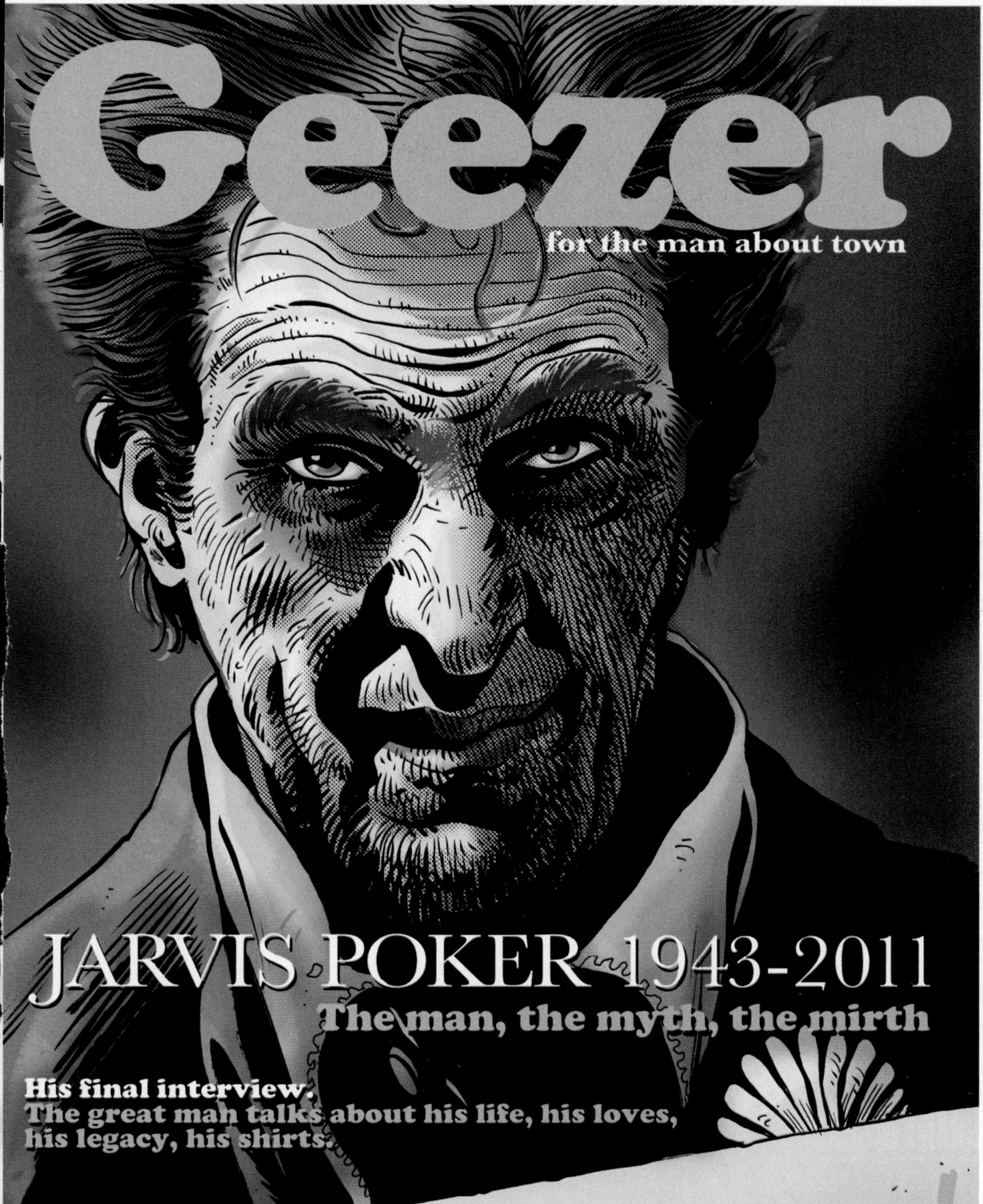
Geezer
for the man about town
JARVIS POKER 1943-2011
The man, the myth, the mirth
His final interview.
The great man talks about his life, his loves,
his legacy, his shirts.

Above: Unpublished art for a spoof magazine cover, which was to have been the final ad in issue 6. R.I.P. Jarvis.

Hope you enjoyed the behind-the-scenes look at our little piece of Britain!

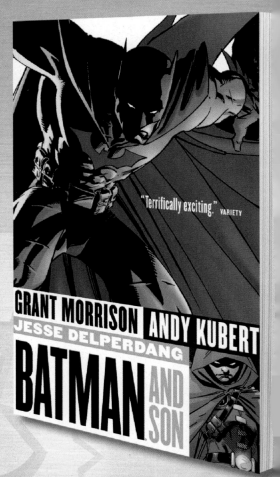
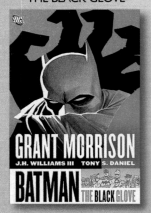

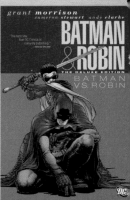

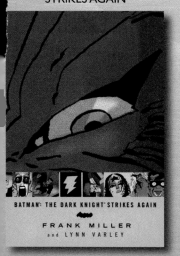

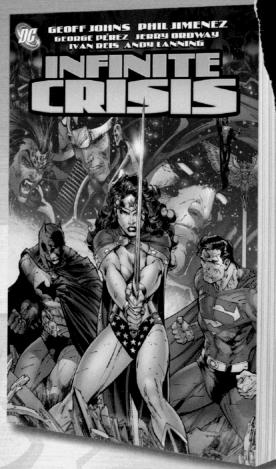